Historical Sketches

OF

POCAHONTAS COUNTY, WEST VIRGINIA

BY

WILLIAM T. PRICE

Hath this been in your days, or even in the days of your fathers? Tell your children of it, and let your children tell their children, and their children another generation. —Bible.

Marlinton, W. Va.
Price Brothers, Publishers
1901

Facsimile Reprint

Published 1990 By
HERITAGE BOOKS, INC.
1540 Pointer Ridge Place, Bowie, Maryland 20716
(301)-390-7709

ISBN 1-55613-347-2

Preface.

This volume seems to be the spontaneous outcome of circumstances, or in a sense has simply grown up "without observation." Most of the contents came the compiler's way without ever suspecting their future appearance in book form, by casually noting down what he saw and heard while moving around among the homes of our people, recording interviews with the older venerated persons, or recalling what was suggested during the thirty or forty youthful years of the almost forgotten past, and were published from time to time in the Pocahontas Times.

Referring to the Biographic Notes, we quote from the Bath News an article by Joseph T. McAllister, himself a historical student of more than ordinary ability: "These sketches are from notes made as occasion offered, and they can not be prized too highly. It is very hard for one man unaided to gather these facts, and it requires no little time to edit them. We sometimes think very lightly of such things, and are too much inclined to let the dead past bury its dead, and live alone in this work-a-day present. But we should remember that along this western Virginia the Scotch-Irish worked out a vast problem and wrought a vast change in the then existing form of government; that they made history and played no small or mean part in life's great stage; that the simple life they led nurtured men to whom we are indebted for countless blessings, and that no incident of their lives is too small or insignificant to be recorded. Only by access to such sketches as those published by Mr Price can the coming historian gather truthfully the materials from which to write. When Green, the great English historian, wrote his immortal work—it was not to set forth the deeds of the kings, or the deeds of the members of the royal household. He wrote what he fondly calls a 'History of the English People.' "

The writer esteems it a privilege granted by the Supreme Being,—in whom we live, move, and have our being,—to have been enabled to collect and put in permanent form the matter contained in these sketches, much of which would soon have faded from the minds of men and lost to present and future generations.

Sincere thanks are due the advance subscribers, without whose assurance of support and co-operation the work would not have been attempted at this time.

WILLIAM T. PPICE.

Marlinton, West Virginia,
    July 19, 1901.

Contents.

SKETCHES OF POCAHONTAS COUNTY

Section I.

SOME PRELIMINARY WORDS.

A Hebrew Prophet utters this impressive admonition: "Hear this ye old men and give ear all ye inhabitants of the land, hath this been in your days, or even in the days of your fathers? Tell ye your children of it, and let your children tell their children, and their children another generation."—Joel 1, 2–3.

The duty inculcated by these earnest words we,— the Editor; the venerated, aged persons whose memories have with so much fidelity preserved the traditions and the oral unwritten history that have been transmitted from their pioneer ancestry to their children and children's children; the advance subscribers; and the printer publishers,—hereby endeavor to perform.

These sketches are designed to illustrate, in some measure, the history of Pocahontas County, located as it is in one of the most remarkable regions of the whole habitable earth. The territory referred to extends from the Ohio Valley to the Blue Ridge, and from the Potomac to the sources of New River. There may be other regions of like limits equally favored with the bounties of nature, but none to surpass it, when all things are duly considered. The spontaneous resources for sustaining human and animal existence exceed all ordinary means of estimating. The streams were alive with fish and aquatic birds; the forests teemed with uncounted herds of bison, elk, and deer, bears, wolves, panthers, wild cats, foxes and smaller animals of great variety roamed at will. Flocks of turkeys, grouse, quail, and the wild pigeons abounded in fabulous profusion. The branches of as noble trees as ever grew, —trees that would be the pride of royal parks,—were occupied by throngs of birds of bright and varied plumage and sweet notes, thus making the solitary forest scenes beautiful and more than sweetly vocal.

When the pioneers came they found this wilderness paradise just as God the Creator fashioned it, already peopled by a branch of the human race, men, women, and children, that had been here for centuries. There were indications that these had been preceded by a still older class of occupants.

As to the American Indians found by the pioneers, the question of their origin, who they were and whence came they has been a much discussed ethnological problem for the past four hundred years by Spanish, English, French, and American scholars. Egypt, China, and Norteastern Asia, as well as Northwestern Europe, have passed under searchingly profound consideration as sources whence the aboriginal people of North and South America have migrated at prehistoric periods. The language, religious traditions, manners, and usages of the Indians that occupied the region whereof our county forms a part seem to some writers

suggestive of Hebrew origin, and might be a remnant
of the so termed Lost Tribes of Israel. On this theory
the Book of Mormon was written, and our intelligent
readers know something of what has resulted whenever
the Mormon question is broached.

But as the question now stands, that of origin as to
what nation or nations of the old world whence the
American Indians have come, the state of the problem
is so perplexing that positive truth is not conceded to
any one theory. Plausible conjecture is the most that
is conceded for the best considered theory of origin.

Hu Maxwell, who has investigated such historical
themes with conspicuous ability, says:

"In Mexico to-day the Indians, Mayas, and Aztecs
live side by side, and their features and general characteristics show them to be radically.the same people,
not different races. They are at least as much alike as
are Germans and Spanish, the Greeks and the French,
and the common origin of these nations is not difficult
to trace. It is neither proper nor profitable to enter
at length upon the consideration of the origin of the
Indians. It is a question which history has not answered, and perhaps never will answer. If the origin
of the Indians were known, the origin of the people
who built the mounds would be near at hand. But the
whole matter is one of speculation and opinion. The
favorite conclusion of most authors is that America
was peopled from Asia by way of Behring Strait. It
could have been done. But the hypothesis is as reasonable that Asia was peopled by emigrants from America who crossed the Behring Strait. It is the same dis-

tance across, going west or coming east, and there is
no historical evidence that America was not peopled
first, or that both the old world and the new world
were not peopled at the same time; or that each was
not peopled independently of the other. Since the
dawn of history, and as far back into prehistoric times
as the analysis of languages can throw any light, all
great migrations have been westward. No westward
migration would have given America its inhabitants
from Asia, but a migration from from the west would
have peopled Asia from America. As a matter of fact
Behring Strait is so narrow that the tribes on either
side can cross to the other at pleasure, and with less
difficulty than the Amazon River can be crossed near
its mouth.''

In our sketches we will not spend much time on
theories of origin, but give earnest attention to facts,
and the fact now before us is this, the pioneers found
the land they had come from beyond the ocean seas to
possess, already occupied by their fellow men, claiming the land as theirs from prehistoric times. The
tribe of Indians that laid special claim upon our region
by actual possession was the Shawnee; and as the
Shawnee had been nurtured and reared in such a surprising goodly land, he ranked among the superior
members of the North American aborigines.

The Shawnee Indians preceded the pioneers in actual possession and long use of hunting grounds well-
nigh coextensive with the limits already indicated.
These Indians had the Ohio Valley as their home place
so to speak. Nearly all of the aborigines that waged

border warfare lived in Ohio adjacent to the present limits of West Virginia, whence they would come to make good their claims to their hunting grounds, and for more than twenty-five years waged cruel hostilities against the pioneers.

The French Jesuit fathers, as early as 1640, had taken and published a missionary census of the total number of Indians in the territory east of the Mississippi, north of the Gulf of Mexico, and south of the St. Lawrence River and the Lakes. The territory referred to in that missionary census includes what now claims our consideration. According to this census the Indians numbered about one hundred and eighty thousand.

It thus appears that the Jesuit Fathers took much pains to inform themselves about this region, and had secured the confidence and attachment of the Shawnees. These alert, tireless, shrewd missionaries always knew a good thing when they saw it, and they seemed to have felt that no brighter gem was in their reach, with which to adorn the tiara of the Holy Father at Rome, than the natural Paradise reported by the Shawnee braves and Huron hunters as their own hunting grounds. No doubt rested in the souls of these devoted missionaries that their paramount duty was to secure and make good for the use of the Holy Father this goodly heritage of the heathen, for it was his as the vicegerent of Christ, to whom God had promised the earth and the fullness thereof. They were ready to sacrifice all the delights of sense, all the luxury of personal ease, and even life itself, to make good a claim so divine.

Nothing in the annals of missionary endeavor is

more pathetically interesting than what these devoted Jesuit fathers voluntarily endured, in their efforts to propagate the faith, as they express it. First came the missionaries, followed in due time by the French engineers, and the goodly land was explored. The missionaries were quickened in their zeal and confirmed in their faith when they discovered so much that was suggestive of Palestine in so many features. What Moses said and what they had read in the 8th of Deuteronomy about the Holy Land being a land of brooks of water, of fountains and depths that spring out of valleys and hills; a land whose stones are iron and out of whose hills brass might be dug, the Fathers found all duplicated here, and they were not slow to perceive its possibilities could make it materialize into a "land of wheat and barley and vines and fig trees and pomegranates; a land wherein bread would be eaten without scarceness," and nothing really good be lacking, and be moreover a land of oil, olive, and honey.

Since apostolic times no class of men have on record or have displayed more selfdenying energy than the French Father missionaries at the time referred to. Some of these previous to 1640, and at various periods since down to 1774, explored every nook and corner of our region worth looking after, guided by their Shawnee adherents. It is believed that the remains of one of these fathers, or engineers, were plowed up in the Indian Draft, some years ago, near where the Edray branch joins the main stream.

To have a proper appreciation of what it all cost the pioneers in their efforts to have and to hold what is now the place of our homes, it would be well to learn something of Shawnee character, as men and warriors.

The leaders that gave our pioneers the most trouble were Pontiac, Chief of the Ottawas; Cornstalk, Killbuck, and Crane. Killbuck annoyed the settlements for a long series of years, and when hostilities ceased went to his home in Ohio, and thereafter paid occasional visits to Wheeling. He became blind, and lived to be more than a hundred years old.

Killbuck had for a comrade, whose efficiency as a warrior made him nearly as dangerous, named Crane, because of his unusually long neck and legs. Crane was an ugly thorn in the flesh, especially to those of the settlers that located on the South Branch, and made himself a conspicuous nuisance never to be forgotten. But little record is to be found of his exploits, but enough is known to give him the distinction of being considered nearly as dangerous as Killbuck.

The Shawnees, the aboriginal people, were here to repel the pioneers for the reason they regarded the land as theirs by inheritance from their fathers, at whose burial mounds they observed solemn rights of worship, and whose exploits they so fervently chanted in war songs and funeral dirges.

Indian troubles continued about thirty years with brief intervals of precarious peace. It is believed on very reliable tradition that for ten years before his death at the battle of Point Pleasant, October 10, 1774, Colonel Charles Lewis was never at home more than a month at a time.

The pioneer Scottish Virginians, ancestors of so

large proportion of our Pocahontas people, were remote from the seat of the colonial government, poorly provided with means of defense, and were exposed to all the troubles arising from the long and bitter struggle between the French and English for supremacy in the Mississippi Valley. History makes no formal mention of expeditions numbering hundreds of men going out as armed rangers upon the frontier. Nothing but a few unnoticed Acts of Virginia Assembly, acknowledging and commending such services, are available to show that companies of "Rangers," "Independents," or "Volunteers," led by a Lewis, a McClenachan, a Cunningham, a Preston, a Dickinson, a Dunlap, a Moffett, an Alexander, or some one else, armed and equipped at their own charges, penetrated the forests to punish or disperse hostile parties of Indians.

For in times of avowed peace the Indians would allege nominal or supposed wrongs, and thereupon murder defenceless families, then disappear stealthily as panthers, hastening away to their well-nigh inaccessible strongholds beyond the mountains. The Indian leaders, moreover, were foemen worthy of any antagonistic steel. The Emperor Pontiac appears to be the first to wage war against the Scottish Virginians. He was a war chief of the Ottowas, the most influential of the northern tribes, and was conspicuous among the native heroes whose devotion to the interests, of their people, wisdom and eloquence in council, skill in strategy, bravery in battle, have made for them a fame that the proudest warriors of all time might well envy.

One writer speaks of Pontiac as a person of remarkable appearance and commanding stature. Another says that in point of native talent, courage, magnanimity, and integrity he will compare without prejudice with the most renowned of civilized rulers and conquerors. It was Pontiac's war in 1763 that required the utmost strength of the Colonies and the strongest support of the British Government to withstand and overcome. It was in obedience to Pontiac's orders and plans that raiding parties pressed far into panic stricken settlements, and among the massacres were the Big Levels and Muddy Creek in Virginia, and the merciless slaughter in the Valley of Wyoming.

Ten or eleven years later another terrific Indian war blazed forth. This was conducted by the Shawnee chief Cornstalk, who when a young warrior was under Pontiac. The Shawnees held all other men in contempt as warriors. Mr Stuart speaks of Cornstalk as distinguished for beauty of person, for agility and strength of frame, in manners graceful and easy, and in movements majestic and princely. He commanded the Indian forces at Point Pleasant. During that very memorable action he was frequently seen moving rapidly along the lines of picked braves, and his marvelous voice was heard above the din of conflict cheering on with his battle cry "Be Strong! Be Strong!"

Colonel Wilson, a British officer, says: "I have heard the famous orators of Virginia—Patrick Henry and Richard Lee— but never have I heard one whose powers of delivery surpassed those of Cornstalk."

As seen and regarded by us as we write, had Cornstalk been successful at the battle of Point Pleasant,

the war for Independence could not have occurred
when it did, and very probably never taken place. For
English cavaliers, the French and Spanish missionaries
with their Shawnee and other Indian adherents would
have made it too uncomfortable for the Scotch-Irish
and the Hugenots to remain, and there would not have
been a Pocahontas County to write history about, as
we know it, and are now preparing. The tide of that
very eventful and pivotal battle was turned against
Cornstalk and his chosen brnves by the management
of Jacob Warwick, a pioneer of Pocahontas County,
who now sleeps in his lowly grave six miles west of the
Warm Springs, Virginia.

The close of Cornstalk's eventful career in life is
one of the most touching events of the kind on historical record since the death of Socrates. Impelled by a
magnanimous sense of duty unsurpassed in all barbaric
history, in order to be faithful and true to the treaty of
peace he had made with the pioneers, Cornstalk came
to the fort at Point Pleasant, the scene of his humiliat-
ing defeat, to inform the garrison of efforts made by
British emissaries to incite the Indians to war against
the Virginians during the Revolution. He and his son
Ellinipsico were detained as hostages.

In the meanwhile some of the garrison, infuriated
by the treacherous death of a comrade by an Indian
tramp, resolved to be avenged upon the hostages.
Soon as Cornstalk divined their purpose, he turned to
his son and said: "My son, the Great Spirit has seen
fit that we die together, and has sent you here to that
end. It is His will—let us submit. It is all for the

best." He then faced the persons making ready to slay him, bared his bosom, received seven shots from deadly mountain rifles, and fell lifeless. With him departed the spirit and prestige of the Indian power on the frontier. In thinking of this wonderful person, how very aptly the words apply:

> "The Lord of all
> The forest heroes, trained in wars,
> Quivered and plumed and lithe and tall
> And seamed with glorious scars."

Such historical allusions seem needful to aid us now living in forming some adequate conception of what our worthy ancestors had to encounter and overcome in their endeavors to build up their homes, for themselves, and for their sons and daughters, their children and childrens' children. So comparatively silent is general history concerning border warfare that none but special students of pioneer times have anything like a correct apprehension how dangerous and skilful were Indian warriors fighting for hunting grounds, fishing streams, and ancestral graves. While it may be that little, relatively speaking, has been recorded of the events that make up pioneer history, yet it is impossible for those of us who revere our ancestral worthies not to revert often in thought to those sad twenty-five or thirty years in which the weapons must have been fashioned and the characters formed and matured for the stupendous war that was to be fought before the Rose of Sharon planted by Scottish-Virginia hands should bloom and adorn this goodly land and diffuse

all around its liberty inspiring and soul saving frag-
rance.   With so much at issue in a conflict to be led
by savage and civilized leaders of the highest endowments, there is something so sublimely portentous in
its significance as to prompt every pious patriot to exclaim in all fervency of spirit:

> "Sound, thou trumpet of God, come forth Great
>   Cause, to array us.
> King and Leader appear!   Thy soldiers sorrowing
>   seek thee."

Having thus considered the character of the Ottowa
and Shawnee leaders opposing the early settlers, we
will give some attention to the characteristics of our
pioneer ancestors, so as to comprehend in a measure
how they became qualified to meet and overcome the
opposition confronting them, and by their marvellous
success opened this "goodly land" for our use and
daily comfort, and known and loved by us as "home,
sweet home," amid the West Virginia hills.

Of the persons most prominent in the early history
of our pioneer ancestry, special mention should be
made of Dr John Craig, for the reason that he exerted
so much telling influence upon the immediate lives of
those persons who pioneered the counties of Pocahontas, Greenbrier, Monroe, and Kanawha.   He is moreover a type of the persons whose names were embalmed by so many of our ancestors with all their hearts
could give, "their praises and their tears."

Dr Craig was Master of Arts by graduation from
the University of Edinburg, Scotland.   For twenty-

five years he ministered to the Old Stone Church, in Augusta County, walking five miles to preaching Sabbath morning, and when Indians were troublesome would carry his own trusty rifle along with Bible and Psalm Book. Services would open at 10 a. m., recess of one hour for lunch at noon, then preaching until sundown. Sometimes, on Sacramental occasions, a candle was needed to read the closing hymns. Then some of the congregation would ride ten or twelve miles to their homes, and after doing up the household chores, would go to bed at midnight. One of his sermons still extant is laid off in fifty-five divisions.

When Braddock was defeated, mainly by the skillful management of Pontiac in 1754, thus leaving all west of the Blue Mountains exposed to Indian incursions, the inhabitants in utter consternation were talking about safety in flight somewhere back to Pennsylvania or over the mountains towards Williamsburg, so as to be near the seat of government, and the safety it implied, the undaunted preacher was opposed to all such schemes. In his journal he thus writes:

"I opposed that scheme as a scandal to our nation, falling below our brave ancestors, (in Scotland) making ourselves a reproach among Virginians, a dishonor to our friends at home, an evidence of cowardice, want of faith and noble Christian dependance on God as able to save and deliver from the heathen; and withal a lasting blot forever on all our posterity."

This valiant soldier of two banners,—the banner of the Cross, and the banner of civil and religious freedom,—advised the erection of forts. In his journal he

writes: "My own flock required me to go before them
in the work, which I did cheerfully, though it cost me
one-third of my estate; but the people followed me and
my congregation in less than two months was well for-
tified."

There are numbers of people living in Pocahontas
today whose ancestors assisted in the erection of the
forts referred to. With such an example, his people
maintained their homes most bravely through all the
fiery trials of that period so eventful in results, as far
reaching as the civilized world and even to the regions
beyond. What remains of this brave patriots recorded
views indicates that his was a mind characterized by
keen, practical sagacity, generous sentiments, and judicious magnificence of reasoning powers. Hence it
was he correctly appreciated the actual needs, advantages, perils, and prospects of his surroundings.

Obtuse indeed must one be who fails to perceive
something splendid, wonderful in such a man, guided
as he had been by a dream in Ireland to his place of
service in the wilds of the Virginia Valley. Before
leaving Ireland, and while frequently praying for Divine guidance where to go, he had a dream that profoundly impressed him, and it was ever vivid to his
memory. After coming to America he followed the
stream of immigration up the Valley of Virginia until
he came to Fort Defiance, a locality that corresponded
with his dream. He at once selected it as a place for
his home, where he dwelt, labored, died, and was buried. Honoured for all time be his memory. May his
example of life and faith like all

"the actions of the just,
Smell sweet and blossom in the dust."

The people upon whom such influences of living and
practicing were exerted, and from whose habitations
invincible defenders went to vanquish foemen like
Pontiac, Logan, and Cornstalk, and famous generals
from Europe, were mainly of Scotch Irish extraction.
The best of such blood is very good, but candor demands the admission that the worst is about as bad as
his Majesty the Prince of the Power of the air would
have it. These warlike, clannish, iron-handed people
did not seek Pennsylvania or the Virginia wilderness
to avoid debt or retrieve broken fortunes, as is said of
the Cavalier English, neither were they in quest of a
refuge where they might praise God as they pleased,
yet compel others to do like them, as is often insinuated of the Pilgrims of Plymouth Rock. The Scottish-
Virginians came for the most part because there was a
fascination in the roominess and liberty that a new
realm promises. Moreover there was something attractive for such inquisitive, daring people in the adventures and dangers that abounded.

And they remained the same unyielding characters,
whether contending for Christ and His covenant in the
old world among the Grampian Hills, or reclaiming
the Alleghanies of the New from Indians, ferocious
beasts, and venomous reptiles. Unrestrained by re-
deeming grace, these people were of fiery temperament
free-and-easy, sport loving, gallant, fighting at the
drop of a hat, racing horses, playing at cards, pitting
game chickens, indulging in whiskey freely as water,
swearing with an emphasis and rhetorical jingle truly

surprising.   With their faults, nevertheless, they were endowed with resplendent virtues of personal character and when individuals became pious it was not half-way doings with them.

In their religion the Pauline phase had precedence, and so they believed and were sure that God abhors sin with no degree of allowance and deals sternly and righteously with unrepentant sinners.   Their belief in the Divine sovereignty was such as to imbue them with that unrelenting persistence under difficulties that so eminently prepared them for the part they were led by Providential guidance to perform, in subduing the pathless wilderness and forming new states.

In regard to the Scottish Virginia women, be it ever remembered in their praise that they were more than equal to their arduous duties in those eventful times. Society was enriched and adorned by the presence of wives, mothers, and sisters whose characters were refined by the sweet uses of adversity, and whose piety was developed and invigorated by most searching tests. The mothers were keepers at home, teaching the children and servants the catechism, and attending church once a month, more or less as opportunities presented. These robust, home.loving, sweet-souled ladies wrote no books, recited no poems nor read essays, yet were none the less fitted to do their all-important part in placing deep and firmly the foundations of the institutions civil and religious that are the precious heirlooms of their descendants.

One of the last ladies left of the pioneer days in Augusta County, was Mrs Margaret Humphreys, near

Greenville. Until quite recently, there were living persons who had listened to her graphic descriptions that conveyed the liveliest impression of the times when the Valley of Virginia was a frontier settlement. Where now may be seen the beautiful farms and substantial houses, her active memory recalled the log cabins, the linsey-wolsey, the short gowns, the hunting shirts, the moccasins, the pack horses, the simple living, the shoes and stockings for winter and uncommon occasions, the deer and the rifle, the fields of flax and the spinning wheel, the wool and the looms; and with them the strict attention to religious concerns, the catechising of children, the regular going to church, the reading of the Bible, and keeping Sabbath from the beginning to the end of the day; the singing of hymns and sacred songs, all blended, presented a beautiful picture of enterprise; economy, and religion in laying the foundations of society.

The compiler of these Pocahontas Sketches well remember seeing and hearing of parties in his younger days, of Scotch-Irish lineage and members of churches reared by their pioneer ancestors, who brought their love affairs to a happy understanding by the means of the hymn book or the Bible. One morning before services began in one of the oldest of the Valley churches a youthful, enamored member politely handed his hymn book to a lady friend in the pew just before him, with a pin stuck in the stanza he wished her to read. Whereupon she read these significant words:

"Let the sweet hope that thou art mine

My life and death attend,
Thy presence through my journey shine
And crown my journey's end."

The young lady in place of blushing and whispering "Oh this is so sudden," took another plan, for she seemed to know at once of a hymn that would meet the emergency in kind and enable her to give as good as he had sent. Returning the book with the selfsame pin for a pointer, he read therein as follows:

"All that I am and all I have
Shall be forever thine.
Whate'er my duty bids me give
My willing hands resign."

The reader is left to figure out what it all came to in the lives of these young people.

Another party, of similar lineage and training, settled matters one afternoon after returning from public worship in another ancient church. They were left in the "company room" all alone, and thereupon the young man disclosed the paramount desire of his heart. This made the young lady look and feel somewhat embarrassed. But she arose and approached the centre table on which was placed the "Big Ha' Bible" in its place of honor. She looked up the 37th Psalm, and turning to her lover friend invited him to read the verses as she pointed them out. He was quickly at her side, and as her hand passed slowly from verse to verse he read what to them both ever after were memorable verses:

"Trust in the Lord and do good; so shalt thou dwell in the land and verily thou shalt be fed. Delight thyself also in the Lord, and he shall give thee the desire of thine heart. Commit thy way unto the Lord, trust also in him and he shall bring it to pass."

From all that remains of the former presence of the Indians in our region, they never occupied it as a place for fixed permanent habitation, but for temporary resort in late Spring, Summer, and early Autumn. The existing traces of Indian occupancy all indicate such to have been the fact. At Clover Lick, Marlinton, and on the Old Field Fork of Elk are found the most that now remains indicating Indian temporary occupancy.

The most interesting trace of the kind in question is found in a meadow near Gibson's on the Old Field Fork of Elk River, twelve miles from Marlinton. This meadow was cleared about forty years ago by William Gibson, and takes the place of one of the thickest patches of laurel and alder brush that the late William Gibson says he ever worked at in all his life. After it was cleared and put in meadow, a circle appeared about 132 feet in diameter, formed of a strange grass that grows, or has not been seen, anywhere else. Mr Gibson saw similar grass in Indiana.

This circle is formed of two figures representing rattlesnakes in the act of mutually swallowing each other. One figure—the yellow rattler—symbolizes light. the black rattler typifies darkness; both combined represent the succession night and day, and illustrates the Indian idea of Time, that mysterious something that gives and takes life, having the power of life and death.

Here the hunters would assemble to invoke the favor of this mighty, mysterious deity, upon whom the contemplated pursuit of game, so essential to their subsistence and of their squaws and papooses, depended. Or if about to go on the war path, the braves would rally here as a rendezvous, and with their dark and bloody rites and ceremonial dances performed within or around this circle would seek to placate the same mysterious power for success over their enemies in the pending battles.

The contrast of the aims and purposes of the Indians and the pioneers is instructive and deserves more than a passing notice.   With Ottowas and more particularly the Shawnees, mere subsistence in the easiest way was the paramount question at issue, and for such a purpose no region surpassed this for their uses.

With the pioneers, homes were what they wanted, where fathers and sons could be settled in communities.   Along with subsistence they desired social comforts, and advantages of intelligent christian worship, and securing these their hopes and aspirations seemed realized.   For their cherished hopes and aims our region was equal to most and surpassed by none under the sun.   At the present day among their descendants the making of money and the enjoyment of all that money secures is the paramount issue.   Mere commercialism, in a more or less modified sense, is the spirit of the new order of affairs with the posterity, the children's children of the pioneers.   And for this new

phase of human endeavor our region is equal to most
and surpassed by none for all the elements of commercial wealth in the forests and mines, in the streams and
oil wells.

Before concluding the first section of the Sketches
of Pocahontas County; I would like to have the attention of our younger people and secure their sympathetic interest. It is my fervent desire and pleasing hope
they will give these sketches of their native county
close and studious attention, as it was and is for their
special benefit these pages are sincerely intended and
in a sense dedicated. In the good Providence of God,
as I firmly believe, my beloved readers, I have been
permitted to occupy sweetly responsible relation to you.
I deem it one of the highest honors ever conferred upon me to have the privilege of serving you with my
own best thoughts, and the thoughts of others consent-
ing to lend the aid I so much need to make these pages
all that I would have them be.

While for good and sufficient reasons my own con-
tributions may not be marked by their depth of thought
or logical or rhetorical power, still I know what con-
duces to earnest and useful thought when I read and
study the writings of the foremost thinkers of the
times, wherein great all important matters are considered, and I intend for my readers the best results ob-
tainable from such sources. I do this believing that
those young West Virginians who may honor these
sketches with their attention are equal to anything I
have been capable of apprehending, and that even
children so termed are worthy of something better than

mere child's play in their reading.

The way to improve is to fix the mind on some proper model or example and try to be conformed to it, and not conform the model to the actual state of the mind. To write and talk in a childish way, it seems to me, amounts to nothing more than making oneself childish, and leaving those to be instructed about where they were at first.

So far as my influence is permitted to reach the readers of these pages, I am going to write and have been writing indeed as if I were writing for devoted, sincere christians, deep and earnest thinkers and highly cultivated persons, for these are just the persons I wish all reading young people to be, and which they must be in fact to stand worthily in the solemn position to which they are likely to be called. There is no doubt in my mind, and it is a conviction that I have permitted myself with much hesitancy indeed, that our young people will be called to meet and decide the most momentous questions that have claimed the attention of men since the Reformation.

I am informed from highly trustworthy sources that no people more successfclly withstood the upas-like overshadowing of the Moslem power than the Hellenists. The reason given is that the highest and the lowest, the youngest and the oldest, vie in the veneration they show for ancestral examples. Their histories, their romances, their traditions, their legends, and their poems keep the glorious exploits of their ancestry ever fresh in their memories, and every Greek wishes to live and die worthy of such illustrious fathers. We have something better to emulate than they. The young Greek cherishes the memory of Solon, Pericles, Themistocles, Demosthenes, Socrates, Plato, and other names of surpassing lustre, but for real merit and goodness what are such names in comparison with those whom every young West Virginian may revere and emulate;—Washington, Henry, John Craig, and Charles Lewis.

The future of our great country will soon pass into the keeping of these very young people, for whose benefit these sketches are sincerely intended. Hence it is the genuine wish of all right feeling people that our sons and daughters may be such as one of God's holiest men of old prayed for:

"Rid me and free me from the hand of aliens whose mouth speak fraud, and whose right hand is a right hand of falsehood. So that our sons may be plants grown large in their youth; our daughters as corner stones, polished for the building of the temple."

A GEOLOGICAL AND GEOGRAPHICAL, AND CLIMATOLOGICAL OUTLINE.

SECTION II.

Our courteous readers are earnestly entreated to keep in mind a clear perception of this fact, that the world-renowned region whose history we are endeavoring to illustrate in some measure, reaches from the Ohio Valley to the Blue Ridge; from the Potomac to the head streams of New River and the Kentucky border.

Intellectual or scientific culture has been so highly developed in our times that for a writer to be up to date in writing up a region like ours, some facts pertaining to its geography, climate, soil, and geology are expected. Geography is a description of the surface as it appears at the present time, while geology takes into account not merely the present surface features but changes that may have affected the surface in the past, with whatever as far as may be known or understood lies beneath the surface.

Like geography, the climate deals mainly with present conditions, but geology opens up glimpses of climate that prevailed ages since. As to soil, when properly studied it will be found needful to know and apply the teachings of geography, geology, and climatology. Geology first claims attention, being older than present geography or climate.

Geology deals with the opinion, for which reasons may be deduced, or given from known phenomena that there was a time the heat of the earth was so intense that all substances beneath or upon its surface were in a molten state of fluidity, and whirled through illimitable space an incandescent, white-hot globe, composed of all the minerals. Its component elements,—iron, gold, silver, rock, all else whatsoever,—were molten, and consequently the earth was larger than now, and the nights and days were of greater length. After the passage of measureless cycles, the surface cooled forming a crust on the still hot globe that had been sparkling and scintillating, and then was the first appearance of "rock," as the word is now understood.

At this first cooling the surface may have been rough, but there were no mountains of any marked altitude, for the crust was not strong enough to hold up any mountains such as now exist. All underneath still remained melted, and probably for unnumbered years after the crust began to form there was no rain, though the air was fuller of moisture than now. The rocky crust continued so hot that a drop of rain would be instantly changed to steam. But in the course of time the crust became cooler and showers began to form and fall. In respect to this period of our earth's history we have no guide but inferences from the teachings of astronomy, assisted in part by well known chemical facts. All attempts to describe our world at that period must be philiosophically conjectural or speculative, and all descriptions would be about as applicable to one part of the earth as another. So far as known to us, no eye but God's ever saw and recognized as such one square mile of the original crust of the incandescent globe in the form it congealed from the melted condition. As the ages rolled away some parts of the cooling earth were broken up by fire, rains, winds, and frosts, and buried other parts with the sedimentary sand thus formed.

There is convincing evidence to the effect that even now the cooling process has not proceeded very far; the surface has only attained a partial degree of coolness, while the interior mass is hotter than the most intense furnace heat. Large areas of the earth's surface have been ffaected by stupendous upheavals and depressions, and these are believed to be owing to the settling down of the solid rock crust in one place and the corresponding uplift in another. There is ample reason for thinking that at a distance of twenty miles or less beneath the surface the temperature would be that of molten iron. There is equally good reason for believing that twenty or thirty miles from the surface of the earth into space, on a line from the earth's centre, a temperature would be reached that the warmest day in those altitudes the thermometer would register a hundred or more degrees below zero.

This should impress us to notice how narrow are the limitations of all human life. Above us in what appears sunny regions, the measureless cold of space; beneath is the fire that feeds on solid rock.

There is geological information to the effect that in a well near Wheeling, West Virginia, the temperature at 4462 feet was 110 degrees; and a descent of less than a mile raised the temperature sixty degrees. In the vicinity of Pittsburg a well five thousand feet in depth had a temperature of 120 degrees. In Germany there is a well 5740 feet deep, which gives a temperature of 135 degrees. From all this it appears that only the outer crust of the earth is cool, and the interior characterized by intense heat.

Upon the crust of the earth becoming sufficiently cool, rains would wash down the higher portions, the sand and sediment thus gathered would be spread over the lower places. This sediment becoming hardened composed the first layers or strata of rock. Some of the oldest layers were very thick at the sea bottoms, and when heated from internal warmth were melted, the stratified feature disappeared, and then they were called "amorphic" or formless rocks. By some granite is regarded as a rock of this kind.

The earth in the process of cooling, shrank in proportion, and the surface became shriveled and wrinkled in folds, large and small. The largest of such folds were mountains, with the seas occupying the depressed places. About that period the first springs, streamlets and rivers appeared, feeling and threading their way wherever the best channel could be found. In the meantime it would still rain and be frosty too, and the rain and frost would attack the higher ridges, and the rocky slopes almost destitute of soil, and the washings would be borne to the seas, forming other layers of rock on the bottoms, and so the accumulation kept on, with some diversity of rate at times, from that era to the present time 1901.

It comes so near being all, that we say that all rocks in this region were formed in the depths of the ocean; formed of sand, mud, and gravel, or of shells, or of a mixtute of all, the ingredients of which were glued together with silica, iron, lime, or other mineral substances held in solution. These rocks when raised by upheaval from the water formed the dry land, and have been fashioned into valleys, ridges, gorges, and the various indentations of surface seen almost everywhere within the limits of West Virginia.

These primeval rocks are occasionally visible as "bed rock" in streams, and alluvial bottoms, and sometimes forming cliffs and tops of peaks and barren mountains, "bald knobs," and the like. But in our region the underlying rocks for the most part are hidden by soil. At the deepest, however, this soil is only a few feet thick, and were it all cleared away there would be visible everywhere a system of ledges and bowlders, conformable to every height and depression now making up the salient features of the surface; the thickness of these rocks in the aggregate about four miles. To the scientific mind this fact satisfies him, and he feels sure, until there is positive evidence to the contrary, that sand and shells four miles deep, in the past were spread out over the bottom of the sea, and these deposits after being hardened into rock by interior heat, were upheaved, and then arranged and cut into the valleys and rugged inequalities so apparent to us all in this our day and generation.

Let it be remembered too that this stupendous rock building was not all done at one time, for this region, or much of it, has been several times under and above the sea, especially where the coal measures are found. Across it time after time has the coast line moved back and forth, this being shown by the rocks themselves.

The expert geologist is able to decide from the fossil shells and plants in a stratum the period of the earth's geological history when that layer was formed, and he can, moreover, determine, the oldest and the newest in a series of strata. And yet the fossil shells and plants may not be all at his command, for the position of the layers to one another is often a sure indication of the oldest and the newest, for the sedimentary sands having been deposited in layers one above another, it may be inferred those on top are not so old as the lower, unless it be in instances not usual or common in our region, where strata have been folded so much as to have been broken and turned over. In such an event, the older rocks may be found above the newer.

Unmeasured though the creative ages be, as recorded by the mountains and cliffs of our goodly land, still the most ancient of our visible ledges are young compared with the ledges of other localities in the world at large, or even of contiguous provinces. The Laurentian Rocks of Canada, more than five miles in thickness, formed like ours by the slow accumulation of sandy deposit, yet that series of rock formations was finished up, and possibly partly worn away, ere the first handful of sand, or the first shell of which anything is now known to us by our rocks, had been placed at the bottom of the Cambrian Sea, under which West Virginia was submerged.

Here thoughts arise that stagger our powers of loftiest imagination. Because of the inconceivable ages required for depositing shell and sand four miles deep astounds the mind, what is to be thought of that vaster lapse of ages, pointing back to the cycles of the young world, all of which was passed, and left their impress in stone, before the corner stones of our Virginia mountains were placed by the architect of the universe. And what is more, this does not certainly bring us to the beginning as yet, for no expert geologist knows it for a fact that the Lourentian rocks are oldest of the layers, and if they should be, still back of them opens that nebulous era, penetrated only by astronomical light, during which the unstratified rocks were in process of formation, from whose pulverized and disintegrated material all subsequent formations have been built up.

The geological eras of special use for our present purpose are the Laurentian, Cambrian, Silurian, Devonian, and Carboniferous.

But meagre traces of the Laurentian period are visible in our State. So with us the Cambrian era is virtually the oldest, and our local interest in geological studies begin with it.

In the Cambrian era, there was a mass of land to the west of us, including what is now Ohio, Indiana, Illinois and beyond. On the east of us was another vast continent of land, reaching from Maine to South Carolina, comprising what is now the Atlantic coastal plain, and extended eastward an indfinite distance, much of it being what is now the basin of the Atlantic Ocean. Between these two bodies of land in the Cambrian era there was a narrow sea from the Gulf of St. Lawrence to Alabama. The trend or line of the eastern coast of tnat Cambrian sea is believed to have been what is now the general direction of the Blue Ridge range, and so West Virginia was at the bottom of that sea. This sea of ours seems to have survived the Cambrian age, the Silurian, the Devonian, and the Carboniferous.

During the Cambrian age, sand washed from the land forming the eastern coast, spread over the bottom of the sea and formed the lowest or oldest layer of rock found anywhere in West Virginia in anything like abundance. On this rock the West Virginia hills are built or founded. This Cambrian sandstone is so deeply covered as to be seen only in places where it is exposed by the folding of strata, or where rivers have eroded very deeply. For the most part the Cambrian rock is buried thousands of feet under subsequent formations. During the Silurian era the Cambrian sea seems to have commenced receding, and the washings of the uplands, it is probable, began to accumulate on the low plains and widening valleys as a deep fertile soil. In the meanwhile too, over a large part of West Virginia that was still under the sea, thick beds of limestone were formed of shells, mixed more or less with sediment.

Shell fish lived and died in the waters of the Cambrian sea during the Silurian period, and when dead sank to the bottom.   A consideration of this fact explains the diverse origin of sandstone and limestone. Limestone is the product of the sea, while sandstone is of material washed from the land into the sea, by rains and swollen streams.   During the period denoted by the close of the Cambrian and the beginning of the Silurian eras, the limestone deposits formed beds from three to four thousand feet in thickness.

Afterwards when that part of the Cambrian sea was separated from the Gulf of St Lawrence by an upheaval in what is now the state of New York the Devonian age was ushered in, which was a wonderful rock builder in the north.   In Pennsylvania the Devonian rocks were nine thousand feet thick; in parts of West Virginia seven thousand feet; in southern Tennessee twenty-five feet; and the Devonian rocks disappeared in Alabama.

The sediments forming the Devonian rocks were fine grained, and formed shales, medium sandstones, and some limestone occasionally.   When the tedious, wearisome Devonian era came to a close, it was succeeded by the Carboniferous geological age.

It was during the Carboniferous period occured the longest summer that has ever been, when over the northern hemisphere there was no winter, and there was a season of vegetation and plant growth such as had never occurred on earth previously, or would ever occur again, in all probability.   It was during this phenomenal summer that our coal fields were formed. In the Carboniferous era the deposits ranged from two thousand to eight thousand feet in thickness in different parts of the state of West Virginia. Moreover there is evidence that there was during this period a breaking up and redistribution of a vast gravel bar that had been somewhere out of the reach of the waves far since the earlier ages. This aggregation was composed of quartz pebbles, in sizes varying from a grain of sand to that of a cocoanut, all worn and polished as if rolled and fretted in turbulent mountain streams or by the waves on the beach for centuries. By some means or other these pebbles were spread in layers in the depth of the sea, thousands feet thick, and were cemented together forming coarse, hard rocks, and known as "conglomerate," "pudding-stone," "bean-rock," and "millstone grit."

A heavy stratum of those stones forms the floor of the coal formations. It is the opinion of some geologists that the pebbles represent the most indestructible remnants of mountains once abounding in quartz veins, but were washed away before the middle or the carboniferous era.

The hard quartz resisted the grinding process that pulverized the other rocks and remained as pebbles in beds or bars until some great upheaval or depression swept them into the sea and spread them out in layers. Their quantity was simply wonderful, for rocks composed of them cover to a considerable depth thousands of square miles.

The distinguishing product of the Carboniferous age were the coal formations that were placed while the Cambrian Sea was undergoing the convulsions and uphevals that permitted West Virginia to emerge from

the depths of sea and become the "goodly land" it now
appears.   It was a fearful collision of the elements.
The basin of the sea was raised up, became dry land
then was again submerged in the deep and gloomy
recesses of the Cambrian Sea.

A mighty effort was apparently made by the land to
repel the waters that had so long maintained the supremacy.   The contest was of vast proportions and
long continued. during which first the land then the
waves had the advantage.

Backward and forward for hundreds of miles would
the Cambrian Sea alternately rise and recede.   The
struggle was prolonged for myriads of years but finally
the land prevailed and the Cambrian billowy contest-
ant in the strife retreated to the west and south as far
as the Mexican Gulf.

Victorious West Virginia became dry land and has
thus remained to this hour, so well has she maintained
her position.

While these changes from sea to land and from land
to sea were going on during a part of the Carboniferous
age the coal fields were being formed, Unlike the
rock formations, coal beds are made above the water
or at its immediate surface.   These deposites are
formed of the trees and plants of varied kinds which
grew so excessively luxuriantly during that longest
summer time of the ages mentioned elsewhere as prevailing over the northern half of our planet in the
Devonian period.

Every coal mine represents some morass, large or
small, wherein plants and trees of fabulous size grew,

fell and were buried for ages. The areas in which the coals were in process of formation were probably depressed and occasionally submerged for some thousands of years, and during the submergency sand and mud settled over it and hardened into stone. And when the hardened deposit would be uplifted materials for another coal deposit would accumulate.

This alternation of coal and rocks means an alternate upheaval and submergence of the land, the coal being formed on land, the rocks in the water. This alternation occurred during the period when the Cambrian Sea, successively advanced or receded across West Virginia while the Carboniferous era was slowly nearing its eventful termination.

There were other geologic periods after the Carboniferous, but they need not be specially noticed in a book like this, because very limited traces remain of their existence in our region. The reason why this should be the case seems to be that after the Carboniferous period West Virginia land was above the sea and therefore no sediment could be deposited to form rocks, and so there would be comparatively little for a lasting record to be impressed.

From the Cambrian age to the Carboniferous, the strata underneath West Virginia becomes thicker and deeper.

From the Carboniferous era to the present era, from the recession of the Cambrian waters, the layers of rock have been modified by the wearing and tearing of the elemental collisions and so the aggregate kept becoming thinner and thinner. And so the strata have been

folded, upraised by subterranean explosions and worn
away by the erosive influences of flowing streams.
There are places where the Carboniferous have not
been worn away; while there are other places where
river gorges have reached the lower of the Devonian
rocks. In some other localities the vast silurian layers
have been penetrated, and in some places the penetra-
tion has deeply reached the Cambrian rocks.

As to the glacial age, which was the counterpart of
the summer age, during which our coals were formed,
but little remains in West Virginia to show that this
empire of steadfast, inconceivable cold once swayed its
ice sceptre in our region. There is but little reason to
doubt, however, that during the glacial era the cold in
West Virginia was intense, and there may have been
glaciers among the highlands, but all traces wellnigh
erased,

Hu Maxwell, a distinguished West Virginia student
and writer, seems to have a passion for geological
themes, and thus expresses himself:

"When we look out upon our great valleys, the
Kanawha, the Potomac, the Monongahela, or contem-
plate our mountains, rugged and near, or robed in distant blue, rising and rolling, range beyond range,
peak above peak; cliffs overhanging gorges and ravines; meadows and uplands; glades beyond, with
brooks and rivers; the landscape fringed with flowers
and clothed with forests; we are too apt to pause before fancy has time to call up that strange and wonderful panorama of distant ages when the waves of a vast
sea swept over all, or when only broken and angular

rocks thrust their shoulders through the foam of the
ocean as it broke against the nearly submerged ledges
where since have risen the highest peaks of the Alleghanies and the Blue Ridge.

"Here where we now live have been strange scenes.
Here have been beauty, awfulness, and sublimity, and
also destruction. There was a long age with no winter. Gigantic ferns and rare palms, enormous in size
and delicate leaves and tendrils, flourished over wide
areas and vanished. And there was a time when for
ages there was no summer. But we know of this from
records elsewhere, for its record in West Virginia has
been blotted out. Landscapes have disappeared. Fertile valleys and undulating hills with soil deep and
fruitful have been washed away, leaving only a rocky
skeleton; and in many places even this has been ground
to powder and carried away, or buried under sands and
drift from other regions."

This is about the most about geological themes we
have room for in these pages.

Let it be noticed however, before the subject is dis-
missed, that what has been written about the geological
history of our home region may grate somewhat strangely and even harshly on the minds of some of our more
devout, Bible loving readers. Unless these readers be
superior in mental balance to a great many eminent
writers of the remote as well as the recent past, of Biblical interpretation, these readers will feel that such
geological views jeopardize the integrity and even the
truth of Bible teachings, in the estimation of all persons who may incline to believe geological history of
the creation as the writer does.

The expression "In the beginning God created," is capable of two interpretations. One might mean "beginning" in the absolute sense, before all worlds whatsoever,—the "unbeginning beginning," as Augustine termed it. This is the "beginning" of which Wisdom seems to be speaking in Proverbs (7, 22–31), as if that beginning was everlasting.

Then there is another explanation which gives to the phrase "in the beginning" a relative significance. In this sense it would mean the beginning of time, when the creation of matter began, when the heavens and the earth were brought into existence in their first form, and thus it marks the initial time period of history. But the "unbeginning beginning" refers to that mysterious beginning mentioned in the first verse of John's gospel, when the "word was toward God, and the word was God." The "beginning beginng" marks a period when God made a beginning in his governmental relations with the universe, and it is the "beginning" referred to in Genesis; first chapter and first verse.

It should soothe all anxious fears about Bible truth being dimmed by geological facts to remember that the Historic Bible only dates its events from the "genesis" of all things, and its reconstruction from confusion and emptiness when the Spirit of God brooded upon the waters. Bible history passes from creation in the "beginning beginning" clear across inconceivably vast cycles of changes to the period of reconstruction and completion by one single leap. Bible history simply states that in the beginning God created the heavens and the earth. Then the whole of the creative ages, the geologic periods intervening down to the creation of man, are passed over in silence. When the time arrived for man to appear, then it was God made kosmic order out of chaotic confusion. And here begins inspired history, written by Moses "the man of God," the higher professional critics to the contrary, notwithstanding.

Our worthy readers will please fix this idea in their memories, that there are three initial points to be observed: first the "unbeginning beginning" of John's Gospel, 1st verse; second, the beginning made by God in the creation of the matter of the universe, the heavens and the earth; third, the beginning of the present order of things, with man at the head, as made known to us by Moses. Then moreover the reader will please observe that we not only have history in the Bible but prophecy also.

The historic Bible reveals what we ought to know of the world before the creation of man, while the prophetic Bible reveals what is best for us to know of the hidden future of this present creation, and what is to come after the present creation shall have fulfilled its purpose and shall have passed away. Consequently this truly wonderful Book of all books tells of a palingenesis—a regenesis—of the heavens and the earth—a new heaven and a new earth, wherein dwelleth righteousness.

In Mathew (19, 29) our Lord speaks of the palingenesis, or new order of things to be set in motion and established in the universe.

Peter foretells the heat and fire out of which the earth will emerge in "the day of God."—(2 Peter, 3c).

. John with his eagle vision beheld the future and tells of the unbounded and endless life, peace, and hapiness of the age yet to come. (Rev. 21, 1–8.)

One of the Wesleys speaks of the Bible in this manner: "The Bible is here as a fact. Only three ways to get here, written by bad men or good men, or by the inspiration of God. Bad men would not write it; good men would not palm off a fraud; and so it must have been written by holy men as they were moved by the Holy Ghost."

Unless the reader be superior in mental balance to a large number of eminent writers on Biblical interpretation, in the more remote as well as the quite recent past, these readers will feel that such geological views jeopardize the influences of Bible teachings on the minds of all who may be inclined to adopt them as true. Now let it be remembered that the phrase "in the beginning God created the heavens and the earth" is susceptible of two interpretations, which have been mentioned elsewhere. Thus viewed, the historic Bible with its "genesis" of the heavens and the earth, leads us to the period when God pronounced the results of His creative ages to be very good.

At this juncture; strangely and mysteriously a something occurred of which Milton speaks:

> "Earth felt the wound,
> And sighing throughout her mighty frame
> Gave signs of woe, that all was lost."

Henceforth the prophetic Bible deals mainly with God's redemptive ages and dealings with man. "The heavens, even the heavens are the Lord's, but the earth hath he given to the children of men."

The Prophetic Bible opens with these words: "And the Lord God said unto the serpent, Because thou hast done this thou art cursed above all cattle, and above every beast of the field; upon thy belly shalt thou go, and dust shalt thou eat all the days of thy life. And I will put enmity between thee and the woman, and between thy seed and her seed; it shall bruise thy head and thou shalt bruise his heel."

Now with its palingenesis and redemptive ages, the prophetic Bible leads us to and leaves us at the place where the "seed of the woman," whose testimony is the spirit of prophecy, proclaims: "Surely I come quickly. Amen." To this the loved disciple responds "Even so come, Lord Jesus." As the seal is stamped and the prophetic Bible closes up, the unending ending is ushered in.

The devout Bible reader realizes that though eye hath not seen, nor ear heard, neither hath it entered into the intellect of man to conceive of the things God hath prepared for those who love him, yet the spirit of the Lord in the prophetic Bible has afforded such glimpses and premonitions that the now unseeable, unhearable, and unthinkable prepared things are virtually revealed. To those receiving what is written with implicit trust, the Bible imparts a hopeful assurance that is unspeakable and full of glory, as well as a peace that passes all understanding. Beloved reader, may it

be yours as well as mine to taste and see that the prophetic Bible is good, as well as the historic Bible.

> Let every kindred, every tribe
>   On this terrestrial ball,
> To Him all majesty ascribe
>   And crown Him Lord of all.
>
> Oh that with yonder sacred throng
>   We at His feet may fall;
> We'll join the everlasting throng
>   And crown Him Lord of All !

By Him all things consist, and without Him was not
anything made that was made.

Passing on from this brief consideration of the geological history of our region, something will now be
said of the geographical features for which West Virginia is so widely and justly celebrated.

In forming and modifying the surface features of
our state two movements have been at work, one vertical, the other horizontal. The vertical movement
elevated extensive areas and formed plateaus not
mountains; the horizontal movement folded and dou-
bled up the strata of rocks, and these foldings, when
sufficiently large, are the mountain ranges, and in our
region both of these movements have acted in the
same area.

By a sweep of the imagination let us think of the
West Virginia mountains as being so leveled as to
form a plain surface. Such a surface when examined
would show that West Virginia has a dome-like surface gradually rising from three or more directions.

This imagined surface form, without the mountains, is what has been imparted by vertical upheavals, that have occurred since the Carboniferous age, unmodified by the horizontal movement. This dome-shaped form shows a great swelling of the surface, coming to an apex at the interblending sources of the Potomac, East Monongahela, Cheat, Elk, James, and Greenbrier rivers, for the highest point of the surface must needs be indicated by the varied courses of the rivers, thus showing that the surface through which they flow slopes in various directions.

Now from this imagined surface, with the mountains all brought low, it appears manifestly that even without mountain ranges, parts of West Virginia would be still high, and this being the fact, it becomes interesting to inquire how our mountain ranges were formed, and why nearly all the highest summits can be grouped in a few counties.

The layers of rock were pushed horizontally by two forces, one from the northwest, the other from the southeast. Rains and streams have been disintegrating, carving these mountains so formed by these pushings and foldings, somewhat modifying their original aspects, but leaving their main characteristics. The first upheaval was vertical, and from it the surface of West Virginia assumed the dome-like contour, as has been imagined by us a little while ago. The next upheaval caused by a horizontal pressure folded the layers of rock that formed the dome-like surface, and thus made mountain ranges.

Now if we keep in mind that these mountain ranges

in crossing the original surface after the first vertical
upheaval, ran up one slope, across the summit and
then down the opposite slope, it is readily understood
why there should be so many of the highest points
grouped in an area so limited. Measured from the
general level of the country where they stand, the
West Virginia mountains are from one thousand to two
thousand feet in altitude.

The general level itself, however, at the highest
part is about three thousand feet above sea level and
thus it is a mountain one thousand feet high where it
stands on a base three times as high will tower four
thousand feet above the sea, and so it follows that the
highest peaks in our state are found where the ranges
cross the most elevated parts of the plateau or general
level. Hence we perceive the reason why the highest peaks cluster about the head springs of the Greenbrier, Monongahela and Potomac Rivers.

The most elevated point in our State is Spruce mountain in Pendleton County, which stands 4,860 feet
above the sea.

The lowest point is found in the Potomac Channel at
Harper's Ferry, 260 feet above sea level. The difference between Spruce Mountain and Harpers Ferry is
4,600 feet, which difference indicates the vertical range.

The general level of Pocahontas County is about
3000 feet above the sea. Where it enters Pocahontas
the bed of the Greenbrier is 3300 feet above the sea,
which is 300 feet lower than the point where Shavers
Fork of Cheat River leaves Pocahontas.

Among the peaks grouped about the river sources of

our State, the following are in our own county: Bald Knob, 4800; Mace Knob, 4760; Spruce Knob, 4700; Bear Mountain, 4600; Elleber Ridge, 4600; Watering Pond Knob, 4600.

Scientists are not fully assured whether the vertical upheaval that raised the West Virginia plateau, or the horizontal compression that elevated the mountains has yet ceased, or not. On one point, however they seem agreed, and that is the work of tearing down is not at rest. To persons versed in scientific researches and observations it seems very certain that mountains, hills, cliffs, uplands, even the valleys and the whole system of underlying rock must ultimately pass away and their materials be spread over the basin of some sea. Rains and frosts, stormy winds, and unforseen chemical processes will complete the work of disintegration. What seems to the eye everlasting rock will become sand, which will go out with the currents and channels of our rivers until the streams themselves no longer have currents, lost in some all prevailing sea.

As to the climatology of our region, observations and tabulated comparisons show a greater diversity in West Virginia than in almost any other section of the United States of like limits.

West of the Alleghanies the climate differs materially from that east of the range, while in the elevated region between east and west the phases of climate are different from either. The dome-like topographic feature characteristic of the State's surface is largely responsible for this climatic diversity in an area so very limited. As a result the vertical range is over four

thousand feet which places a portion of the land to in-
tercept the westerly currents of air, and another portion to catch the eastern winds, while still other parts
are so situated as to be exposed to every wind that
blows. As a rule the sections east of the Alleghanies
have a warmer and dryer climate. In the mountain localities the summers are rarely very hot if ever, while
the winters are usually very cold. Near the highest
Alleghanies the thermometer some times falls 30 degrees below zero, while the highest temperature in summer is seldom above 90 degrees.

There are traditional reports of a snow in 1780 in
the northwest part of the State that was more than three
feet on the level. In 1831 at an elevation of 1000
feet there was a three foot snow between the mountains
and the Ohio River. In 1856 at an elevation of 1500
feet there was a forty-two inch snow along the mountains and valleys west of the Alleghanies. Indications
of snows six or eight feet deep have been seen near the
summits of high mountains, where stumps of trees
have been seen eight or more feet high, cut for browse
or fuel while the snow was encrusted. In the same region west of the mountains on May 5, 1854, a four
inch snow fell. In 1854 the summer west of the
mountains was almost rainless.

The dryest summer spoken of in Pocahontas was in
1838. Swamp deposits became so dry as to burn like
punk, and when ignited would smoulder and smoke
like charcoal pits. June 5, 1859 frost killed almost
every green thing in the interior and northern parts of
the state. In the Little Levels corn with four or more

blades was frost bitten at that time. Some of it was saved by persons clipping the frosted blades with shears.

As to rainfall the annual average for the whole State including melted snow is about 47 inches. West of the mountains the precipitation is greater than it is in the east, but on the western side of these mountains near the crests is the greater precipitation.

There are two directions whence the rains and snows of this region usually come—the east or the west-south west, while partial or local storms may arrive from any point of the compass. In the main, eastern storms are limited to the region east of the Alleghanies since the clouds that bring the rains come from the Atlantic Ocean. The two systems of rains that characterize West Virginia climatology have for their dividing line the uplands following the summits of the Appalachian Range from Canada well nigh to the Gulf of Mexico. The clouds from the Atlantic move up and over the gentle slope from the coast line of the Atlantic to the mountains, precipitating rain or snow as they float along the air currents. Upon reaching the abrupt eastern face of the Alleghanies, exhausting their force of propulsion, and giving out what remains of their moisture, rarely ever cross to the west side. From this it appears that the Blue Ridge is not sufficient to repel or seriously interfere with the transition of the clouds over their serrated summits, while the Alleghanies are barriers against eastern storms especially. Sometimes there are terriffic rainstorms about midway to the summits as the clouds strike and break upon the rugged sides, while at the summit little or no rain falls. It was upon such an occasion that persons now living in our county looked down upon from Paddy's Knob, one of notable AllegLany peaks on the northeast border of Pocahontas county. During this terrffic tempest they saw lightning flash and play, heard the thunders crash and reverberate beneath them. It has been observed too that clouds crossing high mountains rarely precipitate much rain on the leeward side of the propelling currents of air.

Let this study of cli natology be closed by an inquiry where originate the rains and whence do they come to western part of our State. These rains do not come from the Atlantic for the Alleghanies are in the way of the clouds, and and winds that bring rain to the western section blow towards, not from the Atlantic and repels the clouds from that source of rain supply. It is moreover a well ascertained fact that scarcely an appreciable portion of the rainfall over the world at large is ever taken up from the land. Though it may be true that it matters not where rain or snow is known to fall it is from vapor drawn up by the sun chiefly from lakes seas and oceans. In settling the question as to the rain and snow supply for the western slope of our mountain State, which irrigates the lands to the Ohio and indefinitely the regions beyond, the most available method in reach is to take the bearings of the currents of air on which the clouds are wafted, and trace them to their place of starting. The bearing of these rain briuging currents of air is something west of southwest. In tracing this bearing our readers are led to the Pacific ocean on the Mexican coast, whence the Equator would be reached in the course of two or three thousand miles. Upon touching the Equator turn at right angles and a thousand miles farther in this south-easterly course, that part of the Pacific would be reached which extends from South America to Australia and most probably that here our readers would find themselves at or very near the starting point whence the winds start on their mission of carrying the rains and the snows that we receive on the western slopes of our state. It would require more time and space to elaborate the evidence that favors this opinion than can be spared in these sketches, so accurate and complicated it is in the scientific observations and inductions required. So let it suffice or satisfy us to know surely that the vast atmospheric systems of currents and counter currents have been traced and recorded on charts until they are nearly as well known as are the courses of the rivers on the continents of our earth.

Reflecting minds are very profoundly impressed when they observe the rains pouring down in summer showers, or the snowflakes gyrating in the wintry storms, by thinking of the distance passed over by the clouds overhead, and the burden carried, that is represented by a sheet of water nearly four feet deep and spread over a surface of twenty thousand square miles. All this too lifted from the South Pacific ocean by the sunbeams and every year borne through the air ten thousand miles and poured in blessed profusion on hill, mountain, vales, meadows, and gardens making them pleasing fruitful and "filling our mouths with good things."

DISTINCTIVE NATURAL FEATURES, MINARAL SPRINGS, STREAMS.—PIONEER METHODS AND SOCIAL CUSTOMS.

SECTION III

From now on we will devote ourselves strictly to the limits of Pocahontas County, West Virginia. Preliminary words on the outlines of general history, and what was written concerning geological, geographical, and climatological features characteristic of the region wherein Pocahontas forms a conspicuous feature, were all intended to impress ourselves and readers with some idea how wonderfully the lines of habitation had fallen to our pioneer ancestors in such a remarkable region, and what a goodly heritage is ours could we but justly appreciate it all.

By an act of the Virginia Legislature at Richmond, assembled in 1821, Pocahontas County was formed of territory detached from the counties of Bath, Pendleton and Randolph aggregating 820 square miles. Colonel John Baxter of Stony Creek was very active in bringing about the organization of the new county. Two counties were provided for, one to be named Alleghany, the other Pocahontas. The intention was to name the county embracing the crown of the Alleghanies, "Alleghany," the other lower down "Pocahontas," but owing to a clerical oversight the intended names were interchanged.

The geographical position of our county, is defined from 37 degrees 40 minutes to 38 degrees 45 minutes North Latitude; from 79 degrees, 35 minutes to 80 degrees 24 minutes West Longitude. Approximately, Marlinton's geographical position is indicated by the intersection of N. L. 38 degrees 13 minutes and W. L. 80 degrees 8 minutes. The true meridian station mark of sandstone is located in the courthouse grounds 11.9 feet north-east of courthouse steps. The distant mark, north of station mark 957.5 feet on south side of Marlin's Mountain. August 16, 1898, the magnetic declination was 3 degrees, 31 minutes W. Mean annual change 3 seconds approximately.

Pocahontas is an eastern border county' Alleghany top being the line between Pocahontas and Virginia. From the centre of West Virginia Pocahontas county is located to the south-east. Among the distinctive features of the north portion of this county is the fact of its being a part of the high region where nearly every river system of the Virginias find their head springs. The entire county has a great elevation, some of the highest peaks in the State being within its limits. Greenbrier River rises in the north highlands and flows for the entire length of the county through the central portions. Williams River is in the western part of the county, and joins the Gauley in Webster County. In the eastern limits of the county is Knapps Creek, rising in the Alleghany in the vicinity of Frost, and joins the Greenbrier at Marlinton. This junction of streams, where the bright waters meet, forms the rich alluvial delta where the first corn ripened in Pocahontas, and on which Marlinton is building up.

Deer Creek and Sitlingtons Creek from the east; Leatherbark, Warwicks Run, and Clover Creek from the west are important tributaries to the Greenbrier, in north Pocahontas. In central Pocahontas, Thorny Creek and Knapps Creek, with its branches Douthards and Cochran's creeks, Cumming's and Brown's creeks, from the east; Stony Creek and Swago Creek from the west are the main tributaries of the Greenbrier. In south Pocahontas, Stamping Creek and Locust Creek, and Trough Run from the west, and Beaver Creek, Laurel Run, and Spice Run from the east are the tributaries of Greenbrier River.

The Elk region in the northwest is drained by the Old Field Fork, Slaty Fork, and Big Spring Branch of Elk River.

Concerning Knapps Creek, there is an interesting tradition to the effect that it derives its name from Knapp Gregory, believed to be the person of solitary, eccentric habits, who reported to parties in the lower Valley of Virginia that he had seen water flowing towards the west, which report led to Marlin and Sewall's exploration of this region and their locating at Marlin's Bottom, 1749.

The site of Knapp Gregory's cabin is near the public road about opposite Mr Peter L. Cleek's residence, two miles from Driscol. Traces of the fireplace and the dimensions of the cabin yet visible. Early in spring the grass appears here more luxuriantly than elsewhere and earlier, for the spot seems to be especially fertile, an often observed characteristic of places where buildings have disappeared by gradual decay.

Knapp Gregory is reported to have disappeared from the Creek suddenly and mysteriously. When seen last he was in pursuit of a deer near the Lockridge fording. It was supposed by some that he might have been drowned, while others suspect that he may have been killed and robbed by some suspicious looking characters that had been seen about the same time, by scouts from Augusta County.

East Pocahontas is mountainous and in former years heavily timbered with white pine and much other valuable timber, and abounds in iron ores. Central Pocahontas consists largely of limestone lands, much of it is nicely cleared, and cultivated in grains and grasses. West Pocahontas has more mountains, vast forests of timber of varied valuable kinds, and the indications are to the effect that much coal of great commercial value is ready for development. Heretofore this region was called the Wilderness, or Wilds of Pocahontas, having been, comparatively speaking, an unbroken and wellnigh an impenetrable region.

Throughout Pocahontas County there is such an abundance of purest, freshest waters as beggars all ordinary powers of description. Literally it is a land of "springs and fountains," beyond the dreams of poetic diction to portray realistically. Some of these springs gushing from the earth, even in midsummer show undiminished volume, and with a temperature but little above that of iced water. The entire county is seemingly underlaid with vast reservoirs, whose dimensions puzzle the imagination, for from the level land as well as from the mountain sides pour forth great springs, many of them with volume sufficient to propel water mills. Larger streams thus starting from a hill-side sometimes disappear, only to appear elsewhere from some unexpected opening in the earth. Of this it is believed that Locust Creek furnishes a notable example in its relation to Hills Creek.

Among the mineral springs for which this county may soon become famous, mention may be made of the Lockridge Spring, near Driscol; the Curry Meadow Springs, at Huntersville. James E. A. Gibbs, the sewing machine lock-stitch inventor, when a young man in delicate health, was employed to build a barn for William Fertig, forty or fifty years ago, a short distance below the Curry Spring. While at work he used the water because it was convenient to get at. To his grateful surprise his health improved and he became a vigorous person, and yet lives to pay a tribute for what this water was the means of doing for the benefit of his health.

The Peter McCarty group or springs at the head of Brown's Creek, four miles from Huntersville; the Pritchard and Price Springs at Dunmore, three miles from Forrest Station on the Greenbrier Railroad; the Spring-House spring near the head of Clover Creek. All these Springs have a local reputation for remarkable cures and they seem to be analogous in their properties to the Capon Spring in Hampshire County.

Dr J. B. Lockridge had Prof Mallett, of the Virginia University, to make a qualitative analysis of the Driscol Spring. Like the Capon Springs, the Driscol Spring has been found to contain silicic acid, soda, magnesia, bromine, iodine, and carbonic acid, and therefore good for bathing and drinking, promising relief for rheumatism, gout, dyspepsia, dropsical affection, calculus, and renal troubles. Within the radius of a mile of Dunmore are the Moore Blue Sulphur spring, the Kerr magnesia, and chalybeate water.

Near Edray several mineral springs are known and for more than fifty years have been used with beneficial results, such as the Warwick sulphur, Duffield chalybeate, Duncan's chalybeate, and Smith's magnesia, on the west branch of the Indian Draft; Clover Lick Salt Spring, Moore's magnesia Spring, near Marlinton; Moore's alum spring, or as some call it, natural lemonade spring on Brown's Creek. On Laurel Run, four or five miles, east of Hillsboro, is a remarkable group of springs, consisting of a fresh water spring and a purple sulphur spring welling up from the same rock within a radius of a yard or so. The effects of these springs used to be the wonder of the gossips and wet nurses fifty years ago.

In the matter of natural scenery Pocahontas County can display some charming mountain views from points like Droop Mountain Summit, where the Lewisburg Pike reaches it and overlooks Hillsboro and vicinity; Gibson's Knob, overlooking Clover Lick, a point from which, under favorable conditions of weather and sky, House Mountain in Rockbridge and the Peaks of Otter

may be discerned.   Several years ago, about the time
a new tin roof was placed on Lexington Court - House
the late William Gibson saw saw the scintillations of
reflected sunlight.   The distance to Lexington is about
eighty miles; Peaks of Otter, one hundred and ten.
Grassy Knob, near Greenbank; Paddy's Knob, east of
Frost; Kee Rocks, and Buck Knob, overlooking Marlinton, and the High Rocks, overlooking Millpoint
and vicinity; the "Bend," overlooking Edray; Mount
Seeall, overlooking the Hills and Knapp's Creek Valleys; Briery Knob, that looms up so visably in lower
Pocahontas, all afford prospects to be appreciated must
be seen and enjoyed.   The sunrise prospects challenge
description worthy of the best endeavors of Ruskin or
a Maurice Thompson to put in words.

Some four or five years since two ministers had occasion to travel over the Drooping Mountain at an
early hour.   This mountain overlooks much of southern Pocahontas and northern Greenbrier, commanding
an entrancing view of Hillsboro and its charming rural
surroundings of Groves, fields and orchards.   It was
very misty on the morning referred to, and as the ministerial equestrians passed from Hillsboro their view
was   shut off   on   every   side by the dense va-
pory barriers. They slowly ascended the broad but
devious road up the mountain side towards the summit.
Upon reaching the crest of the mountain the sun was
seen some hours high in all its glorious power and
light.   If the Psalmist had been there he would have
spoken of the sun as a bridegroom coming out of his
chamber and rejoicing as a strong man ready to roll

away the mists that were over the hills, the vales and streams, keeping them from view. We paused at the point most favorable for our outlook, and time was spent contemplating the scene, feeling that we knew of no words that would at that moment fitly express our emotions. In the meantime a radiant power more than ninety million miles away had come and was working miracles all about us. The vast surface of the lake-like cloud beneath our feet began to rise and roll like the waves of a miniature ocean, and the sunbeams beautified all these white waves. They seemed to gather themselves into Delectable Hills, and from their radiant tops spires of vapors enchanting with nameless beauties reached upward towards the sun. And as one would tower above others near, it seemed to draw them along with itself till all had vanished in upward viewless flight. Drops of dissolving mist were on the leaves. Like pearls they hung the bushes with brilliants, and shone like diamonds on the grass.—Had that morning been without cloudy mists, the morning scene would have been divested of more than half of its unspeakable beauties and suggestive lessons. Such a scene as was witnessed by those ministerial friends on Drooping Mountain was well fitted to remind them, and all others who pause, and think upon like morning scenes amid our mountains, of the fact that it was when alone upon a mountain that Elijah saw the glory of the Lord. It was when alone upon the mountain "the Lord spoke unto Moses as a man speaketh unto his friend. Then and there Moses received the promise of final rest. A piously intelligent person while

visiting alone, the mountains of Switzerland, wrote in
this manner to friends at home, "It is good to be
among the mountains alone—good for both the mind
and heart." It seems to be almost universally conceded that mountain solitudes are very conducive towards
developing elevated types of piety rightly improved.
By this, however, is not meant that christians or those
desiring to be christians are nearer to heaven, in place,
upon mountain tops than in their homes in the valleys
and chambers for secret prayer, though on the mountain tops they be seemingly and impressively nearer the
blue sky and its starry gems. When the mind is in a
devotional receptive mood there is something very congenial between the mountain tops and prayer and spiritual glory.

Where every thing seems to be more or less unique,
as in Pocahontas, natural curiosities individually do
not cut much figure, yet special mention may be made
of the cliffs at the end of Droop Mountain, which have
but recently become famous, and will be one of the
features of tourists entering our county by rail up the
Greenbrier; the "Ice Cave" of Droop Mountain. the
"Cranberry Meadows" west of Hillsboro; the Falls of
Hills Creek; the Turkey Buzzard Cave, near Mt Vernon, the Black Hole near Linwood, the Saltpetre Cave
at the head of Swago Creek; the Overholt Blowing
Cave, surpassing the historic Windy Cove of Old
Millboro in Bath, near McClintic's Mill, four miles
from Marlinton; the stone footlog and rock parlor ta-
ble at the head of the Dry Branch of Swago; the
Buttermilk Spring on Gauley, about opposite Gibson's

across the mountains; and "Gun Boat Rock," near Split Rock.

Killing frosts early and late made tha working of land a precarious source of subsistence until a comparatively recent period in the history of our county. As late as 1810, the fact that corn would ripen at Marlin's Bottom enough to be fit for meal was nearly a year's wonder. Gardens for onions, parsnips, cucumbers, pumpkins, and turnips; patches for buckwheat, corn, beans, and potatoes, for many years comprised the most of pioneer farming enterprise in the way of supplementing their supplies of game and fish. The implements used for clearing and cultivating these gardens and truck patches were of home manufacture, and for the most part rather rudely constructed, as mere makeshifts are apt to be.

The people were very frequently molested when at work, by the Indians. And on this account the men would carry their guns with them and have them always in ready reach, and while at work they would be on the look out lest cunning scouts in ambush would shoot them down while at their endeavors to win their living in the sweat of their faces.

It being scarcely possible to keep a work horse because of the raiding Indians, most of the labor of farming had to be done with hoes. In course of time when horses and oxen could be kept and used, plows were in demand. The first plows were made entirely of seasoned hardwood. An improvement was made by attaching an iron plate to the plowing beam, and the "shovel plow" was evolved.

To smooth and pulverize the earth for planting, the place of the harrow was supplied by a crabapple tree or a blackthorn bush, pressed down by heavy pieces of wood fastened on by hickory withes or strips of leatherbark, and some nice work was done by these extemporized harrows. The first harrows that superseded the crab and blackthorn, had wooden frames shaped like a big A, and the teeth being made of seasoned hickory or white oak.

The first scythes that were used to cut the meadows were hand-made by the neighborhood blacksmith, and were hammered out instead of whetted to put them in cutting order. The sneathes were straight sticks, and in mowing the mowers were bent into horizontal, semilunar fardel shapes, as if they were looking for holes in the ground, or snakes in the grassy weeds.

For handling hay or grain, forks were made of bifurcated saplings of maple or dogwood, carefully peeled and well seasoned. The writer remembers with pleasure a dogwood fork presented to him by his father, and this fork compared with the hickory rod kept in pickle for lazy, absent-minded boys, was a thing of beauty and the joy of many a summer day in the meadows. It became smooth as ivory, and was the last of wooden forks I have ever seen used, and the last shocks I built with it were in the meadow just above the Island, more than fifty years ago.

When the pioneers came to need more land than mere patches, they would chop three or four acres "smack smooth" and a log rolling was in order. By invitation the neighbors for miles would meet with their teams of horses or oxen, to assist in putting up logheaps for burning. This being done a feast was enjoyed, and all returned homewards.

The next thing was to burn the heaps. Outside the clearing a wide belt was raked inwardly to prevent the fire from "getting away." The preferred time for using fire was usually some night when all would be still and calm. The first thing was to burn the clearing over, thus making way with smaller brush, undergrowth, and other "trash." It was an impressive sight to witness as the smoke and flames of the burning heaps arose like pillars of fire by night, while the men, sweaty and sooty, passed among them keeping up the fires.

Another interesting pioneer social gathering was the "raising" of the dwelling or a barn. Nothing pecuniary was expected, simply a return of like service when notified. "Huskings" were popular at a certain period. In some communities they would come off in the day as a matter of business, not recreation or frolic. But the typical "husking" was prepared for with some elaborate preparation, The ears would be pulled from the stalks, husks and all, and placed in ricks. This "husking" usually came off on some moon lighted night. A managing "boss" was chosen who arranged the men on opposite sides of the rick, and the contest was who would be the first to break over the crest line. Finding a red ear was considered good luck and so every ear would be noticed as it was broken off. Whoever scored the most red ears was the champion of the "husking bee." While the fathers and sons were thus

laborously but joyovsly disporting themselves at the
corn ricks, the mothers and daughters were gathered
at the house, some cooking, others busy at the "quilting." About 10 or 11 o'clock the "husking" and the
"quilting" were suspended, supper served and then
came the "hoe down," wherein heavy stumbling toes
would be tripped to the notes of a screeching unruly
violin, such fiddling was called "choking the goose,"
or when there was no fiddle in evidence some one only
"patted Juba" about as distinctly as the trotting of a
horse over a bridge.

As a rule pioneer festivities were orderly, yet once
in a while there would be a few persons at the huskings who prided themselves in being and doing ugly.
Somewhere about the premises there was some body or
some thing that they would speak of as "Black Betty."
After a few clandestine visits to where "Black Betty"
was, the consequences would be that colored Elizabeth
with her songs, yellings and a few fights would get in
her work, and thereupon a fistcuff or two would impart
interest to the gathering, and make the occasion the
talk of the neighborhood until some other exciting matter came around.

In the early times now under consideration it was
an essential matter that about every thing needed for
comfortable use about the home should be home made
or at least somewhere in the immediate neighborhood.
Thus it came that pioneer wives and daughters were
not only ornamental but exceedingly useful in promoting the comforts and attractions of their homes by the
skill of their willing hands. Every household of any

pretentions to independence or thrift had a loom, spinning wheels, little and big, a flax breaker, sheep shears
wool cards, and whatever else needful for changing
wool and flax into clothing and blankets.

Sheep were raised on the farms and were usually
sheared by the girls and boys. The wives and daughters would thereupon scour, card, spin, weave and knit
the fleeces into clothing:

The flax was grown in the "flax patch," usually a
choice bit of ground. When ripe the flax was pulled
by hand, spread in layers until dry upon the ground
where it had been pulled, then bound in bundles, carried away and spread very neatly over the cleanest and
nicest sod to be found, most commonly the aftermath
of the meadow. Here it remained with an occasional
overturning until it was "weathered," or watered. After an exposure of three or four weeks, or when weathered completely, the flax was gathered, bound in bundles, stored away in shelter until cool frosty days in
late fall, winter or early spring would come, when it
would be broken by the flax breaker, then scutched by
the scutching knife over an upright board fastened to a
block. Then what was left of the woody part by the
breaker and scutching knife would be combed out by
the hackle, and was now ready for spinning and weaving as flax or tow. The tow could be held in the hand
and spun for coarse cloth, "tow linen." The flax,
being the straight and finer fibre, would be wrapped to
the "rock," attached to the little wheel and spun for
the finer fabrics. The rock was a contrivance made by
bending three or four branches of a bush together and

tying them into a kind of frame-work at upper end.
Flax was most commonly put through the entire process from planting to wearing without leaving the farm
on which it was grown.

The growing of wheat in Pocahontas in quantities
sufficient for self-support was not thought of in early
times.   Ploughed in with the the bull tongue or shovel
plow, brushed over by a crab brush or thorn sappling,
and in many instances simply laboriously dug in with
a hoe, it was a precarious crop, owing to freezing out,
blight or rust.   The harvests were gathered with the
sickle.   The reaper clutching a handful of grain in his
left hand would sever it with his right.   The handfuls
were bound into sheaves and then stacked into dozens.
Ten sheaves upright with heads pressed together and
all sheltered and kept in place by the other two sheaves
being broken at the band and spread out like fans and
laid over the top.   These dozens having dried out were
carried by wagon or sled and stacked.   When on steep
ground the dozens would be brought off on stretcher
shaped contrivances attached to a man's shoulders.   At
first the threshing was done by flail, and fifteen bushels
was a good day's work.   In value one bushel of wheat
was equuivalent to two bushels of corn, and exchanges
were made on that ratio.   Where crops were comparatively large flailing was superseded by "tramping out"
by horses freshly shod.   In this innovation the half
grown boy was much in demand as he could ride one
horse and lead a second.   Two or three pair of horses
would hull out forty or fifty bushels per day.   After
tramping awhile the horses would leave the floor and

rest while the straw would be shaken up and turned over, and then the tramping would be resumed until the grain was all out. In separating the wheat from the chaff the first method was to throw shovelfuls up when the wind was high to blow the chaff away, and then the wheat was cleaned by a coarse seive, which was shaken by hand, and the chaff would come to the top and raked off in handfuls. This was improved on the "winnowing sheet," usually worked by two men, while a third would shake the wheat from a shallow basket. Finally the "winnowing sheet" gave way to the windmill or wheat fan, when the farmers became so advanced in circumstances as to feel themselves able to pay thirty or forty dollars for one.

After "horse tramping out," came the threshing machine, and the sensation produced by its advent surpassed anything that has ever occurred in our county, unless it was the coming of the cars, the 26th of October, 1900. This machine, known as the "chaff-piler," was introduced about the year 1839, by William Gibson, of Huntersville, W. Va. It was operated by Jesse Whitmer and John Galford, late of Mill Point. It was a small affair, simply a threshing cylinder in a box, propelled by four horses, and when in operation the wheat would fly high and low as if it was all in fun. An immense sheet was spread on the ground, and this was enclosed by a wall of strong tent cloth about eight feet high, on three sides. A person with a rake removed the straw as it came out. He would have his face protected with heavy cloth, for the wheat grains would sting. After the "chaff-piler"

came the separator, at first propelled by horses, and
then more recently by steam. At the present time
most of the crops are separated by the "steamers."

When it came to be possible to raise corn fit to eat
in the limits of our county, its preparation for the table was a matter of prime importance. One of the
earliest contrivances was the "hominy block." This
was made from a large block of some hard wood, most
commonly white oak, eighteen or twenty inches in diameter, hollowed out at one end by burning and then
trimmed into the shape of a druggist's mortar of huge
proportions. For burning out the cavity a hole was
bored by a two inch auger, then a red-hot bolt of iron
was inserted. This iron bolt was frequently a coup-
ling pin of a wagon. When this could be used no
longer to advantage, then hard dry wood—elm was
preferred—was obtained, and a fire was kindled in the
hole and kept burning until the cavity was of the desired size. The top was large, but it narrowed down
until it assumed a funnel shape, and held a peck or
more of grain. The grain had been slightly softened
by soaking in tepid water, and was reduced by the use
of a wooden pestle, usually made of tough material
thick as a man's wrist, an iron wedge inserted at one
end, made fast by an iron band.

Pounding corn for a family of eight or ten persons
was an all day business, and part of the night on Sat-
urdays. When pounded the grain would be in a more
or less fine condition, and by using a seive made of
deer's skin stretched over a hoop and perforated with
holes, before the wire sifters were known, the coarse

and fine could be separated. The fine meal would do for "johnny cake," which is derived from "journey-cake," baked on a board, and for bread, while the course could be either repounded, or cooked as it was for hominy.

After a time this wearisome pounding was alleviated by a sweep pole; superseding the hominy mortar and sweep pole was the hand-mill, formed of two circular hand-stones. The lower was the bed-stone, the upper was the runner, and both were closely fitted by a wooden hoop, in which there was an opening for the discharge of the meal. In the runner there was a central opening into which the grain was fed. Another opening was drilled near the edge of the runner, into which one end of a pole was fitted, while the other end was put through a hole in a board fastened to the joists above. With one hand grasping the upright pole, the miller turned the runner, and with the other fed the grain into the central opening. The grinding of one bushel was counted a day's work.

Hand mills served their purpose, and tub-mills—the first water mills—came into use. In the tub-mills, the upper stone was stationary while the lower one turning against it reduced the grain to meal. The plan of construction was this: A perpendicular shaft was fixed in the lower stone or runner, and on the other or lower end of the shaft was a water wheel four or five feet in diameter. This wheel being sunk in a stream of water, its force caused the wheel to revolve and thus turned the stone fixed to the upper end of the shaft.

After the tub-mills came the "grist mills," with the

horizontal shafts, the lower stones stationary and the upper ones the runners.

In thinking over what has been written concerning pioneer farming experiences, the writer feels safe in saying that if the successors of these early settlers could see and handle the rude and clumsy, hand made appliances devised and used by the pioneer busy hands in their toilsome, dangerous endeavors for a livelihood they would be greatly surprised, and would be prone to regard them as implements of sorely tedious torture, were they compelled to make use of the same in their bread-winning pursuits in 1901.

It would be a serious mistake however to think in that way of our worthy forbears, because they passed many hours of genuine enjoyment. Their fewer wants easily satisfied, rendered them as well contented, if not better as a rule, than their descendants now living their strenuous lives in pursuit of luxuries of dress, housing, and food that would have been the envy of princes and kings in pioneer days.

So far as tested, all the cereals now produce large yields in Pocahontas County. Wheat, corn, rye, oats, millet, and buckwheat may be produced in ample abundance. Though there be quite a number of good mills, yet they are so located that there are communities who think it to their interest and convenience to carry their wheat to the Warm Springs or Monterey to be ground, and considerable is imported, owing to its being cheaper than the home product.

The climate of this county has passed through a great change the past eighty or ninety years. About that long since it was a rare thing for corn to ripen anywhere in the region now forming the limits of Pocahontas. While it may be true that considerable corn was planted, yet the intention was to have merely soft corn, to fatten a beef or pork in case the mast failed, or be scarce.

About 1810, Major William Poage, then living at Marlin's Bottom, (now Marlinton), had a field of corn near the mouth of the Creek that was looking very promising. He was asked by a neighbor how much corn fit for bread did he think he might have from that splendid looking field. Major Poage, after some thoughtful hesitation, replied very cautiously that he ventured to think there was a probability of there being eight or ten bushels. This was spoken of as the marvel of the season, that out of three or four hundred bushels of corn raised at Marlin's Bottom, there might be eight or ten fit for bread, johnnycake, pone, and hoecake, and the happy people thought things now looked like living.

It is within the memory of living persons when ripe corn was the seldom exception, not the regular rule, on Elk, where fine crops are the rule of everything that is eatable, and that too in notable abundance and of prime quality.

As the climate and soil now are in Pocahontas, they are found to be adapted to the production of tobacco of a very good quality, and for most of the staple fruits, specially the peach and apple.

In the limestone belts bluegrass grows spontaneously and there are places where the bluegrass sod rivals the

famous Kentucky bluegrass. To use the language of
an unknown writer, "Timothy, clover, and numerous
other choice varieties contest the right of the bluegrass
to the field; so we find them growing together, each
trying to choke out the others and to climb high enough
to choke out all the rest." So far as is observed, this
bluegrass producing sod is common over the greater
part of the county, and there is but a small percentage
of its territory where grasses may not flourish. As a
result a great deal of livestock has been and is produced. The cattle, for marketing qualities, equal any in
the State. Pocahontas mutton has a reputation pecu-
liarly its own, and the genuine commands the best
market figures. There have been times, and to some
extent such is the case now, where buyers from other
States have come and canvassed Pocahontas County
for live stock, seemingly not willing to wait until the
cattle or sheep could be taken to them at their homes.
Blooded horses equal to the best for quality and service, have been raised in this county.

It is believed that when the lumber enterprises shall
have finished their operations and the lands no longer
wanted for the merchantable timber, there will be still
grander opportunities opened up for farming, fruit
producing, and stock raising, and then Pocahontas may
rank among the best in any of the States in that line
of home making and industrial endeavor.

Very much of Pocahontas was heavily timbered and
as the variety and quality was equal to most and surpassed by no other county in the State, before the vast in-
roads were made on these timber resurces in the last

fifteen or twenty years. Still there is an enormous supply yet remaining after all has been done by rafts, drives and loaded freight cars. For twenty years or more an interesting feature were the lumber camps here and there in the woods where hundreds of men were comfortably housed and fed on the fat of the land in various parts of the county, mainly east of the Greenbrier. On the higher elevations west of the Greenbrier and in the western and north-western part of the county are vast reaches of black spruce forests, now in such demand for wood pulp of which the paper is made for post cards, books and newspapers. There remains much oak, cherry, poplar, chestnut and the more common forest trees in marked profusion. The value of timber standing not long since was estimated at over two million dollars.

During the construction of the Greenbrier Railway the past two years (1899–1900) several quarries of sandstone were opened along the line or nearby, and the material pronounced equal to the best for construction purposes.

For burning and fluxing purposes limestone is very abundant, and much of it lies very near vast iron ore deposits.

Near the Little Levels in south Pocahontas very pretty marble has been found, and the mountains on the west of the Levels contain vast amounts of black and white marbles. The specimens of which are very beautiful and promise great commercial value. These formations may be of ready access to the main stem of the Greenbrier Railway by short tramways from Seebert and Locust, and possibly points intervening.

The entire county from end to end east of the Green-brier abounds in iron ore indications, principally the brown hemetite and the reddish fossiliferous. The fossiliferous is not in thick veins or very widely distributed, but of the brown hemmetite the supply is regarded as virtually inexhaustible. The veins of ore are large, of excellent quality and distributed over a vast area. In character the ores are pronounced the same as the ores of Monroe and Greenbrier counties. The ore veins of these counties are regarded as extensions of the veins found in Pocahontas.

As to coal resources but little, comparatively, has as yet been ascertained by actual development. While some investigations have been made, but very little coal has been mined for home use and none for exportation. In west Pocahontas in the Gauley and Williams River region, there is a large area underlaid by the New River coking coal veins ranging from two feet thick to eighteen feet, and as far as tested this west Pocahontas coal proves equal to the New River coaking coal. This is the coal that has made the New River region in Fayette County and the Mercer or McDowell coal districts farther south so renowned as coke producing localities. This West Pocahontas county coal is about, as to mileage, the nearest coking coal to the iron producing centres of the two Virginias. Railway transportation and mine development seem to be all that is wanted to bring about a lively demand for this coal. Transportation and development appear now from current enterprizes to be questions of only a short time.

As to the means of travel and communication in pioneer times, it seems that for years the pass ways to and from places in our county and elsewhere beyond were the trails made by buffaloes and Indians. At first the brush was trimmed away and widened for pack-horses, then for sleds, then for wagons, as progress required. The pioneers seem to have noticed that it would be advisable to avoid the trails along the streams and valleys, and follow the crests of leading ridges, and so new paths were blazed accordingly and came to be used, hence the steepness of the old roads may be accounted for in great measure. It was much more practicable to escape an ambuscade on a crest or summit, than when hemmed in by a valley hill sides. With a tenacity worthy of a better purpose the pioneers clung to the old paths with marked conservatism. The sons prided themselves with the idea that what was good enough for their fathers was good enough for them. About 1836, however, there seems to have been an awakening on the matter of better roads to and from the county. The Warm Springs & Huntersville Turnpike was projected, and completed about 1838, with Henry Harper and Wm. Gibson, a Huntersville merchant, contractors. It was a grand high way for that period, and awoke a sensation much like our people felt at seeing cars coming to Marlinton. Every stream was bridged from Huntersville to the Warm Springs, and the means of communication at the time between those places seemed to be all that was desired or could be reasonably expected. Capt. William Cackley was in the Legislature that authorized

and chartered the road, and, to use his own terse language, he had a "time of it log-rolling his bill
through;" the expletives are here respectfully omitted.

The Staunton and Parkersburg Pike was made two
or three years later. It was located by the celebrated
Crozet, one of the great Napoleon's loyal engineers,
who refugeed to the United States after Waterloo had
made it rather uncomfortable for him in the old country.

About 1854 the Huttonsville and Marlinton Turnpike was located by Engineer Haymond. In the same
year he engineered the Lewisburg and Marlinton Turnpike, and the Greenbrier Bridge at Marlinton. Colonel
William Hamilton, of Randolph County, contracted
for the road work from Huttonsville to Marlin's Bottom. Lemuel Chenoweth, from Beverly, built the
bridge in 1854,–56. Captain William Cochran superintended the Lewisburg Road, and all of these enterprizes were completed by 1856. During the war between the States these highways, like so many other
things, were virtually laid waste. The efforts to re-
pair and keep them in proper condition have been
many and varied, and much unfriendly criticism evoked
as to the policy and management of the county authorities. As to road affairs, times change and people with
them, and it seems citizens need time for living and
learning. No doubt the time will come sooner or later
when the interests of the public highways will be committed to the management of persons specially qualified
for the business, like law, medicine, or politics.

As mountains and grasses are so characteristic of

our county, some reflections as to the part they perform in their Creator's plans may be in place. The hills and mountain, of Pocahontas, when contrasted with people who own them as property and live in homes overshadowed by them, seem as to existence "everlasting hills." Yet the truth is these mountains are just as perishing as we are. Their veins of flowing fountains weary the mountain hearts as the crimson pulses do ours. The natural forms of the iron or stony crags are abated in their appointed time, like the strength of the muscles and sinews and bones in a human old age. It is but the lapse of the longer periods of decay, which in the sight of their Creator distinguishes the duration of the mountain from that of the moth or worm.

By our bountiful Father of Mercies mountain ranges are appointed to fulfil their offices with a view to preserving health and thus increase the happiness of the human race in general. The first of these uses is to give motion to water. Every fountain and river, from the shallow streamlet that crosses the road in trembling clearness, to the calm and silent movings of the Potomac, the James, or the Ohio, all owe their motion, purity, and resistless sweeping powers to the elevations of the earth ordained for that purpose. Gentle or steep, extended or abrupt, some determined slope of the surface is essential before the waters of any stream could overtake and refresh a single plant or tree after the long pilgrimage by clouds from the Southern Pacific Ocean.

We are living among the highlands, a veritable goodly land of the sky, where we may walk and meditate beside the grassy or flowery margins of our mountain streams, what opportunities we have to consider how beautiful and very wonderful is that arrangement, in virtue of which the dews and rains falling to the ground should find no resting place to loiter after coming so far away, but should find instead, prepared and fixed channels traced for them, from the ravines of the central crests, down which they rush and roar in turbulent ranks of foam, towards the dark hollows beneath the banks of lowland meadows, pastures, and planted fields, round which they must circle among the stems and beneath the leaves of the growing plants, so essential to human comfort and enjoyable existence.

These pathways for the dews and rains and melted snows are so arranged that by some definite rate of movement the waters must evermore descend, sometimes slow, sometimes swift, but never pausing. The daily existances they must glide over being marked out for them at each successive rising of the sun, or dawning of the morning, the place that knew them yesterday to know them no more, and the gateways of guarding mountains opened for them in cleft, or chasm, or duly tunnelled. Thus nothing is to hinder them in their mission to the growing, life-sustaining fruits, grasses, and grains, while from afar the great heart of the parent ocean seems to be ever calling these blessing-imparting waters back to herself, as if "deep were calling unto deep."

It is well to remember, too, that this office of imparting motion to water is not exhausted on the surface, for a no less important office of the hills is to direct the flow of springs and fountains from subterraneous reservoirs. While it may seem marvelous to see the waters coming up out of the ground beneath our feet, yet this is no miraculous happening, for every fountain and well are supplied from a reservoir somewhere in the hidden chambers of the hills, so located as to involve some degree of fall, assuring pressure sufficient to secure the constant outflowing of the stream.

The second use of mountains is to keep up a constant change in the nature and currents of the air. A difference in soils and vegetation would have in a measure caused changes in the air, even if the earth had been level. This change would have been far less than what is caused now by the chains of hills, which divide the earth not only into districts but into climates, and cause perpetual currents of air to traverse their passes in a thousand different states, by moistening with the spray of waterfalls, beating the air hither and thither in the pools of rushing torrents, closing the air within clefts and caves where the sunbeams are never seen, and all becomes cold as autumn mists. By means of the hills this cooled air is sent forth again to breathe lightly across the velvet fields of grass upon the slopes, or be scorched among sunburned shales and grassless crags, and then when pierced by strange electric darts flashes of mountain fire, the air is suffered to depart at last, chastened and pure, to refresh the far away arid plains.

The third important office of the mountains is to

bring about perpetual change in the soils. Were it not for this office cultivated ground would in a series of years be exhausted and would require to be upturned most laborously by human appliances. Elevations provide for this a constant renovation. The higher mountains suffer their summits to be broken into fragments and to be cast down in sheets of mossy rock, replete with every ingredient needful for the nutriment of plant life. These fallen fragments broken by frosts and disentegrated by torrents into various conditions of sand and clay—materials which are distributed perpetually by the streams farther and farther from the mountain base. The turbid foaming of angry looking waters in time of flood, tearing down banks and rocks are not disturbances of the beneficent course of nature, but are operations of laws necessary to the existence of man and to make the earth beautiful. This process may be carried on more gently, but not less effectively, over the entire surface of the lower undulating districts. Each filtering thread of summer rain trickling through the short turf of the uplands is bearing its own appointed burden of earth to be thrown on some new natural garden for some one to work and enjoy long years in the future.

Of all the good and perfect gifts lavished upon a bit of goodly land, it would be difficult to find anything more suggestive of edifying thought than the grass of the field. It is something mysterious to examine not only when gemmed with the dew drops of morning, or quivering in the mirage of noon, but with the sparkling threads of aborescence, "each a little belfry of

grain bells all achime." When a single blade of grass
is plucked, one of countless millions, and one examines
intently for a time its narrow sword shaped strip of
fluted green, nothing is perceived of notable goodness
or entrancing beauty. In that blade of grass may be
noticed very little that is strong and a very little tall-
ness and a few delicate lines meeting in a dull unfin-
ished point. So the blade of grass by no means appears to be a creditable or much cared for sample of
the Creator's workmanship, made to be trodden upon
by men or roaming beast, a little pale hollow stalk fe-
ble and flaccid leading down to the dull brown fibres
of roots. And yet when we carefully ponder over its
uses and the place grass occupies in promoting man's
physical good, we are inclined to the opinion and so
express ourselves that of all the gorgeous flowers that
bloom in our mountain air and shed their balmy fra-
grance upon the summer breezes, and of all the strong
and goodly trees, pleasant to the eyes or good for food,
like stately palms and towering pines, strong oaks and
ash trees, scented orchards, or gracefully burdened
vines, there is not one so universally loved and sought
after by mankind of every clime and nation, or by the
Creator so highly graced as that narrow point of feeble
green—a blade of grass.

For floral scenery our Pocahontas forests, in the season of wild flowers, are as enchanting as fairy dreams.
The dogwood and the service bloom,—Indian sign for
planting corn, the Shawnee Flower, rivaling the magnolia of the far South; the notable variety of honey-

suckle blooms, so warmly recommended by ardent ad-
mirers as most suitable for the West Virginia state emblematic flower; rhodadendron and ivy, along with so
many curious flowering plants, open up vistas of surpassing loveliness.

Exotic flowers have been cultivated with notable success. The first rose geranium ever potted in our county was brought to Huntersville by Miss Margaret Ann
Craig, from Waynesboro, Va., about the year 1843.
It flourished nicely, and she was very generous in giving away the slips. She carried it on horseback, in
her hand, a tiny slip, clipped off with scissors, slit at
the end and kept open by inserting an oat grain, wrapped in moistened paper. This wrapping was moistened
every few hours at some spring or brook by the wayside, during that journey of nearly a hundred miles.

Flowers are seemingly intended for the solace of humanity, of all age., classes, and conditions. Little
children and quietly contented people love flowers as
they bloom in forests, lawns, or gardens. Luxurious
and pleasure loving persons rejoice in flowers when
gathered for some festive occasion. The flowers are
the home-loving rural cottagers treasure, while in towns
and villages a few flowers adorn as with scraps of rain-
bow the windows of the toiling inmates, in whose souls
linger a longing for the covenanted place of Divine
care, of which the lily and the rose are the emblems.

Notwithstanding this general admiration for flowefs,
the writer feels inclined to make this criticism at a
venture, that were this apparent love of flowers
thoroughly probed there are but few people, compara-

tively care about flowers as flowers. Many indeed are
fond of finding a new shape of blossom, thus caring
for the shape as the little boys care for the kaleido-
scope. Many may like a pretty display of flowers on
the benches or in the pit, as they admire a fine service
of silver or gold plate on the table. Many are scien-
tifically interested in flowers, though the interest of
these scientists may be in the nomenclature rathen than
the flowers themselves, and some enjoy them as they
grow in their gardens like radishes and peas.

Being persuaded as I am that I shall have among
my readers some young people who are thoughtful,
observing and inquiring in their character, I would
write something about the stones that are so very plen-
tiful in our county for their special consideration.
Shakespeare, the foremost of all names in English literature, speaks of a cast of intelligence or intellectual
culture that enables one so cultivated to see sermons
in stones and good in everything. There are but few,
if any natural, objects from which more can be learned
than from stones, as they seem so well fitted to reward
all patient, intelligent observers. As to other objects
in creation nearly all can be seen to some gratifying
degree by the hasty impatient observer whose glances
must be transient, on the spur of the passing moment or not at all. They have no patience with the
objects unless they are pleasant in being hastily seen.
Trees, clouds, cliffs and rivers are highly enjoyable
even by careless observers in being, but the stones over
which they walk have for the careless nothing in them

but stumbling and objects of offense. No pleasure is languidly to be derived of the stones as from clusters on the vines or fruits on the overshadowing boughs. Impatient observers find nothing delicious to their tastes or good of any kind in stones. Even to the patiently studious at first sight all that the stones seem good for is to symbolize the hard heart and unfatherly gift referred to in our Lord's question, "Will a father give his famishing son a stone in place of bread?"

But yet when some of my younger readers will do as I confidently anticipate they will, and give the stones their thoughtful reverent consideration they will to their pleasure find in stones more bread or food for thought than in any other lowly feature of all our interesting Pocahontas landscape. For a stone when duly examined will be found to be a mountain in miniature, as a sparkling drop of dew may be regarded as a miniature sun. The fineness of the Creator's work is so exquisite that in a single stone a foot or more in diameter may be compressd as many changes of form and structure on a small scale as have been needed for mountains on a large scale. When moss is taken for forests, grains of chrstal for crags, the surface of a stone, in by far the most instances, is more pleasingly interesting than the surface of an ordinary mountain by reason of more fantastic forms and richer colors. The moss does not conceal the form of the rock but gathers over it in little brown bunches like pin cushions made by mixed threads of dark ruby silk and gold, rounded over more subdued films of white and gray, with lightly crisped and curled edges, like

autumn frost on fallen leaves, and minute clusters of
upright orange stalks with pointed caps; and fibres of
deep green, gold and faint purple passing into black,
and following with unimaginable fineness of gentle
growth the undulations of the stone until the stone is
so fully charged with color it can receive no more.
Then in place of looking rugged or cold or stern or
anything a rock is held to be at heart, the moss makes
it appear clothed with a soft dark robe, embroidered
with arabesque of purple and silver. Though the moss
be so meek in character, yet it was the first of Heavens mercies visible to our earth, at the opening of the
redemptive ages referred to elsewhere, veiling, as it
did, with silent softness, the first dintless rock. Moss
is the most significant emblem of pity for the ruined,
covering as it did with strange and tender honor the
scarred disgrace of ruin, and laying quiet finger on the
heaving, trembling stones to teach them rest, in which
they now repose. Words have not been coined to express really what the mosses are. No known words
are delicate enough, perfect enough, or rich enough in
their diction and significance to express what should
be told of the rounded mosses of furred and radiant
green, the starred divisions of rubied bloom, fine film-
ed as is the spirit could spin porphyry, as glass is spun
with seemingly magic skill. Where can the phrases
be found in oratory or poetry to describe properly the
traceries of intricate silver and fringes of amber, lus-
trous, arborescent, burnished through every fibre into
fitful brightness and glory, traverses of silken change,
yet all subdued pensive, and framed for simplest offices

of graceful duty. The mosses will not be gathered, like the flowers, for May Queen crowns, or tokens of incipient love as the buds are, but of the mosses the wild birds make their nests, and wearied children their pillow. As the earth's first mercy, so the mosses are the earth's last gift to her departed children. When all other service is hopeless and vain from plant and tree, the soft moss and gray lichen take up their watch by the tombstone and the burial mound. The woods, the flowers, the gift bearing grapes and cereals did their offices for a time, but the lichen and the moss do service forever. Trees for the builder's use, flowers for the bridal altar, cereals for the table, mosses for the grave.

USES OF BIOGRAPHICAL HISTORY.—NOTES ON FORMATION OF THE COUNTY.

SECTION I V

What was writtens in sections 1st, 2d and 3d was designed to impress upon our minds something like a just conception as to how interesting and instructive is the story of the Divine providential leadings of our ancestral people, that guided them to homes in the primeval forests. Moreover we endeavored to realize how impressively beautiful was and is the heavenly handiwork manifested in fashioning, locating, and adorning the "goodly land," wherein God has permitted our lines to fall, and suffers us to hold as our pleasant heritage.

What was written about the origin of our wonderful region was to illustrate what appears to have been God's method of working in His mysterious way His Creative wonders to perform. In virtue of which He moves and works upon the scheme of a continuous progressive change, according to certain laws and by means of resident forces, and it is our matured, steadfast opinion that our Lord Jesus Christ, through the Eternal Spirit, is the Resident Force of the creative ages, and of Christianity pure and simple the great fact characteristic of the redemptive ages now in process of unfolding.

One of the wisest of recently living thinkers very happily remarks: "To live in the presence of great truths and eternal loves, to be led by permanent ideals, that is what keeps a man patient when the world ignores him, and calm and unspoiled when the world praises him."

One of the foremost statesmen of the United States in our day thus defines American civilization to be that gradual amelioration of manners, and that improvement of the human race in character which increases the comforts and happiness of mankind.

If we know our own minds, it ever has been and still is our heart's desire and fervent prayer to give due heed to these Apostolic words: "Finally, brethren whatsoever things are true, honest, just, pure, lovely, of good report; if there be any virtue, and if there be any praise, think on these things."

We would enjoy ourselves, and have all others to participate with us in that mental culture and soul elevation imparted by the teachings of ancestral history, purity of morals, and material civilization in the best sense and highest practical benefits.

Now in this fourth section and what may follow, the paramount aim will be to urge ourselves to the duty of remembering every day and every hour that were it not for people,—men, women, and children,—there would not have been any materials for these sketches; and were it not for people there would be none to read our story; none to occupy and appreciate whatever is good and charming in our Pocahontas environment.

What the soul is to the body, so are the people to any country, and as the body without a pure soul becomes worse than useless, an offensive nuisance, so does a country without people of the proper tone and character. Hence it is that after all the people are the really important subject, whose history is intrinsically valuable for the purpose now in hand. The kind of people that are wanted and for which so many of our best citizens are so anxious to find and choose for leaders, are described in these pathetically earnest lines:

"God, give us men—a time like this demands
  High minds, great hearts, true faith and ready hands;
  Men whom the lust of office does not fill;
  Men who possess opinions and a will;
  Men who have honor; men who will not lie."

"For as the body without the spirit is dead," so a county without a live people is dead also. The poet Dante centuries since uttered an aphorism that had it been duly heeded would have increased the happiness of our race immensely. It was to this purport, "Knowledge and wisdom thrive on well remembered facts." In too many instances it is to be regretted that writers of history as well as interpreters of historical writing have virtually assumed premises to deduce facts when in their avowed honesty of purpose as truth seekers and teachers of men they should have first searched out the real facts and from truthful facts formed their premises for the arguments setting forth their views and teachings. Our aim was and we feel sure that we have succeeded in learning and duly recording

in sections previous such facts that if well remembered by our readers, they will be favered by thriving on
such knowledge and wisdom as will be profitable to
them all not only in this life, but in the life to come.
In the light of the knowledge and wisdom sought to
be imparted by these sketches, it is fondly hoped that
our readers will be helped in whatever efforts they may
be making to live clear of the sordid souless commercialism or selfishness that threatens to prevail over the
earth like waters on the face of the great deep, and
which is so rapidly becoming the spirit of the age, and
according to inspiration has ever shown itself as the
procuring cause of wars and rumors of wars.

And here we would pause and take special notice of
the boys of Pocahontas County and present some
thoughts to this effect: It is believed that there are a
good many who would make fine men, were they to go
about it in the proper manner.   Most of them have had
their muscles well developed by the labors of the farm;
many of them have been improved by attending school
and pursuing their studies under more than ordinary
difficulties, and thus developed practical common
sense.   May it not be hoped, therefore, that all our
youths will aim to make the best of their opportunities
and become first class in whatever calling they may
make their life's work.   Diligence in business, f:erven-
cy in spirit, serving the Lord, will attain the highest
success to be attained in the present state of existence
and endeavor.   Due respect for holy things is the beginning of highest wisdom, and good success have all
they that carry out the directions given us by the Cre-

ator.   He knows what is best for us to follow as a rule
of conduct, and in the end it will appear that those are
best off for the present and future life who do his commandments.

To help ourselves towards attaining satisfactory view
points, the following studies in applied history, illustrating principles pertinent to our ancestral history, are
submitted to the studious consideration of all persons
interested in our local history, The writer feels sure
that all readers who may give such consideration to
these studies will find their minds duly broadened and
will be qualified to realize more correctly the import
and significance of the "short and simple annals" of
our pioneer ancestors by perceiving the ruling and
guarding hand of God in the varied events of their lives.
Though their minds influenced by their providental surroundings may have devised and planned their ways,
yet it was the Lord that directed their steps and established their undertakings, and so, after all, the noblest
study of living Pocahontas people is the study of the
Pocahontas pioneer people who were used by the Divine Disposer of Events in shaping up affairs as we now
happily or otherwise find them to be in our day and
generation.   And, moveover, it will be a salutary lesson in morals to be reminded that as we are so depend-
ant upon those gone before, even so those who may
succeed us will either be grateful for our having lived,
or may have memories bitter as the worm-wood and
the gall.   None can possibly live unto themselves, and
while it may be a solemn thing to remember this and
try to live rightly, "walk humbly, love mercy and act

justly," it is a far more solemn thing not to remember
this and thus leave names to be remembered with
shame and tears.

The uses of historical study may be very beneficial
if judiciously pursued. Its leading purpose should be
to enable each generation to benefit from the experience
of those who have lived before their times and thus advance to higher lines of action, and have in view nobler
aims, and thus be not obliged to start afresh from
points occupied by predecessors when they entered on
the duties of their day and generation. To make real
progress it is better, if possible, to begin where those
preceding us have left off, taking up the battle of life
on the ground where they have fallen, and carry on
the struggle towards final victory.

Persons knowing but little of those gone before are
very likely to care but little of those coming after them.
To such, who are careless about historical research,
life seems a mere chain of sand, while life ought to be
a kind of electric chain, making our hearts throb and
vibrate with the most ancient thoughts of the past, as
well as the most distant hopes of the future. The continuity of history is something marvellous indeed. In
virtue of this continuity it may be shown that there are
many things that we owe to Babylon, Ninevah, Persia,
Egypt, and Phœnicia.

Those who carry watches derive from the Babylonians the division of the hour into sixty minutes. This
arrangement may have its faults, yet such as it may be
it comes down to modern citizens from the Greeks and
the Romans, and they derived it from Babylon. The

sexagesimal division is strictly Babylonian. About 150 B. C. Hipparchus learned it in Babylon, and about 150, A. D., Ptolemy gave the sexagesimal division wider currency. Then in succeeding centuries the French, when applying the decimal system to almost everything else, respected the dial plates of our clocks and watches and let them retain their sixty Babylonian minutes.

Every person who has ever written a letter is indebted to the Romans and Greeks for the alphabet. The Greeks received their alphabet from the Phœnicians, and the Phœnicians learned theirs in Egypt. Students in Phonetics all assert that ours is a very imperfect alphabet, yet such as it has been and may be now, we owe it to the old Phœnicians and Egyptians. In every letter we trace with pen, pencil, or typewriter there lies imbedded an ancient Egyptian hieroglphic. The letter A has the face of the sacred ox, which the Egyptians were ready to venerate with honors almost divine.

As to what we may owe the Persians, it may seem that it could not be very much, as the Persians were not a very inventive people, and the most of their vaunted wisdom they chiefly learned from their neighbors the Assyrians and Babylonians. Nevertheless we owe them something in a way they never intended. We ought to thank the Persians from our inmost hearts for allowing themselves to be defeated so disastrously at the battle of Marathon. It is enough to make one shudder to consider what the world would have come to had the Persians conquered the Greeks and destroy-

ed that wonderful people. So far as we can see from
our point of view, had the Persians been victorious at
Marathon, Greeks, Romans, Saxons, Anglo-Saxons,
and American people would have been Parsees; or Fire
Worshippers.

Another thing to be remembered that we owe to the
Persians is the relation or ratio of silver to gold in our
bimetallic currency. This relation was, no doubt, first
arranged in Babylonia, as the talent was divided into
sixty mina, and the mina into sixty shekels, the sexagesimal system being applied to money as well as time.
This system may owe its popularity to the fact that
sixty has more divisors than most other numbers. This
bimetallic arrangement of 13 to 1 assumed its practical
and historical importance in Persian financial affairs,
and spread from them to the Greek colonies in Asia,
and from there to America, where it has maintained
itself with slight variations down to the recent past.

We have seen how closely the world is held together
by the continuity of history, and how, for good or for
evil, we are what we are—not so much by ourselves—
as by the toil, the sufferings, the conflicts, the character, and the achievements of those who came before us.
Our true intellectual ancestors, whatever the blood may
have been composed of that coursed their veins, or the
bones that formed their skulls. Philosophers assure
us that the law of gravitation that orders and governs
the course of the planetary worlds in their vast and
tireless journeys through the illimitable realms of space
likewise governs the destiny of the smallest grain of
sand on the seashore as effectively as if it were the

only one. So, in a sense, the continuity of history reaches the destiny of empires, but has its influence on the individual as well. Hence it should be the desire of every one to know something of the past, and by the knowledge thus gained, construe the duties of the present and act for the well being of the future.

In reference to our ancestors, it may be inquired why did they come here? What were the impelling motives explaining their leaving the old world and seeking homes in the pathless regions of the western or new world? Their lot for centuries was assigned to those sections of the earth in northern Europe, and subsequently northern America, whose climates are of such a character that the seasons succeed each other in a manner as requires constant effort for existence. In such latitudes life is and always must be a struggle more or less arduous. There seems to be something in the air that makes the people who breathe it feel there is no time for rest. There must be always a toiling and a building up of ones own happiness out of the materials possessed by their neighbors, for their own personal self interest. Even when homes are as comfortable as can be made, with all the available appliances of civilization, it is a question whether such persons have more real enjoyment in life than the sons of the forest had in their wigwams or tepees on the vales of Pocahontas.

Owing to climatic influences, life with our ancestors was a hard, continuous struggle for mere existence, and hence the accumulation of wealth became a necesity, to provide for the uncertainties of old age, or the requirements peculiar to their complex social relations. The European climate with its long, cold. and dreary winters in many localities, the difficulties of cultivating the land, the conflicting interests between rival communities, developed the instinct of self preservation to such an extent that most of the virtues and many of vices of European people can be traced back to climatic causes, The character we inherit was formed under the influences mentioned, and so by inheritance, by education, and by necessity we are what we are, in large measure.

The life of our ancestors in Europe and America was a fighting life; hence our highest ideal of life is a life of action and endeavor.   Hence our people work until they can work no longer, and are ·proud to die with the axe or plow handles in their hands, thus choosing rather to wear out than rust out.

Nothing interests what we term the better and more respectable and prosperous element of our population than the history of what they or their ancestors have accomplished by diligence in business in rearing homes starting business enterprises, or in improving our commonwealth.   As the result of this restless characteristic, unsatisfying accumulation of earthly possessions, conveniences, and accomplishments, it comes almost naturally to imagine that human life is made perfect thereby, and in many instances so attractive that persons have been known to be sorry to leave what has been gathered together by their energy and self sacrifice.

Then, by way of contrast, let the subject in hand be

considered from another point of view. A branch of
the Teutonic race found homes in a far different climatic latitude, and as life comes easy it goes easy. Under such influences the people are never tired of speaking of life as a journey from one village to another,
not as a home or resting place permanently. Hence
we find them moralizing in this vein: "As a man jour-
neying to another village may enjoy a night's rest in
the open air, but after leaving such a resting place for a
night proceeds on his journey the next day; thus father
and mother, wife and wealth are all but a night's rest
to us; so wise people do not cling to them forever."

In one part of the world whence our ancestors came
climate impresses the idea that manly vigor, silent endurance, public spirit and domestic virtues illustrate an
important feature of the destiny or mission humanity
has to fulfil on earth. In another part of the world
whence many Americans trace their ancestry, the genial skies, balmy breezes and flowery vales illustrate or
impress the idea that another phase of human nature,
the passive, the meditative and reflectively sentimental
that prompts people to look upward and ontward to
something not themselves. Thus time is had to inquire
whether something could be understood of true significance of the mystery we speak of as life on earth.

The lines have fallen to us in places highly conducive to the development of both phases of human character, and if this article would so impress the readers
they would greatly conduce to the contentment and
stimulate to making the best of available opportunities to acquire active, energetic, resolute and acquisi-

tive habits of living, along with due attention to whatever promotes meditative patient, seriously thoughtful views of matters pertaining to the higher needs of intellect and spirit. This places within our reach the possibility of presenting to the world noble examples of all around humanity with sound bodies and sound minds.

In reference to the ancestry of our people it may be inferred that our citizenship is of a composite character, German, English, Irish, Scotch, and French.

Such names as these, Lightner, Harper, Yeager, Arbogast, Herold, Halterman, Burr, Siple, Sheets, Casebolt, Shrader, Burner, Sydenstricker, Varner, Hevener, Cackley, Gumm, Overholt, indicate German descent.

Moore, Gillispie, McCarty, McLaughlin, Cochran, Waugh, Hogsett, McNeel, Kerr, Lockridge, Drennan, Gay, McCollam, McCoy, Beard, Baxter, Slaven, Hannah, Hill, Kincaid, Irvine, McElwee, Wallace, Curry, Hamilton, Sharp, Friel, McCutcheon, imply Scotch-Irish or English-Irish ancestry.

Warwick, Matthews, Renick, Clark, Gibson, Johnson, Galford, Buckley, Kennison, Adkison, Barlow, Gatewood, Jackson, Brown, Wooddell, Hull, Cooper, Duffield, Auldridge, Duncan, Beale, Sutton, Callison, indicate English antecedants.

Maupin, Ligon, Dever, Tacey, Dilley, Bussard, and Large are of French extraction.

Poage, Pritchard, Price, Ruckman denote Welch extraction.

Kee, Doyle, Kelley, Loury, Cloonan, Scales, Rorke,

leave us in no doubt that the Emerald Isle is their fatherland.

These representatives of nationalties have blended and affiliated so that the characteristics of each fused, and the outcome is a composite citizenship, versatile in their tastes and aptitudes, fitted for a destiny in harmony with the progressive tendencies of that eventful period, the wonderful 19th century.

It is noticeable that the predominating element, as to numbers, trace their ancestry to the north of Ireland, and are either Scotch Irish or English Irish. This is explained in this manner.

About 1611 there was a district in Ireland that was largely depopulated by forfeiture of lands when O'Neil of Tyronne was defeated. Puritans from England and Reformers from Scotland were induced to occupy the abandoned property. These persons in turn had to seek elsewhere a refuge from oppression when there came a change in Irish affairs. Having been Scotch or English people living for a time in Ireland, they were called Scotch-Irish. In common usage the term is applied to both English and Scotch, as the Scotch seem to have largely predominated.

About the time when on the lookout for a refuge, the Virginians wanted a living wall for protection against Indian raids from beyond the Blue Ridge. Now when it became known that Germans, Scotch-Irish, and French Hugenots were willing to settle on the frontier; liberal concessions were made by the Virginia colonial authorities, and it was not many years—1732 to 1750—a line of settlements were formed, and the desired

living fortifications provided for. Therefore in the
course of fifteen or twenty years subsequently to 1740,
the more inviting sections of the counties of Monroe,
Greenbrier, and Pocahontas were settled by a goodly
number of enterprising families of the same type of
people, inured to hardships and familiar with privations. These people had an experience of life along
the frontier with its perilous emergencies for a period
of thirty or more years of danger that developed strong
elements of character along with a goodly degree of
intellectual vigor. These people placed the highest
value on education, and though their advantages were
limited, they made the very best of their opportunities.

The Scotch-Irish trend of religious belief gives a
high tone to the human intellect and awakens the
highest aspirations of man's spirit nature; thus these
early settlers had by inheritance the highest religious
standard and the highest civilization of their times.

All history teaches, more or less plainly, that God
has established His worship and the ordinances of the
kingdom that is coming, to sustain and nourish the religious and intellectual life of His people. Now whenever these are wanting or neglected, the religious or
higher life becomes feeble. While, therefore, the pioneers of this region came from such an ancestry as
has been described, with such inherited proclivities, it
should not be considered strange the temptations of
frontier life and the comparative destitution or neglect
of religious ordinances resulted in much irreligion, and
consequent immorality. For all experience and observation go to show that when people of good parent-

age and of favorable opportunities do fall, they fall heavy and far. When people go back on their God, there is nothing between them and the horrible pit and mirey clay of sensuality, and of every hateful and hurtful propensity.

Nevertheless be it remembered to their never to be forgotten praise there were persons among our ancestors whose piety was as pure gold refined, and many homes were reared where genuine godliness was maintained. Many of these settlers endeavored to cherish the traditions of their covenanting ancestors, and of the martyrs whose blood stained many a beautiful vale in Scotland, and thus tried to live as worthy sons and daughters of an ancestry so worthy.

Now putting all that has appeared in these articles on applied history in review, we may learn something of the motives that impelled our ancestors to select their homes in this region.

They possessed an energetic spirit that prompted them to desire a place where they could acquire a competency of earthly goods, so needful in times of disability, and for the decrepitude of advancing years. These people came among the mountains seeking refuge from civil and religious wrongs, and have a sanctuary where God could be worshipped, none daring to molest or make them afraid. They felt it a duty to provide for their households, and here land was to be had in goodly portions and sufficient to locate sons and daughters near the parental home, so ardent were their family affinities.

These reflections on applied history are now submit-

ted to our readers for their consideration, to be discussed in any way most in harmony with their opinions.
The writer's ambition is that his people should have a
history, and a future likewise, that may be worthy of
praise and emulation.

"Should critics say my work is bad,
  I won't indulge in wail or woe,
I'll simply smile and go my way
  And say the critics do not know.

"But should they pat me on the back,
  And say they think my work immense
I'll take a rosier view of life
  To think they show such rare good sense."

Affairs having so far progressed, the formation of a
new county was mooted and due arrangements made.
A resolution to that effect was passed by the Virginia
Legislature, March, 1821. Thomas Mann Randolph
was the Governor who signed the bill, and being a descendant of Pocahontas, "the virgin queen of a virgin
world," as General Skeene used to speak of her, this
may have had something to do with the name selected
for the county.

One of the most memorable days in the social and
civil history of Pocahontas County was the 5th day of
March, 1822, when the first court was held at the residence of John Bradshaw, at Huntersville, a log tene-
ment that stood where the Lightner House now stands.

John Jordan, William Poage, James Tallman, Robert Gay, John Baxter, George Burner, and Benjamin
Tallman were present and handed in their commissions

as Justices of the Peace, signed by Governor Randolph.

Colonel John Baxter administered the oath of office, each member qualifying four times, in virtue of which multiplied qualification the members of the new court were solemnly obligated to the faithful performance of official duties; fidelity to the Commonwealth of Virginia; support the national Constitution; and oppose dueling. William Poage, Jr., then administered the four prescribed oaths to Colonel John Baxter, and the proclamation was made that the court was duly open for business.

John Jordan was sworn in as High Sheriff, giving bond for $30,000, with Abram and Isaac McNeel as sureties or bondsmen. Josiah Beard was appointed Clerk, with Thomas Beard, George Poage and James Tallman bondsmen, on a bond for $3.000. Johnson Reynolds, of Lewisburg, qualified as Attorney for the Commonwealth. Sampson L. Mathews was recommended for appointment as Surveyor of Lands. William Hughes was appointed Constable for the Levels District, with William McNeel and Robert McClintock as sureties in a bond of $500. James Cooper was appointed Constable for the Head of Greenbrier, with William Slaven and Samuel Hogsett as bondsmen.

These proceedings occupied the first day, and court adjourned until 10 a. m. the following morning.

When Court convened March 6, 1822, all were present except Robert Gay. John Jordan, the High Sheriff, moved the Court that his son Jonathan Jordan be appointed Deputy Sheriff. The motion prevailed, granting the request, whereupon the four oaths, as already described, were duly administered by the Clerk.

James Callison, William Edminson, John Hill, John Cochran, Alexander Waddell, John McNeill ("Little John"), Robert Moore, Martin Dilley, Benjamin Arbogast, William Sharp, William Hartman, and Joseph Wolfenberger were appointed overseers of various roads, completed and prospective, in the county.

Robert Gay—still out of court—was appointed Commissioner of the Revenue. When informed of this appointment he appeared in court and gave bond in $1000 with William Cackley and John Baxter sureties, whereupon he was duly qualified.

Attorneys Cyrus Curry from Lexington, Rockbridge County, and Johnston Reynolds, from Lewisburg, Greenbrier County, were licensed to practice law as the first two members of the Pocahontas Bar.

The next business transacted at this historic term of the court appears to have been the organization of the 127th Regiment of the State militia as a part of Virginia military establishment. The folowing citizens were nominated as "fit and proper" to fill the requisite offices, and the Governor and Council were requested to issue commissions to them: John Baxter, Colonel; Benjamin Tallman, Lieutenant-Colonel; William Blair, Major; Boone Tallman, William Arbogast, Henry Herold, Isaac Moore, and Milburn Huges, Captains; Andrew G. Mathews, Robert Warwick, William Morgan, William Young, and James Rhea, Lieutenants; Jacob Slaven, James Wanless, Samuel Young, James Callison, Ensigns.

Mr Abram McNeel was recommended to the Governor for Coroner.

Travis W. Perkins was granted license to open a hotel.

Thus organized, Pocahontas took her place among the counties of Virginia, and Huntersville was designated for the County Seat. A location near George Baxter's present residence, in the vicinity of what is now Edray, had been selected by a committee on location and reported on favorably as the place for the permanent location of the County Seat. Inducements by John Bradshaw were so enticing and favorable, and the people at the head of Greenbrier so anxious on the subject, that Huntersville prevailed, and the report of the committee on location was overruled.

In 1800 the population of the region coterminous with the present limits of Pocahontas County amounted to about one hundred and fifty-three persons, and were for the most part members of the first families that had permanent homesteads, whose heads were John McNeel, Thomas McNeill, Moses Moore, Peter Lightner, Henry Harper, John Moore, Felix Grimes, Samuel Waugh, James Waugh, Aaron Moore, Robert Moore, Timothy McCarty, Robert Gay, Jeremiah Friel, Jacob Warwick, John Slaven, John Warwick, Sampson Mathews, Josiah Brown, John Sharp, William Sharp, William Poage, John Baxter, Levi Moore, and John Bradshaw.

From the census returns it appears that in 1830 the population of the county was 2,542; in 1840, 2,922; in 1850, 3,598; in 1860, 3,958; in 1870, 4,069; in 1880, 5,591; in 1890, 6,813. in 1900, 8,572.

According to these official returns, the population of the county has increased from 2542 in 1830, to 8572 in 1900. The percentage of growth about 70.

From 1830 to 1860, the period before the war between the States, the percentage of gain was about 35. From 1860 to 1900 the percentage of gain was about 53. From 1890 to 1900, the gain was 20 per cent, and was larger than any previous decade, and readily accounted for.

The smallest rate of gain was between 1860 and 1870, about 2 per cent. In this decade the war occurred. The next less rate of gain was between 1850 and 1860—about 9 per cent. This indicates that just previous to the war the county was about ready to progress backwards, such was the disposition of people to look for homes in the far West, and the western counties of the State.

BIOGRAPHIC.

Section V.

JACOB MARLIN AND STEPHEN SEWALL.

The first persons of English or Scotch-Irish antecedents to spend a winter in what is now Pocahontas County, were Marlin and Sewall. This was the winter of 1750–51. Their camp was in the delta formed by Marlin Run and a slough or drain near the east bank of Knapp's Creek.

In the course of time—having agreed to disagree—they separated and were found living apart, by Colonel Andrew Lewis, Marlin in the cabin and Sewall in a hollow tree. Upon expressing his surprise at this way of living apart, distant from the habitation of other human beings, Sewall told him they differed in sentiments and since the separation there was more tranquility, or a better understanding, for now they were upon speaking terms, and upon each morning "it was good morning, Mr Marlin, and 'Good morning, Mr Sewall!' "

Under the new arrangement, Sewall crossed the slough, and instead of building another cabin, went into a hollow sycamore tree on the west margin of the slough, quite near where the board walk now crosses, and about in line with a walnut tree now standing on the east bank of the drain and the court house.

The lower part of this tree bore a striking resemblance to a leaning Indian tepee. The cavity could shelter five or six persons, and the writer has been often in it for shade or for shelter from rain or heat.

At the top of the cone, some eight or ten feet from the ground, the tree was not more than twenty inches in diameter, and at that height was chopped off about the year 1839, to avoid shading the crops. Thus the stump was left, a great convenience for shade or shelter, until it disappeared during the War, being probably used for a camp fire.

These persons differed, Sewall told Colonel Lewis, about their "relagian." There is a traditional hint that "immersion" was the theme of contention. But it is more than probable that one was a conformist and the other a non-conformist to the thirty-nine articles of the English rubric. This is known to have been a very live question of those times, both before and after.

This new arrangement did not last long, and Sewall in search of less molestation about his religion, withdrew about eight miles to a cave at the head of Sewell Run, near Marvin. Thence he went forty miles farther on to Sewell Creek, west Greenbrier, and was found and slain by Indians. How impressively this illustrates the evils of religious controversy, so called.

"Against her foes religion well defends,
Her sacred truths, but often fears her friends.
If learned, their pride: if weak their zeal she dreads
And their heart's weakness who have soundest heads;

But most she fears the controversial pen,
The holy strife of disputatious men,
Who the blest Gospel's peaceful page explore,
Only to fight against its precepts more."

It is moreover interesting in this connection to recall the fact that on the banks of Marlin's Run is the burial place of a little child that was dashed to death by an Indian warrior in 1765, when overtaken by a party of Bath and Rockbridge men, seeking to rescue Mrs Mayse, her son Joseph, an unmarried woman with an infant in her arms, a Mr McClenachan, and some other captives. This burial place is a few rods diagonally from the east angle of Uriah Bird's barn on the margin of the rivulet. The infant corpse was buried at the foot of the tree where it had been found a few minutes after its death. The burial took place just a few hours later, before the pursuers set out on their return. The grave was dug with hunting knives, hatchets, and naked fingers. The little body laid in its place very tenderly, and the grave partly filled with earth. The covering of the grave was completed with rather heavy stones, to prevent foxes or other animals from getting at the remains.

Thus died and was buried the first white child known to history west of the Alleghany Mountains.

Joseph Mayse, 13 years old, was rescued at that same time, somewhere between the Island and the mouth of Indian Draft. In 1774 he fought in the battle of Point Pleasant, where he was wounded, and after suffering from the injury for forty-six years, his

leg was amputated.   He recovered, and lived a number of years thereafter, a busy man of affairs.   He died
"serene and calm," April, 1840, in the 89th year of
his age.

In the Richmond Dispatch, April 14, 1901, it is
stated that the last survivor of the Point Pleasant veterans was Ellis Hughes, who passed away at Utica, O..
in 1840, over ninety years of age.   In early manhood
he may have lived in the Lower Levels of our county.
Now if it was known what month Huges died in, it
could be decided who was the last one of the veterans
to bivouac in those "silent tents" that Glory "guards
with solemn round."

MOSES MOORE.

Moses Moore, the progenitor of the largest relationship of the name in the county, came from what is now
Timber Ridge, Rockbridge County, Virginia.   About
1760 he was married to a Miss Elliot, a member of another Timber Ridge family.   Their children were John
born January 29, 17e2; James, born October 5, 1763;
Margaret, born March 29, 1765; Moses, Jr., born February 8, 1769; Hannah, born June 6, 1771; Robert,
born May 27, 1772; Phebe, born February 13, 1774;
William, born September 18, 1784.

At the time of the Drennan raid, when James Baker
and the Bridger boys were killed, Moses Moore was
living on Swago, in sight of what is now the McClintic
homestead.   Phebe, his youngest daughter, remembered how the family refugeed to the fort at Mill Point.
and while the Drenanns and Moores and others were

passing around the end of the mountain they heard the firing at the Bridger Notch, when the boys were killed. This would make it 1786 when James Baker, the first school teacher in Pocahontas, was killed.

During the first years of his pioneer life in our region, he spent much of his time hunting and trapping along Back Alleghany, upper Greenbrier River, and Clover Lick vicinity. He was a close observer of Indian movements, and would make a careful search for Indian signs before resuming operations as the hunting seasons returned. The usual place for the Indians to cross the Greenbrier, in the hunting grounds mentioned, was at a passage narrow enough for them to vault over with a long pole. He would take notice accordingly which side of the river the vaulting-pole would be on, and act accordingly. Finnally the Indians seemed to have found out his strategy, and thereupon vaulted the narrow passage and cunningly threw the pole back to the other side.

This threw the hunter off his guard. It was Satururday; he set his traps, looked after the deer signs, and arranged his camp. The venerable William Collins, yet living (1901), is sure that the camping spot was on what is now the Charley Collins place, on the Greenbrier above the Cassell fording, at a place near Tub Mill where he was captured by the wily Indians.

It was the hunter's purpose to pass the Sabbath at his camp in quiet repose and devotional reading of the Bible he carried about with him for company. He had put a fat turkey to roast about daylight, and was reclining on a bear skin reading a lesson from the Word, preparatory to a season of meditation and prayer before breakfast, a habit so characteristic of the Scotch-Irish at that period. He was interrupted by the breaking of a stick, and upon looking intently and steadily in the direction whence the sound seemed to have come he saw five or six warriors aiming their guns and moving cautiously upon him.

Seeing there was no chance to escape, hemmed in as he was, he threw up his hands and made signs for them to come to him. He put the turkey before them and made signs for them to eat. By gestures and gutteral gruntings they gave him to understand that they would not touch it unless he would eat some first. He did so, and thereupon they devoured it ravenously, and it was no time that scarcely a fragment remained, even of the bones.

Soon as breakfast was over, they started for their home in Ohio. Having passed but a few miles, they halted at what the pioneers afterwards called the Mosey Spring. The spring—one of the most copious and beautiful of its kind—is near the residence of the late David McLaughlin, four or five miles up the Back Alleghany road from Driftwood. The prisoner was securely bound with buffalo thongs and pinioned to the ground. A detachment went off in the direction of Driftwood, and were absent two or three hours. When the party returned they were loaded down with ore. This was carried to a place, where another halt was made and the ore was smelted and reduced in weight, so that one could carry what had required two to bring in as raw material.

The prisoner was taken as far as Chilacothe and the Indians seemed to have been greatly elated over their capture. So much so that as a special compliment to their lady friends it was decided in solemn council of inquiry what to do with the prisoner, that the captive should run the gauntlet. The Indians seem to have knywn of nothing so intensely amusing than running the gauntlet, and of uo compliment more flattering to their favorite lady friends than have fhem to form the gauntlet lines, and leave it to them to torment the captive. Accordingly two lines of squaws were drawn up about six or eight feet apart. One captive had preceded Moore, who was stabbed, bruised and hacked to pieces. This made him think it was only death any way. He entered the line and passed some distance, finally a squaw with a long handled frying pan sturck him. He wrenched the pan from her and knocked her down with his fist and then striking left and right with the handle of the frying pan, he proceeded along the lines, and many of the other squaws ran away. When Moore had scattered them, the warriors crowded around him, patted and praised him, "good soldier," "good soldier," and decided that he should be allowed to live. By degrees he secured the confidence of his captors. In hunting he was very successful and the Indian who was his keeper would give him ammunition, a part of which he would secret. The supply of ammunition was gradually increased, and the time given him to be absent was extended two or three days. With this increase of rations of powder and bullets and extension of time, he ventured to make escape, and got a start so far ahead that the Indians could see no hopeful chance of recapturing him.

It is nothing but just to remark Moses Moore is one of the pioneers of this county who will be among those longest remembered in the future by those interested in our pioneer literature. Moses Moore's descendants have probably cleared more land than any one family connexion; some of them have been and are prominent in public affairs. The following particulars were mainly furnished by the venerable Andrew Washington Moore, one of his grandsons, now (1901) in the 83rd year of his age, residing on Knapps Creek and occupying a part of the old ancestral homestead.

About 1770 Moses Moore settled on Knapps Creek, known at that period as Ewing's Creek, and so named in some of the old land papers. Traces of the original cabin remained for years in the meadow near the old orchard contiguous to Washington Moore's present residence. The tract of land purchased by Moses Moore from one Mr Ewing, for the consideration of two steel-traps and two pounds of English sterling, extended from Andrew Herold's to Dennis Dever's gate by the roadside below the Francis Dever homestead. Besides other improvements, Mr Moore built a mill on Mill Run, quarter of a mile from Isaac Brown Moore's.

The Daughters of Moses Moore.

Margaret Moore, remembered as a very estimable person, married John Moore, a native of Pennsylvania, and they lived where David Moore now resides. Her daughter Hannah was married to Martin Dilley, Esq., and lived where Mrs Martha Dilley, relict of the late Andrew Dilley, now lives.

Her son, William Moore, married Miss Calahan, of Bath County, and settled where Jefferson Moore, her grandson, now lives, whose wife was a Miss Grimes.

Margaret Moore's son, James C. Moore, married Miss Nottingham, and lived on land occupied by his widow and son William. This excellent man was a Confederate soldier and died in battle near New Hope, Augusta County, Va., June 1864.

Another of Margaret's sons, John by name, married a Miss Hannah, of Elk, daughter of Dr John Hannah, ancestor of the Pocahontas Hannahs, and lived on the home place, now held by David Moore. A grandson, Joseph Moore, lives between Frost and Glade Hill. Near his residence the spot is pointed out where Rev Henry Arbogast was slain during fhe Civil War.

Hannah Moore, daughter of Moses, was married to Abram Duffield, on Stony Creek, the ancestor of the Pocahontas Duffields.

Phebe Moore, another daughter, became Mrs Jonathan McNeill on Swago. She was a person highly esteemed for her piety, sound sense, and business energy. For yeart she attended the mill, one of the best of its kind at that time,—in the twenties and thirties. Sometimes that mill would have to run day and night, to supply the custom and avoid grinding on the Sabbath day. There used to be a saying that "an honest miller has hair on the palm of his right hand." Were this a fact, Aunt Phebe's right hand would have been more hairy than Esau's would have been.

There was a Rebecca Moore, who was married to a Mr Cole, and lived in Rockbridge.

The Sons of Moses Moore.

Robert married a Miss McCollam and lived at Edray where William Sharp now lives. Rev Geo. P. Moore is a great grandson of Moses Moore, also Samuel B. Moore, both residents of Edray.

Aaron Moore lived on the Greenbrier, three or four miles above Marlinton. His wife was Catherine Johnson, daughter of John Johnson, who lived on the Jericho Place, a mile north of Marlinton. Charles L. Moore, on Brown's Creek, and Jacob S. Moore, on Elk, are great-grandsons of Moses Moore, the pioneer.

Moses Moore, Jr., emigrated to Kentucky.

William Moore married Christina Dods, of Rockbridge County, and lived on Stony Creek on the place now occupied by the family of the late Dr Page Carter.

Their daughter, Margaret, became the wife of the late Colonel John W. Ruckman of Mill Point.

Another daughter, Jennie, was married to Captain William D. Hefner, who died in battle at Lewisburg during the War.

Their son, Rev James E. Moore, was a widely known Methodist minister.

John Moore, another son of the pioneer, married a Miss McClung, of Greenbrier County, and settled at Mt Vernon, Knapp's Creek. Their daughter Jennie married John Lightner, near Hightown, Highland County. Another daughter, Elizabeth, became Mrs Jacob Lightner, and lived where the late Francis Dever had his home.   There was a son, John Moore, who died aged 18 years.

Isaac Moore, son of Moses, settled near the old home now occupied by I. B. Moore.   His wife was Margaret Wilson, from the vicinity of the Old Stone Church, Augusta County.   Their children were Chesley, Preston, Malinda, who became Mrs Samuel Harper; Washington, Matilda, who became Mrs John Baker; Isaac, Jr., and Moses.

Chesley married a daughter of the late Colonel John Hill, for whom Hillsboro was named.   After her death Chesley married Miss Wanless, on Back Alleghany.

Andrew Washington Moore first married Anna, daughter of Henry Harper, of Sunset, and settled on a part of the Knapp's Creek homestead.   His second marriage was with Margaret Jane, daughter of the late John Dever, of Highland County.

Isaac Moore, Jr., lived at Dunmore.   He and a citizen named Dunkum bought from Andrew G. Mathews his fine farm, and divided it.   Out of their names they jointly coined the word Dunmore and so named the postoffice, which had been previously named Mathewsville.   Isaac Moore married Alcinda Arbogast, daughter of the late William Arbogast of Green Bank.   Their daughters are Mrs George H. Moffett, of Parkersburg; and the late Mrs Dr Charles L. Austin of Green Bank. Their sons are C. Forrest, Harry, Ernest, and Rice. Ernest is Sheriff of Pocahontas County.   Judge C. Forrest Moore resides at Covington, Va.   He presided at the trial of Goodman for fatally shoting, at Gladys' Inn, Va., Colonel Parsons, the proprietor of the Nat-

ural Bridge.   At present he is Attorney for the Covington Paper Mills.   He has been largely instrumental
in bringing the varied resources of our county into
practical notice.   Forrest Depot is named for him.

Moses Moore lived on the home place.   His wife
was Isabella, a daughter of Thomas Campbell of Highland County, and still survives her lamented husband,
who was a person eminent for his christian character.
She has her home with her son I. Brown Moore, who
was recently (98–99) a member of the West Virginia
Legislature.

The study of pioneer history is deeply interesting, and very beneficial when the reader traces
the lines of descent, and duly reflects upon the contrast
of what has been and what is now.   By doing so intelligently, we are prepared to some extent to realize
what is due the memory of those whose bravery, industry, and selfnenial made it possible for us to have
the comforts we now enjoy.

As long as the Moores retain their characteristic industry, prudent economy, honesty in their dealings,
and pious proclivities, they will be a blessing to our
county in the future, as they have been in the past, and
are now.

RICHARD HILL.

Richard Hill, whose ancestral blood courses the
veins of a great many worthy citizens, now claims our
special notice in this paper.   It is generally believed
he came to this region soon after the armies of the Rev-

olution were disbanded, from North Carolina. He was one of the more distinguished of the early pioneers as a scout and a vigilant defender of the forts.

Upon his marriage with Nancy McNeel, daughter of the venerated pioneer of the Levels, John McNeel, he settled on Hill's Creek, on lands lately occupied by Abram Hill's family. As long as Hill's Creek flows and murmurs his name will be perpetuated. There were three daughters, Elizabeth, Martha, and Margaret; and seven sons. Thomas, John, Abraham, Isaac, William, Joel, and George.

Elizabeth became Mrs John Bruffey, and lived on Bruffey's Creek. In reference to her family the following particulars are given. Nancy Bruffey married Levi Hooker, from Connecteiut, a dealer in clocks, and settled in Missouri. Eliza Bruffey became Mrs Robert Moore, near Edray. Late in lire her family went to Iowa. George P. Moore, now of Edray, is one of her sons. Davis and Clark were the other two, now in Iowa.

Martha Bruffey married James Ewing, and lived some years near Marlinton, and finally settled in Nicholas County, West Virginia.

Margaret Bruffey married organ Anderson, now of Hills Creek.

Julia Bruffey was married to William McClure, on Little Anthony's Creek.

Lavinia Bruffey married Claiborne Blaine and went west.

Harriet Bruffey was married to Wesley Cruikshanks and went west.

Bradford Bruffey married Miss Mary Watts, of Greenbrier. T. A. Bruffey and Mrs Ida Sarver are his children.

Murray Bruffey married Miss Lizzie Craig, and lives in Nicholas County.

John Bruffey, Jr., married Maggie Hill, daughter of George Hill, son of the pioneer.

Martha Hill was married to George Gillilan, of Greenbrier County, near Falling Spring. In reference to her family the following particulars are in hand:

Richard Gillilan married Miss Mary Handley, and lived near Frankford. Richard's daughter, Jennie, is now Mrs Wallace Warwick Beard, of Hillsboro. Another daughter, Sarah, became Mrs Stuart, and went west; and another daughter, Mattie, was married to Cyrus McClung, of Frankford.

Margaret Hill, daughter of the pioneer, was married to Samuel Gillilan, brother of George Gillilan, just mentioned, and settled in Illinois. Her children were Electa, Talitha, Nancy, Lydia, John, Samuel, and Shadrach Chaney. Shadrach Chaney, while a mere boy, was sent to mill, and was killed upon his arrival at the mill by another lad, who claimed to be in ahead of Shadrach. His mother's grief was inexpressible, as may be readily believed.

Thomas Hill, in his day a very prominent citizen of Pocahontas, married Anne Cackley, daughter of Valentine Cackley, Sr., of Mill Point. First lived on Hills Creek, and then located near Hillsboro, where he spent most of his life. Their family were five daughters and three sons: Martha, Mary, Nancy, Eveline,

Lavinia, William, Richard, and George.

Colonel John Hill married Elizabeth Poage, and lived near Hillsboro. When far advanced in years, he migrated to Missouri, and located in Davies County. So many families from this region have gone to that county that it might be called the Missouri Pocahontas. In this family were seven sons and four daughters. Margaret, who became Mrs Chesly K. Moore; Nancy, (Mrs William McMillion); Elizabeth and Mary, who married in Missouri. The sons were Richard, William, John, Thomas, Robert, Davis, and George.

Abraham Hill married Sallie Burr, daughter of Aaron Burr, of Greenbrier County, and lived on the old Hill homestead. In his family were nine sons and one daughter. John, Richard, Thomas, George, Aaron, Joel, Doctor, Peter, William. and Rebecca. This daughter was first married to the late William Cackley, near Mill Point. She is now Mrs A. J. Overholt. Lee Cackley is her son, living on Stamping Creek.

The writer remembers Abraham Hill with feelings of strong attachment, for many reasons. He wrote me several letters while I was a student at college, manifesting great interest in my personal welfare and speaking words of christian encouragement, all of which I reciprocated to the best of my abiiity. He came near sudden death while baiting for wolves with poison. A puff of wind blew some of the strychnine into his face; he never recovered fully from the effects, though he survived many years.

Isaac Hill did his wooing in the Lower Levels, and won the confidence and affections of Jennie Edmiston, and settled on Hills Creek.   Two sons and two daughters composed his family: Nancy, Rebecca, William, and Richard.

William Hill, son of Richard, married Ann Ray, near Locust, and settled in Nicholas County.   There were three sons and two daughters in this family: Elizabeth, Nancy, John, Archibald, and Joseph.

Joel Hill, son of the pioneer, paid a number of visits to Greenbrier County, and when he came home with his young wife, Rebecca Levisay, his friends found out what the attraction had been.   In this family were six daughters and two sons.   Mary Frances is now Mrs Sherman H. Clark; Ann Eliza was married to Oscar Groves, of Nicholas County; Martha was married to Mansfield Groves, of the same county; Melinda became Mrs Levi Gay, near Marlinton, first wife; Caroline was married to D. A. Peck, first wife.   Her daughter is now Mrs Adam Young.   Lucy was married to William Curry.   Mrs T. A. Bruffey is another daughter.

Allen Hill was in Missouri at the breaking out of the War.   Being suspected for cherishing Confederate sympathies, he was slain by over zealous Union partisans.

Richard Washington Hill married Margaret Watts, of Greenbrier County, and lives on the homestead.   He served a term as Sheriff of Pocahontas County.

George Hill, son of Richard Hill of honored memory, married Martha Edmiston.   He was married twice. By the first marriage there were four sons and a daughter: Margaret, Franklin, Claiborne, Isaac, and William.   George Hill's second marriage was with Rebecca Cruikshanks. By this marriage there were four sons and two daughters: Henrietta, Minnie, Wallace, Joel, Chalmers, and Sterling.

This venerable man died early in the forties, full of days and greatly respected- The writer was at Colonel John Hill's home when he returned from the burial of his father, and listened for hours to his reminiscences of his grand old father; but alas, so much has faded from his memory that he would like to write.

Richard Hill, whose family history we have just endeavored to illustrate, with the assistance of our lamented friend, Mrs Nancy Callison, his worthy granddaughter, seems to have keen endowed with a charmed life. It would be better to say that in the providence of God he had a mission to perform, and was immortal until that service should be accomplished.

The Indian brave that slew James Baker, one of the first schoolmasters in this region, had shrewdly planned to shoot Baker in the act of crossing the fence and kill Richard Hill with his tomahawk before he could be able to recross and escape to the Drennan house, near Levi Gays.

While Richard Hill was repairing his broken rake in the rye field at Edray, near the grave yard, an Indian in the fallen tree top aimed repeatedly at his breast, and put his finger on the trigger time and again, and every time something seemed to restrain him. The Indian thought it was the Great Spirit, and seemed to have felt it would not do to kill a friend of the Great Spirit, and thus incur his anger.

Then while scouting in the mountains toward Gauley he was thrice aroused by alarming dreams, and when the morning dawned he discovered that an Indian had tried three times to steal upon him and kill him while he was asleep.

There is also a tradition that a detachment of Indians were in ambush for several days near Mr Hill's home on Hill's Creek, for the special object of capturing or killing him, as they had come to feel there would be little or no use to raid this region while he was alive or at large- They had taken up the idea that the owner of such a nice house would dress much better than anybody else, and would not work with his own hands. They saw men at work in reach of their guns, but none of them dressed to suit their ideas as to how Mr Hill would be attired. It so turned out that Mr Hill was one of the hands, and it was his workday dress that beguiled the Indians and prevented his being shot at or captured.

Richard Hill was one of nature's noblemen, who relied more on pure, genuine character than mere superficial appearances, and therein lay the secret of his safety and success. A pure character and a genteel appearance make a lovely sight, but a genteel exterior and an impure character make a nuisance that is simply unendurable to all except human John Crows or vultures.

ADAM ARBOGAST.

The Arbogast relationship is identified to a marked degree with the history of our Pocahontas people, and

justly claims recognition in these short and simple annals. So far as known, the original progenitor of the
Arbogasts in Pendleton and Pocahontas was Michael
Arbogast, who must have been one of the original
pioneers of what is now Highland County, in "Indian
Times." He settled there some time previous to 1758.
Fort Seybert on South Branch, about twelve miles
northeast of Franklin, was the chief place of refuge for
all the pioneers in that section when there was danger
of being pillaged, slain, or carried into captivity by
raiding parties of Indians, led for the most part by
Killbuck. Captain Seybert is reported to have made
the remark, when his fort was taken in 1758, that if
the Arbogasts had been there he could have held the
place in spite of the Indians.

Michael Arbogast had seven sons: Adam, George,
Henry, John, Michael, David, and Peter,—the two
last named were twins. The sons, excepting John,
were all very powerful and stalwart in their physique,
and were often more than two hundred pounds in
weight.

Adam Arbogast married Margaret (Peggy) Hull,
daughter of Adam Hull, near Hevener's Store in what
is now Highland County, Va. They came to the head
of the Greenbrier, near Travellers Repose, in 1796,
and settled on the place now occupied by Paul McNeel
Yeager. Here he built up a home in the primitive
forest, and reared his family. His sons were Benjamin, William, Adam, and Jacob. The daughters
were Susan, Elizabeth, Mary, Barbara, and Catherine.
Barbara and Catherine died in youth. In reference to

the sons, another paper was prepared, illustrating the history of Benjamin Arbogast's family, whose sons were Solomon, Henry, Adam, John, and Benjamin, Jr., the distinguished teacher and pulpit orator. In that paper there are some omissions that are supplied here:

Margaret, daughter of Benjamin Arbogast, Sr., became Mrs John Yeager, late of Alleghany Mountain, of whose family fuller particulars may be looked for in the Yeager Sketches.

Mary (Polly) married Hamilton Stalnaker and lived in Randolph.

Another daughter of Benjamin Arbogast became Mrs Henry Wade on Back Creek. In rererence to her family the following particulars are in hand:

Benjamin Wade was a physician and settled in Missouri.

John Wade was also a physician and lives at Burnsville, Braxton County, where Wilson Wade also lives.

Madora Wade, now Mrs Gawyne Hamilton, lives in Braxton.

Naomi Wade married Joseph Gillesoie, and also lives in Braxton.

Harriet Wade became the second wife of William Cooper, near Green Bank.

Delilah Wade became Mrs Joseph Wooddell, near Green Bank. In reference to her children are these particulars:

Clark Wooddell lives in Renick's Valley.

Preston Wooddell, a gallant Confederate soldier, was slain in the battle of Winchester.

Warwick Wooddell was killed at the battle of Cold Harbor. Aaron Wooddell was also a Conrederate soldier.

John Arbogast, a son of Benjamin Arbogast, Sr., was killed near Glade hill by a falling tree. Joel Arbogast, his son, is a prosperous farmer in Kansas.

William Arbogast, of Adam the pioneer, married Jane Tallman and lived at Green Bank. Frequent and fuller references to him and his family appear in other papers.

Jacob Hull Arbogast, of Adam the pioneer, married Elizabeth Wiison Bright, of Highlrnd, and settled on the West Branch of the Upper Greenbrier, on the place now in possession of Colonel J. T. McGraw. His family consisted of four sons and three daughters.

Margaret became Mrs Levi H. Campbell, and lives in Elkins.

Eliza Jane is Mrs Adam Shuey' and lives at Fisherville, Augusta County.

Harriet Elizabeth is now Mrs B. M. Yeager at Marlinton. B. M. Yeager is a widely known citizen of our county as a land agent, railway promoter and manager for the Pocahontas Development Company.

Paul McNeel Arbogast married Amanda Bucher, and lives on the Greenbrier not far from the homestead

Jacob Lee Arbogast married Otey Riley, and at the time of his recent decease was a merchant at Travellers Repose.

William Barton Arbogast lives at Travellers Repore.

Jacob H. Arbogact was a man of very interesting personality. He was of untiring energy, and in his time was an extensive dealer in wild land. His name frequently appears in the court records a party to some of the most important and warmly contested land litigation that ever transpired at the Pocahontas bar. He was an ardent supporter of the Confederate cause, and saw service in the home guards. In the beginning of the war, a few days after the repulse of Pegram on Rich Mountain, in 1861 he refugeed with his family to the East and spent most of the war times in Augusta County. He carried but little with him, and so lost his household effects and live stock along with his dwelling. In 1865 he returned and began life afresh at the old Greenbrier homestead. But few places in West Virginia were more completely desolated than the head of Greenbrier by the ravages of war.

Adam Arbogast, Jr., of Adam, the pioneer, first married Rachel Gregg, or Zebulon Gregg, and settled near the homestead. There was one son by this marriage, Napoleon Bonaparte. The second marriage was with Sarah McDaniel. In reference to the children of the second marriage the following particulars are given:

Huldah married Paul McNeel Yeager, and lives at Travelers Repose.

Eliza Arbogast became Mrs Frank McElwee and lives at Elkins.

Alice Arbogast married Early Snyder and lives in Crabbottom.

Rrchel became Mrs C. C. Arbogast and lives near Arbovale.

Ella is now Mrs Benjamin Fleisher and lives in Highland.

Ada died in youth.

The son Peter D. Arbogast married Hodie Burner, lived awhile at Arbovale, was a Justice of the Peace: he lately resigned and is now studying medicine at the University of Virginia.

Adam Arbogast, the pioneer, lived to be nearly one hundred years old. He recovered his second sight and for years had no need of eye-glasses. Coming to this region early as he did, and having grown up in the period of Indian troubles, he had many thrilling adventures to relate. Upon one occasion his dogs treed a panther in an immense hemlock tree for which the upper Greenbrier is so celebrated. He called on John Yeager, his nearest neighbor, for assistance in capturing the dangerous animal, one of the largest of its kind. John Yeager was a famous and fearless climber of forest trees. A torch was procured and he began to climb, holding it in one hand. When he had located the panther, he laid the torch on two limbs, descended the tree until ne could reach the rifle that Mr Arbogast had loaded and primed for him. He thereupon returned to his torch and by its light shot and killed his game.

Upon one occasion the pioneer had arranged for a bear hunt on Burner's Mountain. When reaching the point designated, he was disappointed in not meeting his hunter friends. He killed a bear however, and as it was growing late and there were signs of a coming storm, he went into shelter, and soon a hurricane occurred. The next morning he sound there was not a standing tree anywhere near; the dog was gone, the bear fast under fallen timber, the gun broken to pieces, and he was safe without a scratch or bruise. He had to go home for an axe to chop the tree off the bear and get help to bring it in.

What gives these stories their interest, it all occurred just as he told it. Like the Father of his Country, Adam Arbogast could not and would not tell anything but the truth as he saw it.

ROBERT GAY.

Robert Gay, Esq., the subject of this sketch, was one of the most prominent personalities of his time in the affairs of early pioneer days. He was a native of Augusta County, and was brought up to manhood on the banks of the Calf Pasture River, between Deerfield and Goshen. Just before the Revolution he came to this region and settled first on Brown's Creek.

His first wife was Hannah oore, daughter of Levi Moore, Senior, who homesteaded and settled the place near Frost now occupied by the family of the late Samuel Gibson, Esq.

Afterwards Mr Gay located on the east bank of the Greenbrier, about opposite fhe mouth of Stony Creek, near Marlinton. Subsequently he built a new house on the west bank, traces of which are yet visible at the Lumber Yard. The timbers of this house are now in the dwelling occupied by Colonel Levi Gay. These are among the oldest specimens of hewn timber in the county. The tradition is that the old house now owned by M. J. McNeel is the first building of hewn timber ever erected in the county. Here the venerable pioneer spent his last years.

He figured prominently in the organization of the county, was a brave patriot, and widely known and much esteemed. He was a special friend of Jacob Warwick's family, and pleasant relations have ever existed between the descendants of the two old pioneer comrades and attached personal friends.

Mr and Mrs Robert Gay reared a worthy family of six sons and three daughters. The sons were Samuel, George, John, Andrew, Robert, and James; the daughters were Jennie, Sallie, and Agnes.

Jennie married William Cackley, one of the most prominent citizens of his time, and lived many years near Huntersville, on the place now owned by the family of the late Joseph Loury, Esq. Mr Cackley finally moved to Missouri, late in life.

Sally became the wife of James Bridger, and for a long while lived at the Bridger Place, higher up the Greenbrier. This family went to Iowa.

Agnes married Alexander Gillilan, and her family moved to Missouri.

Samuel Gay married Alice Cackley, eldest daughter of Frye Cackley and Polly his wife, who came from near Winchester, and located ar Mill Point, about 1778. Joseph C. Gay, on Elk, and Mrs Polly Gibson, on Old Field Fork of Elk, are their children. Two of their sons, George and William, were slain during the War. Hannah sacrificed her life waiting on her sick friends and relatives during the War. Sarah Ann was the first wife of the late Jacob Waugh, of Stony Creek. S. D. Waugh and Mrs A. Coombs are her children.

George Gay married Susan Lightner, whose parents were Peter Lightner and Alcinda (Harper) his wife, on Knapp's Creek. This son lived several years in the Levels, on the farm now occupied by F. A. Renick. Afterwards he moved to Iowa, and prospered.

John Gay married Miss Margaret B. Clark, a lady from Cecil County, Maryland. He spent his entire life on the old homestead near Marlinton.

James Gay married Miss Abbie Callison, sister of the late Mrs Julia Poage, of Poage's Lane. John R. and Quincy Poage, well known citizens, are her nephews.

This humble effort is put forth to perpetuate the memory of a very worthy man. In peace and in war his country could rely upon him. He belonged to that pioneer citizenship of whom Washington thought in a dark hour when he exclaimed: "Give me but a banner and rear it on the mountains of West Augusta, and I will rally around me the men that will lift my bleeding country from the dust and set her free!"

Having reared a very worthy family, having been prominent in public service in this section of Virginia, before and since the organization of the county of Pocahontas, his life came to a close March 22, 1834. His remains were borne to the old burying ground on Stony Creek, near the Edray crossing, in sight of his home.

Mrs Hannah Gay survived him in widowhood more than twenty-five years. In August, 1859, on a visit to Sally Bridger, something happened to enrage the bees and upon going out to see, she was attacked by them and before she could be rescued she was fatally injured, and died August 15, 1859, at a very advanced age. She was borne to rest at the side of her noble husband, and thus passed away one of whom it was testified by many that she was one of the "best old ladies that ever lived in her neighborhood."

The writer cordially agrees with that sentiment, when he remembers how kind, and even affectionate, she was toward him while he was a mere youth. "Keep on trying to do right, Billy,—there will be better times for you some day." These words he fondly treasures in his memory, and for fifty years has seen and felt how wise and useful such words are.

BENJAMIN ARBOGAST.

This paper is composed of fragmentary notices of one of the early settlers of the Glade Hill neighborhood. Benjamin Arbogast, Senior, the progenitor of a well known branch of the Arbogast relationship, settled early in the century near Glade Hill, on the lands now in possession of Cornelius Bussard, Clark Dilley, and others. In his home were five sons and three daughters: Henry, Solomon, John, Adam, Benjamin, Carlotta, Sally, and Delilah.

Carlotta became Mrs Jonathn aPotts, and lived in Upshur County.

Sally became the second wife of Ralph Wanless, near Mt Tabor.

Delilah was first married to Joseph Wooddell, near Green Bank. Her second marriage was with Frederick Pugh, of same vicinity.

In reference to the sons, we have the following particulars, gathered from a variety of sources:

Henry Arbogast married Anna Warwick, on Deer Creek, and settled on a part of the homestead. Their sons Warwick and Newton died while young. Jamieson married Sarah Grimes, and settled on Elk.

Marshall Arbogast married Rachel Nottingham, and lives in Randolph County.

Sally Arbogast became the wife of George Arbogast and lives near Glade Hill.

Margaret was married to Martin Clark Dilley, and lives on part of the homestead.

Minta became Mrs Bud Stalnaker, and lives in Randolph County.

Henry Arbogast was a person of high natural endowments; was widely known in our county, and was greatly respected for many good qualities. He was a local preacher in the pale of the Methodist Episcopal church, and "cried aloud and spared not" when denouncing the fashionable foibles of his times. The writer once heard him preach a sermon from the text: "Pray without ceasing." The sermon was largely taken up in a description of the Magic Carpet, we read about in the Arabian Nights Entertainment, and then used it as an illustration, showing that the prayerful soul has in prayer something far more to the purpose than the magic carpet ever was or could be. He was an enthusiast in his religious views. To him Methodism was the chief of all the prevailing "isms,"—the one "ism" that was "altogether lovely,"—and he made no secret of it.

During the war between the States he was a sincere, decided, but harmless sympathizer with the Union cause. When last seen alive he and his neighbor Eli Buzzard were in charge of a squad of persons claiming to be Confederate Scouts. A few days afterwards these two civilians were found dead near the roadside, about half way from their homes towards Frost. From the attitude in which his body was found it is inferred that he died in the act of prayer, heeding the text referred to above.

Solomon Arbogast married Nancy Nottingham, and lived on part of the homestead. In reference to his family the following particulars are noted:

Allen first married a Miss Curry; his second marriage was with a Miss Gillespie.

George married Sallie Arbogast.

Charles was a Union soldier and died in the war.

Lizzie married Gilmer Sharp and lives near Frost.

Mary married William Cooper, near Green Bank.

Rachel became Mrs Samuel Sutton and lives beyond Green Bank.

Caroline first married the late James Ruckman; her second marriage was to Michael Scales, and lived near Mill Point.

John Arbogast, son of Benjamin, Sr., married Margaret Yeager and lived near Glade Hill. He was killed by a falling tree, leaving a widow and three sons.

Adam Arbogast married Clarissa Sutton, and lived near Green Bank. They were the parents of five sons and three daughters: John, Brown, Christopher, Ben-

jamin, Reed, Dorinda, now Mrs David Shears; Eliza,
who became Mrs James Sutton; and Emma, now Mrs
J. Trace, all three near Green Bank.

When a little girl, Mrs Clarissa Arbogast had her
arm crushed in a cider mill. She was given up to die
by the physician sent for from an adjoining county.
The late Captain John McElwee, ancestor of the Mc-
Elwee relationship in our county, had the nerve to take
his joint saw and razor and amputate the arm above
the mortified part. The patient recovered and lived to
rear the five sons and three daughters just named.
What Mrs Arbogast could not do with her good left
arm in housekeeping was not worth doing. She died
quite recently.

Benjamin Arbogast, of Benjamin, Senior, married
Miss Gibbons, a sister of the gallant Colonel S. B.
Gibbons, Tenth Virginia Infantry, who died May 6th,
1862, on the McDowell battle field,—shot through the
head the moment he reached the line of fire, leading
his men into action.

Benjamin Arbogast, Junior, was one of the most remarkable persons that ever lived in our county. Upon
attaining his majority he was appointed constable. and
he magnified his office and worked it for all it was
worth. He frequented the courts, and seemed to have
been infatuated with the lawyers of loose habits and
alcoholic propensities, and proficient in the history of
the four kings. He aspired to the distinction of beating them at their own game, for they seemed to be
what a gentleman should be. He soon acquired his
coveted distinction of being the fastest young man in

the county.

When about twenty-five years of age he came under the influence of Charles See, who taught in the family of Colonel Paul McNeel, and there was kindled in our young friend's mind an irresistible desire for a college education. He learned the rudiments of Latin and algebra from Mr See, went a session or two at Academy and then away to Dickinson College, in Pennsylvania, and was graduated among the best in his class. In the meantime he had professed piety, entered the ministry, and became a noted pulpit orator, and one of the most distinguished teachers of the high schools under the auspices of the Methodist Episcopal church, South. He died a few years since at Winchester; leaving a reputation long to be remembered by his denomination. Recently one of his surviving children, an accomplished daughter visited Marlinton.

The writer tenderly cherishes the memory of this remarkable Pocahontas man, for he often manifested special friendship for me, and we have had many good talks together. We last met in Winchester, in October, 1874. He introduced me to Norval Wilson, father of Bishop Wilson.

JOHN McNEEL.

John McNeel, the ancestor of the McNeel relationship in our county, appears to have been the first to occupy the Little Levels by permanent settlement. He was a native of Frederick County, Virginia, but passed much of his early life in or near Cumberland, Mary-

land. He seems to have been fond of athletics, and
in a pugilistic contest his antagonist was so badly
knocked out as to be regarded fatally injured. To avoid
arrest and trial for murder, he refugeed. He followed
the trend of the Alleghanies. A long while was spent
in their gloomy solitudes, and his sufferings of mind
and body can not be even imagined by any of us.
Finally, going deeper and deeper into the wilderness,
he came at last in view of the Levels, about 1765.

As he overlooked this section from some neighboring eminence, he saw much to remind him of his native
region. An extensive, wooded plain, bordered by
mountain ranges of unsurpassed beauty, and very fertile. He decided, as every thing looked so much like
the old home scenery, to settle here; and chose a site
for his cabin near the present home occupied by Hon.
M. J· McNeel. Traces of this cabin have been seen
by many persons yet living, between the gate on the
public road and his residence. If the spot could be
identified, it would be well to mark it with a piece of
the marble recently found in such fabulous quantities
close by.

Here the solitary man brooded over his supposed
guilt, prayed with his broken heart for pardon, and
hunted for his food, subsisting almost entirely upon
venison and trout. One day while hunting he met
Charles and Edward Kinnison, from his old home, who
had come out here prospecting for a situation. He
learned from them that the person he boxed with was
not dead, not even seriously hurt. This was indeed
good news, and then and there he felt free from all

bloody stain, and he could return without fear of molestation.

John McNeel insisted upon his friends to share his cabin with him. He assisted them in making a selection for a home adjoining his tract. The three then set out on their return to the lower Valley of Virginia.

While on this visit home John McNeel married Martha Davis, who was born in Wales in 1740, and soon after their marriage they came out to the Levels. A few acres were soon cleared off, and plenty to subsist upon was raised.

Mr McNeel seemed deeply impressed with a sense of gratitude to God for his providential care, after all his wanderings and fears to permit the lines to fall to him in such a pleasant, wealthy place, that he built a house for worship, the White Pole Church.

In a few years the Dunmore war opened up. The three friends,—McNeel and two Kinnisons,—went into camp at Lewisburg, and joined the expedition to Point Pleasant, October 10, 1784. They survived that eventful and important contest, came back, but not to remain very long. They went across the eastern mountains and enlisted in some company that went from Frederick County, served during the Revolution, and then took up the peaceful tenor of their lives where they had left off. There is a pathetic tradition that while Mr McNeel was absent to Point Pleasant a child was born and died before his return. The mother with her own hands prepared the coffin and the grave, and buried it. They reared five children, two sons and three daughters.

Miriam married John Jordan, and lived near Locust on what is now known as the Jordan Place, owned by Isaac McNeel. They reared three daughters and five sons. Particular mention of these in the John Jordan paper.

Nancy McNeel, second daughter of the pioneer, married Richard Hill.

Martha, the pioneer's third daughter, married Griffin Evans, moved west and settled on the Miami River.

Our venerable pioneer reared two sons, Abram and Isaac.

Abram first married a Miss Lamb. Her brother, William Lamb, was greatly esteemed by Abram McNeel, and he named his son for him. William Lamb was an expert Artisan. The late Captain McNeel had a clock made by this person that was one of the most elegant specimens of its kind to be found anywhere. There was one daughter, Elizabeth, who was married to William Hanna, of Greenbrier County.

Abram McNeel's second wife was Miss Bridger, relative of the slain Bridger Brothers. By this marriage there were three sons, Washington, who died in youth; John; and Abram, who went west. The daughters of this second marriage were Margaret, who married the late William Beard of Renick's Valley, and she has been dead but a short while.

Martha married Bayliss Butcher, and went west. One of her sons practiced medicine in our county a few years since, Dr F. Butcher.

Miriam, another daughter, married Christopher Beard, and her son Dr Beard is a prominent physician in Lewisburg.

Nancy McNeel married James Rankin, and lived on the Greenbrier at the mouth of Locust.

Mary was a lifelong invalid, and never married.

Abram McNeel's third wife was Magdalen Kelly, of Monroe County. At the time of their marriage she was the widow Haynes. Rev James Haynes is a grandson of her first husband. The children of this third marriage were Henry Washington and William Lamb.

Henry Washington has lived mostly in the west, and has led a busy life for many years, and is there now.

Captain William Lamb McNeel, lately deceased, lived on the old homestead. He held many positions of trust, and met the expectations of his most admiring friends, in the camp, the legislature, and in business affairs.

Isaac McNeel, the other son of the pioneer, settled upon lands now held by the family of the late Jacob McNeel, M. J. McNeel, W. T. Beard, and C. E. Beard. His first wife was Rachel McKeever. By this marriage there were four sons, Paul, John, Richard, and Isaac. The daughters were Hannah, Martha, Nancy, and Rachel.

Hannah married Benjamin Wallace, of Bath County Virginia. Dr Matt Wallace, an eminent physician at Mill Point, lately deceased, was her son. Her daughter, Rachel, became Mrs William Hefner, a prominent citizen of Braxton County. Her other daughter Elizabeth married Christopher Jordan.

Martha McNeel married David McCue, of Nicholas

County.

Nancy, the third daughter, married William C. Price late of Huttonsville, Randolph County.

Rachel McNeel married Jacob Crouch, of Randolph County.

In reference to the sons of the first marriage it will be remembered that Colonel Paul McNeel was one of the most widely known citizens of his day.

John McNeel's sons are Isaac McNeel and Hon. M. J. McNeel, of the Levels.

Richard McNeel's daughter, Mary, is the wife of W. T. Beard, whose sons, Edgar and Lee, are well known.

Isaac McNeel served as Sheriff a number of years, and went west.

By his second marriage, Isaac McNeel, son of John, the pioneer, to Ann Seybert, daughter of Jacob Seybert, mouth of Stamping Creek, there were two sons, Jacob and Samuel Ellis. The latter died a soldier in the war.

The daughters of the second marriage were Catherine, who became the wife of Charles Wade, of Green Hill, Virginia; Elizabeth married Jacob Sharp, near Edray; Miriam married Joseph McClung, of Nicholas County; Magdalen married Dr Robert Williams, of Bath, Virginia.

This brings the chronicles of the venerable pioneer's family down within the memory and observation of the living. His life was of no ordinary interest. His righteous memory should be in everlasting remembrance. He was the first to "wail with judicious care" amid these mountains the hymns sung by his ancestry amid the moors of Scotlond, the men of the moss hags.

But very little, if any of the lands he preempted has passed out of the possession of the relationship, now in the third and fourth generation, a very remarkable circumstance in the history of American families.

John A. McNeel, a great grandson, furnishes the following data:

"The knowledge I have of my great-grandfather is purely traditional, but with one link of tradition, and that one my father, the late Paul McNeel, of Pocahontas County. John McNeel, Senior, was born in the year 1745, and was 80 years old when he died, his death occurring in 1825. Paul McNeel was born within sight of his grandfather's house, in the year 1803. He was consequently 22 years of age at his grandfather's death. There was an intimacy between these two people, as I have often learned from my father, that was only ended by the death of the older McNeel.

"Paul McNeel was taken at an early age to live with his grandparents. I have heard him relate an incident to fix his very earliest recollections of his grandparents which was this: His grandmother had given him a piece of wheat bread and butter, (quite a luxury then), and set the little boy down to eat it. When left alone a large tomcat came up to divide the boy's meal. A fight followed, and the boy threw the cat in the fire, where there happened to be a bed of coals. The coals stuck to the cat's fur, the cat ran and screamed until the boy was scared out of his wits. He too ran home as fast as he could. This occurred when Paul McNeel was six years old, in the old house in the rear of M. J. McNeel's residence.

"As I say, Paul McNeel at a tender age became an inmate of his grandparent's home, and to a great degree received his early training from them. The death of his mother, Mrs Rachel McNeel, occurred in 1818, when he was only 15 years old, rendered his dependence on his grandparents the more necessary. There is a field belonging to the estate of the late Jacob McNeel that my father has frequently in passing pointed out to me, which he and his grandfather planted in corn (they doing the dropping) in 1825; and in connection he told how active of body and sound of mind his grandfather was at eighty, and soon after this the old gentleman was seized with pneumonia and died.

"I have related these two incidents—the beginning and ending of the acquaintance of these two people—to show you how thoroughly I have been taught, both by "legend and lay," to know and revere the character of the venerable pioneer. The exact spots where the "White Pole Church" and the "First Camp" were built have been pointed out to me; and, as you suggest both should be marked by a slab of the marble that is found in such abundance close by.

"Martha Davis, the wife of this gentleman, was a Welch girl, a Calvinistic Methodist, born in the year 1742, being therefore several years older than her husband. She survived him five years, being 88 years old at the time of her death. You speak of the death of her child during the absence of her husband to Point Pleasant. Of this I have frequently heard, and that she with her own hands prepared the body of her child and performed the first burial rites ever performed at the McNeel graveyard.

There was another matter this lady was the first to do, and for which her name deserves to be kept in dear remembrance, and by this latter act to the living generation she has set an example of the highest christian character: and that was to bring with her to her new mountain home as a part of her dowry, a Bible printed in the Welsh dialect. A noble exemplar! This is the first Bible that there is any record of having ever been brought to the waters of the Greenbrier.

"The date fixed by you as the time when John McNeel, Senior, arrived in the Levels, 1765, is correct. He was then in his 20th year, and now when we reflect that this was the year succeeding when the Indians had made the most fearful massacre of the white people in the Valley of Virginia, and the the Ohio River Valley was an unbroken wilderness, we wonder at the adventurous spirit of this remarkable man.

"Of the traditional history that I have heard of him the thing that impressed me most of all was his wonderful sincerity of character and strength of purpose in his daily life. This feature of his character had a powerful influence on his grandson, Paul McNeel, and contributed in no small degree to his success in after life. And in conclusion I will say that during the 27 years it was my pleasure to know my father, I never heard him mention the name of John McNeel, Senior, but with the words of praise upon his lips. And the deep hold that Methodism has held in the Levels of

Pocahontas for the last hundred years can be explained
when I say that the man and woman who built the
"White Pole Church" laid the foundation of the Methodist Church; and let us trust that the influence of this
humble christian man and woman will descend from
generation to generation, and like the mantle of Elijah
prove a blessing on whomsoever it may fall."

JOHN SLAVEN.

One of the notable families in our local annals was
the Slaven relationship, whose ancestor was John
Slaven, who came from Tyrone, Ireland, about the
middle of the previous century. He first settled in
Rockingham County, and then came to what is now
Highland County, Virginia, and located permanently
at Meadow Dale, on property now held by Stuart
Slaven and James Flesher. His wife was a Miss Stuart.
Traces of the old home are still to be seen near James
Flesher's residence, who is a descendant by the fifth
remove.

In reference to John Slaven's sons, we learn that
Henry and Reuben went to Ohio and settled in the
famous Scioto Valley. Daniel Slaven located his home
on Clinch River, Tennessee. Isaiah Slaven married
Martha Stuart and went to Montgomery County, Ky.
in 1792, about the time that State came into the union,
and settled at Mount Sterling. William Slaven settled
in Smith County, Tennessee.

Stuart Slaven remained on the homestead. His wife
was a Miss Sohnston, a daughter of Jesse Johnston.

He was one of the most prominent and influential citizens of his time. Stuart Slaven's children were Reuben, for so many years one of the leading citizens of his county, and perhaps celebrated more marriages than any magistrate that ever held that office in his section; Jesse, William, Stuart; Nellie, who became Mrs Adam Lightner; Mrs Thomas Campbell; Sallie, who was Mrs Alexander Gilmore; Rachel, who became Mrs Givens, and went west; and Mrs Matilda Wade.

Margaret Slaven was married to the late Benjamin B. Campbell. Her daughters are Mrs S. P. Patterson and Miss Mattie Campbell, of Huntersville; Stuart Campbell, of Belington; Brown Campbell, late of Monterey, and Luther Campbell, at Dunmore, are her sons.

John Slaven, son of John from Tyrone, was twice married. The first wife was a Miss Wade. There was one son, John Slaven, who never married. The second marriage was with Elizabeth Warwick, a sister of Andrew and William Warwick, on Deer Creek. Not long after this marriage he settled on the head of Greenbrier, and he is the ancestor of the Pocahontas branch of the Slaven relationship. By the second marriage there were five daughters and two sons.

He was a person of remarkable muscular powers, and was a Revolutionary veteran, a noted hunter and successful trapper. He had thrilling descriptions to give of the many bloody engagements he passed thro, the hazardous risks he ran, and the bitter privations he endured in the service of his country. He lived to an advanced age, and was so weakened by the infirmities of age as to make use of crutches in moving around in his closing days. In reference to his children the following particulars are available:

Sallie Slaven became Mrs Dinwiddie, and lived for a time at the head of Jacksons River; thence went to Hardin County, Ohio.

Priscilla Slaven was married to Joseph Wooddell, of Green Bank, and lived in Pike County, Ohio.

Anna Slaven married Patrick Bruffey, and lived near Green Bank, on property occupied by John Hevener. Patrick Bruffey was a very useful and prominent citizen; a skilled workman in stone, iron, and wood; and filled most of the official positions in the gift of the county.

Mary Slaven became Mrs John Wooddell, near Green Bank. The late Mrs M. P. Slaven, Hon W. J. Wooddell, and J. S. Wooddell, Esq., were her children.

Margaret Slaven became Mrs Samuel Ruckman.

William Slaven, son of John Slaven the pioneer, was born July 6, 1798, and was married in 1819 to Margaret Wooddell, daughter of Joseph Wooddell, at Green Bank. She was born June 27, 1800.

They were the parents of six sons and two daughters. Their names were Charles, who died seeking gold in California; William Patrick, James Cooper, Henry, Nathan—a Confederate soldier killed at Fort Donelson; and Elizabeth, who became Mrs Osborne of Gilmer County.

William Slaven's second marriage was with Nancy Cline, of Lewis County, and there were five daughters and four sons by this marriage. Mary, Sarah, Caroline, Martha, Lucy Frank, Lanty, Roland, and Perry. William Slaven's descendants mainly live in Jackson, Wirt, Lewis, and Gilmer counties, and are reported to be prosperous and good people of that section of West Virginia.

While living in Pocahontas County, William Slaven was a person of marked prominence—a member of the Virginia Legislature, magistrate, and Assessor. More than sixty years ago he concluded to move to Lewis County. Assisted by John Wooddell, his household effects were carried over Cheat mountain to Lawyer See's near Huttonsville on pack horses, there being only a bridle path at the time. He lived awhile on Leading Creek, Lewis County; thence went to Wirt County, near Burning Springs; and finally to Jackson County, a few miles from Ravenswood. In his new places of residence, after leaving Pocahontas, he was honored with places of trust, served the public as magistrate and deputy sheriff, which at that time meant the full, active duties of sheriff. He leaves the reputation of being always an efficient, trustworthy business man.

Jacob Gillespie Slaven, son of the pioneer of that much named region, Head of Greenbrier, Upper Tract, Travelers Repose, married Eleanor Lockridge, daughter of Lanty Lockridge, Senior, on Knapps Creek. These persons passed the most of their married lives on the head of the Greenbrier, in a widely known and attractive home. In their time there was an immense travel along that road, Staunton and Parkersburg Pike. The most of communication between the western and eastern parts of Virginia was by this route. Governor

Joe Johnson and Stonewall Jackson have stopped over here to enjoy trout and venison. Everything seemed prosperous and pleasant with Jacob Slaven until the terrible ravages of war laid his home in ashes, and exiled the happy inmates. The family consisted of eight daughters and four sons. We lay before our readers the following particulars concerning these sons and daughters.

Harriet, who was greatly admired for her personal attractions, became Mrs Patrick Gallaher and went to Missouri.

Elizabeth was married to Colonel William T. Gammon, a citizen of marked prominence. She now lives at Odessa, Missouri.

John Randolph Slaven, late of Huntersville, married Margaret P. Wooddell, lately deceased.

Lanty Lockridge Slaven married Isabella Burner, and settled on Back Alleghany, where his widowed wife with her sons, Jacob, Charles, and Gratz, resides.

Mary P. Slaven was married to Jesse B. Slaven, at Meadow Dale, where she died and is buried.

Warwick Slaven married Mary Riley and lives near Green Bank.

Martha Slaven became Mrs J. T. Hoggsett, and lived near Mill Point at the time of her death a few years since.

Adalaide Eleanor Slaven was first married (by the writer) to Washington Arbogast. He died in 1864, of wounds received in the battle of Spottsylvania Courthouse. Her second marriage was with William L. Brown, Esq and lives at Green Bank.

Margaret Eveline Slaven, now Mrs J. H. Patterson, lives at Marlinton. Mr Patterson is the Clerk of the Pocahontas Circuit Court. He was a Confederate soldier from start to finish, and shared the perils of those who were first in battle and last in retreat.

Sarah Slaven was first married to Peter H. Slaven, and lived at Monterey, Virginia. Their son Emmet lives in Nebraska. Her second marriage was with Arista Hartman, now living in Kansas.

Winfield T. Slaven married Nannie P. Ruckman, and lives near Marvin.

In reference to the daughters, it is interesting to note that Eleanor and Margaret were twins. Mildred and Alice were also twin sisters.

John Slaven and wife, the ancestral pioneers, that had their home on the beautiful banks of the upper Greenbrier, had a married life of fifty-two years, ten months, and twenty-one days. It would be well could their graves be identified, where unheeded o'er their silent dust the storms of the eventful present and the recent past have raged in such ominous fury. The story of their lives helps us very much towards a proper understanding of what it cost to make it possible for the comforts that gladden our lives.

CHARLES AND JACOB KINNISON.

Among the earlier pioneers of the Little Levels were Jacob and Charles Kinnison. They were among the persons who had heard the wonderful intelligence brought in by a half demented neighbor, that he had

seen streams flowing towards the west during his last
excursion in the wilderness regions beyond.   In their
explorations of the Greenbrier Valley they found John
McNeel, a refugee neighbor, near Millpoint.   He gave
them the benefit of his observations, and the three
persons attempted permanent settlements about 1765,
and thus left their old homes a few miles of Winchester, Va., near Capon Springs.

Charles Kinnison's wife was Martha Day.   About
the time of Braddock's defeat she and her mother were
taken prisoners by the Indians, in the Capon neighborhood.   On the morning after the captivity, Mrs Day
remarked to her friends that she believed the Indians
intended to kill her.

"Oh, mother, what makes you think so?" exclaimed
Martha.

"Because they have given moccasins to all the prisoners but me, and have left me bare footed," replied
the mother.

When all were ready to move on a warrior walked
up to Mrs Day and with his war club struck her a stun-
ning blow between her shoulders, knocking the breath
out of her, and then in an instant lifted her scalp-lock.
She was left there in a state of insensibility, and it was
never known whether she recovered consciousness or
died immediately.

The lands settled by Charles Kinnison are now occupied by Sherman H. Clark as a residence.   Charles
Kinnison remained on this place until he was far advanced in life, when he migrated to Ohio.   Mr and
Mrs Kinnison were the parents of two daughters, whose

names are not remembered: and five sons, David, Charles, Mark, Nathaniel and Amos.

David Kinnison was born June 7, 1767. He married Susanna Hughes, a sister of Moses and Milburn Hughes. She was born April 17, 1767. He died in 1835, aged 67 years. She died in 1854, aged 83 years. David Kinnison, soon after his marriage, settled north of Millpoint, where Kenney Hogsett lives. They were the parents of two daughters, Esther, who became Mrs William McNeel, and Elizabeth; and these are the names of the seven sons: Charles, William, Lawrence, Mark, David, James, and Jacob. All these children went west, except Jacob Kinnison, and we have no information as to their families.

Jacob Kinnison married in 1828 Catherine Clendennin, a sister of William and John Clendennin, and settled on the homestead. In reference to their children we have this information: Hannah was the first wife of the late William Morrison, near Buckeye; William married Jane, daughter of Squire John McNeil, and lived on Dry Branch. He was a Union soldier. Hezekiah Bland married Elizabeth Ann Silva, and located in Braxton County; Allen married Rebecca Perkins and lives on the Greenbrier east of Hillsboro; Nancy is now Mrs John D. Rorke, at Marlinton. Sarah Ann became Mrs Isaac Hill on Hill's Creek; John Bland died in early youth; David Dyerly, a Confederate soldier, died during the war. Mrs Catherine Kinnison died in 1864. Jacob Kinnison was a well known citizen, and served many years as constable of his district. He seemed never suited in politics and would sometimes decline voting, and claimed to be a conservative.

Nathaniel Kinnison, of Charles the pioneer, came in from Ohio on a visit, and died near Green Bank.

Amos Kinnison, of Charles the pioneer, married Nancy Casebolt, on the Greenbrier, and settled on part of the homestead now in the possession of John B. Kinnison, two miles west of Hillsboro. Their children were David, Martha, and John Barlow.

David married and settled near Charleston.

Martha became the wife of Zechariah Armentrout, and settled in Nicholas County. John Armentrout, her son, a Confederate soldier, had his head torn off by a solid cannon shot at the battle of King's Saltworks.

John Barlow Kinnison married Deida Gillespie Morrison, and settled on the homestead. He farmed and operated a flourishing blacksmith shop. He was an expert at the anvil, and by patient industry and economy he acquired a fine estate, now occupied by his children.

In reference to his family, we learn that his only daughter Caroline died aged four years.

James Claiborne first married Rachel Kellison; second marriage was with Martha Cutlip, and he now lives on Hills Creek.

Thomas Franklin married Julia Hanna, of Greenbrier County, and lives at the homestead.

John Wesley married Alice Hill, and lives on property recently held by the late Thomas Hill.

George Allen Kinnison married Serena Brock and lives on Hills Creek.

Doctor Morgan Kinnison married Cora, daughter of

Isaac Hill, and lives on Hills Creek.

John B. Kinnison's father, Amos Kinnison, died March 10, 1860, aged 82 years, 2 months, 7 days; his mother, Nancy, died March 18, 1870, aged 84 years, 10 months, 6 days; his wife, Deida, died July 20, 1890, aged 60 years, 2 months, 23 days.

Jacob Kinnison, the fellow pioneer, with his brother Charles, located on lands just east of Hillsboro, lately occupied by his sons, Nathaniel and William Kinnison. There was one daughter Elizabeth, who was never married. Nathaniel Kinnison was never married also, and brother and sister kept house for a great many years. The neatness and generous hospitality that characterized this home made it pleasant for the itinerant ministers for a long while. Nathaniel died February 13, 1859, at a very advanced age, having lived a consistent christian life.

William Kinnison married Nancy Oldham of Locust, and settled on the homestead. There were two daughters and four sons. Sarah became Mrs William Oldham, Elizabeth Mrs James Burnsides, first wife.

The sons were Davis, John, Nathaniel, and William. The three sons first named were Confederate soldiers.

Davis Kinnison ranked among the first class of our county citizenship. He was for many years a magistrate in his district. He received a liberal education at the Hillsboro Academy, mainly under the tuition of Rev Dunlap. Mr Dunlap regarded him as one of the most exemplary young persons he had ever instructed.

Squire Davis Kinnison died in 1893, about 62 years

of age.

Charles and Jacob Kinnison, the pioneer brothers, were skillful workers in wood with the broad axe and whip saw. Some of the first carpenter work ever done in this county was by them and Richard Hill.

Charles Kinnison hewed the logs for John McNeel, pioneer. The building yet stands. He also prepared the logs for the house now dwelt in by Claiborne McNeil, near Buckeye. His services were greatly valued in planning and constructing forts.

Thus with assistance of J. B. Kinnison and Allan Kinnison, something has been attempted to embalm the memories of these good men and their worthy descendants. We believe it is the temper of many of the living Kinnisons to see that the lustre of the Kinnison name shall not be tarnished, but rendered more illustrious by all the facilities that may come to hand.

ARCHIBALD CLENDENNIN,

The Clendennin name has been familiar as a household word to our people for more than a hundred years.

They are the descendants of Archibald Clendennin, who was one of the pioneers of Greenbrier County, and lived in the Big Levels, not far from Lewisburg. The place has been long known as the Ballard Smith homestead.

Charles Clendennin was slain by the Indians in 1763 and was survived by two sons, George and Charles.

In regard to George Clendennin we have nothing authentic. Charles Clendennin was one of the pioneers of Kanawha County, and the city of Charleston is named for him. William Clendennin, a son of Charles, married Sallie Cochran, daughter of John Cochran, and settled on the Burgess place, near Hillsboro, now occupied by John Payne. This occurred about 1780. Their sons were William and John; their daughter Catherine became Mrs Jacob Kennison.

John Cochran was the person who brought in the slain bodies of the Bridger Brothers. His mother was a Miss Hogshead, of Augusta County, very pious person, and her granddaughter Sallie was a very rigid christian person and trained her children in the nurture and admonition of the Lord. She was called a Jewess both "outward and inwardly," as she insisted upon her sons learning some trade. To gratify her conscientious wishes, her son William Clendennin was apprenticed to Bayliss G. Rapp, at Frankford, for seven years, seven months, and seven days. Upon his marriage with Jane Cochran, he settled at the Casebolt mill and finally located on the Seybert Place at the mouth of Stamping Creek. Their children were Mary Ann who became Mrs Buckhannon, and settled in Upshur.

John Clendennin married Rebecca Byrd, and lived at Byrd's Mill in upper Greenbrier.

James Clendennin died in youth.

Sally Clendennin cared for her parents, prospered, and bought the place where she now lives.

John Clendennin, of William the pioneer, learned his trade in a voluntary apprenticeship with Ralph

Wanless, as his mother wished. It is told of John that when a mere child he attended a preaching service at the Hawk Place, on Locust Creek, conducted by Dr McElhenney. When the minister inquired whether any children were to be baptized, John, in the absence of his mother, came forward and presented himself and was baptized, and named himself John McElhenney.

Upon his marriage with Catherine Seybert, he settled at Beard's Mill on Locust Creek, and after many years moved to Highland County. They were the parents of six sons:

William died at the age of eight years and lies in an unknown grave in the McNeel cemetery.

Jacob F. lives in Highland. His first marriage was with Elizabeth Bird, and has two sons. The second marriage was with Mary Bird.

George G. married Louella McNeel, and lives on a part of the old Seybert homestead.

Adam S. was a Confederate soldier from the first of the war, and died in the battle before Petersburg, April, 1865.

Charles R. married Mary Ann Tomlinson, and settled in Highland County. His sons John and Samuel went west.

Stewart died at the age of fourteen years.

In reference to these six sons of John Clendennin it may be noticed that George, Adam, and Charles learned the blacksmith trade, and Jacob tailoring.

Thus we have been able to give a few interesting items illustrating the Clendennin family history as far as identified with our Pocahontas citizenship. The most of this information was furnished by George G. Clendennin, of Mill Point, in a recent interview.

Since writing the preceding it has come to mind that the Andersons, on Hills Creek, are descendants of Archibald Clendennin by the third or fourth remove. Rev W. S. Anderson, Principal of the Alleghany Collegiate Institute; Rev C. M. Anderson, are among them.

This sketch will be closed by a historic reminiscence that has been widely published, and is perhaps already familiar to many.

A party of sixty or more Indians, led by Cornstalk, appeared very suddenly in west Greenbrier, in 1763, and came to the Clendennin home, where they found perhaps seventy-five persons, men, women, and children, to spend the day in social enjoyment and help their neighbor Clendennin feast on three fat elk he had just brought in. Though not invited or expected, the Indians upon their arrival were kindly received and bountifully feasted as welcome guests. While all this good cheer was going on, the people never dreaming of danger, as peace had been prevailing for the past two or three seasons, and the Indians had been coming and going in a most friendly manner, an aged person afflicted with a chronic sore, consulted with one of the older Indians and inquired if he knew of anything that would cure it. In a bland and assuring manner he told her that he thought he knew of the very thing that would cure her. Then drawing his tomahawk he killed her instantly, and before the people had time to think, nearly all the men in the house were killed by this single warrior medicine man.

Mrs Clendennin fought like a fury; reproached the
Indians in terms of the severest invective, calling them
cowards and all the mean names she could think of,
while the warriors brandished their tomahawks and
scalping knives over her head, and slapped her face
with her husband's bloody scalp, threatening instant
death if she did not hush up and behave herself.

The captives were taken at once to Muddy Creek in
charge of a detachment, while the rest continued the
raid as far as Kerrs Creek in Rockbridge County.
Upon their return in a few days, preparations were
hastily made to retreat to the Ohio.   On the day they
started from the foot of Keeneys Knob, Mrs Clendennin gave her infant to one of the captives to carry.
The captives were placed in the centre of the line, with
warriors for vanguard and rearguard.   While crossing
the mountain she slipped into a thicket of laurel and
concealed herself in a hollow tree.   The child soon became very fretful, and this led the Indians to suspect
that the mother was missing.   One of the warriors
said he would "soon bring the cow to her calf."   He
caught the child by the feet and beat its brains out
against a tree, threw it in the path, all marched over
it, and its intestines were trampled out by the horses.

After nightfall Mrs Clendennin came out of her hid-
ing place and returned to her home, ten miles away.
She found her husband dead in the yard, with one of
the children in his arms, where he had tried to escape
over the fence.   After covering the dead with rails she
went into the cornfield near by and waited for day.
During the night a great fear came upon her, as she

imagined she saw a man standing within a few steps from her.

Mainly with her own hands she prepared a place under the porch for the last resting place of her beloved dead, and then soon after refugeed to Augusta County, where she remained a year or two. She finally returned to her home in Greenbrier, and was afterwards married to Ballard Smith, the ancestor of the distinguished family of that name, so prominent in the annals of the Greenbrier citizenship.

JOHN H. RUCKMAN.

Among the citizens of our county in later years from the forties to the sixties, that took a lively interest in everything that promised to promote the interests of education, morality, and the prosperity of the county generally, John Hartman Ruckman deserves more than a brief notice.

He traced his ancestry to one Samuel Ruckman, a native of England, and born in 1643. The Ruckmans had lived awhile in north east Wales, bordering England, and thence came to Long Island, New York, in 1682. Thomas Ruckman, son of Samuel Ruckman, the Welsh emigrant, was born on Long Island in 1682, and his son James Ruckman, another link in the ancestral chain, was born in New Jersey in 1716. James Ruckman's son, David Ruckman, was born in New Jersey in 1747. David Ruckman is the progenitor of the Ruckman relationship in Highland and Pocahontas Counties. He came to what is now south east High-

land County, Virginia, and settled in lower Back
Creek Valley, about 1784. The place is now occupied
by William Price Campbell, whose wife is a daughter of
David Ruckman, a grandson of the pioneer.

The settler married a New Jersey wife, who seems
to have been a person of high aspirations, and longed
for something far better than she could get in New
Jersey. Marvelous accounts seemed to have been reported about the beauty, wealth, and happiness of
Southern homes. That in Virginia people lived in
houses with earthen floors, discarding the use of wood.
She seemed to have gathered from this that the floors
were of mosaic work, such as princes have about their
houses in the old country. Upon reaching the place
of destination, and finding what earthen floors meant
on the Virginia frontier, her disappointment was so
intense that she wished to return at once; but circumstances were such that this was impossible, and so the
situation was accepted, went to work, and a home was
reared out of the Virginia forest. Her name was Susannah Little.

David and Susannah Ruckman were the parents of
four sons and four daughters: Elizabeth, Sophia, Mary, and Hannah; Samuel, John, James, and David
Little. One of these worthy people, David L., died
on the homestead reared by their own industrious, mutually helpful efforts, July 11, 1822, and is buried on
a gentle eminence that overlooks the scene of the
toils and cares from which they now so silently rest.
She survived and came to Pocahontas with her son
David, and died about 1845, far advanced in age.

John H. Ruckman, in whose memory this biographic paper is specially prepared, was the eldest son of Samuel Ruckman, Esq., of Highland County. Samuel Ruckman just named was the eldest son of the pioneer, and was born in New Jersey, November 17, 1783. His first wife was Nancy Hartman, from beyond Greenbank. They were married July 18, 1809, and settled on Back Creek. There were one son, John H., and two daughters, Mary and Nancy, in the first family. Samuel Ruckman's second wife was Margaret Slaven, from Pocahontas County, and her children were James, Elizabeth, Asa, and David Vanmeter.

Mary Ruckman married Isaac Gum. She is survived by two sons, Isaac and Aaron Gum.

Nancy Ruckman was married to William Wade, went west, and is survived by several children.

James Ruckman died in youth.

Elizabeth Ruckman was married to John P. Ervine. She is survived by three children, James, Mary, and Anna.

Asa Ruckman married Cornelia Brown, and went west.

David V. Ruckman married Anna Herring, daughter of the late Bethuel Herring, of Augusta County. Their children were Kate, now Mrs Wise Herold; Lucy now Mrs Edward Wade, Anna Laurie, now Mrs William Price Campbell; Margerie is the wife of Rev Cocke, of Missouri; Sarah is at home; David Glendye Ruckman lives in Augusta; Samuel Ruckman, a youth of more than ordinary promise, died when a student.

Colonel D. V. Ruckman's second wife was Miss

Lizzie Eagle, daughter of the late Samuel Eagle.

John H. Ruckman was born in Highland County, (then Bath), November 11, 1810. He married Mary Bruffey, November 7, 1833. She was a daughter of Patrick Bruffey. He first settled on the old homestead on Back Creek, and then moved to Pocahontas, about 1845, to the Bradshaw place near Millpoint. He finally located on the Greenbrier, opposite the Stamping Creek junction, where he built a fine residence and spent several years. Mr and Mrs Ruckman were the parents of eight children: Caroline, Sydney, Charles, Samuel, James A., William Patrick, David Newton, and Polly Ann. It is a sad reflection that not one of these sprightly sons and daughters is now alive.

Caroline became Mrs William J. Cackley, near Millpoint, and died soon thereafter. Charles Ruckman was a Confederate soldier, became a prisoner of war, and was for some time a prisoner at Fort Delaware, and on his return homeward died at Baltimore from the effects. Samuel Ruckman, a younger Confederate soldier, died at Greenbank, occasioned by fatigue and exposure. James Atlee Ruckman died in battle at Port Republic. William Patrick, David Newton, and Polly Ann died in childhood.

Sydney Ruckman, the eldest of the sons, was a Confederate soldier, and survived the war. He married Almira Campbell, daughter of the late William Campbell, who at the time occupied the home opened up by David Ruckman the pioneer. It was the writer's pleasure to officiate upon the occasion, and was made the recipient of one of the most liberal fees ever known to be given for such a service in that vicinity. After all the perils of war, he came near losing his life in a time of peace in a rencontre that is alleged to have been the principal reason of the famous Atchison lynching at Monterey. It is reported that all this was done in direct opposition to Sidney's wishes, and that he was always sorry it ever happened, as he felt himself fully able to look out for himself. He finally went to Oklahoma, and on his way to meet and bring home his wife, visiting in Kansas, he died under sudden and sad circumstances, September, 1896, at the hands of suspected parties, who were pursued and dealt with in a very summary manner. He is survived by his wife and two sons, Charles and William.

John H. Ruckman's second wife was Mary Wooddell, near Greenbank. In 1863 he sold out his possessions in Pocahontas and moved to Georgia, where he died a few years since. Mrs Ruckman married again, and is now Mrs Wilson.

The writer cherishes the memory of this man with feelings of special interest. He owes something in the way of mental stimulus to his influence.

"William, do you know that if you were to try you might become something of a man in time? My advice is, set your aim high, and see what it may all come to you yet."

"Well, Mr Ruckman, you talk differently from what I generally hear about myself. A person who knows me much better than you do told me that I was about the biggest fool in all this country, and sometimes I feel as if it might be so."

Some little time after this interview, I was at his house for dinner, and when we took our places he invited me to invoke the blessing, and so at his table my first effort of the kind was ever made.

For some years we were confidential friends, but finally our paths drifted far apart and we saw and knew but little of each other face to face, but in memory he was often present to my mind, and he is now, as I pencil these memorial paragraphs, seemingly near enough to grasp his hand and greet him the time of day. He was a scrupulous member of the Methodist Episcopal Church, an ardent advocate of temperance, and intensely devoted to the welfare of his country.

EDWARD ERVINE.

Among the citizens of prominence in the organization of the county was Edward Ervine, late of the Greenbank District. His residence was at the head of Trimble's Run. This homestead is now occupied by his son Preston, and David Gragg, a son in law.

Mr Ervine was born April 2, 1790, near Miller's Iron works, Augusta County, and lived there until manhood. He married Mary Curry, who was born June 20, 1794. Upon leaving Augusta County soon after his marriage, he settled on Back Creek, near the Brick House at the mouth of the Long Draft. They were the parents of ten children, seven sons and three daughters. The daughters were Mary Ann, now Mrs

George Tracy; Margaret Jane, born 1827, now Mrs Charles Philips; Frances Elzedie, born 1829, became Mrs Jacob Tomlinson, late of Kansas.

In reference to the sons of this pioneer Edward Ervine, we have the following particulars, furnished by his son, Preston Ervine :

Benjamin Franklin Ervine born 1816, married Mary daughter of Robert Kerr, who were the parents of these children : Eliza, now Mrs James Hughes; Edward Newton, on Buffalo Mountain homestead; Margaret, recently deceased, who was for the most of her useful life an inmate of Hon. S. B. Hanna's family, on Deer Creek. She will be long remembered for her very interesting character.

B. F. Ervine entered the Confederate service, was captured on the Upper tract in 1861, and died a prisoner of war soon after.

James Addison Ervine, born 1818, married Elizabeth, daughter of Patrick Bruffey, and lived on the Nottingham place, and were the parents of six daughters and three sons. The sons were William, Calvin, and James Patrick. The daughters were Mrs Stephen Lockridge, late of Highland County, Mary, Harriet, Elizabeth, Caroline, and Rose. Soon after the war J. A. Ervine moved to Missouri and located near St. Louis

William Frye Ervine (born 1824) first married Elizabeth Kerr and settled on property now owned by Marion Ray. Mrs Brown Arbogast is their daughter.

Second marriage was with Mary Jane Burner. The children of this marriage were John Preston and Amy, now Mrs Joe Riley.

Third marriage was with Mrs Elizabeth Jane Taylor, widow of William Taylor, daughter of the late Frederick Burr, near Huntersville. The children of this marriage are Mrs Mary Burns, of Bath County, and McNeer Ervine, on the Burr homestead on Browns Mt.

Robert Hook Ervine (born 1831) married Mrs Isaac Hartman (nee Matheny) and settled near Pine Grove. Their one child, Bertha, died at the age of seven years.

Edward Augustus Ervine (1833) married Mary Ann daughter of Henry Beverage, and moved to Centreville, Upshur County, where he now lives. They are the parents of four daughters and two sons, Vernon, George, Amanda, Laura Ann, Nancy Jane, and Sarah.

Preston Cunningham Ervine (1836) married Margaret Rebecca Beverage, and settled on a section of the parental homestead. His family consists of four sons and eight daughters; Mrs Susan Varner, of Georgia; Mrs Alice Arbogast, Mrs Emma Kellar, Mrs Nannie Rader, Mrs Clara Arbogast. David Lee married Virgie Sutton, daughter of Samuel Sutton, and lives at the homestead; Cora Ella, now Mrs Jesse Orndorf; Houston died tn 1897 in his 20th year. Lola Grace and Sadie Florence at their homes.

Charles Washington Ervine (1838) married Serena, daughter of Solomon Varner, and settled in Upshur County, near Centreville, where he died in 1896. Their children were Baxter, Florence Rebecca, now Mrs McWhorter in Buckhannon; Bryson, Ida, now Mrs John Gawthrop, near Centreville; Walker lives in Upshur, Brady in the far west, and Gertrude.

The foregoing are some of the particulars that illustrate the family history of Edward Ervine, a citizen of marked prominence in his day in county affairs. He became a citizen of this region some time before the organization of the county, and was one of the first members of the County Court. Upon his removal from Back Creek he settled on lands bought of Bonaparte Trimble, who lived in Augusta County, not far from Buffalo Gap. The improvements at the time of his purchase consisted of a primittve cabin, an acre or so of cleared land, and, as the reader has just been informed, reared a large family.

He held the office of magistrate for almost his lifetime, celebrated numerous marriages, presided at a great many trials, and issued more warrants than can be readily enumerated. His disposition was jovial, and his humor seemed inspiring, and wherever he went he seemed to diffuse good humor and cheerfulness. For a long while he was a member of Liberty Church, and was a model specimen of the plain, straightforward, Scotch-Irish Virginian. It appears from the Curry records in Augusta that Mr Ervine was a lineal descendant of one of the three Curry brothers who came to the Valley of Virginia with the earliest emigrants.

In the leadings of an all wise providence, Edward Ervine's lot fell to him in a sparsely populated country The type of religion he inherited in Scotland and the north of Ireland tended to blend in personal character indomitable industry, wise provision, and satisfying comfort, and the ideal of his endeavors was to have a home of his own amid fields and meadows. Of such homes an eloquent writer says : ''The homes of our land are its havens of peace, its sanctuaries of strength and happiness. Hence come those principles of probity and integrity that are the safeguards of our nation.''

ANDREW EDMISTON.

Andrew Edmiston, Esq., of Scotch-Irish ancestry, late of the lower Levels, is the subject of this biographic memoir. The immediate ancestry of the Edmiston relationship is traceable to Matthew Edmiston, who came to Augusta County, Va., from Chester County, Pa., among the earliest settlers of Augusta County, about 1740, or very soon thereafter.

James Edmiston, a son of Matthew the ancestor, was one of six children and was born in Augusta County, October 7, 1746, and died October 7, 1817. James Edmiston's wife was Jane Smith, from Ireland, who was born October 17th, 1746, and died May 20th, 1837, aged 91 years. Andrew Edmiston, son of James, was born July 22d, 1777.

Soon after his marriage with Mary (Polly) Gilliland, January 8th, 1807, Mr Edmiston settled near Locust, on lands now owned by George Callison. In reference to Mrs Polly Edmiston, let it be noticed here that she was a daughter of the first Mrs James Gilliland,—

Lydia Armstrong, born October 17th, 1755, and deceased July 23d, 1817. Mrs Polly Edmiston was born July 4th, 1790, and was a bride at 17 years of age. Her death occurred January 2, 1877, surviving her husband thirteen years. James Gilliland, her father, was born in Augusta County, March 16th, 1749, and died February 14th, 1844, near Falling Spring, Greenbrier County, aged 95 years. He married for his second wife Mrs Jane Smith Edmiston, the widowed mother of Andrew Edmiston, in February, 1819. By this marriage Mr Gilliland became Andrew Edmiston's step-father, as well as father-in-law, a relationship so unique as to challenge a parallel in the history of Pocahontas marriage relationships.

This James Gilliland's father was named Nathan Gilliland, about whom we have no particulars. By the first marriage there were six sons, Robert, James, Nathan, William, Samuel, and George; and six daughters, Jane, Sarah, Elizabeth, Nancy, Lydia, and Mary (Polly), the last named the wife of Andrew Edmiston.

What lends interest to what has just been said about James Gilliland's first family is the fact that there are cogent reasons for believing that Hon. Mark Hanna, of Ohio, is a descendant of one of the above named sisters.

It is also interesting to mention that Andrew Edmiston was a lineal descendant of Sir David Edmiston, cup-bearer to James 1st of Scotland; also of Sir James Edmiston, standard bearer of the royal colors in the battle of Sheriffmuir, (1715). In the Revolutionary war Mr Edmiston's ancestors were distinguished, and nota bly at the battle of King's Mountain. Several of his grandsons were good Confederate soldiers in the late war between the States.

Mr and Mrs Edmiston were the parents of five sons and five daughters: Lydia, Elizabeth, Jane, Martha, Mary, James, George, Matthew, Andrew Jackson, and William.

Lydia Edmiston was married to Richard McNeel, grandson of John McNeel the original settler of the Levels, and lived near Millpoint.

Elizabeth Edmiston became Mrs James Gilliland, of James, Senior, and settled in Davies County, Mo. Jamesport, a town of 1200 population, was located on his farm, and hence was called Jamesport.

Jane Edmiston became Mrs Abram Jordan, mentioned elsewhere as having gone west. So far as known to the writer, she is now living in Kansas with her daughter, Mrs William Renick.

Martha Edmiston married Franklin Jordan, and settled in Missouri, where she died leaving no surviving children.

Mary Edmiston was an invalid all her life and never married. She went with her brother George Edmiston to Missouri.

Matthew Edmiston married Minerva Bland, in Weston, and settled there. His name appears in the history of our State as one of the most distinguished of our native born public characters. In Lewis' History and Government of West Virginia, mention is made of this distinguished man as follows:

"Judge Edmiston was born September 9, 1814, at Little Levels, Pocahontas County, where after receiving a common school education, he was admitted to the bar in 1835. Four years after he removed to Lewis County, which later he represented in both branches of the General Assembly of Virginia. In 1852 he was chosen a judge of the circuit court, in which position he continued until 1860. He was elected to a seat in the Constitutional Convention of 1872, but because of ill health did not qualify. He was appointed a judge of the Supreme Court of Appeals in 1886, but one year before his death. Judge Edmiston died June 29th, 1887, at his home in Weston, Lewis County."

Judge Matthew Edmiston reared a large family. Of his five sons, four became physicians and one a lawyer. Each distinguished himself with marked credit in both private and professional life. One by one they fulfilled the destiny of their career and answered the final summons of life, until to-day but one survives. He possesses the distinction of having been named for the subject of this sketch. Hon. Andrew Edmiston resides at Weston, Lewis County. Of him well may it be said, "His has been a life of great influence and usefulness." Possessing in a marked degree those sturdy elements and attributes of manhood which have always characterized the Edmiston family, he has brought added lustre to the name. Electing to follow in the footsteps of his eminent father, he has graced and dignified the high calling of the law. Prominent

in politics and state-craft, he has steadily advanced in
the esteem of the public until he has erected for himself a monument of honor and influence that will testify
in all future time to his worth and greatness.   Whether
engaged in the discharge of the duties incident to political office or in the less prominent walks of life, he
has always served his constituency alike with the same
unfaltering fidelity.   The name of Andrew Edmiston,
of Weston, is conspicuously identified with the political
history of West Virginia.   To few men is given such
wide power and influence.

James Edmiston married Mary Hill, daughter of
Thomas Hill.   He lived a number of years near ˉMill-
point, on the farm now held by C. Edgar Beard.   Mr
Edmiston was a member of the Pocahontas Court, and
for years was prominent in county affairs.   Late in
life he went west.   Mrs Minerva Beard, of Lewisburg,
is his daughter.

George Edmiston married Mrs Nancy Callison, relict
of Isaac Callison, and a daughter of John Jordan, and
lived many years at the homestead.   He was a busy,
enterprising man, and was engaged in many business
enterprises with the late Colonel Paul McNeel.   He
finally moved to Missouri, where his family resides.

· Andrew Jackson Edmiston married Rebecca Edmiston, a daughter of James Edmiston, son of William
Edmiston, brother of Andrew Edmiston.   After the
decease of her husband, Mrs Edmiston became the
wife of Jackson Jones, of Nicholas County.

William Edmiston, the youngest of Andrew Edmiston's sons, spent some time with Judge Edmiston at Weston, where he attended school. He then went several terms to Rev Dunlap, principal of the Pocahontas Academy at Hillsboro. When he attained his majority he started to Missouri with Anthony C. Jordan. While on a steamer in Missouri waters he was seized with cholera and died on the boat. The towns were quarantined in a very rigid manner, and all landing was prohibited. Hence the crew were compelled to bury their passenger at a lonely, uninhabited spot, not very remote from St. Charles, Mo. His friend Jordan went ashore to assist in the burial, but would not return to the boat, and finished his journey to Davies County on foot, after successfully eluding the quarantine guards by keeping away from the public routes of travel.

In his youth and early manhood Andrew Edmiston seems to have had a consuming passion for athletic exercises, boxing, wrestling, and feats of muscular endurance. There was living at the time one Thomas Johnson, near the head of Stony Creek, who claimed to be the champion hard hitter of all that region. He heard of young Edmiston's exploits as an athlete, and these exploits created some doubt as to which was the "best man"; and to settle the question the ambitious Stony Creek champion sent a challenge to the champion of the lower Levels, that if he would meet him he would find out that though he might be the best the Levels could show, that he would soon find himself no-

where on Stony Creek if he just dared to show himself
up there. This fired young Edmiston, and made him
as hot as the furnace we read of in Daniel. He may
have sought rest but he did not find any that night,
and so he set out by the light of the morning stars for
West Union.

He walked from his home near Locust to John
Smith's, head of Stony Creek—fifteen or more miles—
before breakfast to dispute the question of "best man"
with Tom Johnson on his own Stony Creek ground.
Without stopping for rest or breakfart he sailed into
Johnson, tooth, fist, and toenail. In the first round
Johnson landed a terrific blow on Edmiston's shoulder
that dislocated Edmiston's arm, and yet he continued
the contest until he saw his opportunity, and overpowered Johnson until he called out enough.

John Smith then took charge of the victor, the now
best man of Stony Creek and the Levels, and gave
him his breakfast, and by noon he was back at Locust.
He felt the effects of that dislocation all of his subsequent life. Slight exertion would ever after make his
injured arm fly out of place at the shoulder.

In his later years he professed a change of heart and
became a member of the M. E. Church. His sincerity
was respected by all who knew him best, and regarded
genuine. Mr Edmiston died April 15th, 1864, aged
87 years. When the dying day came, when he was to
pass over to the bright forever, it was found that he
had nothing to do but to die. God had not cast him
off in the time of old age, nor forsaken him when his
strength failed. At evening time it was light with

this venerable man, and he could realize the power of words like these: "I will go in the strength of the Lord God; I will make mention of thy righteousness, even of thine only."

JEREMIAH FRIEL.

The Friel relationship trace their ancestry to one Daniel O'Friel, a native of Ireland, who probably came to Augusta county with the Lewises, 1740. He settled on Middle River, between Churchville and Staunton. His children were James, William, Jeremiah, and Anna. James O'Friel went to Maryland, Eastern Shore. William settled in Highland County. Anna became a Mrs Crawford and lived in Augusta.

Daniel O'Friel seems to have been a person of considerable means. He sold his property for Continental money, with a view of settling in Kentucky. The money being repudiated, he was unable to carry out his plans. Upon Jacob Warwick's invitation, Jeremiah O'Friel came to Clover Lick. Mr Warwick gave him land on Carrich Ridge. This land was exchanged with Sampson Matthews, Senior, for lands on Greenbrier, now occupied in part by his descendants.

Jeremiah Friel's wife was Anna Brown, daughter of Joseph Brown, who was living at the time on Greenbrier River. Their first home was on Carrich Ridge, then afterwards they lived on the river. Their children were Joseph, Daniel, Josiah, John, Catherine, Hannah, Ellen, Mary, and Jennie.

Joseph Friel married Jane McCollam, and lived on the home place. He served on the first Pocahontas grand jury. His children were Jeremiah, William, George Washington, a Confederate soldier, 31st Virginia Regiment, and died at Stribling Springs in 1862; Hannah, and Mary Ann, now Mrs Joseph Dilley.

Daniel Friel married Anna Casebolt, daughter of Henry Casebolt, on the Greenbrier near Stamping Creek, and settled on a section of the homestead. Of their children, Andrew Harvey married Anna Johnson, went first to Iowa, thence to Tennessee, where he died in 1871. Barbara became Mrs Lindsay Sharp; Sabina Martha became Mrs Stephen Barnett. Montgomery Allen was a Confederate soldier attached to the 31st Virginia Infantry. He married Rachel Christine, daughter of Rev James E. Moore, and lived near Huntersville.

Josiah Friel married Mary Sharp and lived on part of the John Sharp homestead. Their children were Ann; Sally, Mrs James E. Johnson; Mrs Nancy Grimes, near Millpoint; Ellen, Mrs George Slaven; John, and Israel, who lives on Droop Mountain.

John Friel married Jennie Brown, daughter of Josiah Brown, and settled on a section of the Brown homestead near Indian Draft. In reference to their children the following particulars are in hand: James Twyman lives on the Dry Branch of Elk. He was a Confederate prisoner for three years. Josiah Franklin, Confederate soldier—31st Virginia—died in battle at Port Republic. William Thomas, Confederate soldier —18th Virginia Cavalry—survived the war, and was drowned in Valley River, near Elkwater, in 1879.

Mary Jane became Mrs James Gibson, on Elk, and died recently. Mary Frances was the first wife of Sheldon Hannah, on Elk. John Friel was a Confederate soldier, though exempt by age from military service, and died in the army on Alleghany Mountain, December, 1861, shortly after the battle.

Catherine was married to James Sharp, on Elk. In reference to her children these interesting particulars are available: Jeremiah Sharp was a Union soldier and died in the service. John Sharp was a Confederate soldier—62d Regiment—and died in battle at Beverly in 1864. Josiah Sharp was a Confederate soldier, attached to the Greenbrier Cavalry. He survived the war, married a Miss Dotson, and lives near Falling Spring.

Daniel Sharp was a Confederate soldier—62d Regiment. He was captured on Elk, and was killed at Tolley's (two miles below Mingo) in an effort to rescue the prisoners.

Morris Sharp, Confederate veteran—62d Regiment—was wounded at Winchester so severely that the surgeons decided on amputating his left arm. He emphatically and persistently refused to submit to the operation. The wound healed and he now lives, and when last heard from he was in charge of Henry Clark's mill on Spring Creek.

In reference to the pioneer's daughters, we learn that Hannah Friel was married to Jefferson Casebolt, and lived near Stamping Creek. Her daughter, Martha Casebolt, became Mrs John A. Alderman, and Barba-

ra Ann was married to John Donahue, and lived in
the Levels.   Jennie became Mrs Tharp and went west.
Ellen Friel became Mrs John Dilley, and lived near
Edray.   Mary Friel became Mrs William Dilley, and
settled in Huntersville.

The compiler in his attempt to illustrate the history
of Jeremiah Friel's family has been mainly aided by
his grandson, the late M. A. Friel, who took special
pains to collect authentic information.   It may be interesting to say about him that he stands on the old list
as the first subscriber to "The Pocahontas Times"; and
he claims to have owned and used the first kerosene
lamp in Pocahontas, in 1865.

Jeremiah Friel was in the expedition to Point Pleasant, 1774, in the same company with Jacob Warwick.
He was one of the soldiers detailed under Jacob Warwick to provide a supply of meat for the contemplated
advance on the Indian towns in Ohio, in the morning
of that memorable battle, and was at work in the
slaughter pens when the battle was going on.   The
hunters and butchers were rallied by Jacob Warwick
and crossed over.   At this the enemy mysteriously
ceased firing and began to withdraw across the Ohio
River, supposing that Colonel Christian had arrived
with reinforcements.   The importance of that action
by Jacob Warwick and his men need not be dwelt
upon here.

Jeremiah Friel and his sons were noted reapers.   At
that day there was cooperative harvesting.   Squire
Robert Gay's wheat was usually the first to ripen.   Beginning there, all hands from James Bridger's down,

would come halloing and singing, waving their sickles, eager to see who would cut the first sheaf and make the best record. Then from field to field up the river the harvesters would progress until Bridger's harvest was reaped; thence to William and John Sharp's, and Josiah Brown's, and sometimes to Robert Moore's, at Edray. Then the sickle club would disband with great hilarity for their respective homes.

Late one evening at Friel's the harvesters quit without shocking up all that had been reaped and bound. Jeremiah Friel observed: "Boys, it is so late and you are so tired I believe we will let these sheaves rest till morning." But after supper he noticed it lightning ominously in the west and north. He roused up all hands out of their beds, provided pine torches, and away all went in torchlight procession to the field and finished up the shocking just before midnight. This harvest scene must have been strangely picturesque. Before day it was raining torrents attended with terrific thunder and lightning.

He was a jovial companion for his sons and encouraged them from infancy in the favorite pastimes of the period, running foot races, wrestling and boxing. A favorite amusement when raining and the boys had to stay in doors, was a mode of swinging called "weighing bacon." A loop was fixed at one end of a rope or trace chain, the other end was thrown over a beam or joist. The feet were placed in the loop, and then seizing the other end with the hands they would swing. It requires practice and nice balancing to swing, although it looks very easy to one that has never tried it.

We would not advise any one to try it without providing a big pile of straw to fall on.

When the Virginia troops were on the march to Yorktown, Daniel O'Friel's team was pressed and Jeremiah was detailed to take charge of it. This was about the most of the service he was called on to render during the Revolutionary war.

Several years before his death he was riding through the woods one dark night. The horse passed under a tree with wide spreading limbs, and Mr Friel was so severely injured in his spine that he was virtually helpless the remainder of his life. He died in 1819, sincerely lamented by his relatives, neighbors and friends.

PETER LIGHTNER.

Forty or fifty years ago, one of the most generally known citizens of our county was Peter Lightner, on Knapps Creek. He was tall in person, active in his movements, always in a good humor, and one of the most expert horsemen of his times, and perhaps realized as much ready change swapping horses as any other of his citizen contemporaries. He could come so near making a new and young horse of an old dilapidated framework of an animal as was possible for anyone to do who has ever made a business of dealing in horse-flesh.

Near the close of the last century, he settled on Knapps Creek, on land purchased from James Poage, who emigrated to Kentucky. Mr Poage had built a mill which Mr Lightner improved upon, and for years accommodated a wide circle of customers, who had gotten tired of hominy and hominy meal pounded in a goblet-shaped block. The pestle by which the trituration was done was usually a piece of wood like a handspike, with an iron wedge inserted in one end, and fastened by an iron band to keep it from splitting. This mill was a precious and valuable convenience, and brought comfort to many homes, and some of the most toothsome bread ever eaten in our county was made of meal from Lightner's mill. Some families had hand-mills, but they were about as hard to operate as the hominy block, or mortar with the iron-bound pestle.

It is believed Mr Lightner came from the neighborhood of Crab Bottom, near the headwaters of the South Branch of the Potomac. His wife was Alcinda Harper, a sister of Henry Harper, the ancestor of the Harper connexion in our county. She, therefore, brought that pretty name to Pocahontas, and there have been many Alcindas in her worthy descendants and relatives.

The property owned by Peter Lightner is now in possession of Hugh Dever and the family of the late Francis Dever, Esq., a few miles from Frost.

Mr Lightner's family consisted of one son and four daughters.

Jacob Lightner, their only son, married Miss Eliza-Moore, who was reared on the farm now occupied by Andrew Herold, Esq., near Frost. Her father was John Moore, a son of Moses Moore, the noted pioneer, and her mother was a McClung, of the Greenbrier branch of that noted connexion. Jacob Lightner's children were Peter Lightner, who died at home; John

M. Lightner, once a member of the Huntersville bar, and moved to Abilene, Texas, where he died a few years since; Samuel M. Lightner was a student of Union Theological Seminary, and had about completed his studies for the Presbyterian ministry when he entered the army. He married Miss Sally Mildred Poage, in Rockbridge County, and died a few months after his marriage, at Batesville, Virginia, and was buried at Falling Spring Church near the Natural Bridge. His widow married Rev Edward Lane, D.D., a distinguished missionary to Brazil, where he died much lamented. For some time Mrs Lane has resided in Staunton, Virginia, to be near her daughters who were pupils of Miss Baldwin's Seminary.

Alcinda, one of Jacob Lightner's daughters, was a noted beauty, and very popular. She became the wife of the late James B. Campbell, of Highland County, Virginia.

Mary, another daughter, married Rev John W. Hedges, of Berkley County, a widely known Methodist minister of the Baltimore Conference.

Alice, the youngest daughter never married.

The eldest daughter of Peter and Alcinda Lightner, was named Elizabeth. She was married to Joseph Sharp at Frost. Mr and Mrs Sharp were the parents of Abraham and Peter Sharp at Frost, and Henry Sharp at Douthards Creek. Polly Sharp married John Hannah; on Elk, and was the mother of the late Bryson Hannah, of Frost, and Mrs George Gibson, near Marlinton.

Phebe Sharp first married the late Henry Harper, Jr.,

who died of an accidental wound inflicted while fixing
a gate latch near Sunset schoolhouse.   She afterwards
married Mr Abe Rankin.   Susan Sharp became the
wife of the late William Burr, on Brown's Mountain,
near Huntersville- Mr Burr died suddenly in F. J.
Snyder's law office, whither he had gone to look after
some business affairs.

Rachel Sharp lives near Frost on the old home place.

Susan Lightner, another daughter of our worthy
pioneer, Peter Lightner, was married to George Gay,
a brother of the late John Gay, Esq., near Marlinton.
For many years Mr and Mrs Gay lived on the farm
now in the possession of F. A. Renick, Esq., near
Hillsboro, until their removal to the State of Iowa.

Polly Lightner and the late Sheldon Clark, Esq., were
married and settled in the Little Levels, where their
son, Sherman; now lives.   Mr Clark came from the
state of Connecticut, and made an immense fortune by
merchandising and farming.   He was a highly esteemed citizen, and by strict attention to his own business
he prospered much.   Mr Clark is survived by four
sons: Sherman, Henry, Alvin, and Preston.

Sherman H. Clark, the eldest, married Mary Frances
daughter of the late Joel Hill, and lives on the old
Clark homestead.

Alvin Clark married Mary Agnes, daughter of the
late Josiah Beard, and resides east of Hillsboro.

Henry Clark lives near the head of Spring Creek.

Preston Clark married Josephine Levisay, near
Frankford, and lives on the George Poage property,
west of Hillsboro.

There was another worthy brother, Peter Clark, whose wife was Martha Blair. He died several years since on a farm south of Hillsboro.

The history of Sheldon Clark illustrates the Pocahontas possibilities in reach of those who are moral in habits, diligent in business, honest and strictly upright in their business relations. The advancement of such may be slow, but it will be sure and enduring, and the results bring comfort and influence to those who inherit them, a rich heritage to childien's children.

Phebe Ann Lightner was married to John Cleek, on Knapps Creek, on the place now occupied by the homes of their sons, Peter L. and the late William H. Cleek, and their daughter, Mrs B. F. Fleshman.

The annals just recorded of these persons may be brief and simple, but yet how very suggestive as one reflects upon them. From these biographical notes material may be gathered illustrating pioneer sufferings and privations, thrilling romance, tragic incidents in peace and war.

JOHN BARLOW,

Among the worthy pioneers of our county, the venerable John Barlow, ancestor of the Barlow connexion, is very deserving of remembrance. He was the only son of Alexander Barlow, of Bath County, who was a French emigrant, and had married an English emigrant, whose name was Barbara. He was living in Bath when the Revolutionary war came on. Entering the service of the colonies he fell in battle, according to authentic tradition.

This soldier's widow married Henry Casebolt and lived at the Auldridge Place on the mountain overlooking Buckeye.

Our pioneer friend was born November 26, 1781, and when he reached manhood, he found employment very readily for he was honest and industrious. There will always be a place for such as long as there remains work to be done. Alexander Waddell, who lived on the Moore place near Marvin, had him employed. Young Barlow and one of the daughters became attached, and were married in 1806. The engagement occurred while Martha Waddell and Yong Barlow were getting in a supply of firewood. She drove the sled while he chopped and loaded. It is not often that wood is chopped and hauled under such pleasingly romantic circumstances. At the time of their marriage the groom was 25 and the bride 16.

John and Martha Barlow began home keeping at the "Briar Patch," on Buckley Mountain, now known as the Pyles property. A point that commands a very extensive view. Afterwards Mr Barlow bought a piece of land from Thomas Brock, on Redlick mountain. Here he built up a home, reared his family, and spent the greater part of his married life. This property is now owned by his son, Henry Barlow.

They were the parents of ten sons and five daughters: William, Alexander, James, John, Nathan, Josiah, Henry, Amos, George, and Andrew. The daughters were Elizabeth, who became the wife of the late William Baxter, Esq.; Miriam, who married Sam-

uel Auldridge; Mary Ann married James Auldridge;
Ellen, who died at the age of four years; and a daughter unnamed, dying in infancy a few weeks old.

The eldest son, William, moved west and settled in
Schuyler County, Missouri. Of this large family but
three are now surviving. Henry Barlow, near Edray,
on the old homeplace. He has been a merchant and
grazier, and has been very successful in business.
The second survivor, and one of the youngest of the
family, is Amos Barlow, of Huntersville. He is a
merchant and farmer, and prospered greatly in bus
iness affairs. He is President of the County Court,
and widely known.

It is worthy of mention that when our worthy pioneer
bought the Brock land he paid for it in venison at fifty
cents a saddle or pair. Mr Barlow estimated the number of deer killed by him at fifteen hundred. On the
most lucky day of all his hunting career he killed six
deer and wounded the seventh. He never kept count
of the bears, panthers, wildcats. turkeys, and foxes
shot by him. The elk and buffalo were virtually ex-
terminated before his hunting days.

He was an expert marksman, and passionately fond
of shooting, but the rules of his church—the Methodist
Episcopal, of which he was one of the original members on Stony Creek—forbade shooting for prizes. A
shooting match was arranged for in the neighborhood,
and he attended as a spectator. The main prize was a
quarter of beef. Near the close of the match a neighbor proposed to Mr Barlow to shoot in his place as his
substitute. After much solicitation he consented, took

careful aim, and pierced the centre, thus gaining the savory prize of fat beef. A scrupulous fellow member felt in honor bound to report to the Presiding Elder, and have the offending brother duly disciplined for the credit of religion. The Elder had him cited to appear before the quarterly conference for trial. Brother Barlow meekly obeyed, and put in his appearance. When his turn came on the docket, the Elder said:

"Well, Brother Barlow, you are charged with shooting for a prize. What did you do?"

"I merely shot once," replied Mr Barlow, "to accommodate a friend, not for the purpose of getting a prize for myself."

"Did you win the prize."

"I did."

"Did you get the beef?"

"Only so much as my friend sent me for a mess."

"Was it good beef?"

"Yes, very nice."

"Well," says the Elder, after some apparently serious reflection, and solemn groanings ot the spirit, "I see nothing wrong in what Brother Barlow has done, so I will just drop this case and proceed to the next matter of business."

During his last days, while kept at home and out of the woods by the infirmities of age, our venerable friend was asked if he would like to live his life over again. He replied; "I have no wish to live my life over again, but there is one thing I would like to do, and that is to have one more good bear hunt on Red

Lick Mountain."

This aged and interesting man passed away January 23, 1866, verging 85 years of age. His devoted wife died October 7, 1872, aged 82.

Conscientiously honest themselves, they believed everybody else to be honest. They were Israelites in deed, in whom there was no guile. On them and their children rest the blessing promised to the meek and the pure in heart; provided, they cherish purity and meekness as their venerated pioneer ancestors did.

FELIX GRIMES.

This paper is devoted to the memory of two persons whose numerous descendants have formed an influential element of our citizenship for the past 75 years.

Felix Grimes, the pioneer, and his wife, Catherine, were natives of Ireland. The ship on which they sailed came near being lost during a storm in mid-ocean. At one time the masts were touching the waves, and water pouring in over the ship's side. The passengers and some of the sailors were in frantic terror,—some were praying, some cursing and swearing, and some wildly screaming with fright. The captain and some of the crew were self-possessed enough to urge the passengers to the opposite side of the vessel, and it righted at once, and the voyage was made in safety thereafter. It took three months to make the crossing. The landing was at New Castle, most probably, and some time was spent in Pennsylvania. Following the tide of emigration, these persons finally located a home on the uplands overlooking the valley of Knapp's Creek from the west, nine or ten miles from Huntersville. It is believed they settled here about 1770.

The original name was Graham, but it came to be abreviated to Grimes, and has so been written and pronounced all along.

Felix Grimes settled in the unbroken forest on lands now occupied by Morgan Grimes, the heirs of the late Davis Grimes, and others in that vicinity- The original site is now in the possession of Margaret Grimes, near Mt Zion church. Traces of the pioneer home are yet discernible near her residence. It was here these worthy persons reared their family, consisting of five sons and four daughters: Margaret, Mary, Sally and Nancy; Arthur, John, Charles, Henry and James.

Margaret Grimes married William Montgomery and settled in Licking County, Ohio. Nancy was married to Rev Samuel C. Montgomery, a Methodist minister, in the same county. Mary married Henry Montgomery of Ohio; and Sally married a son of Alexander Waddell, the Marvin pioneer, and moved to Gallipolis, Ohio.

Arthur Grimes, eldest son of Felix, married Mary Sharp, a sister of the late William Sharp, near Verdant Valley, Their children were Rachel, who married Solomon Buzzard; Henry, who married Hester Buzzard, daughter of Reuben Buzzard, of Pendleton county. Henry's sons were Peter and Franklin: Zane and Hugh, near Frost; David, in Harrison county. David and Hugh were Union soldiers, also Zane. Jane married Leonidas Bowyers. She died in Highland county.

Her sons, Cicero and James Leonard Bowyers, went to Parkersburg, West Virginia. John Grimes died in Buckhannon during the late war between the States.

David G., son of Arthur, married Mary Grimes. daughter of James Grimes, of Felix, the pioneer. Their son, Hanson, married Mary Nottingham, daughter of Mr and Mrs Harvey Nottingham, near Glade Hill. Hanson's only child, Minnie Grimes, is now Mrs Earl Arbogast, of Greenbank.

Margaret, a daughter of David G., first married W. H. Sims. After his decease she married Erasmus Williams, now living near Hot Springs, Virginia, and is the mother of fourteen children. Amanda, another daughter of David G., married Charles O. W. Sharp, and is the mother of eight children. Her son Hanson is in Central America, and Frank is in Louisiana.— Leah another daughter of David G., married the late Rev George Preston Hannah, She is the mother of seven children, four living and three dead. Mr Hannah was an esteemed and useful minister of the M. E. Church.

Rebecca, of Arthur, of Felix, married Thomas Drinnan, settled in Buckhannon, thence to Parkersburg. thence to Chilicothe, Ohio. She was the mother of four children. One son, Franklin, and three daughters, names not remembered.

Arthur Grimes, Jr., son of Arthur of Felix, married Rebecca Cumpston and lived a while on the old homestead, then moved to Upshur county. His son Newton died young; Lavinia married Silas Helmick; Rebecca Jane is married and lives in Upshur county; Angeline is the youngest.

Hon. John Grimes, son of Felix, the pioneer, married Elizabeth Burner, of Travelers Repose and lived near Academy, on the farm now owned by Pocahontas county as an infirmary. There were six children: Henry died in youth; Abraham married a Miss Callison, and finally moved to Gallia County, Ohio, as did Wesley and Fletcher; Nancy married a Mr Morrison and settled in Upshur county; Elizabeth married William McCoy and went to Ohio. Late in life Mr Grimes went to Ohio to be with his sons. He was a person of fine appearance and possessed natural endowments of a high order, and made the most of his limited opportunities for mental improvement. He represented Pocahontas as a Democrat in the House of Delegates, 1841-42. Upon his motion charters were granted for three academies, Hillsboro, Huntersville and Greenbank. He was a very prominent member of his church, the Methodist Episcopal.

Charles Grimes, the third son of Felix the emigrant, married Martha Bussard, daughter of Reuben Bussard, Senior. Their family consisted of ten children. John Wesley died young. Morgan married Jane, daughter of Major Daniel McLaughlin, near Greenbank. Morgan's children are John Wesley, at home. Cora is the wife of the Rev Jasper N. Sharp, a member of the West Virginia M. E. Conference. Mantic is Mrs George Bambrick, and Onie Jane is at home with her parents. Morgan Grimes was a Union soldier during the war between the States, and so was his relative W. C. Grimes.

William Davis Grimes, another son of Charles Grimes, married Margaret Paugh and settled on a section of the old homestead. He recently died, and is survived by his widow and two children—Ida Missouri who married Clay Dreppard, and Elmer E. Grimes.

Susan L., a daughter of Charles Grimes, married Samuel Auldridge. She was the mother of five children: Tillotson lives at Buckeye; Charles died in Greenbrier; Luther lives near Mill Point; Kenney in the Levels; Elizabeth married William Clendennin.

Margaret Grimes, daughter of Charles Grimes, married Hugh Carpenter and settled on Thomas Creek. She is the mother of five children. Charles went to Texas; Hanson and Fletcher live near Dunmore; Rachel married Craigan Grimes, a teacher of schools and lives near Millpoint.

Elizabeth Catherine, another daughter of Charles Grimes, died during the War,—a young woman of much amiability of character.

Another daughter of this Charles Grimes, Mary Cullum, was married to Rev George Poage Wanless, a widely known and much esteemed Minister of the M. E. Church. Towards the close of his long and useful ministerial service he was Presiding Elder of the Roanoke District. At his death he was a citizen of Montgomery County, Virginia. Her children were Josie Loretta, wife of Bently Olinger, of Price's Fork, Va., who was killed while at work on New River Bridge. Della Wanless married William Snedegar, on Droop Mountain, who is now a merchant at Lafayette, Virginia. Samuel Wanless is a young Methodist minister. Virgie is the wife of U. S. A. Hevener, a Methodist minister, now in Tennessee. Fannie died young.

Another daughter of Charles Grimes of Felix, the emmigrant, was named Loretta Jane. She is the wife of William Jefferson Moore, who lives on a part of the John Moore homestead. She is the mother of nine children.

Rachel A. Grimes, another daughter of Charles Grimes, was married to A. Jackson Moore, on Back Alleghany. She has seven children.

Martha S. Grimes, of Charles, became the wife of Peter H. Grimes; and settled in Ola, Iowa. The names of her six children are Thelia, Seba, Mary, Ezra, Brumby and Henry.

Henry Grimes, son of Felix, died in youth.

James Grimes, the last of the sons of Felix, the pioneer, married Mary Burner of the Upper Tract, a sister of the late George Burner. James settled on that section of the Felix Grimes lands now held by Mrs Mary Fertig. There were nine children, Abraham, who married Margaret Brady, daughter of Samuel Brady, and settled in Webster, and reared a large family. Rev Addison Grimes, book agent, is one of Abraham's sons. Abraham died several years since, aged seventy years.

Another son of James, Allen Grimes, married Francis Weiford, and after her death married Fannie Silva, and lived on Stamping Creek. His children are Craigin B. Grimes, Elizabeth, who is the wife of Thomas Rigsby of Webster county; Georgiana, wife of Henry

Boblitt on Stamping Creek; J. Barnett Grimes, of
Stamping Creek, a prominent teacher; James Grimes
on Stamping Creek; Mary, wife of Willard Overholt;
and Lucy, the wife of Emmett Notingham, on Stamping Creek.

George Grimes, of James, married Nancy Friel,
daughter of the late Josiah Friel, and settled above
Millpoint; George C. Grimes married Eleanor Weiford
and moved to Iowa, and reared seven children. Rettie, Scott, Granville, William, Esta and Ziona are the
names remembered by their friends; Bryson died in
youth, just before the War; Catherine married Leonard Bowyers, as his second wife; Mary married David
Grimes; Elizabeth married James Weiford, of Hillsboro.

This brings the chronicles of the Grimes relationship within the memory and observation of their living
friends, and a basis is furnished for the use of some future compiler, The writer gratefully appreciates the
patient and efficient assistance rendered him by Morgan Grimes, and Mrs Mantie Bambrick.

Jacob Warwick and Felix Grimes seem to have been
on very friendly terms. He once asked James Grimes
what he would charge for managing his affairs. While
James was trying to estimate what he would be willing
to do it for, Mr Warwick remarked that all he realized
for what he was doing was what he could eat and wear.

Arthur Grimes and Levi Moore, son of Levi, the
pioneer, and afterwards a member of the Legislature,
went on a scout to Clover Lick to see if Indians were

around. Seeing no sign they went to the house, placed their guns just outside the door, and finding a bed within, lay down and fell asleep. Arthur dreamed of being bitten by a rattlesnake, sprang out of bed and awakened Moore. The dog was growling at Indians stealing toward the house. The men seized their guns and escaped, leaving the dog shut up in the house. The dog soon came to them, however. The Indians fired the building, cut a pair of moccasins from a dressed deer skin belonging to old "Ben," and amused themselves by striping the feathers from two live roosters to see their antics.

When they reported to Jacob Warwick about the affair, he told them that whenever he dreamed of wild turkeys he was sure of having trouble with Indians very soon.

DAVID GIBSON.

David Gibson, a pioneer of Pocahontas county, and progenitor of the Gibson connexion in our county, came from Augusta county, near Waynesboro, Virginia, about 1770. He located near Gibson's Knob, two miles south of Hillsboro, now in possession of Isaac McNeel. He reared a large family, but few of their names are known to the writer. One of his sons, John, moved to Indiana, where his descendants now live; a daughter, Mary, died in youth; Sally married Sampson Ochiltree and lived near Buckeye, where Henry Lightner now lives; Elizabeth married Joseph Buckley and

lived on the neighboring farm, now owned by Levi
Gay; Jennie married a Mr Blake.

David Gibson, another son, located on the Old Field
Fork of Elk about 1823, and began life in the woods.
The Hannah brothers had preceded him a year or two.
David Gibson's wife, Mary, after whom Mary's Chapel
el is named (a neat house of worship on Elk,) was a
daughter of the late William Sharp, near Edray. Her
mother was Elizabeth Waddell, daughter of Alexander
Waddell, a pioneer settler near Millpoint, the place
now occupied by Joseph Smith and others.

The Gibson family on Elk consisted of five sons and
three daughters. William, the oldest, lived on Elk.
His wife was Polly Gay, daughter of the late Samuel
M. Gay, near Marlinton; John married Margaret Townsend, near Driftwood; David, a well-known physician,
married Elizabeth Stalnaker, daughter of Warwick
Stalnaker, of Randolph; James Gibson married Jennie
Friel, daughter of John Friel, who was killed in battle
on Alleghany Mountain, December, 1861; Jacob Gibson married a Miss Wamsley of Randolph, and was
killed during the war near Huttonsville in a skirmish
with Jenkin's Cavalry; David Gibson's daughter, Elizabeth became the wife of James McClure, near Edray;
Mary married Rankin Poage, at Edray; Nancy became
the wife of Samuel M. Gay, on the Indian Draft.

Mr Gibson built up a comfortable home, in which he
was assisted by his industrious sons and daughters.
The habits of thrift learned from their parents have
been successfully kept up, and prosperity attends them
in their affairs, and all have comfortable homes and are

prospering.   His home was open to the stranger that
might come along.   His confidences were sometimes
abused and imposition practiced · upon him, but that
made no difference with his treatment of others.   For
years his home was at the service of the preachers, and
thus most of the preaching on Upper Elk was at his
house.   It was a great undertaking to locate in the unbroken forest and build up a home and rear the family
these worthy people succeeded so well in accomplishing.
All such should be remembered and their services
gratefully appreciated, and the story of their lives told
for the instruction and encouragement of the generations following.   The righteous, the honest and industrious should be held in lasting remembrance.

VALENTINE CACKLEY.

During the last century but few names have been
more familiarly known in our county, before and since
the organization, than the Cackleys.   The ancestors of
this relationship were Valentine Cackley, Senior, and
Mary Frye, his wife, from the lower Valley not far
from Winchester, at Capon Springs.   They located at
Millpoint about 1778.   These worthy people were of
German descent.   The original name was Keckly, and
came to be spelled Cackley by the way it was pronounced.   Their sons were Levi, William, Joseph,
Valentine, Benjamin, and their daughters were Alice,
Mary, Anne, and Rebecca—six sons and four daughters.

Alice, the eldest daughter, became the wife of the

late Samuel M. Gay. who resided on the farm now
held by the heirs of the late George Gibson, on the
Greenbrier above Marlinton two miles. Mr Gibson
was her grandson. Mrs Gay was a very estimable person, and the story of her life would make thrilling
reading.

Mary Cackley was married to Willette Perkins, and
went west.

Anne Cackley became the wife of Thomas Hill.

Rebecca Cackley was married to John Ewing. Her
family went to Ohio. She was the mother of eleven
sons. The youngest was named Eleven Ewing. It is
believed that the famous Tom Ewing, statesman and
orator. and as such was the pride of Ohio, in his time
was of this family.

Levi Cackley married Nancy Bradshaw, daughter of
John Bradshaw the founder of Huntersville, and settled on Stamping Creek, where some of his worthy descendants yet reside. Jacob, Levi, and William were
the names of his sons. Rev A. M. Cackley, D. D.,
of the Baltimore conference, is a grandson.

William Cackley, son of Valentine, married Jennie
Gay, daughter of Robert Gay, and first settled on the
property now owned by Mathews Ruckman, near Millpoint, and also operated a store. Having sold his farm
to the late D. L. Ruckman, he moved his family to a
farm on Cummings Creek, near Huntersville, where
he resided for many years, farming and merchandizing
and in public office. A singular occurrence was connected with this removal to Huntersville. Mrs Cackley had become tired of her flock of pigeons and tried

to leave them back, but to her surprise the pigeons were on the oak tree near the dwelling the next morning.

Mr and Mrs Cackley were the parents of five sons and four daughters: Robert, Claiborne, Frye, Davis, and John; Mary, Leah, Hannah, Ann and Sarah Jane. Mary became the wife of J. J. Clark, merchant from Staunton- Leah became Mrs John Hogsett and lived on Elk. Hannah was married to William Floyd and lived at Sutton, Braxton County.

William Cackley was a captain in the war of 1812. His kindness to his company endeared himself to the soldiers and their friends and gave him great popularity. He was a Jacksonian Democrat; went several terms to the Legislature; was Sheriff of the County. Late in life he moved to Illinois, where most of his surviving posterity reside.

Valentine Cackley, Junior was married to Mary Moore, from Eastern Virginia. Their daughter Caroline was the first wife of Harper McLaughlin; and their son, William H. Cackley, once a prominent citizen of Pocahontas, now a merchant in Ronceverte.

Valentine Cackley took the census for Pocahontas County in 1840. He had the lower mill erected at Millpoint. Joseph Cackley owned the upper mill, and after selling out to Sampson Mathews, he migrated to Ohio, married and settled there.

Benjamin Cackley staid awhile on his share of the homestead, now known as the Lee Place, and sold out to his brother Joseph and went to Jackson County, O.

The youngest son of Valentine Cackley, Senior, was

named Jacob. He seemed to have been excessively fond of of athletic sports—running, wrestling, and pitching quoits. One of the most popular diversions of that time seems a singular one to us. It was to see who could throw a pumpkin the highest and catch it while falling. Another diversion was skipping flat stones over the water. One day while thus amusing himself, with several others, on the mill race, Jacob suddenly collapsed and was carried into the house. He had overexerted himself by an underhanded throw, and received internal injuries, and died from the effects a most excruciating death. As a final resort quicksilver was given him, the effects of whicn were agonizing in the extreme. Dr Althair was the attending physician.

Valentine Cackley, the pioneer, accumulated an immense landed estate. His home was about the location occupied by Isaac McNeel's residence. It seems at one time to have been within the limits of the fort. The fort was about where the garden is. Persons yet living have seen relics picked up by parties working in the garden. He encouraged and promoted useful industries. A firstclass mill, for the time, was built; a tannery projected, a tilt hammer started, and a store carried on. While the venerable pioneer could overlook a wide prospect from his home, and while he was not quite "the lord of all his eye could survey," yet he could lay claim to a goodly portion of what was in sight east, north, and west of Millpoint. The name of such a person is worthy of remembrance, for he left a very important and influential part of our county much better off than it was when he settled therein.

DIANA SAUNDERS.

Soon after the war of 1812 there came to our county one of the most interesting and eccentric personalities that our older people remember anything about, Mrs Diana Saunders, late of Rocky Point on Dry Branch of Swago. She was the widowed mother of four children, Anna, Eleanor, Cyrus, and Isaac. Her cabin home was built near the head springs of Dry Branch, almost in speaking distance of the Rocky Point schoolhouse, and just below.

Cyrus Saunders lived in Madison County, Va., and was a merchant and a citizen of prominence.

Isaac Saunders, upon attaining his majority, went to Fayette County, married, and settled on the banks of New River not far from the Hawk's nest. His sister Anna made her home with him for a time, and then became Mrs Ewing of Fayette County.

Eleanor Saunders was married to Barnett Adkisson, from Madison County, and lived on Spruce Flat on the head of Swago, on the place now occupied by James Adkisson. In reference to her children we have in hand the following particulars, communicated by John Adkisson.

Catherine first became wife of William Tyler, from Madison County, and then Mrs Jacob Weiford, near Millpoint.

William Adkisson, whose wife was Martha Jones, from Madison County, lived on Spruce Flat.

Abel Adkisson, whose first wife was Susannah,

daughter of the late Daniel Adkisson, and whose second wife was Frances Hughes, lived on the head of Swago, where his son Oliver Blake now lives.

Daniel Adkisson married Mary Holmes of Madison County, and settled on Spruce Flats.

Isaac Adkisson married Martha Young, and lived at the "Young Place" on Rich Mountain.

Frances Adkisson first became Mrs James W. Silvey and lived at the head of Swago. She was afterwards married to the late Joseph Rodgers, and lives near Millpoint.

Nancy married Benjamin Taylor of Nicholas County and settled on New River. He was a hatter by occupation.

Martha Jane Adkisson married James Arthur, of Webster County, and went to the western part of the State.

Lucinda Adkisson, the youngest of Eleanor's daughters, was married to Rev Joshua Buckley, and lived at Buckeye. Some reference to her family is made in other sketches.

But few persons have left their impress upon the writer's memory more vividly than Mrs Diana Saunders. As to her personality, she had been formed in "Nature's choicest mould" and in her youth must have been the peer of Edgar Allen Poe's "rare and radiant maiden." The writer recalls one or more of her granddaughters as among the most perfect models of feminine form and feature that he has observed anywhere.

From the way Granny Saunders used to spean of

Jim Madison, Jim Monroe, and Tom Jefferson, and wonder how such finicky, limber-jointed, red-headed, fiddling and dancing customers had ever been made Presidents of our United States, it is inferred that her blooming youth must have been passed in Orange and Albermarle atmosphere.

The writer was frequently told by his lamented mother that when he was an infant about six weeks old he had the whooping cough so severely that he was given up to die. As a last resort Granny Saunders was sent for in all haste, and when she arrived the baby was to all appearances cold and dead. The doctress ordered a tub of hot water, plonted the baby in, soaked him awhile and gave him a good rubbing. She then called for a razor and a goose quill, scarified the little body between the shoulders, inserted the quill and gave him a blowing up until the infant began to blow for himself. He came to and recovered, and has been blowing seventy years on his own hook, figuratively speaking. There have been times in his life when the writer has felt rather regretfully that Granny Saunders managed her case so well as to keep him from dying at that safe time. Now, however, he feels thankful to God for what she was able to do. He deems it a most wonderful privilege to have lived the life the Supreme Being has allotted to him. Though this life has been humble and obscure, full of mistakes and blunders, still, blessed be His Holy name, for life and its wonderful hopes for the hereafter, when the Lord comes.

It would be hard to exaggerate the useful services performed by Mrs Saunders for a half century

or more, when there was no resident physician nearer
than the Warm Springs or Lewisburg. For years and
years her time was virtually spent in the homes of the
suffering. Stormy nights, swollen, raging mountain
streams and torrents were braved by this heroic woman
to be with the sick in their distress.

While it is true the most of her services were rendered in scenes over which the thickest veil of privacy
should be ever drawn, yet it may not be out of good
form to say that she never lost her self possession. The
patient might be to all appearances in extremis, with
less than a step between her and death in the throes of
of maternity, all present convulsed with grief and apprehension except Granny Saunders. She would dip
her pipe in the ashes, ejaculate prayers along with the
puffs of smoke, and sit down by the patient: "Hold on
old girl, we can't spare you yet; pick your flint and try
it again. I have been praying for you, and the good
Lord Almighty never goes back on his word to old
Granny Saunders."

In the course of an hour or so, Granny Saunders
looks up the "old man." When she finds him she
opens her arms as if to embrace him. He draws back
exclaiming, "Oh Granny, don't do that!" "Well, you
ugly beast, if you won't let me kiss you, come in and
see what a pretty thing the good Lord has sent your
old woman. How it could be so pretty no one could
tell without seeing the mother!"

One of the most praiseworthy traits in the character
of this grand woman was her abhorrence of "doggity
ways," as she would tersely put it. She was greatly

worried by the way a young man seemed to be treating a girl in whom she felt a motherly interest. Appearances seemed to indicate that the "young rascal of a puppy" had plucked the the rose, but left the thorn with her heartbroken young friend: or in other words had fooled her upon a promise of marriage.

One day, it seems, the young man met her in the road, and he said: "Granny Saunders, if you do not quit talking about me as I hear of you doing, I shall have to sue you for slander."

The old lady cleared her decks for action, rolled up her sleeves and shook her fist under his nose. "I am ready for you here, at the court house, or anywhere else, outside the bottomless pit. There is where pups like you are bound to go, so I will not promise to have anything to do with you there. I cannot blame a Beaver Dam evening wolf for coming over here and stealing a lamb, for it is built that way, and can't know any better, but when I see a customer like you, with good looks, good natural sense and belonging to a decent family, guilty of things the Old Boy would be above doing, I must tell you, I do say I must tell you the dirtiest, yellow, egg-sucking dog in all Pocahontas is an angel to what you are. If the devil knows you as I do, and thinks of you as I do, he will put you on one of his hottest gridirons all by yourself, as not fit company for any other lost soul."

Granny's words seem to have been "winged ones." The suit was never brought for slander, he mended his ways, looked through his Bible and found a verse in Paul's writings that convinced him that the easiest way out of the tangle would be to marry as he had promised.

If there could have been kept a faithful record of all her doings and sayings it would have made a book by itself, nothing like it in extant literature. She had an entertaining story of the time the troops were on the march to Yorktown, and about Washington stopping at the yard fence and calling for water. Her mother sent her out with bucket and gourd, fresh from the well, and watered the thirsty general and staff attendants. "They took their water, and I tell you they all drank a few, and then the grandees rode away with high heads and stiff upper lips, looking at me as if they thought it was about all that I was fit for, to handle the water gourd for their pleasure."

She had many stories that thrilled the little folks. One was about a child being born in 1775 that only lived a few minutes. Before it died it said just as plainly as could be spoken by a grown person:

"A warm winter and a cold spring,
  A bloody summer and a new king!"

One of her most popular lullabys had this refrain:

"Sleep all day and cry all night,
  Whippoorwill, whippoorwill."

Persons yet living remember the reply she once made to the salutation, "Well, Granny, how are you to day?"

"Poorly enough, to tell you truth. O dear, I am just here and that is all. I have pains in my face, pains in my ears, pains in the top of my head, at the back of my neck, between my shoulders, in my arms, in my breast, in my body, in my knees, in my ankles, in both my big toes." Then pausing a moment as if trying to think of more places for pains, she would raise her eyes toward heaven and devoutly exclaim, "But praise the Lord, bless His Holy Name, I have a good appetite!"

Late in the fifties or early in the sixties, she went to make her home with Isaac and Anna, on New River, where she died fifteen or twenty years ago, aged about a hundred and three years as most of her acquaintances believe. Dear old friend, the Creator has not sent many like her to our part of the world as yet.

LANTY LOCKRIDGE.

One of the most widely known of Pocahontas families in former years was that of the ancestor of the Lockridge relationship, at Driscol, four miles east of Huntersville. It was a place of resort for visiting lawyers to and from Huntersville on public occasions. Pleasant mention is made of the kind treatment received and of the nice and bountiful table comforts enjoyed in the memoir of the late Howe Peyton, and in some published reminiscences of George Mayse, of the Warm Springs.

Lancelot (Lanty) Lockridge, the progenitor of the name in our county, came from the Lower Bull Pasture, in Highland county, about four miles up the river from Williamsville, Bath county. Mrs Lockridge was Elizabeth Benson, of the same vicinity. Some of her near relatives migrated to Ohio, from whom Joseph Benson Foraker traces his name and ancestry, and who is now in the Senate of the United States, colleague of M. A. Hanna, from Ohio.

Mr and Mrs Lockridge were of pure Scotch-Irish descent. Early in the century they settled on Knapp's Creek and built up a prosperous home and reared a large family, four sons and five daughters: Andrew, Matthias, Lanty, James T., Elizabeth, Nelly, Harriet, Rebecca and Martha.

Andrew Lockridge married Elizabeth Gillilan, daughter of John Gillilan, near Millpoint, and moved to Missouri.—Matthias Lockridge went to Missouri in early manhood, married Miss Crow, a Missouri lady, and settled there.—Lanty Lockridge married Caroline Cleek, daughter of John Cleek, and first settled on the "Gay Place," near Sunset, then on the "Harper Place," near Sunset, finally moved to Ord, Nebraska, where his sons Lee and Augustus now reside.

Col James T. Lockridge married Miss Lillie Moser, of South Carolina, and occupied the homestead, which was his home during life. He was a citizen of marked prominence, Colonel 127 Virginia Militia, magistrate, merchant, sheriff and member of Virginia House of Delegates. Their children, two sons and two daughters, are Horace M. Lockridge, of Huntersville; Mrs Florence Milligan, of Buena Vista; Dr J. B. Lockridge, of Driscol, and Mrs L. W. Herold, a popular school teacher and instructor in instumental music.

Elizabeth, eldest daughter, became the wife of the late Henry Herold, who moved to Nicholas county, where most of her family settled. The late Washington Herold, near Frost, was one of her sons.

Nellie, the second daughter, was married to the late Jacob Slaven, of Travelers Repose. Their children were four sons and eight daughters.

Harriet, third daughter, was married to the late John McNeel, near Millpoint. The tradition is that Nellie and Harriet were married the same day—a double wedding. Their family numbered two sons and three daughters: Isaac, Mathew John, Eveline, who was married to the late Adrew D. Amiss of Buckeye. Mr Amiss was a clerk in one of the government departments at Washington, and attended to considerable public business in Pocahontas during his life. Rachel was married to the Late Dr Wallace. Elizabeth McNeel married Jacob Crouch, of Randolph County.

Rebecca Lockridge, the fourth daughter, was married to the late Joseph Seybert, and lived first on the Waddell place, near Millpoint, then on the place occupied by Henry Sharp, on Douthard's Creek, and lastly on the farm now held by Wllliam L. Harper, near Sunset. Their sons were Lanty and Jacob. Lanty died a prisoner of war at Elmira, New York. Jacob married Mary Jones, of Greenbrier County, and lived a prosperous citizen of Rockbridge County. There were two daughters, Maria and Elizabeth. Maria Seybert was married to Andrew Herold and now lives near Frost. Elizabeth Seybert was married to the late William D. Gibson, of Highland County. Joseph, Kemper, and William Gibson are her sons. Eva Rebecca Gibson married David Kyle, of Rockbridge County;

Clara Gibson is a teacher in the public schools of Highland; Elizabeth Gibson married J. M. Colaw, of Monterey, Va.; Catherine Gibson is a popular teacher in the Rockbridge public schools.

Martha Lockridge, the fifth daughter, was married to Roger Hickman, of Bath County. Her children were Lanty Hickman, now of Tucker County, and Elizabeth, who is Mrs Stuart Rider, of Bath County.

It has been a pleasure to the writer to collect the material for this sketch, for many of the persons mentioned therein were among the cherished friends of his youth.

As to the personal appearance of this venerable man, it was a common remark of those who had seen Henry Clay that there was a striking resemblance in the form and features of the two men, and that those who had portraits of Henry Clay had nothing to do but scratch out the name and write Lanty Lockridge in place of it, and they would have his picture and one that everybody would recognize. The writer never saw Henry Clay, but he has been often impressed with the portrait he has seen, and is always reminded of our venerable friend by the striking resemblance, so apparent to those who were acquainted with him.

JOSHUA BUCKLEY.

It appears from Authentic tradition that the pioneer settler of the Buckeye neighborhood, four miles south of Marlinton, was Joshua Buckley, at the junction of

Swago Creek with the Greenbrier. It was about the year 1770 or 1775. He came from Winchester, Va., and his wife, Hannah Collins, was a native of Newtown, few miles south of Winchester. John Buckley, their eldest child, was but two weeks old when his parents set out in the month of March on their pack horses for their new home.

Upon their arrival they occupied a deserted hunter's camp, and on the same day Mr Buckley took the suffering, jaded horses to John McNeel's, in the Levels, to procure keeping for them awhile, thus leaving wife and child alone. The wolves howled all night, and she could hear the snapping of their teeth, but she disclaimed all fear. This camp was occupied until a cabin could be built and ground prepared for potatoes and buckwheat.

This family for the first summer subsisted on a bushel and a half of meal, brought with them from Winchester, with potatoes and venison. Mr Buckley could go up Cooks Run and pick out a deer as conveniently as a mutton may now be had, and even more easily.

One of the daughters, Mrs Hetty Kee, the ancestress of the Kee family, when a little girl remembered seeing the Indians very often, and frequently heard them on the ridges overlooking Buckeye, whistling on their powder charges, and making other strange noises as if exchanging signals.

Mr Buckley raised one crop of buckwheat that he often mentioned to illustrate how it would yield. For. fear the corn might not ripen enough for bread, he dropped grains of buckwheat between the rows by hand and covered with a hoe. He planted a half-bushel of seed and threshed out eighty bushels. He carried the nails used in roofing his barn from Winchester. They were hammered out by hand, and cost seventeen cents a pound.

There were frequent alarms from Indian incursions. The women and younger children would be sent to the fort at Millpoint. The older boys would stay around home to look after the stock, with instructions to refugee in a certain hollow log if Indians should be seen passing by.

About the time Joseph Buckley became a grown man, his father had five hogs fattening at the upper end of the orchard. One night a panther came and carried the whole lot to Cooks Run, piled them up, and covered them over with leaves and earth. The father and his sons watched for several nights, and finally the old panther came with her cubs. She was shot and the cubs captured and kept for pets. One was given away, and the other kept until almost grown. It took a great dislike to the colored servants, named Thyatira and Joseph. Young Joe Buckley took much delight in frightening the servants. He would hold the chain and start the panther after them, and would let it almost catch them at times. This would frighten the servants very mvch, and they cherished great animosity towards the pet, and threatened to put it out of the way. This made the young man uneasy about his panther, and he would not leave it out of doors at night fearing the servants would kill it, and so he made a place for safe keeping near his bed. The beast would sleep by his side, purring like a kitten, though much louder.

One night the young man was awakened by something strange about his throat. When became conscious he found his pet was licking at his throat, slightly pinching at times with its teeth, then lick awhile and pinch a little harder- This frightened the young man so thoroughly that he sprang to his feet, dragged it out of doors and dispatched it at once.

JOHN SHARP.

Among the persons settling in what is now Pocahontas County early in the century, John Sharp, Senior, a native of Ireland, is richly deserving of more than passing notice. He is the ancestor of the families of that name that constitute such a marked proportion of the Frost community, and have been identified with that vicinity for the past 91 years. Previous to the Revolution he came in with the tide of Scotch-Irish imigration that spread over Pennsylvania and New Jersey, and thence moved south, and finally located in Rockingham County, Virginia. His wife was Margaret Blaine, whose parents resided in the vicinity of Rawley Springs. She was a relative of Rev. John S. Blaine, one of the pioneer Presbyterian pastors in our countyr

After a residence of several years in Rockingham County, Mr Sharp came to Pocahontas to secure land for the use of his large and industrious family, and he succeeded well, and saw them well fixed in life all

around him. He reached Frost in 1802, and settled
on the place now occupied by Abram Sharp. There
were six sons and as many daughters. The daughters
were Margaret, Anna, Isabella, Elizabeth, Rosa, and
Polly. Margaret became Mrs Henry Dilley and lived
on Thorny Creek. Anna was married to Daniel Mc-
Collam, who finally moved to Ohio, Isabella became
Mrs Alexander Rider, who lived so long on the top of
the Alleghany, seven miles east of Huntersville. Elizabeth was the wife of Rev James Wanless, a widely
known minister, and lived on upper Thorny Creek,
where John F. Wanless now resides.

Rosa Sharp was married to the Rev William J. Ry-
der, on Back Creek. Her family mostly went west—
to Illinois. Rev Stewart Ryder, of Bath, is her son.
He was for several years an itinerant minister in the
Baltimore Conference. Aaron Ryder, who liver near
Frost, is another son.

Mary Sharp became the wife of William Hartman,
and settled in Upshur County. Her children were Joel
Susan, Elizabeth, and Mory. Joel Hartman married
Jonathan Yeager's daughter Rachel. Mary Hartman
became Mrs Jeter; Susan Hartman became a Mrs Harper, all of Upshur County.

In reference to the six sons that were of this family,
and the brothers of the six sisters whose history is
so briefly traced, we learn the following particulars from Mrs Elizabeth Sharp, the aged relict
of the late John Sharp, a grandson of the pioneer John
Sharp. This venerable lady has a remarkable history.
Left alone during the war, she supported her young

and numerous family, paid off mortgages on the land, and came through the great trouble out of debt.

The pioneer's sons were John, Robert, Daniel. William, James, and Joseph.

John Sharp married Rebecca Moore, daughter of Pennsylvania John Moore, and settled on land now occupied by Joseph Moore, who is a grandson of John Sharp, Senior.

Robert Sharp died in early youth.

Daniel Sharp married Margaret Palmer, of Augusta County, and settled on Buffalo Mountain, beyond Greenbank. Daniel finally went to Lewis County, and settled on Leading Creek.

James Sharp married Margaret Wanless, and settled on the head of Thorny Creek. There were five sons and two daughters in his family. William, Andrew, Robert, James, and Lindsay were the sons; and Jane, who became Mrs Nicholas Swadely, and Nancy, who married James Moore, now of Nicholas County, were the daughters. Nicholas Swadely moved to Ritchie County. Lindsay Sharp lives on the old homestead. Andrew Sharp lives on Back Creek, and was 97 years of age July 3, 1897. He was able at that time to do considerable work with his axe and brush-hook.

William Sharp married Margaret Nesbitt, of Rockbridge County, and settled near Frost. There were a son and three daughters. Mary Paulina married Stephen Wanless, and lived on Back Creek. Her husband was killed by a vicious horse. Eliza Jane, became Mrs David Hannah, of Fayette County. John Sharp, the one son of this family, married Elizabeth

Slaven Wade, of Highland County, and settled on the
place near Frost where his widow now lives. There
were five sons and four daughters.

The sons were Charles Osborne Wade, William Alexander Gilmer, John Benjamin Franklin, Aaron
Uriah Bradford. Little Bradford died at the age of
seven years, his mother's darling, and though many
years have passed she weeps at the mention of his
name. Matilda Ursula died at sixteen months. Margaret Ann died aged sixteen years. Martha Ellen
and Marietta Emmeretta Virginia are yet living.

Gilmer Sharp married Nancy Elizabeth Arbogast,
and settled a mile from Frost on the west branch of
Knapps Creek, in the pine woods, and opened up a
nice home. His family consists of seven sons and two
daughters: Upton Porter, William Bradford, Clifton
Chalmers, Ernest Gilmer, George Mervin, Charles
Letcher, Minnie Ursula, and Nancy Elizabeth Daisy.
Minnie is now Mrs Ellis Bussard, near Glade Hill.

J. B. F. Sharp, great-grandson of the pioneer, married Mary Alice Gibson, of Bath, rnd now lives near
Frost. Henderson Wickline, Carrie, Bessie, Ellen,
and Ruth are their children.

C. O. W. Sharp, another son of the same family,
married Amanda Grimes, and settled near Frost.
There were slx sons and three daughters: Hannibal
Hamlin, Charles Hanson, David Franklin, George
Winters, Summers Hedrick, Austin John, Trudie
Montgomery, Isa Amanda, Esta Medora.

Martha Ellen Sharp, one of the surviving sisters, became the wife of Abram Sharp, near Frost. He was a

Union soldier. Their family consists of six sons and four daughters: Joseph Averill married Sarah Vint and lives on Browns mountain. John Washington married Mary Ann Simmons, of Highland, and lives near Frost. Their sons are Anderson Butler, Stewart Holmes, Aaron Abraham, and Lincoln, who died at the age of four years. The daughters are Julia Quebec, who is Mrs William Shrader and lives near Frost; and Cuba Truxillo, who died December, 1895; greatly lamented; Elizabeth Rachel, and Mary Hannah Susan.

The other surviving member of Mrs Bettie Sharp's family is Marietta Emmeretta Virginia, who married Thomas R. Kellison, and lives near Mountain Grove. Her family of three sons and six daughters are named as follows: John Benjamin Franklin Lightbourne, Charles Hackie, Thomas Bonar, Elizabeth Lugertie Moomau, Anna Amanda Jane, Ella, Marietta Constance, Hattie, and Lucy.

The last of the sons of John the pioneer is Joseph Sharp, who married Elizabeth Lightner and settled on the homestead, now held by Abram Sharp. The late Peter Sharp, near Frost, was a son of Joseph Sharp. He was a Confederate soldier. His wife was Mary Ann Herron, daughter of Leonard Herron. Three of his sons are Methodist preachers. Oscar is a local preacher; William and Jasper are in the itinerary; Samuel died recently, and Ashby is Constable of Frost District. Alice is Mrs Alexander Kiricofe, and lives in Augusta County. Azelia married Rev C. M. Anderson.

Another son, Henry Sharp, married Caroline Curry,

daughter of the late J. Harvey Curry, of Dunmore, and lives on Douthard's Creek, near Driscol. Their family numbers seven daughters and two sons: Clara, now Mrs Henry Overholt; Docia, now Mrs Warren; Effie, Mrs J. E. Campbell, of Covington; Lizzie, Mrs Mack Ervine; Bertha, Lucy, and Pearl- Gilbert Sharp is at home, a well known machinist. Albert Sharp resides at Marlinton, where he is a well known citizen, and has performed an active part in the construction of improvements.

Thus far we have been able to illustrate to some extent the history of John Sharp, the settler. As was intimated, the great motive that prompted his coming to the head of Knapps Creek was to get land. In this he was successful. His landed possessions reached from the Gibson farm, near Frost, up the West Branch to Armnius Bussard's, near Glade Hill. He had property in the Hills, on Thorny Creek, and on Buffalo Mountain beyond Greenbank, and the most of these lands yet in the possession of his descendants.

He was small in person, blue eyes, light hair, and of florid complexion. He was constantly employed. Mrs Sharp was quiet in all her ways, very diligent in her duties, and patiently met and endured the toils and inconveniences of living in the woods. These persons were pious, and some of the first religious meetings ever held in the vicinity of Frost were at their house.

DAVID HANNAH.

This paper is prepared to pay a tribute to the memo-

ry of a pioneer citizen of our county, the late David
Hannah, of the Old Field Branch of Elk. He was a
son of David Hannah, Senior, who was the progenitor
of the Hannah Family, one of the oldest in Pocahontas. David Hannah, Senior, was a native of Ireland.
He married a Miss Gibson, who was reared in Augusta
County, and settled at the mouth of Locust Creek soon
after the Revolutionary war. He possessed some practical knowledge of medicine of the botanical school,
and did a good deal of practice in frontier times. He
was probably the first person that ever practiced physic
in lower Pocahontas. Dr and Mrs Elizabeth Hannah
were the parents of six daughters and four sons.

Ann became Mrs Joseph Oldham and Lucinda married William Oldham. Their homes were near the
source of Locust Creek. Mary Hannah was married to
John Mollohan, and lived in what is now Webster
County. Elizabeth Hannah became Mrs William Bennett, and lived in Harrison County. Jennie Hannah
was married to the late Samuel Whiting, on Droop
Mountain, where the Whiting family now lives. Her
son Ebenezer married Sallie McMillion and lived on
the Whiting homestead. Nancy Hannah became the
wife of James Cochran, and lived near the Greenbrier
border.

William Hannah and John Hannah died in youth.

Joseph Hannah married Elizabeth Burnsides, on
Greenbrier River, and settled on Elk, where his son,
John Hannah, lately lived, over eighty years of age.

David Hannah, Junior, the subject of this article,
married Margaret Burnsides, on the Greenbrier, east of

Hillsbore, a daughter of John Burnsides and his wife, Mary Walker, of Augusta Couty. Her family and the family of General J. A. Walker, of Wytheville, Va., are closely related. He was one of the last commanders of the Stonewall Brigade. He settled on Elk, and reared a large family of worthy sons and daughters.

Isabella Hannah was married to the late John Varner, and settled at Split Rock, a few miles down Elk, and built up a good home with their industry and economy. Their children were Margaret, now Mrs Clinton Slanker; David Varner, a Confederate soldier killed in war; Mary Varner, afterwards Mrs Robert Wilson, and lived near Lexington, Va. John Varner and Samuel Varner, at Linwood; Susan Varner, now Mrs William Snyder, in Iowa; William Varner, at Old Field branch; Alice Varner became Mrs John Stewart, near Valley Head; Jennie Varner was married to Hamilton Snyder, and located in Taylor County, Iowa; Benjamin Varner married Ella Moore, of Knapps Creek, lived awhile at the Split Rock homestead, and finally moved to Ohio where he now resides.

Elizabeth Hannah was married to Marinus J. VanReenan, and settled in Iowa. Mr VanReenan was a native of Holland, His father's family was attached to a band of Holland emigrants, who were induced to colonize on Laurel Run in 1842, by the Rev John Schemerhorn, of New York. The highlands of Pocahontas were not congenial to persons from a populous Holland city in the Netherlands, and after grievous privations the colony disbanded. Some went west; others remained in Pocahontas, and are excellent people. The Stultings came in this band also. The names of Elizabeth VanReenan's children are David, Robert, and Mary.

John Burnsides Hannah married Margaret McClure, and located on part of the "Old Field" homestead, and has lately died. The following particulars are given in reference to their children: Mary is now Mrs John Beverage, near Clover Lick; Samuel David married Amanda Moore, and settled on the Hogsett place; Wallace died while young; William Boude, whose wife was Miss Birdie Dilley; John Ellis married Malinda Catherine Sharp, and settled on the homestead; Nancy was married to Fletcher Dilley, and lives near West Union; Ivie Viola; Edgar Russell, and Lena Mary died while young.

David Hannah, the third of the ancestral name, was first married to Rebecca Moore, daughter of the late Isaac Moore, of Edray. Second marriage to Margaret Jane McClure, daughter of Arthur McClure of Lower Pocahontas, and settled in Iowa; thence moved to Missouri. The names of his children were James, Joseph, Mary, Margaret, and Julia.

Robert Hannah married Jennie Burk and settled in Iowa. John is the name of the only one of his children known to the writer.

William Hannah, one of the twins born to Mr and Mrs David Hannah of Pioneer memory, married Catherine Rhinehart of Randolph County, and settled on Pine Flat, head of Swago. William's family were three sons and a daughter. James married Maggie Auldridge, a daughter of Thomas Auldridge, and lives near the head of Dry Creek. Eugenius married Jennie

Kellison, and lives near Poage's Lane. Margaret is Mrs Kenny Kinnison, on Swago. Burleigh married Miss Lula Perry, on the Greenbrier.

Joseph Hannah, the other twin son of the pioneer, married Elizabeth Cool, daughter of John Cool, of Webster Countyt and lives in that county.

The writer remembers the personality of the venerable pioneer very vividly. In early youth I saw him frequently, and he was very interesting to me fron the fact Mr Hanna had been off to the war of 1812. To me an old soldier seemed more than human. He had an interesting way of relating his adventures, and was fond of talking about the war. He was at his best when telling how he felt when aroused one morning before day to get ready for an attack, as the British were reported as coming. He arose and put on his accoutrements quickly as possible, and took his place in the ranks and moved off to fight. His hat kept falling off as he marched until it became so troublesome that he was determined to find out the reason why it would not stay on his head. It had never been so hard to keep on before because it was a good fit. When the troops halted he examined his head and found the hairs were all on end, stiff as bristles, and were pushing the hat off as fast as he could put it on. The hair kept stiff until the order was given to return to camp, when it all became limber enough, and the hat was no more trouble. He found out afterwards that the whole scheme was to try the new soldiers to find out how they would conduct themselves when ordered into battle. This was near Norfolk.

The story, however, he seemed the most fond of telling was about his experience in the hospital tent. Before his term of service had expired he was prostrated by fever and given up as a critical case, and very strict orders were given not to let him have a drop of anything cool to drink. He noticed that there was whiskey and water on the table for the nurse's use, and he determined to have some at all hazards. The attendant came to him and found the young soldier so weak and stupid that he seemed to know nothing, and was unable to lift even his hand. So the hospital man thought there would be no risk to run were he to leave the bottle and pitcher on the table while he would step out and get some fresh air. Soon as his back was turned the sick soldier crawled to the table, mixed the liquor and water, and drank till he could drink no more and crawled back to his bunk, and when the nurse returned he was surprised to find his patient apparently asleep and the skin showing a tendency to moisture. Finally the sweat broke, and when the doctor came to look at him, and seemed much pleased with the change in the patients condition.

"You were mighty near gone, old fellow, and if we had not kept cold water away from you, where would you be now?"

The soldier kept his secret, and as he was beginning to get stronger the liquor was kept our of sight. He thought he would have mended much more rapidly if things had been left on the table as before.

The old soldier worked hard in building up his home

and the privations he and his family had to endure
would seem unbearable now.   He was kind and hos-
pitable to a fault, ready to share the last he had with
the visitor that might desire shelter and food.   He was
much esteemed by all of his acquaintances.

Finally the end came.   One of the prettiest places
near his home was selected and they placed him to
sleep under the green sod that his own hands had helped to clear away.

JOSEPH HANNAH.

Among the earliest settlers of the Elk region was
Joseph Hannah, a son of David Hannah, who lived at
the mouth of Locust Creek.   He married Elizabeth
Burnsides and early in the century settled on the "Old
Field Fork of Elk."

His home was on Mill Run near where William
Hannah, a grandson, now lives.   This immediate
vicinity seems to have been a place of more than ordinary importance in prehistoric times.   One of the most
frequented Indian trails seems to have been from Clo-
ve, Lick up the Creek to the Thomas Spring; thence
over the mountain, crossing at the notch near Clark
Rider's farm; thence down by James Gibson's to Elk.
Here is the "Magic Circle," mentioned elsewhere in
this book.   Nearly a mile further down was the encampment where about two acres of land had been de-
nuded of trees for camp fires, and this was the "old
field" that gave this branch of Elk its name; and was
the first piece of ground planted by Joseph Hannah.

Mr and Mrs Hannah reared a large family of well-behaved, industrious children. This family did a good part in the industrial devolopment of this thrifty section of our county. In reference to their children the following particulars are given.

Joseph, William, Robert, and Sally died in childhood or early youth.

John Hannah married Mary Sharp, daughter of Joseph Sharp, near Frost. Their children were Sarah Jane, who became Mrs Aaron Fowlkes; Margaret Elizabeth, who was married to the late John Hall; Rachel Ann was married to the late George Gibson, near Marlinton; Martha Susan, now Mrs James Gibson; Amanda Pleasant, the wife of William Lee Hambrick; Mary Ellen, who died young. Joseph Bryson Hannah, late a merchant at Frost. Sheldon Clark Moore, on lower Elk, whose wife was Martha Moore. His children are named Georgiana, Davis, Albert, Virgie, Effie, Clark, Hugh, Feltner, Jane, Lee, and Frederick. Andrew Warwick Hannah, whose wife was Dora Hannah, daughter of Henry White, of Driscol. Their children Levie, Sadie, Lucy, Mary, Maggie, Bessie, and Marvin. William Hamilton Hannah, who married Sarah White, sister of the person just mentioned. Their children: Andrew, William, Myrta, Forrest, Bryson, Carrie. George Luther Hannah married Emma Bell McClure, daughter of Arthur McClure, of Locust. She expired suddenly while attending public worship in Mary Gibson Chapel a few years ago. Henry Hannah, Peter Hannah, and John Hannah, Junior, died young, during the late sad war between the States of our glorious Union.

David Hannah, son of the "Old Field" pioneer, married Hester Sicafoose, from lower Crabbottom, and settled on Elk. In reference to their children we have the following information:

Sarah Hannah was married to Silas Sharp and settled near Linwood. Her son, Luther David, is a well-known merchant at the old homestead. Her daughter Mary Ella Frances is the wife of Robert Gibson, and Melinda Catherine is the wife of J. E. Hannah, at the "Old Field." Henry Hannah married Margaret Mc-Clure, and is now a merchant at Renick's Valley, Greenbrier County. Another son, Rev George Hannah, married Leah Grimes, and his late residence was in Upshur County. Melinda is now Mrs John Rose, and resides in Webster County near the Randolph border. Mary was married to Samuel Gibson, and settled near the homestead. Otho and Joseph Hannah died young.

Jane Hannah, daughter of the pioneer, was married to Joseph Barlow, one of the sons of John Barlow, and lived on Red Lick Mountain, settling in the unbroken forest, and built up a nice home. In connexion with clearing many acres of dense forest, he had a tannery, a blacksmith shop, cooper shop, made and repaired shoes, and could do neat cabinet work and carpenter work also. The number and variety of fruit trees planted about his home is the wonder and admiration of all that have ever seen his orchard.

Elizabeth Hannah was married to Dr Addison Moore and lived near Edray.

Mary Hannah was married to Henry Buzzard, and settled on Cummings Creek, near Huntersville.

Joseph Hannah was a person of impressive personal appearance. His memory was remarkably retentive, and his conversational powers something wonderful. He had committed to memory, it is believed by some, the greater portion of the Bible, and he could recite the Scriptures for hours at a time,—having a special preference for the historical narratives of the patriarchs and the wanderings of the Israelites and the conquest of the Promised Land under Joshua. He saw in these historical narratives illustrations of the life now to be lived by Christian people, and it was one of the greatest pleasures of his old age to have his neighbors assemble and repeat these narratives in their presence.

Some years since an article written by a distinguished minister in Bath County stated that Simon Girty, the renegade was summarily put to death by being burned in a log heap by an enraged and desperate body of men in the Little Levels. Joseph Hannah wat referred to as an eye witness of the dreadful affair, or as having some personal knowledge of it. Mr Hannah's children say they never heard their father say a word about such an occurrence happening to anybody in this county, under any circumstances of provocation whatever. Simon Girty's grave is now to be seen near the city of Detroit, so he was not burned in a Pocahontas log heap.

When a mere lad Joseph Hannah was sent by his father to Elk, to look after the live stock in the range.

He often went to fort with his family in his youth and early manhood. He was remarkably active in his movements, and very fleet of foot. He would often tell of a jump he made when a practical joke, or 'trick' as he called it, was played on him by Richard Hill, Adam Bumgardner, one Mullins, and a colored man named Dick. Young Hannah and Dick were hoeing corn. The jokers explained to Dick what they were up to, and Dick cheerfully promised to act his part. While the two were hoeing away, a shot was fired from ambush. Dick fell and made a dreadful outcry, rolled and kicked about in seemingly terrible agony. Young Joseph Hannah fled precipitately towards the house and in the race leaped a gully. When matters came to be understood and quiet restored, the leap was measured, and it was forty-two feet from track to track. Mr Hannah was fond of telling his friends that he had ''jumped the decree.'' ''Decree'' mean what ''record'' now means in races and athletic games. In ''jumping the decree'' he ''broke the record'' by two feet.

When the writer first remembers seeing Mr Hannah he was of very venerable appearance. His gray hair was combed back and plaited in a cue that hung down between his shoulders. The last time I ever saw him we were spending the night at Sampson Ocheltree's. in the winter of 1849. The two old men were in busy conversation until a late hour, and most of the talk was about the children of Israel and the dealings of God. The fire was getting low, the candle about burned out, when Mother Ocheltree observed it was about time to get ready for bed. At this suggestion Mr Hannah arose and in a very soft solemn tone repeated and then sang a hymn. He then knelt in prayer and poured out his full heart in humble, trusting prayer, in the tone and manner of a loving child to a kind and more loving father. The memory of that prayer, heard fifty years ago, imparts a pleasant glow to my feelings while writing these memorial sentences.

DANIEL McCOLLAM.

One of the oldest families in our county is that of the McCollam relationship. While it is not certain, yet there is good reason to believe that the pioneer ancestor was named Dan. McCollam. From some interesting correspondence had by James McCollam's family with a lady in New Hampshire there is no reason to question that he was of Scotch-Irish descent, and the son of a physician a graduate of the University of of Edinburg, and lived in New Jersey. The name of the pioneer's wife cannot be recalled.

Mr McCollam, the ancestor, came from New Jersey in 1770, or thereabouts, and settled on Brown's Mountain near Driscol, which is yet known as the "McCollam Place," now in the possession of Amos Barlow, Esq. His children were Jacob, Daniel, William, Rebecca, Mary, and Sarah.

Jacob McCollam first settled on the "Jake Place," a mile or so west of Huntersville on the road to Marlinton; thence he went to Illinois, and was killed by a falling tree.

Daniel McCollam married Anna Sharp, daughter of John Sharp, the Frost pioneer, and settled first on the Bridger Place near Verdant Valley, thence to the Marony Place near Buckeye, and finally settled in Noble County, Missouri. Two of his daughters remained in Pocahontas, Mary (Polly) who became Mrs John Buckley. Her son was the Rev Joshua Buckley, a venerable and greatly respected citizen of Buckeye who died April 23, 1901, at the advanced age of 92 years. The other daughter, Jane McCollam, was married to the late Joseph Friel and lived on the Greenbrier about five miles above Marlinton, where some of her family yet reside. Rachel and Nancy went with their father to Missouri. Rachel became Mrs Van Tassell and Nancy became Mrs Brown. Daniel McCollam set out to visit his former home, and while coming up the Ohio he was exposed to the smallpox. He at once went back and died of the disease in his western home.

Rebecca McCollom was married to the late Robert Moore, Senior, of Edray. Isaac Moore, Esq., Robert Moore, Junior, and Jane Moore, the wife of the late Andrew Duffield, near West Union, were her children.

Sarah McCollam was married to John Sharp, and lived on the place occupied by J. Wesley Irvine, near Verdant Valley, who is her grandson. Ellen, who became Mrs Amaziah Irvine; Mary, who became Mrs Josiah Friel; Rebecca, who was Mrs John R. Duffield; and Nancy, who was Mrs Willlam Irvine, were her daughters.

Mary McCollam was married to Thomas Brock and

lived on the "Duffield Place," now held by Newton Duffield. Her children were Daniel Brock, who married a Miss McClung, of Nicholas County; William Brock, Robert Brock, and Margaret, wife of the late William Duffield, near the Warwick Spring.

William McCollam married Sally Drinnan, daughter of Lawrence Drinnan, whose home was on Greenbrier River, on the upper part of Levi Gay's farm, very near the bank of the stream. It is to be remembered as the place where James Baker, one of the first school teachers, was slain by an Indian warrior about 1786. Soon after his marriage he settled near the summit of Buck's Mountain, about 1798, perhaps three hundred yards of the residence now occupied by his son, James McCollam, Esq. Traces of the old home are yet visible. His family consisted of five sons and six daughters. John, Lawrence, William, Isaac, James, Sarah, Susan, Nancy, Matilda, Rebecca, and Ruth.

John McCollam went to Lincoln County, Tennessee, where one of his descendants became an eminent Baptist minister.

Lawrence McCollam died in 1861.

William McCollam died in youth.

Isaac McCollam married Margaret Thomas, daughter of John Thomas, and settled in Randolph County. Fletcher McCollam, near the head of Stony Creek, is a son of Isaac.

James McCollam first married Anna Jane McCoy and settled on Buck's Mountain near the old homestead. George W. McCollam, a well known citizen, is his son. His second wife was Miss Mary Anna

Overholt.

Sarah McCollam, daughter of William McCollam, became Mrs Absalom McCollam and lived on Hill's Creek. The late William Morrison, at Buckeys, was her son.

Susan was married to the late James Kellison, on Brier Knob, head of Hill's Creek. Daniel Kellison, Esq., at Mingo Flats, Randolph County, is her son.

The daughters, Nancy, Matilda, and Rebecca were never married. They lived to be elderly persons, and were esteemed for their good character, industry and lady-like deportment, and made themselves very useful in many ways. All of them were so kind and skilful in waiting on their sick neighbors.

Ruth McCollam was married to William Kee, Esq., near Marlinton.

Thus far it has been placed in our power to illustrate the family history of these worthy people.

William McCollam was one of the original members of the Stony Creek M. E. Church, and while he lived was prominent in meetings and the official proceedings. Upon one occasion while the parents were absent attending meeting or visiting the sick, the house caught fire and was consumed with the most of its contents. At the time of the burning, John, the eldest son, was about eight years old; Lawrence was about two. In the confusion the baby boy seems to have been forgotten, and when John asked where the baby was he was told by one of the little girls that he was in the cradle asleep. John pressed his way through the smoke and heat at the risk of his life, and brought his brother out alive, but in doing so both were so badly burned as to have scars upon their persons long as they lived.

This man toiled on however; rebuilt his home, opened more land, and in the meanwhile eleven children had gathered around his table. At the time when his care and presence seemed most needed, it seemed good to the God he loved to call him away from a responsibility so important. The sugar season had just opened —the morning was such as to indicate a heavy run, and much wood were needed to keep the kettles boiling fast enough. On the 4th of March, 1818, he had morning prayer, sang a hymn of praise to Him that watches the sparrow when it falls, and went forth cheerfully to his work. A large red oak tree suited to his purpose was selected, which soon bowed and fell beneath his stalwart strokes, but somehow a limb from another tree in its rebound smote him with such furious force that he never seemed to conscious of what had happened. This occurred about a mile from home, near where James Hannah lives.

Though all this was sudden, there has never been a misgiving about the certainty of his having found rest from his honest toils and efforts to meet his duties, the rest that remains for the people of God. He had learned from his Scotch ancestry to sing:

"The sword, the pestilence, or fire,
  Shall but fulfill their best desire,
  From sin and sorrow set them free,
  And bring thy children, Lord, to thee."

JACOB WARWICK.

The compiler of these memorials, deeply impressed that something should be attempted to perpetuate the memory of these persons—Jacob Warwick and Mary Vance, his wife—has availed himself of such facilities as have been in reach. He is largely indebted to John Warwick, Esq., Judge James W. Warwick, and Mrs Elizabeth McLaughlin for the information from which these sketches are compiled. All these persons have since died, at a very advanced age. This article first appeared in the Southern Historical Magazine for August, 1892. Mrs McLaughlin, a daughter of William Sharp, lived with Mrs Warwick at intervals, as a friend and visitor in the family, and for whom Mrs Warwick manifested special attachment.

The father of Jacob Warwick came to Augusta County, from Williamsburg, Va,, during colonial times, between 1740–50. He was a Lieutenant in the service of the British Crown, and was employed in surveying and locating land grants in Pocahontas County, which County included territory of which States have since been formed.

Lieutenant Warwick located and occupied the Dunmore property for his own use. He married Elizabeth Dunlap, near Middlebrook. He was one of the English gentry whose families settled in Virginia in consequence of political reverses in England, and whose history is so graphically given in Thackeray's Virginians.

After operating extensively in lands; and securing

the Dunmore property in his own name, Lieutenant Warwick concluded to visit England. He never returned, and being heard of no more, he was given up for dead. In the meanwhile, Mrs Warwick settlrd on the Dunmore property, had it secured by deed to Jacob and afterwards married Robert Sitlington, but remained at Dunmore a number of years after her second marriage. Jacob Warwick seemed to have remembered but little of his own father, and always cherished the highest filial regard for Mr Sitlington. When Jacob attained his majority, Mr Sitlington moved to his own property near old Millboro, the estate now occupied by Mrs Dickinson, daughter of the late Andrew Sitlington. Upon her decease, Mrs Sitlington left a bequest of one thousand dollars to Windy Cove Church the annual interest of which was to be paid to the pastor of that congregation. For a long while it was managed by the Messrs Sloan. In the hands of Stephen Porter it was finally lost through financirl failure.

Upon reaching legal age and coming into possession of his estate, Jacob Warwick was married and settled at Dunmore. Just here let it be stated, that when it was decided that Lieutenant Warwick was dead, the grandfather of David Bell, of Fishersville, Va., was appointed guardian of Jacob Warwick. William and James Bell were the sons of this guardian, and James Bell was the father of William A. Bell and David Bell well remembered citizens of Augusta County.

Dunmore was Mr Warwick's first home after his marriage. His wife was Miss Vance, daughter of Colonel John Vance, of North Carolina. He died on

Back Creek, at Mountain Grove, Va. Colonel Vance's family moved to the vicinity of Vanceburg, Ky., except Samuel Vance, Mrs Warwick, and Mrs Hamilton. The last named was the mother of Rachel Terrel, of the Warm Springs, and John Hamilton, Esq., of Bath County. Governor Vance, of Ohio, and Senator Zeb Vance, of North Carolina, are of the same family connection. The Vances, originally, from Opecquon, near Winchester, Va.

In business trips to Richmond, to sell horses or cattle, Mr Warwick formed the acquaintance of Daniel Warwick, a commission merchant, who attended to business for Mr Warwick, and thus became mutually interested and were able to trace a common ancestry.

Mr Warwick remained at Dunmore a number of years. His children were all born there. He was industriously and successfully occupied in accumulating lands, and managing large herds of cattle and droves of horses. His possessions on Jacksons River were purchased from a certain Alexander Hall, of North Carolina. Mr Hall owned from the Byrd place to Warwickton. One of his sons, being charged with horse theft, the penalty being death by hanging, refugeed to Bath County. The elder Hall came to Dunmore to see Mr Warwick, and proposed to sell this land to provide means to send his refugee son to Kentucky so as to elude arrest. Mr Warwick had sent out one hundred head of cattle to be wintered in the cane brakes. This herd was taken by Hall as part payment for the Jackson River lands. The cattle rated at eight pounds a head (about forty dollars.) The Clover Lick lands were rented from the Lewises.

The accounts from Kentucky were so flattering that Mr Warwick decided to settle there. He actually set out for the purpose of locating and securing a new place for a new home. The persons in advance of the party with which he was going were slain by Indians near Sewall Mountain, and when Mr Warwick and those with him came up and saw their slain friends, all returned home. Mrs Warwick thereupon became so unwilling to emigrate from her Pocahonias home, that her husband concluded to exchange his Kentucky possessions with one Alexander Dunlap for a portion of the Clover Lick lands. The Dunlap patent called for four hundred acres of land; the actual survey made six hundred. There was a suit between Lewis and Dunlap about this possession. When matters as to these lands became satisfactorily arranged, Mr Warwick moved to Clover Lick, and lived in a row of cabins. After a few years he and Mrs Warwick thought it might be better for their children to live on the Jackson River estate. They moved to Bath, and remained there until the marriage of their son Andrew.

Upon their return to Clover Lick, the log cabins were deemed unfit for occupancy, and arrangements were made to build a spacious mansion. Patrick Bruffey was employed to prepare the material. He began work in Mr Warwick's absence. Mrs Warwick instructed Mr Bruffey to hew the timbers so as to have a hall or passage, as it was then termed. He did so. When Mr Warwick returned, and found what had been done, he was not pleased with his wife's plans, and had the logs changed accordingly.   Mr Bruffey hewed the logs and dressed the plank, but did not build the chimneys.   Mr Wooddell, near Greenbank, furnished the plank for sixty pounds (nearly three hundred dollars.) The nails were forged by hand at the Warm Springs.

Several mounds have been discovered near Clover Lick,   In searching for material for the foundation of the large new house, the builders gathered some nice stones from a rock pile.   They found human remains, and when Mr Warwick heard of it he emphatically ordered the stones to be replaced, and told them not to molest anything that looked like a burial place. Greenbrier Ben often spoke of the opening of a grave just in front of the Chapel; and from the superior quality of the articles found with the remains, all were of the opinion it was the tomb of a chief.   Mr Warwick directed it to be carefully closed, and the relics were not molested.

One of the main objects in having the new house so spacious was that it might be used for preaching services, and there was preaching there more frequently than anywhere else in this region, during a number of years.   This historic mansion was finally removed to give place to the handsome residence reared by Dr Ligon, and which was burned in 1884.

The main route for emigration from Maryland, Pennsylvania, and other points north and northeast, passed by Clover Lick to Kentucky and Ohio.   As many as forty and fifty would be entertained over night.   This made Clover Lick one of the most public and widely known places in the whole country.   The approach from the east avoided hollows and ravines, keeping along high points and crests of ridges, so as to be more secure from ambuscades and Indian attacks. The original way out from Clover Lick, going east, after crossing the Greenbrier near the mouth of Clover Creek avoided Laurel Run, kept along the high point leading down to the river, and passed close by the McCutchen residence. Mrs Warwick had the first road cut out, up the Laurel Run, in order to bring the lumber for the new house from Wooddell's in the Pine Woods, now Greenbank and vicinity. She gave the enterprise her personal attention.

Quite a number of interesting incidents are given by tradition illustrating the character of Mrs Warwick. While renting Clover Lick, her husband and others were making hay. A shower of rain came up very suddenly and dampened their guns and horse pistols. Late in the afternoon the men fired them off, so as to load them with fresh charges. Some one hearing the report of firearms in quick succession brought word to Mrs Warwick, at Dunmore, that the Indians were fighting the men at the Lick. She at once mounted a large black stallion, put a colored boy on behind, and went at full speed and swam the swollen river in her effort to see what happed. This colored boy is old "Ben," who died at Clover Lick, and is remembered by many of the older citizens.

Upon another occasion, when the Shawnees were returning from one of their raids to the east, forty or fifty of their warriors were sent by Clover Lick with the intention, it is believed, to pillage and burn. A scout

from Millboro warned Mr Warwick of their movements.   With about twenty others he waited for them
in ambush on the crest of the mountain south of Clover
Lick.   The fire was very effective, and every man killed or wounded his victim.   The Indians in their surprise hastily retreated, and were pursued as far as Elk
Water in Randolph County.   Upon hearing of the result, Mrs Warwick at once followed her husband
and friends, attended by servants carrying provisions
for them.   She met them at the Big Spring on their
return, and the weary hungry party were greatly re-
freshed by her thoughtful preparations.

She was eminently pious, and was a member of the
Windy Cove Presbyterian Church.   She never felt herself more honored than when ministers would visit her
home and preach.   The visiting minister would receive
a nice horse, or something else as valuable, as a token
of appreciation.   She was conscientiously rigid in her
domestic discipline.   Her brother once made this remark; "Mary, I used to think you were too strict with
your family, and you have been blamed for it.   I see
now you are right.   You have not a child but would
knee in the dust to obey you.   I let my children have
more liberties, and they do not care near so much for
me."

The Rev Aretas Loomis came from Beverly, for a
time, every four weeks, and preached at the Warwick
residence.   She was highly emotional, and during the
services often appeared very happy.   As to her personal appearance she was tall, slender, and blue eyed,
hair slightly tinged with auburn, and lithe and agile in

her carriage. So she was distinguished for symmetry of person, beauty of feature, and force of character, all of which she retained even to an advanced age. She was very benevolent, and her kind deeds were done upon the principle of not telling the left hand what the right might be doing. Persons in her employ would always be overpaid. Polly Brown, whose lot it was to support her blind mother, received two bushels of corn every two weeks, and no one knew where the supply came from at the time. A person named Charley Collins, who was renowned as an athlete, and whose name is given to one of the meadows of Clover Lick, did a great deal of clearing. It was reported that he was but poorly paid, but before Mrs Warwick was done with him his family was doubly paid by the substantial gifts dispensed with her open hands.

Among her many other generous deeds, it is told how a rather worthless character, disabled by frozen feet, was received into her house, clothed and fed until he could walk. His name was Bosier. This man afterwards died from the effects of a burning tree falling on him, against which he had made a fire, while on his way from Big Spring to Mace's in Mingo Flats. George See, a grandson of Mrs Warwick, heard his cries and came to him. In his efforts to rescue him, he exerted himself so laboriously that he was never well afterwards.

It should be remembered also, that Mrs Warwick, in her old age, gathered the first Sabbath School ever taught in Pocahontas County. In the summer her servants would lift her on her horse, and she would then

ride about four miles to a school house near where the
Josiah Friel cabin stood, now in the possession of
Giles Sharp. The exercises would begin at about nine
o'clock. There was no prayer, no singing; but she
would read the Bible, talk a great deal, and give good
advice. The scholars would read their Bibles with
her. The exercises would close at two in the afternoon. After this continuous session of five hours Mrs
Warwick would be so exhausted as to require assistance
to arise and mount her horse. It was her custom to
go to William Sharp's, dine and rest awhile, and then
go home later in the day. To use the language of one
of her scholars, the late Mrs Elizabeth McLaughlin,
who died near Huntersville in 1895, aged over ninety
years: "She would give such good advice. If all
would do as she told them, how well it might have
been. She was the best woman to raise girls I ever
saw, if they would take her advite how to act and how
to do. She has talked to me for hours, and it was
often thrown up to me that old Mrs Warwick made me
proud because I tried to do as she advised me."

The school was mainly made up of Josiah Brown's
family, John Sharp's, William Sharp's, and Jeremiah
Friel's. The lamented Methodist preacher, Rev James
E. Moore, once belonged to her Sabbath school, and
received from her his earliest religious instructions.
By common consent it is agreed that he did more for
his church than any two ministers who have ever
preached in this region.

Not a great while before her death, during one of
Mr Loomis' ministerial visits, she received the com-

munion. Upon receiving the elements, her emotions became so great that her husband and children, fearing results, carried her to her own room. For four weeks she was helpless from nervous prostration. All her children from Bath and Pocahontas were sent for. She died at the ripe age of eighty years, in 1823, at Clover Lick, and there she was buried. There were no services of any kind in connection with her burial.

The purpose of these sketches is already manifest to the discerning reader—to rescue, if possible, from total oblivion the name and services of an obscure but eminently worthy person. Jacob Warwick was one of the persons who made permanent settlements in what is now Pocahontas and Bath counties Virginia and West Virginia.

It has been already stated that he commenced his business life at Dunmore; purchased Clover Lick, where he resided for a time; then moved to his immense possessions on Jacksons River, and then returned to Clover Lick. In addition to these estates he acquired some equally as valuable. He endowed his seven children with ample legacies, and besides bequeathed a competency to ten or fifteen grandchildren.

Mr Warwick was an alert and successful Indian fighter, and had a series of conflicts, narrowly escaping with his life on several occasions; yet he was never sure of killing but one Indian. Parties now living remember seeing a tree on the lands of John Warwick, near Greenbank, where Jacob Warwick killed that Indian in single combat. It always grieved him that he had certainly sent one soul into eternity under such sad circumstances.

Owing to his accurate knowledge of the mountain regions far and near, his services were in frequent demand by land agents and governmental surveyors. He and others went to Randolph as an escort for a land commission in the service of the colony. It was during the period when Kilbuck scouted the mountains with bands of Shawnees and Mingoes. Colonel John Stuart, of Greenbrier, says: "Of all the Indians the Shawnees were the most bloody and terrible, holding all other men—Indians as well as whites—in contempt as warriors in comparison with themselves. This opinion made them more fierce and restless than any other savages, and they boasted that they had killed ten times as many white men as any other tribe. They were a well formed, ingenious, active people; were assuming and imperious in the presence of others, not of their nation, and sometimes very cruel. It was chiefly the Shawnees that cut off the British under General Braddock, in 1755—only nineteen years before the battle of Point Pleasant—when the General himself and Sir Peter Hackett, the second in command, were both slain, and the mere remnant only of the whole army escaped. They, too, defeated Major Grant and the Scotch highlanders at Fort Pitt, in 1758, where the whole of the troops were killed or taken prisoners.'

At the time Mr Warwick went over to Randolph with the commissioner, the season had been inclement, and it was believed the Indians would not be abroad. Indeed, such was their sense of security the party did

not think it worth while to arm themselves on setting
out on their business. While in the lower valley about
Huttonsville, however, it was reported by one Thomas
Lacky, a person of somewhat questionable veracity,
that he had seen fresh Indian signs. As Mr Warwick
and his party were unarmed, six citizens and friends of
the escort armed themselves and proposed to go with
them to the place where Lacky had seen the Indian
trail. Upon coming near the place, Andrew Sitlington's horse showed fright, thereupon his rider saw Indians, but for a moment could not speak. This attracted Mr Warwick's attention, and looking in the same
direction ne saw the Shawnees creeping along to reach
a suitable place to cut them off. He gave the alarm—
"Indians! Indians !" Finding themselves discovered
the warriors fired hastily, wounding one of the party
and Mr Warwick's horse. The horse sank to the
ground as if dead, but as Mr Warwick was in the act
of throwing off his cloak for flight, the horse rose and
darted off at the top of his speed, and carried his
rider safely home to Dunmore before night. Those
that were mounted all escaped—Jacob Warwick, James
McClain, Thomas Cartmill, and Andrew Sitlington.
Of those on foot, John Crouch, John Hulder, and
Thomas Lacky escaped. The following were killed:
John McClain, James Ralston, and John Nelson.
When these were attacked they were near the mouth of
Windy Run. One man was killed running across the
bottom. Three of the men escaped by climbing the
bank where they were; two others, in looking for an
easier place to get up the bank, were overtaken, killed

and scalped.   Not very far fro n this place is the laurel
thicket where Colonel Washington was killed in 1861.

The horse was found to be wounded in the thigh.
The ball was extracted, and the noble animal lived
long and became very valuable for useful endurance.
Most of the way home the day he was wounded that
horse carried two persons a distance of thirty miles.

Upon a subsequent occasion Mr Warwick went to
Randolph County.   It was night when he returned.
His horse shied at something in the road, which he at
once recognized as the fresh husks of roasting ears.
The presence of Indians was at once suspected, and
upon approaching the house cautiously it was found
that the row of cabins were burned and the premises
ransacked.   In their glee, the Indians had caught the
chickens, picked all their feathers off and let them go.
The place had been left in the care of a colored man
named Sam and Greenbrier Ben, aged ten or twelve
years.   Sam made good his escape to the woods, but
Ben hid in a hemp patch so near the cabin that when
it was burned he could hardly keep still, his buckskin
breeches were so hot.   From his retreat Ben saw the
Indians pick the chickens, leaving their tails and top-
knots, and laugh at their grotesque appearance.   He
saw them run the wagon into the fire, after the cabin
near the spring had become a smouldering heap of
coals.   This wagon was the first that ever crossed the
Alleghanies.   It was brought from Mountain Grove,
up Little Back Creek, about three miles above where
the Huntersville road first crosses the stream going
east; then across Knapps Spur, along by Harper's

Mill; then straight across to Thorny Creek, through the Lightner place, past Bethel Church, to the Saunders place on Thorny Creek; thence up the ridge to the top, and then along down to the Knapp place on the Greenbrier River; thence to Clover Lick.

The most memorable event of his life, however, was his being in the expedition to Point Pleasant, under General Andrew Lewis. The march from Lewisburg to Point Pleasant—one hundred and sixty miles—took nineteen days. It is most probable that he was in the company commanded by Captain Mathews. This conflict with the Indians was the most decisive that had yet occurred. It was fought on Monday morning, October 10, 1774.

It is a matter of regret that the recorded history of this battle does not accord full justice to the memory of a very deserving person. It is conceded by all, so far as there is any record, that up to the time when there occurred a lull in the battle the advantage was with the Indians. The question arises, why should a warrior as skillful as Cornstalk call a halt in the full tide of success, and suddenly cease firing and pressing upon a receding foe, with victory just in his grasp?

Had it not been for this, no troops could have been safely detached for a flank movement. Flank movements are only a good policy for those who are pressing the enemy, and not for the retreating party. When Cornstalk ceased to press, the victory was decided in favor of the Virginians, and lost to him. Had the battle been lost to our people and the army sacrificed, unspeakable disasters would have befallen all settlements west of the Blue Ridge mountains; the Revolution would have been deferred for all time, possibly, and the whole history of America far different from what has been.

How is that lull in the battle to be accounted for, which resulted in victory to the Virginians? Dr Foote says, in his account, which is one of the most minute and extended of all in reach of the writer, that "towards evening, Lewis seeing no signs of retreat or cessation of battle, dispatched Captains Shelby, Hathews, and Stewart, at their request, to attack the enemy in their rear. Going up the Kanawha, under the cover of the banks of Crooked Creek, they got to the rear of the Indians unobserved, and made a rapid attack. Alarmed by this unlooked for assault, and thinking the reinforcements of Colonel Christian were approaching, before whose arrival they had striven hard to end the battle, the savages became dispirited, gave way, and by sunset had recrossed the Ohio. Colonel Christian entered the camp about midnight, and found all in readiness for a renewed attack." (Second Series p165)

Colonel Kercheval, who claims to have derived his information from Joseph Mayse and Andrew Reed, of Bath County, states on their authority "that about two o'Clock in the afternoon Colonel Christian arrived on the field with about five hundred men, the battle was still raging. The reinforcements decided the issue almost immediately. The Indians fell back about two miles, but such was their persevering spirit, though fairly beaten, the contest was not closed until the setting of the sun, when they relinquished the field."

There were persons recently living in Bath, and the writer conversed with one, (September, 1873), almost in speaking distance of the residence where Joseph Mayse lived and died, who are certain that Mr Mayse gave the credit of that cessation in battle and falling back two miles on the part of the Indians, to Jacob Warwick and the persons with him. According to Judge Warwick's statement,—and the writer's impression is that Mr Mayse's statement was emphatically confirmed by Major Charles Cameron, a lieutenant in the battle,—Mr Mayse often repeated the fact that Jacob Warwick, an obscure private in the ranks, was detailed with a number of others, perhaps fifty or sixty in all, to bring in a supply of meat, that rations might be supplied for a forced march to the Indian towns, as Governor Dunmore had so treacherously given orders. These persons crossed the Kanawha about daybreak, and while at work in the hunting grounds and slaughter pens, they heard the firing beyond the limits of the camp, and so far up the Ohio they supposed it to be a salute to Governor Dunmore, who was expected at any time by the soldiers generally. But the firing continuing too long for this, it was surmised the troops were putting their arms in order for the contemplated march over the Ohio. Finally they suspected it was a battle. Mr Warwick was one of the first to ascertain this to be so, and immediately rallied the butchers and hunters, in order to return to camp and join the battle. This was noticed by the enemy, and Cornstalk was of the opinion that Colonel Christian was at hand. He ceased in the reach of victory, and took measures to withdraw from the field, unobserved by our exhausted troops. For nearly two hours they had been falling back, and when the flank movement was made to communicate with the hunters, supposed to be Colonel Christian's advance to join them. What fighting occurred afterwards was with the rear guard of Cornstalk's retreating army of demoralized braves.

If all this be true, and considering the sources of information, the writer sees no reason to doubt its authenticity in the main, it illustrates how important results are sometimes made to depend, in the providence of God, upon fidelity to duty on the part of the most obscure, and it brings to light the leadings of God's hand in human affairs.

This is not written in a complaining spirit, yet one feels like saying, if this be true, what a comment it furnishes on the justice meted out by the historic muse. The reputed hero of Point Pleasant appears in bronze, an honored member of the group wherein stand Henry, Jefferson, and Marshall, while the humble man whose hand turned the fortunes of that most eventful day sleeps in his obscure grave on the west bank of Jacksons River, six miles from the Warm Springs. Were it the grave of Campbell's "Last Man," it could not be in a much less frequented place.

Major Warwick's sons and daughters were all born at Dunmore, Pocahontas County. The eldest daughter, Rachel, remembered when the settlers would fly to the fort near her home, when she was a little girl. The fort was near the spot now occupied by Colonel Pritchard's mill.

She became the wife of **Major** Charles Cameron, a descendant of the Camerons so noted in the history of the Scottish Covenanters. He was in the battle of Point Pleasant, and was there called upon to mourn the death of his three brothers slain in that conflict. In person he was of medium stature, tidy in his dress, wore short clothes, very dignified in his manners, and was never known to smile after the heart-rending scenes he witnessed at Point Pleasant. He was an officer in the Revolution, and served as clerk of both courts of Bath County many years. He reared the late Charles L. Francisco, so long clerk of Bath, as his successor.

Mrs Cameron drew a pension of nine hundred dollars for several years before her death in 1858.

Major Cameron's residence was on Jacksons River, at the crossing of the Huntersville and Warm Springs pike. The two story spring house yet remains in a good state of preservation, the upper part of which he used for his office, where he long and faithfully kept the legal records intrusted to his care, almost one hundred years ago.

One son, Colonel Andrew W. Cameron, survived him. He became a very wealthy and popular citizen. He represented Bath in the Virginia Legislature. He removed afterwards to Rockbridge County and resided on an immense estate near Lexington, so as to secure educational and social advantages for his large family of sons and daughters. He met his death in a sad way in the town of Lexington, where he had gone anxious to hear something of his sons John and Charles in the army.

One of the passengers in the mail coach was a soldier with a musket. In the act of leaving the coach this weapon was discharged, the contents inflicting a wound from which he expired almost instantly.

Dr John H. Cameron, a popular physician of Deerfield, Va., is his eldest son. Mrs Thomas White, Mrs D. White, and Mrs Judge Leigh, of Lexington, Va., and the late Mrs A. W. Harmon are his daughters.

Mrs Jane Warwick Gatewood and Her Descendants.

She was Major Warwick's second daughter, and became the second wife of William Gatewood, of Essex County, a near relative of President Tyler. Their home was at Mountain Grove, Bath County. Their sons were Warwick and Samuel Vance, and their daughters were Mary Jane and Frances.

Warwick Gatewood married Miss Margaret Beale, of Botetourt County, Va., a relative of President Madison. Their daughter Eliza became Mrs Judge James W. Warwick, near the Warm Springs, and Catherine became Mrs Cæsereo Bias, once proprietor of the Red Sweet Springs. Mr Bias was rescued when an infant from a wrecked ship, and is supposed to be of Portuguese parentage. One of their sons, James W. Bias was a very promising candidate for the Presbyterian ministry, and died in North Carolina, where he was spending a vacation in charge of a church. Miss Kate Bias, her daughter, is a very efficient missionary in Brazil.

Colonel Samuel V. Gatewood married Miss Eugenia

Massie, near Alleghany Falls, Va. He succeeded to the old Mountain Grove homestead and built the fine brick mansion there. His daughter Susan became Mrs William Taliaferro, of Rockbridge County. Mary Pleasants, his second daughter, married Samuel Goode of the Hot Springs, Va. William Bias Gatewood, one of the sons, a prominent business man of Loudoun County, has recently died. Colonel A. C. L. Gatewood, another son, resides at the Big Spring, Pocahontas County. He was an officer in the Confederate service, 11th Virginia, (Bath Cavalry), and ranked among the bravest of his comrades. His daughter is Mrs Dr W. T. Cameron, a popular physician in the vicinity of Linwood.

Mrs Jane Gatewood's daughter, Mary Jane, became Mrs Kennedy, a merchant in Memphis, Tennessee, where she died of yellow fever.

Frances, the other daughter, became Mrs Patton, of Rockbridge. Her daughters, Mrs Crockett and Mrs Kent, were highly esteemed ladies of Wytheville and vicinity. Upon her second marriage Mrs Frances Patton became Mrs General Dorman, of Lexington, Va.

Mrs Mary Warwick Mathews and Her Descendants.

This member of Major Warwick's family was married to Sampson Mathews, and for years occupied the old Warwick homestead at Dunmore. Her children were Jacob Warwick, Andrew Gatewood, Sampson Lockhart, Elizabeth, and Jane.

Jacob W. Mathews resided on Sitlington's Creek, near Dunmore. His wife was a daughter of Rev John

McCue, of Augusta County, and who is mentioned in history as a pioneer minister in Greenbrier and Monroe County. There were two daughters, Elizabeth and Mary. Elizabeth married Captain Felix Hull, of McDowell, Highland County. Captain Hull was a prominent merchant and popular citizen. He led a company of two hundred men into Grafton, W. Va., in May 1861. He died in the service of the State of Virginia.

Mary was married to Joseph McClung, a citizen of Greenbrier, near Williamsburg. Mrs Newman Feamster, in the Blue Sulphur District, is her daughter; Mrs Brownlee, of Birmingham, Ala., is another daughter.

Andrew G. Mathews married Mary W. See, and lived several years at Dunmore, and then moved to Pulaski County, Va., where his later years were passed amid very pleasant surroundings. He was a highly respected citizen, and a prominent ruling elder in his church and well known throughout the Virginia Synod.

His daughter Martha married Uriah Hevener, near Greenbank. Mrs James Renick, of Greenbrier County, is one of his daughters. Mrs Ellen Snyder, of Salem, Misses Eliza and Rachel Mathews at the old Pulaski homestead, are also daughters. Charles Matthews of Summers County, is his son. Mrs Samuel B. Hannah, near Greenbank, is a granddaughter of Andrew G. Mathews.

Sampson L. Mathews, the third son of Mary Warwick Mathews, married Nancy Edgar, of Greenbrier County. The town of Ronceverte now occupies the Edgar homestead. He was a very useful and intelligent citizen of Pocahontas. He was the first surveyor

of the county and a member of the court a number of
years. His only child Mary, became Mrs William H.
McClintic, and yet lives. Her five sons were educated at Roanoke College. Hunter was a prosperous citizen of Pocahontas, and met his death April, 1901, by
a falling tree; Withrow is an enterprising citizen of
Pocahontas; George is a lawyer at Charleston; Edward
resides at Seattle, State of Washington. He was
among those who visited Alaska, in 1897, searching
for gold. Lockhart was State's attorney several terms
and represented Pocahontas County in the Legislature.

Elizabeth, the eldest daughter, was married to a Mr
Miller, of Rockingham County, Virginia, emigrated to
Missouri, and died young. Jane married Captain
George Woods, of Albemarle County. Her home
was near what is now Ivy Depot. She was the hap-
py mother of six sons and two daughters.

Margaret Warwick See and Her Family.

This daughter was married to Adam See, who lived near Huttonsville, Randolph County. He was a
well known lawyer, an extensive owner of lands,
an influential citizen and a devoted ruling elder in
his church. There were four sons and seven daughters. The sons were George, Jacob, Warwick, and
Charles Cameron. Eliza, Dolly, Christina, Mary,
Rachel, Hannah, and Margaret were the daugters.

George See's daughter, Georgiana, became the wife
of the late Captain Jacob W. Marshall, who raised
and commanded a very efficient comyany of mounted
infantry for the Confederate service. He was also one

of the original promoters of Marlinton, and was an
active member of the Pocahontas Development Company. F. P. Marshall, Sheriff of Randolph County;
Dr L. J. Marshall, of Marlinton, and Cecil Marshall
are his sons. Mrs Samuel Holt, and Mrs E. I. Holt,
of Hillsboro, are his daughters.

George See's son Adam married Dolly Crouch and
lived at the old home on Elkwater, Randolpoh County
Their daughter Florida became Mrs J. Calvin Price,
near Clover Lick. She and her two beautiful little
boys died within a few months of each other, several
years ago.

Jacob Warwick See married a daughter of the Rev.
Dr. Geo. A. Baxter, one of the most eminent ministers and educators of his day, and settled in Pocahontas, on the property owned by Mr. Uriah Hevener.
The last years of his life were spent in Tucker county,
W. Va.   When more than sixty years of age, he volunteered in the Confederate service, and died in Lynchburg Va., in a military hospital in 1862. His son Rev.
Chas. S. M. See, a well-know minister, was with him
and had his remains carried to Tinkling Spring Cemetery in Augnsta county, where he now sleeps well
after his busy life. In personal apperance he is said to
have borne a very marked likeness to his venerated
grand-father, and no doubt inherited his patriotic spirit
along with his name.

The third son, Charles Cameron, was among the
most popular and widely known citizens of his native
county, an ernest friend of liberal learning, and a
zealous Christian gentleman. His wife was a daugh-

ter of Dr Squier Bosworth, an eminent physician of Beverly. Peter See, a prosperous and influential citizen of Augusta County, an a ruling elder in the old Stone Church, is his son. Mr Peter See's wife, Mary, is a paughter of Mrs Eliza Gamble, one of Margaret Warwick See's daughters, whose husband, Dr Robert Gamble, was a noted physician, a ruling Elder in the Augusta Church, and a very influential citizen of Augusta County.

Dolly See was married to Hon. John Hutton, of Huttonsville, W. Va. This gentleman was a member of the Randolph court, and a delegate to the West Virginia Legislature, and did as much as any other man toward removing the disabilities of southern sympathizers.

Christina See was married to Washington Ward, and lived on the old See homestead, nearly east of Huttonsville. Her sons, Jacob, Renick, and Adam, were all in the Confederate service, and were known by their comrades as men that never flinched from danger nor shirked a duty. All three with their families have migrated to the far west.

Mary See became Mrs Andrew G. Mathews, of whom mention has been made.

Hannah See became Mrs Henry Harper, near Beverly, a ruling Elder in the church and a highly esteemed citizen.

Margaret See was married to the Hon. Washington Long, one of the wealthiest and most influential citizens of Randolph County.

Rachel Cameron See was the wife of Hon. Paul

McNeel, of Pocahontas County. He possessed an immense landed estate, was for years a leading member
of the court, sheriff of the county, and was a member
of the Virginia convention that passed the Ordinance
of Secession. Their eldest son George resides near
Hillsboro. He was a Confederate soldier. Andrew
Gatewood raised a company for the Confederate service. He died a few years since. John Adam was a
soldier, studied law, and now resides upon a fine estate
in Rockbridge County. Eliza, the eldest of the daughters, became the wife of Rev Daniel A. Penick, a
Presbyterian minister in Rockbridge County. The
other daughters are Mrs Edgar Beard, near Millpoint,
and Mrs Captain Edgar, near Hillsboro.

Andrew Warwick and His Family.

Major Jacob Warwick had another son, Charles
Cameron, but he died while at school in Essex County,
Va., aged fourteen. Andrew was therefore the only
son that lived to be grown, and to perpetuate his father's name. He was twice married. His first wife was
a Miss Woods, of Nelson County; the second wife was
a Miss Dickinson, of Millboro Spring, Bath County.

Andrew Warwick's eldest son, James Woods, lately
resided on Jacksons River on a section of the old
homestead. He served a term as Judge of the courts
of Bath and Highland counties. He received the appointment from the Virginia Legislature. He had
never been a lawyer by profession, but such was his
clear perceptions and common sense of the right thing
to be done that he met the duties of his station with

marked ability, and very acceptably to the people generally. He had three sons:

John Andrew was a lieutenant in the Confederate
service; received several wounds, from one of which he
suffered many years. For several years he was in the
west, leading the life of a frontiersman. He died in
1898.

James Woods was a soldier; a teacher and Superintendent of Schools in Pocahontas County.

Charles Cameron, lately deceased, was a cadet of
the Virginia Military Institute, and at one time a civil
engineer in the Mexican Railway service.

Judge Warwick's daughter Mary, is the wife of Col.
A. C. L. Gatewood. Lillie married James A. Frazier,
of Rockbridge Alum Springs. Eliza is the wife of J.
W. Stephenson, of the Warm Springs, a lawyer and
attorney for Commonwealth, Bath County. Another
daughter is Mrs Jacob McClintic near the Hot Springs.

Andrew Warwick's second son, Jacob, married Miss
Ellen Massie, of East Virginia, and most of his life
was spent there. He was an extensive planter, and
much esteemed for his elevated, pure character.

John Warwick, the third son of Andrew, resided in
Pocahontas County. As a member of the court, school
commissioner, assessor of lands, and in other positions
of trust, he was prominent as a citizen, and influential.
His first wife was Hannah Moffett, the only daughter
of Andrew Gatewood, of whom special mention is yet
to be made. His second marriage was with Caroline
Craig, youngest daughter of George E. Craig, merchant at Huntersville, Elder in his church, and a m...

estimable christian gentleman. Miss Emma Warwick, Mrs Ernest Moore, of Dunmore, and Mrs Dr Lockridge, of Driscol, are their daughters. Their sons John Warwick, merchant at Hinton, died in 1896; George Warwick died in Lexington, while a student at Washington and Lee College.

Elizabeth Warwick Woods.

This member of Jacob Warwick's family married Colonel William Woods, near Charlottesville, Va. There were no children born to them. He and his wife were particularly kind and bevevolent: A great many persons remember them with gratitude for their ample hospitality.

Mrs Nancy Warwick-Gatewood Poage and Her Descendants.

This member of Major Warwick's family was first married to Thomas Gatewood, son of William Gatewood, of Mountain Grove; by a previous marriage, Jane Warwick, already mentioned, was the second wife of William Gatewood.

Their home was at Marlin's Bottom, now Marlinton, Pocahontas County. Andrew Gatewood was the only child of her first marriage. Upon relinquishing all interest in the Marlins Bottom estate, he received the Glade Hill property, near Dunmore. He is remembered as a person of uncommon sprightliness. While a student at Washington College, he was regarded as the peer of his classmate, William C. Preston of South Carolina, in studies and oratorical talent in their

academic rivalry. He married Sally Moffett. A son
and daughter survived him, Charles and Hannah. The
daughter became the first wife of John W. Warwick. Her only child was the late Mrs Sally Ligon,
wife of Dr John Ligon, of Clover Lick. She was the
mother of eight daughters and one son: The late
Mrs C. P. Dorr, Mrs Dr McClintic, Mrs Louisa Coyner, Mrs Annette Coyner, Mrs Eva McNeel, Mrs Rosa
Arbuckle, Mabel, Georgia, and Yancey.

Upon her second marriage Mrs Nancy Gatewood became the wife of Major William Poage. Four daughters and one son were born of this marriage.

Mrs Poage died one morning just at the dawning.
Feeling death to be near, she requested Jennie Johnson, who afterwards became Mrs Jennie Lamb, to sing
her favorite hymn:

> "Come, O Thou traveler unknown,
> Whom still I hold but can not see,
> Art Thou the man than died for me?
> The secret of thy love unfold,
> With Thee all night I mean to stay,
> And wrestle till the break of day."

Mrs Poage's eldest daughter, Rachel Cameron, was
married to Josiah Beard, of Locust. At 18 years of
age, Mr Beard was a ruling Elder in the Falling Spring
Church, Greenbrier County, and was the first clerk of
Pocahontas County. During the Civil War, when
over seventy years of age, he was taken prisoner by
Federal troops. Something was said to rouse his ire,
and he challenged the whole squad to single combat.

Their family numbered eight sons and three daughters. William T. Beard, the eldest, was liberally educated, and became an honored, influential citizen. His wife was Mary, the only daughter of Richard McNeel.

Henry Moffett Beard was a Lieutenant in the Confederate service, and for years was among the most prosperous Pocahontas farmers.

Samuel J. Beard has long resided in Missouri.

Joel Early Beard died in the Confederate service. His mother came to church one Saturday morning of a sacramental occasion, to the Brick Church, and the first intimation of her soldier son's death was the fresh grave and the arrival of the body for burial. Her other sons were Charles Woods, John George, and Wallace Warwick were Confederate soldiers, and are influential citizens residing in the Little Levels of Pocahontas. Edwin Beard, the youngest son, is a merchant at Hillsboro. Mrs Alvin Clark, Mrs George McNeel, and Mrs Maggie Levisay are her daughters.

Mrs Poage's second daughter, Mary Vance, who is said to have borne a remarkable resemblance to her grandmother, Mary Warwick, was first married to Robert Beale, of Botetourt County, and resided on Elk Pocahontas, where he died, leaving one child, Margaret Elizabeth, who married Dr George B. Moffett, one of the first graduates in medicine that ever resided in Pocahontas. One of their sons, James Moffett, lives in Chicago. It was at her son's home Mrs Moffett died a few years ago.

Upon her second marriage Mrs Beale became the wife of Henry M. Moffett, the second clerk of Pocahontas, a very excellent man in every respect, and in his time one of the most influential of citizens. Their only son that survived them was George H. Moffett, a member of the Pocahontas bar, ex-speaker of the West Virginia Legislature, and at present a distinguished journalist in Portland, Oregon.

One of her daughters, Mary Evelina, was married to Colonel William P. Thompson, a Confederate officer, whose late residence was in New York, and prominent in the management of the Standard Oil Company. The youngest daughter, Rachel, became Mrs Dr McChesney, of Lewisburg.

Sally Gatewood, another daughter, became Mrs Dr Alexander McChesney, of Charleston, whose daughter, Mary Winters, is the wife of Rev A. H. Hamilton, a well known Presbyterian minister.

Margaret Davies Poage, the third daughter of Mrs Nancy Warwick Poage, was married to James A. Price of Botetourt County, and lived at Marlins Bottom.

Four of their sons were in the Confederate service— James Henry, Josiah Woods, John Calvin, and Andrew Gatewood.

James Henry was captured at Marlins Bottom and taken to Camp Chase. He died in 1898.

John Calvin was severely wounded in the same skirmish, shot down in the river, and afterward rescued by friends. He resides near Clover Lick.

Josiah Woods graduated with distinction at Washington College in 1861. He was a lieutenant in Captain McNeel's company of mounted infantry. He was a teacher, superintendent of schools, and merchant in

Randolph County; a member of the Randolph court, and for a term was presiding officer. He now resides at Marlinton.

Andrew Gatewood Price was in the Confederate service in the Bath Cavalry. He was taken prisoner at Hanover Junction, and died a few weeks thereafter at Point Lookout, July 6, 1864, aged about twenty years. A lady near Richmond, seeing his name mentioned among the missing, wrote some very beautiful lines, that have been widely copied in books and journals, and his name has been sweetly embalmed and his memory not soon forgotten.

Samuel Davies Price married Caroline McClure and lately resided on Jacksons River, where his widow and children now lives.

Mary Margaret Price, the only surviving daughter, was married to Andrew M. McLaughlin, of whom was purchased the land on which the town of Marlinton is built. They reside near Lewisburg, W. Va. Their eldest son, Rev H. W. McLaughlin, is a Presbyterian minister, in charge of the Greenbank and Dunmore churches. Lee and Edgar are their other sons; Anna Margaret, Lula, and Grace are their daughters.

Concerning William T. Price, the eldest son of J. A. and Mary D. Price, the following is taken from Herringshaw's Encyclopædia of American Biography:

"WILLIAM T. PRICE, cleryman, author, was born July 19, 1830, near Marlinton, W. Va. He was prepared for college at the Hillsboro Academy, and graduated in 1854 from Washington College, now called the Washington and Lee University, receiving a gold medal as the first honor graduate.   In 1857, he completed his theological studies at Union Seminary and was licensed the same year to preach.   His time has been devoted mainly to the ministry of the Presbytertan Church—for forty years;—twelve years as home missionary in Bath and Highland counties; sixteen years as pastor of Cooks Creek Church, Rockingham County, Va.; and twelve years as pastor of the Huntersville and Marlinton churches.   He has contributed extensively to religious literature and is the author of several published works.''

William T. Price and Anna Louise Randolph, of Richmond, Va., were married in 1865.   Their children are Dr James Ward Price, Andrew Price, Susie A. Price, a student at the Woman's Medical College of Baltimore; Norman R. Price, medical student; Calvin W. Price, and Anna Virginia Price.

Elizabeth Wood Poage, the fourth daughter, became the wife of Colonel Joel Mathews, of Selma, Alabama. A sad mortality attended her family; a few, perhaps none survive.   Colonel Mathews was an extensive planter, and owned between two and three thousand slaves.   He tendered a colored regiment to the Confederate Congress, but the Government was too punctilious to receive them as soldiers, and put them to work on fortifications.   Major Dawson, a son-in-law, was a member of the Southern provisional congress.

Colonel William Woods Poage married Miss Julia Callison, of Locust, and lived awhile at Marlins Bottom.   His later years were passed near Clover Lick. He served many years as a member of the court.   Two

of his sons, Henry Moffett and William Anthony were
slain in the war.   Henry Moffett was a cavalry officer,
and was recklessly daring.   He fell near Jack Shop.
Mrs Sally W. Beery, of Mt. Clinton, Va., is his only
surviving child.   William Anthony was no less brave,
and lost his life near Middletown, Va., while on a
scout.

The surviving sons of Colonel Poage, John Robert
and Quincy Woods, are prosperous farmers on the
grand old homestead near Clover Lick. These brothers
married sisters, daughters of Jacob Sharp, whose mother was the intimate friend of Mrs Mary Vance Warwick, long years ago.

Authentic tradition preserves some incidents that illustrate 'some of Major Warwick's personal traits.
Soon after the affair at Point Pleasant, he went among
the Shawnees on a trading excursion to secure skins
and furs.   On the last excursion of this kind he traveled as far as Fort Pitt, where he found little Gilmore,
a boy who had been carried a captive from Kerrs
Creek, Rockbridge, Virginia.   To put him out of the
reach of the mischievous boys, his master had lashed
him to a board and laid him on the roof of a log cabin.
Mr Warwick tried to ransom the captive, but too much
was asked by the Indian foster parent, and so he planned to rescue the boy and bring him home to his surviving friends in the Virginia Valley.   He went with
the Indians upon a hunting expedition, and while moving from place to place to place he would frequently
carry the Indian children behind him on his horse,

and by turns he would carry the Gilmore boy too. Sometimes he would fall behind the party, first with an Indian boy and then with the white one, but still come up in time. Finally the Indians placed so much confidence in the trader as to be off their guard, whereupon he withdrew from the party with the captive and started for the settlements, and before the Indians became suspicious of his intentions, his swift horse had carried them safely beyond their reach. After an arduous journey he arrived home in safety and restored the captive to his friends.

Mr Warwick was once at a house raising in the vicinity of Clover Lick. A young man made himself unpleasantly conspicuous boasting of his fleetness of foot. The Major took one of his young friends aside and told him if he would beat that youngster at a foot race and take some of the conceit out of him he would make him a present. The race came off in the afternoon, and was won by the young friend. Mr Warwick was delighted, and told him to come over to the Lick soon as convenient and see what was there for him. When he did so the Major gave him one of his fine colts.

That youth became a distinguished Methodist minister, Rev Lorenza Waugh; traveled in West Virginia, Ohio, and Missouri, and finally went overland to California, where he died in 1899 at the advanced age of 95 years. During the greater part of this extended itineracy he used horses that were the offspring of the horse presented to him by Major Warwick.

In a controversy about land on Little Back

Creek, in Bath County, a challenge passed between him and Colonel John Baxter. This was about the only serious difficulty he ever had with any one, but the affair was amicably and honorably settled by mutual friends.

His grandson, the late John Warwick, Esq., remembers the last visit paid to the old home in Pocahontas. He would have Greenbrier Ben, a faithful servant, to mount a large black mule; take his grandson, a lad of four years, in his arms and carry him from Jacksons River to Clover Lick—between thirty-five and forty miles—the same day. The party of three rested at noon in the home of John Bradshaw, the pioneer and founder of Huntersville. Squire Warwick remembered seeing the hands at work upon the court house, then in course of erection, and the interest manifested by his venerated grandfather, then more than eighty years of age, in what was going on.

In person, Jacob Warwick was tall, stoop shouldered, and exceedingly agile and muscular. His grandson, the late Jacob See, is said to have resembled him more than any one else in personal appearance.

Mrs Mary V. Warwick was a person of highly refined taste, and took all possible pains to make home attractive. When there was preaching at her house, all present were pressingly invited to remain for dinner. Her table service was really elegant, and a prince might well enjoy her dinners. She had a well supplied library of books in the nicest style of binding, and she made good use of them, too.

Mr Warwick was jovial in his disposition, and extremely fond of innocent merriment. He delighted much in the society of young people, and even children. His pleasant words and kindly deeds to young people were vividly and affectionately remembered by all who ever knew him.

After the decease of his wife, most of his time he passed at the home of Major Charles Cameron. He died at the breakfast table. When apoplexy came upon him he was merrily twitting Miss Phœbe Woods about her beau, young Mr Beale. This occurred January, 1826, when he was nearing his eighty-third year.

They carried his venerable remains about a mile up the west bank of the Jacksons River, and in a spot reserved for family burial, he was buried. When the writer visited his grave several years since, the place seemed to be in danger of forgetfulness. A locust tree stood near it and marked the place. Since then it has been nicely and substantially enclosed, and the grave marked by a neatly sculptured marble. In that lonely, but beautiful, valley retreat the strong, busy man has found repose.

THOMAS GALFORD.

So far as now known Thomas Galford, Senior, was the original ancestor of the Pocahontas Galfords. It is believed he came from the Middle Valley and was of Scotch descent. Thomas Galford lived on the place now held by F. Patterson and Charles Nottingham on Glade Hill, and it is the opinion of most persons that he came there just previous to the Revolution.

Thomas Galford had a brother, John, of whom but little is now known. There was a sister, Jennie, who became Mrs Otho Gum and lived at the head of Crab Bottom, Highland County. There was another sister whose name cannot now be recalled who became Mrs John Chestnut, on Little Back Creek, where she has numerous descendants.

Thomas Galford married Naomi Slaven, an aunt of Newlen Slaven, late of Meadow Dale, and they were the parents of two sons, John, and Thomas, Junior; and a daughter, Elizabeth.

John Galford married Jennie McLaughlin, lived on the home place, finally went to Lewis County and settled near Walkersville. There were five sons and one daughter: Allen, John, William, James. Thomas and Naomi.

Naomi Galford died a young woman in Lewis County.

John Galford, Junior, married Frederika Hillery and lived at Huntersville where he conducted a flourishing tannery. Two sons and one daughter, Harrison, George, and Mary, who is now Mary V. Rodgers, near Buckeye, are their children.

John Galford's second marriage was with Mary Simmons, daughter of the late Nicholas Simmons. Hampton and Lydia, now Mrs Lee Overholt, are her children.

Thomas Galford married Margaret Curry, on Back Mountain. Their children John, Brown, Naomi, Abigal, now Mrs L. A. Hefner, on Swago. Lanty A. Hefner was a Confederate soldier from '61—'65, attached to Colonel G. M. Edgar's battalion, They are the parents of nine sons and two daughters.

James Galford married Margaret Anderson in Lewis County. They are the parents of seven children. Everett is a teacher of high schools. Homer lives at Walkersville. James Galford is in fine circumstances financially and a highly esteemed, influential citizen of Lewis County.

Allen Galford married Nancy Cassell and lived on on the Greenbrier near the mouth of Deer Creek. They were the parents of four daughters and three sons. Full particulars are given of his family in the Cassell sketches.

Allen Galford was a well-known citizen and prospered financially. He died not long since aged 82 years. Several years since he sought the forgiveness of his sins and united with the church at the age of 77 years. He left in manuscript a very sincere confession of his faith in the merits of his Savior's atoning blood.

Thomas Galford, Junior, one of the ancestral brothers, was first married to Naomi Slaven, a relative, and settled on a part of the Glade Hill homestead, and thence moved and located on property now held by the late Harvey Curry's family near Dunmore. By this marriage there was one daughter, Jane, who married her cousin, William Galford, son of John Galford, Senior, and first settled on the head of Sitlington's Creek on the farm now owned by her son, William Wellington Galford, and finally moved near Dunmore. The following particulars are at hand about her children:

John Galford, a Confederate soldier in the 31st Virginia Infantry, was wounded at Gettysburg and died at Richmond soon after, in Chimborazo hospital.

Thomas Galford married Lizzie Vint and lived and died near Dunmore.

James Galford died while on a visit to relatives in Highland. His memory is cherished as an earnest, christian man, and a person of promise for good citizenship.

William W. Galford married Ada Mayse, daughter of the late Jubal Mayse and lives at the head of Sitlington's Creek.

Elizabeth Galford, a young woman died at the home place near Dunmore.

Nancy Galford lives on a part of the homestead.

Naomi Galford died soon after reaching womanhood.

Marietta Galford died when nearly grown, of pulmonary affection.

In his second marriage Thomas Galford, Junior, was married to Henrietta Sutton, and there were no children.

Thomas Galford was a very pronounced Confederate sympathizer, and as such he was regarded as a dangerous citizen to be at large in war times. In discharging what they deemed to be their duty, he was arrested by a detachment of Union soldiers, under the command of the late Captain Nelson Pray, and sent to Camp Chase, where he died during the war.

In reference to the pioneer's daughter Elizabeth Galford, the tradition is that when she was fourteen years old she was sent on an errand to the mill, a quarter of a mile east of the residence. The child was never seen afterwards. While parties were carefully searching the creek, Indian signs were discovered and it was at once concluded that she had been taken captive. Vain pursuit was made, and the neighbors hastened to the fort. Indians, believed to be the same party, attacked the fort and killed a man named Sloan, and an Indian was wounded. The Indian was taken to a glade near Arbovale, and secreted until he was able to leave for the Ohio towns. Hence the name "Hospital Run."

Some months subsequently Thomas Galford and Samuel Gregory went to the Indian towns, but could hear nothing of the child. The two men lingered about the town, inquiring for furs and tried to trade with the Indians, hoping thus to get the desired information about the missing child. Hearing nothing, they gave up all hopes, and turned their attention to a pair of fine horses. They stole them, hitched them some distance from the town, and then went back and waited in ambush for the warriors that might come in pursuit. Two were shot down and their ornaments taken, and these were kept for years. The bracelets were burned when Thomas Galford, Junior, lost his house. The captured horses were fine stallions. The bay was called Buck Rabbit and the other Irish Grey. Buck Rabbit was sold to John Bird, the ancestor of the Bird relation, on upper Back Creek. The other was bought by John Harnes, a trader from Staunton.

Thomas Galford, the pioneer, and Jacob Warwick, on returning from a scout, thought they would have sport at the expense of William Higgins and Peter Ingram, whom they found digging potatoes near the fort at the mouth of Deer Creek. Higgins always claimed

there was no indian that could ever make him run.
While the two were busy with their digging, Galford
and Warwick slipped up to the fence and fired simultaneously, hitting the ground close to Higgins and
scattering the dust all over him. He and Ingram ran
with all speed to the stockade and reported that Indians had fired on them. The panic was soon relieved
however, when hilarious laughter instead of war whoops
were heard in the direction of the potato patch.

JOHN R. FLEMMENS.

One of the most unique and picturesque characters
that figure in our local history was John R. Flemmens,
of Laurel Creek. Early in the century residents of the
head of Stony Creek saw smoke rising from Red Lick
Mountain. At first it was thought to be a hunter's
camp. Upon noticing the smoke continuing for some
days, curiosity was awakened, and parties went up
into the Red Lick wilderness to see what it meant. To
their surprise they found a family in camp, arranging
for a permanent settlement.

There were five persons, John R. Flemmens and
Elizabeth Flemmens, his wife; James and Frederick
were the sons, and one daughter, Elizabeth. There
were nice horses and several cows ranging about. The
family had been there for several weeks, yet no one
ever found out when or whence they had come. Had
these persons arrived in a balloon from the clouds at
midnight, their coming could not have been better

concealed than it seemed to have been from the neighbors.

The Flemmens opened what is now the "Rosser Place." But few persons were ever known to labor more industriously than the mother and her three children. Mr Flemmens bought lands from Isaac Gregory amounting to four thousand acres. It was a part of the William Lewis Lovely survey. The papers dated 1777, and this region was then in the metes and bounds of Harrison County. Such a deal in lands sounds fabulous now, or did until the recent operations of Colonel McGraw and others have rather eclipsed the Flemmens' deals on that line. John R. Flemmens at times seemed pressingly anxious to sell large tracts at ten cents an acre. Lands now held by Colonel McGraw, the Whites, Shearers, and others.

On his possessions John Flemmens made an opening, built a house, and preparations were made for an immense barn. The barn was never finished. Some of the hewn timber for the barn was more than two feet across the face and smooth as silk. How such work could be so smoothly done was the wonder of all who may have examined it.

The Flemmens family became noted for sugar making. They would work several hundred trees in the season. On the southern exposures an early camp would be worked, then move to another less exposed, and then move into the north and close the season there. The mother and children would carry the sap for miles in pails supported by straps from their shoulders, and much of the sap was carried up hill. In making arrangements for evaporating the sap, an immense tree would be felled and the kettles supported against it, and then the fires kindled. It was no uncommon thing to see fifteen or twenty large kettles boiling at the same time.

The output would amount to hundreds of pounds. The sugar was generally stirred until it pulverized, and much of it was nearly as fair as brown or coffee sugar.

A good deal of the sugar was taken to Lewisburg and exchanged for more kettles. Mr Flemmens could pack three large iron kettles on one horse. In these excursions to the sugar market, and very frequently at other times, John Flemmens had three horses, driving the foremost, riding the middle one, and leading the third—all arranged random fashion. In this manner he could traverse the bridle paths,—at an early day the common means of communication between places.

The entire family became members of the church.

James Flemmens was fond of hunting, but he met with so little success that his father warned him that if he came home any more without venison, he should not be allowed to waste any more time as he had been doing.

"Worrich pays better than no luck, Jim, in huntin', and so you know what will be up if you don't git nothin' this time."

This was spoken in stentorian tones with a commanding voice, and it seems to have rung in Jimmy's ears to a practical purpose.

That day he had the luck to bring home a venison.

The same day the late venerable John Barlow killed

a deer, but he did not bring it home—left it hanging in the woods, hunter fashion—and it mysteriously disappeared. Suspicious gossip ran high, which the Flemmens meekly endured until they began to think that forbearance was no longer a virtue, and a church trial was demanded to vindicate Jimmy's character from the slanderous insinuations in connexion with the disappearance of the dear.

The preliminaries for trial being duly arranged by the Presiding Elder at Hamlin Chapel, the slandered hunter put in his pleas, with flowing tears and tremulous voice, when the Elder asked the question:

"Brother James Flemmens, did you or did you not take Brother Barlow's deer?"

"I hope not. God knows I hope God does not know I took the deer, as I am slandered with."

Mr Barlow exclaimed; "God does n't know any such thing."

The strife of tongues now promised to become sharp, but the imperious Presiding Elder made it short and decisive by a wave of the hand and a significant look toward the door. Somehow, as the Flemmens thought unjustly, the Elder construed James' plea as a virtual confession that he had spirited away the missing game. He solemnly deposed him from church membership, and thus cleared all others of slanderous intentions.

Soon as the decision was announced, John Flemmens arose an asked for a dismissal: "Give me my name, and give me old Betsy's, too!" Young Betsy tearfully asked for her name also. They all soon found a church home elsewhere.

In the course of events Frederick was the first to die and that too far away from his mountain home under sadly peculiar circumstances. John R. Flemmens called at John Barlow's to pass the night. Mr Barlow had heard of Frederick's death, but did not wish any one to say any thing about it before morning. But one of the boys came in before his father could repress him and said: "Mr Flemmens, do you know that Fred is dead ?"

"Is it possible, Mr Barlow, have you heard that my boy is dead ?"

"Yes," replied Mr Barlow, "I am sorry to say it is even so."

In an instant the bereaved father seemed to be frenzied by his grief. He caught up his three horses and started for home in the night. As he slowly ascended the mountain path his agonized cries could be heard for miles: "O Freddy, my dear son; your poor old father will never see you again. O Freddy, my son, my son !"

While on a visit to Ohio, Mr Flemmens died there.

Mrs Flemmens and her daughter Elizabeth spent their last years in the vicinity of Buckeye. They spun and wove ond industriously earned a living as long as their willing hands coald retain their cunning, and had the respectful esteem of all their neighbors.

AARON MOORE.

Aaron Moore, one of the older sons of Moses Moore the pioneer, hunter, and scout, after his marriage with

Catherine Johnson, daughter of John Johnson, first lived near Frost; but the greater part of his life he dwelt on the west bank of the Greenbrier, four miles above Marlinton, where he had settled in the woods.

John Johnson, the ancestor of the Johnson relationship, and the pioneer of West Marlinton, whose log cabin stood several hundred yards below the bridge, near a large walnut tree, heard that corn had matured in Nicholas. He set out to bring in some of the Nicholas corn for seed, and lost his way in Black Mountain and was bewildered for nine days, having nothing to eat most of the time. In his desperation he tried a morsel of garter snake, but he could not swallow it, and he concluded he would rather die than "eat such eatings as that." Upon coming to a house he was just able to move, and scarcely able to talk enough to make the mistress of the place understand what had happened. She at once proceeded to prepare a bountiful meal, thinking a man as hungry as he was would never know when to quit. In the meantime the proprietor came in and countermanded all this preparation, and directed a little thin mush to be boiled and a little skimmed milk be brought from the spring house. He prepared a saucer of mush and milk and gave the famished stranger one spoonful, and then waited for results. In a few minutes there was a violent emetic disturbance, ann it looked as if he was about to turn inside out. When this subsided, a little more of the mixture was given, with more favorable results, and in a few hours the pangs of hunger were somewhat appeased. Nourishment was carefully dosed out for some days, and he finally made the trip, bringing the corn, which planted one of the first crops ever produced in the vicinity of Marlinton.

By arduous industry and judicious economy Mr and Mrs Moore built up a prosperous home. Their sons were John, James, Samuel, Thomas, Andrew Jackson, Henry, William Daniel, and George Claiborne; and the daughters were Mary, Elizabeth, Catherine, Eliza, and Melinda—eight sons and five daughters.

John Moore married Jane, daughter of Colonel John Baxter, and settled in the woods near Marlinton. Their children were Aaron, William, Theodore, Washington, and one daughter, Catherine, now Mrs Thomas Auldridge, near Indian Draft.

James Moore married Anne McNeill daughter of the late Squire John McNeill, on Dry Branch of Swago, and settled in the woods near Marlinton, on property now owned by John R. Moore. Their children were John Register, Frances, Rachel, George, Henry, Nelson, and Naomi. John Register lives on the homestead. His wife was Mary Baxter, daughter of the late William Baxter, near Edray.

Samuel Moore married Nancy Beale, and settled on the summit of Marlin Mountain, in the unbroken forest and killed ten rattlesnakes on the first acre cleared about his cabin. Their children were Lucas, Martha, Catherine, Margaret, Jennie, William Thomas, Anise, George, Kenney, Rachel, and Melinda—eight daughters and four sons. Mrs Moore was a daughter of Thomas Beale, who came from Maryland soon after the war of 1812. He claimed to have been a sailor in early life, and was one of the defenders of Baltimore, and saw the engagement immortalized by the "Star Spangled Banner." The farm opened up by Samuel Moore is visible from so many points that a lady from Florida called it a revolving farm.

William D. Moore settled on Elk Mountain in the woods. He was married three times. His first wife was Rebecca Sharp; her children were Matthias, Charles L., Elizabeth, Mary, Jacob, and Nancy. The second wife was Mary Ann Auldridge, daughter of Thomas Auldrige, Senior. Her one child was Mary Ann Moore. The third wife was Hannah Beverage. Her children were Amanda, now Mrs S. D. Hannah, on Elk; Susan, now Mrs John Gibson, near Mary's Chapel; Effie, now Mrs A. P. Gay, near Clover Lick; Etta, Joseph, and Ellis.

Thomas Moore, a noted rail splitter and fence builder, never married. He opened up a nice farm on Back Alleghany, where he now resides.

Andrew Jackson Moore was married twice. First wife was Abigail McLaughlin, daughter of the late Major Daniel McLaughlin, near Greenbank. Her children were Ernest and Anise, now Mrs D. Hevner, on Back Alleghany. The second wife was Rachel, daughter of the late Charles Grimes, near Frost. Her children were Virginia, now Mrs Silva, on Stamping Creek, Forest, Samuel, Thomas, and Elmer.

A. J. Moore settled in the woods on Back Alleghany, and opened up a fine farm.

Henry Moore married Elizabeth Auldridge, and settled in the woods near Driftwood, and opened up two nice farms. Their only son, Andrew Moore, lives at the homestead.

George C. Moore married Rachel Duncan on Stony Creek. Her father, Henry Duncan, came from Rockbridge, and was one of the carpenters that worked on the court house at Huntersville. Mr Moore lives on the "Young Place," on Stony Creek.

Elizabeth Moore became Mrs William Auldridge. These persons settled in the woods near Indian Draft. Their children were Hanson, Melinda, and Eliza. Eliza died not long since. Hanson and Melinda are living on the nice homestead opened up by their worthy parents.

Catherine Moore was married to John Burr, and they settled in Burrs Valley, where she is now living.

Eliza Moore became Mrs Price McComb, and they settled in the woods on Cummings Creek, densely covered with white pine, and opened up virtually several nice farms. Their children were Nancy, Charles, George, Wyllis, Andrew Beckley, Henry on the homestead; and Alice, now Mrs George Wagner, at Huntersville.

Melinda Moore was the second wife of the late Captain William Cochran, on Stony Creek. Her children are William Cochran, on the homestead; and Catherine Jane, now Mrs Giles Sharp, near Verdant Valley. Her second marriage was with Joseph Barlow, who lives on the Cochran homestead.

It is instructive to reflect on the memoirs of such a relationship, so largely composed of patient, industrious people, accomplishing what they have done in

developing our county. Nine members of this family
settled in the woods, and by their efforts more than a
thousand acres of wilderness land has been made to rejoice and blossom as the rose.

Mary died in early womanhood, regarded by her
sisters as their special favorite. Two, while not settling in the woods, have shown by their industry and
enterprise how to make the best of more favorable opportunities, and improved what came into their hands
already opened up and improved.

It is not easy to appreciate what it cost—weary toil,
wear and tear of muscle and bodily vigor—to achieve
what they have. Nevertheless, the oldest people tell
us that there was more real contentment and satisfaction and enjoyment in life then than now; for there was
a felt community of interest, and harmonious help and
truly sympathetic endeavor, that seemed to have a
charm not apparent now. Then it seemed a genuine
pleasure to show favors and render assistance, but now
pay seems to be expected for most everything that may
be done in the way of helpful service.

Like most of the persons of his time, Aaron Moore
was a successful hunter and made it profitable. One
of his memorable adventures occurred while on his way
to search for the body of his neighbor, James Twyman
who was drowned in Thorny Creek, January 17, 1834,
and was not found until January 19. Mr Moore lived
on the west bank of the river, while Thorny Creek is
on the east side. He went up the west bank to cross
at Joseph Friel's. As he was threading his way along
the snow covered path, his dog came upon the trail of

a panther, and treed it in a lofty pine near the summit of the river ridge, about opposite Friel's. He shot the animal, left it where it fell to be attended to later on, and then hurried away on his sorrowful duty, canoeing the river at high tide. The body of the drowned neighbor was found stranded on a large rock, that is still pointed out not very far below the mouth of the creek.

When Mr Moore died, his remains were taken to the Duffield grave yard. His faithful wife survived him a few years, and then was carried to rest by his side, where they are now sleeping the years away, in hope of a blessed resurrection. May they stand in their lot at the end of the days.

LEVI MOORE.

One hundred years ago, one of the most widely known citizens in the region now embraced by Pocahontas and Bath counties, was Levi Moore, Senior, a native of Wales. He was the pioneer of Frost, and came to there some time previous to the Revolution, and was among the first to make a permanent settlement. The lands he settled now owned by the Gibsons, Sharps and others. His wife was Susannah Crist and he first settled in Pennsylvania, where he lived until his family, two sons and two daughters were born and the older ones nearly grown.

Hannah Moore was marrried to Robert Gay, the ancester of the Gay relationship, so frequently alluded to in these papers.

From Mrs John Simmons and Mrs Mary Jane Moore we learn the following particulars:

Sally Moore became Mrs John Smith, one of the first permanent settlers of the Edray district, near the head of Stony Creek, of whom special mention is made.

George Moore was at the notable wedding when Jacob Slaven and Miss Eleanor Lockridge were married near Driscol. The tradition is that a practical joke was played by one James Brindley, at which the horse took fright, ran off, and the rider's head struck a projecting fence stake and was instantly killed. George Moore lived a while on the land now held by Abram Sharp, but sold to John Sharp and went to Kentucky. He was back on a visit when his sudden death occurred as just mentioned.

Levi Moore, Junior, was a person of marked prominence in county affairs. In person he was six feet eleven inches in height, and well proportioned. He was a member of the Virginia legislature and was on the commission to locate the court-house, and selected a site near where George Baxter, county surveyor, now lives. His first marriage was with Miss Nancy Sharp, daughter of William Sharp, the Huntersville pioneer, and lived on the Moore homestead. In reference to their children the following items are recorded:

Rebecca Moore was married to Leonard Irvine, on Back Creek, and lived at the brick house where the road to Frost leaves the Back Creek road. Levi Irvine was killed in an accident; Lizzie Irvine was married to Henry Coffee, of Augusta County, Va.; Cornelia Irvine

was married to William Gardner and settled in Web-
ster County; Wilton Irvine married Kate McCarty,
daughter of George McCarty, and settled on Little
Back Creek; Susannah Irvine was married to Cyrus
Kelley on Little Creek; and there is a son, Herron
Irvine.

Margaret Moore was married to Eli McCarty and
lived near Laurel Run. Her daughter, Margaret
McCarty, married the late John Simmons and lived on
the homestead. Her brother, Paul, died in the west.

Martha Moore, another daughter of Hon Levi Moore,
Junior, was married to the late Rev John Waugh, of
Indian Draft. Her children were Levi, Beverly, John,
Samuel, Miriam, Ann and Eveline. Joseph B. Mc-
Neel, on Bucks Run; Rev John W. McNeel, a minis-
ter of the Baltimore Conference, are her grand-children.

Andrew Moore married Rebecca Waugh, daughter
of Samuel Waugh, in the Hills, and settled on Knapps
Creek, thence moved to the head of Stony Creek, and
finally located in Jackson County. He was noted for
his skill in forecasting the seasons and weather.

Levi Moore, the third, went to Nebraska where it is
reported he amassed a large fortune in the fur trade.
Having no family of his own, he adopted his nephew,
John Moore one of Andrew's sons.

The Hon Levi Moore's second marriage was with
Mary McCarty, daughter of Timothy McCarty, a Revolutionary veteran, and the ancestor of the widely extended McCarty relationship in our county.

Rachel Moore, a daughter of this marriage, became
the wife of James Sharp, on Thorny Creek, and mi-

grated to Iowa.

Susannah Crist Moore, another daughter, was married to Stephen Hadden, and also went to Iowa.

Mrs Mary Jane Moore, the third daughter, makes her home with her daughter, Mrs Matilda Moore, near Mt Zion Church.

George Moore, the youngest son, was about as tall as his father. He spent some years in the west. He returned to Pocahontas about 1841, and was a pupil at the first session taught in the Pocahontas Academy, at Hillsboro, in 1842. The Rev Joseph Brown was Principal. He had the profession of medicine in view and was studious to a fault in his efforts to qualify himself. Mr Brown took much interest in the quiet and exemplary student, so intensely anxious for intellectual improvement. After all his hard labor, the young man was seized with pulmonary disease, aggravated by his close application to books, and died at the home of his sister, Mrs Rebecca Irvine, on Back Creek. The writer remembers him well, and he feels the pathos of "the Epitaph" in Gray's "Elegy of a Country Churchyard."

Levi Moore, Senior, located 575 acres of a "British survey on the headwaters of Knapps Creek. After the Revolutiun new requirements were made in order to secure permanent possession. It was to pay a requisite fee, a warrant would be laid, and a patent granted by the federal government. The new papers are dated 1798, and attested by Henry Grimes and Allen Poage, and signed by James Madison, Governor of Virginia.

Previous to this survey George Poage had laid a warrant on two thousand acres, which would have included the 575 acres claimed by the Moores. At first the Moores contested for the British right, but when they found such was not valid they then availed themselves of the provision authorizing exchange of warrants. Levi Moore, Junior, appears in this new arrangement as assignee of Levi Moore, Senior, for lands adjoining the lands of Aaron Moore, who was living at that time on the Herold place. So when a warrant held elsewhere was exchanged for the warrant on the land adjoining Aaron Moore, was agreed upon by Poage and Levi Moore, it came about that when the patent was applied for, George Poage stated the fact that there had been an exchange of warrants, and at Poage's request the title for 575 acres was vested in Levi Moore, Junior, as assignee of Levi Moore, Sr.

This transaction is interesting and instructive, as showing the spirit of the times, and how business men acted on the principles of an enlightened and pure conscience. So far as the letter of the law went, Poage could have held the 575 acres, with all the improvements and good qualities of the land; yet within his breast there was the higher law of a conscience void of offense toward God and man, and he keeps his fellow citizen from suffering from the mistake he made when he relied on the validity of British right, which had been declared null and void by the results of the Revolution. At the time, the warrant elsewhere bore no comparison, in real value, to the warrant for the lands adjoining the lands of Aaron Moore.

The golden rule comes in, and an enlightened conscience decides the matter. The spirit did right when the letter of the law would have been a shield for robbery. It makes us feel proud of our pioneer people to catch glimpses of what manner of men they were.

It is a sad day for any generation or family relationship to have it said of them that, like potatoes, the "best parts of them are in the ground."

The record of this transaction is carefully preserved, and may be consulted time and again in the future as a testimony of what it is to be fair and square.

JOHN MOORE.

"Pennsylvania" John Moore is represented by a worthy posterity, and deserves special mention as one of the Pocahontas Pioneers. He was among the immigrants from Pennsylvania, and as there were several John Moores, the soubriquet "Pennsylvania" was and is attached to his name. Upon his marriage with Margaret Moore, daughter of Moses Moore, scout, hunter, and pioneer, John Moore settled and opened up the place now occupied by David Moore, near Mount Zion Church, in the Hills. Their family consisted of three sons and eight daughters.

Martha Moore became Mrs John Collins, and lived in Upshur County, West Virginia.

Jennie lived to be grown and died of cancerous affection.

Nancy Moore was married to Peter Bussard, and they had their home near Glade Hill.

Hannah Moore married Martin Dilley, and lived where Mrs Martha Dilley now resides.

Pœbe Moore became Mrs Samuel McCarty, and lived where Peter McCarty now lives.

Elizabeth Moore was married to Daniel McCarty, a soldier of the War of 1812, and lived where Sheldon Moore now dwells.

Margaret Moore married Eli Bussard, and lived where their son, Armenius Bussard, now lives.

Rebecca Moore was married to John Sharp, from near Frost, and lived on the place now occupied by Joseph Moore, near the Bussard neighborhood.

William Moore, son of the Pennsylvania immigrant, married Margaret Callahan, of Bath County, Va., and opened up the homestead now owned by William Jeff Moore. In reference to William Moore's family the following particulars are in hand:

James C. Moore married Hester Nottingham, from Glade Hill. Their children are Adam C., William, and Mrs W. H. Gabbert, near Huntersvllle. Adam and William Moore live on the old homestead with their mother. James C. Moore, their father, was a Confederate soldier. He died of wounds received during the memorable seven days fight around Richmond, and was buried near Greenwood Tunnel, Va.

William Jefferson Moore married Loretta Grimes, and lives on the paternal homestead near Mount Zion. They are the parents of these sons and daughters: Mattie Elizabeth, George Ellsworth, Charles King Caroline Frances, Fannie Amoret, Myrtle Florence, Ira H., and Hattie.

Mary Jane Moore, sister of James and Jefferson Moore, was married to Ralph Dilley and lived on another section of the paternal homestead.

This worthy man, William Moore, came to end his industrious, useful life under very sad circumstances. A fire had broken out from a clearing near his home, and with no one with him he endeavored to check its progress. In doing so he seems to have been overcome with fatigue and was suffocated by the smoke and flames. He was therefore found dead in the track of the fire, on the 4th of April, 1866.

John Moore, son of John Moore the Pennsylvania emigrant, married Mary Hannah, one of Joseph Hannah's daughters, on Elk, and settled on a portion of the pioneer homestead now occupied by David Moore. One of his sons, Joseph, married Susan Bussard, and lives near Frost. Another son, David, married Matilda Moore, and lives on the homestead where his father had lived before him. Alfred, another son of John Moore, Junior, lives with his brother, Joseph Moore.

James W. Moore, a son of John Moore, Junior, married Margaret Nottingham, and lives on a section of the Moore homestead.

William Moore, the only son of the James Moore just mentioned, was a Confederate soldier. He was captured near Richmond in 1862, and was never heard from afterwards. He sleeps in some unknown grave, far from his kindred and the friends that remember him so tenderly.

John Moore, the ancestor of this branch of the Moore relationship, was one of the families that came first to Pennsylvania and thence to Virginia, early in the seventies of the eighteenth century. Except by marriage, there is no well authenticated relationship known to exist between his family and the other families of the Moore name—so numerous in our county—and who have performed such an important service in opening up prosperous homes, in the face of such serious obstacles, so bravely and perseveringly met and overcome by them.

We younger people, who were permitted to begin where the pioneers left off, can scarcely realize what it cost in laborious privation, in personal discomfort and inconvenience, in wear and tear of mind and body, to make possible what seems to come to us as naturally as the air we breathe. In a modified sense, the same qualities that were requisite in clearing lands, and rearing homes, and making improvements, in the first place, are needed to retain what has been done, and add thereto. Eternal vigilence is said to be the price of liberty that cost the blood and lives of the brave. So, in a higher sense, enternal industry and economy is the price of a living from the lands reclaimed at such a cost by those who worked and suffered while they lived for our good and their own.

GEORGE KEE.

The late George Kee was one of the early settlers of our county, and deserves a place in the history of the the Pocahontas people. He was a native of Tyrone, Ireland. He and his brother William left Ireland when he was under age, and owing to the shipping regulations was not allowed to embark as a regular passenger. Young Kee went aboard to see his brother off, and concealed himself until too far away at sea to put him off the vessel. The intention was to take him back, but upon landing at Philadelphia he eluded the parties in search of him, and escaped to the country.

He came to America in 1780, landing at Philadelphia after a voyage of thirteen weeks. At Lancaster City the brothers spent some time, and separated at that place and never met again, and Mr Kee never heard anything more of him.

From Lancaster Mr Kee went to Lakeville, near the Susquehanna River, where he staid for some time. From Lakeville he came to Pendleton County, West Virginia, where he met a relative, Aaron Kee. This relative was a merchant, and furnished Gorge Kee some goods, and sent him to Pocahontas County, (then Bath), to dispose of them. He became acquainted with John Jordan, who had been in that business before him, and Mr Jordan had him make his home with him, and for six or seven years he spent the most of his time in the Levels at John Jordans.

It seems, too, that the young Irish merchant was fond of making trips to Joshua Buckley's on the east bank of the Greenbrier, opposite the mouth of Swago Creek. Hetty Buckley, with her smart and tidy ways, took his fancy, and they were married 1800, and opened up their home at the place now occupied by Aaron Kee, a grandson, two miles below Marlinton.

There were six sons and one daughter. Two of the

sons died in childhood.   The four sons that lived to be
grown were Joshua Buckley, Andrew, John, and William.   The daughter's name was Hannah.

Hannah married Timothy Clunen, a native of Ireland, and lived on Bucks Run,   Her children were
Hetty, who became Mrs Sterling Campbell, and lived
on head of Swago; Margaret, now Mrs Luther Kellison
on the Greenbrier near the mouth of Beaver Creek.
Nancy is Mrs Daniel McNeill, at Buckeye.   George
Clunen and Buckhannon Clunen live in Missouri.
Allie Clunen lives in Indiana.   Elizabeth Clunen lives
at the old home on Swago.

Joshua B. Kee, the eldest son of the Kee family,
married Rebecca Stevenson, of Bath County, and settled on the Greenbrier, a mile below Marlinton.   Esther and Rachel were the names of his daughters, and
they both died when about grown.   Joshua Kee was a
person of remarkable mechanical skill.   He could
work in stone, iron, and wood, as well as farm.   His
specialty was gunsmithing, in which he excelled, and
in his time when so much hunting was done this was
of great service to the people.

Andrew Kee married Mary Duncan, on Stony Creek
a sister of the late Henry Duncan.   Her family came
from Collierstown, a few miles from Lexington, Rockbridge, Virginia.   His children were Hannah, Jane,
Nancy, and Esther.   The two latter died during the
war, and had grown to womanhood.   It was about this
time that camp fever and diphtheria ravaged this whole
region, and swept away in some instances all but one
or two of entire families, and Andrew Kee's was one

such. Mrs Kee was the only survivor, and lived a widow more than thirty years.

Andrew Kee lived on the Greenbrier, near Buckeye, on the place now held by William A. Duncan. He was a very expert marksman and successful hunter. It was no uncommon thing for him to shoot squirrels across the Greenbrier with his mountatn rifle, over 100 yards. Many would think it good shooting to hit a deer that distance with such a weapon.

John Kee married Hester Gwin, a daughter of James Gwin, Senior, near Gall Town, Highland, and a neice of Mrs Rebecca Kee, mentioned elsewhere. John Kee lived at the homestead, and the names of his children were James, Alcinda, Dallas, Aaron, Samuel, Susan, Henrietta, and Hester.

James Kee was a Union soldier in the regular service, and died in the war at Winchester, Virginia.

Alcinda became Mrs George McKeever, and lives on Swago.

Aaron Kee married Milly McNeill, and settled on the Kee homestead. Samuel Kee lives with his brother Aaron.

Hester Kee first married William Poage and lived near Edray. Her second marriage was with Henry Poage.

Like his brothers, John Kee was an expert worker in different callings. His specialty was wagon making along with farming.

William Kee, son of George Kee, married Ruth McCollam, and settled on a part of the homestead now occupied by Captain J. R. Apperson. Their children were Eliza, George, Matilda, and William.

Eliza was a young person of much promise, and a highly esteemed and successful teacher. She died December 19, 1861, aged 22 years, and in a week before her father's lamented death.

George M. Kee first married Mary J. Palser, and settled on a section of his father's homestead. Locke and Eliza were the children of this marriage. The second marriage was with Rachel Moore. They have six children. George M. Kee was a Confederate soldier. He has filled several positions in county affairs, as magistrate, commissioner of the court, &c.

Matilda Kee was married to Captain J. R. Apperson, and lived on the homestead.

William L. Kee, who lives near Washington City, and holds a position in the Land Office, is the youngest of William Kee's family. His wife was Catherine Phares, daughter of William Phares, near Elkins.

William Kee, the youngest son of George Kee the ancestor, was a very estimable person, being an honest industrious citizen, he was of great service to the community in which he lived. He was one of the most public spirited citizens of his times. He and his brothers, Joshua, Andrew, and John, built with their own hands and at their own expense one of the most comfortable school houses anywhere in their section of the county, in order to have their children educated. It was near the stone quarry. Mr Kee's wife was Ruth McCollam, daughter of William McCollam and Sally Drennan his wife. They were married in 1837. He died December 25, 1862. She died February 5, 1897, aged 79 years, 9 months, and 14 days.

George Kee, the progenitor of the Kee relationship, was in many respects a very remarkable person. He read a great deal, and reflected on what he did read, and could converse fluently and intelligently on whatever subject that was discussed in books or the public journals. He was the first person that I had ever heard say anything about John Locke, the eminent mental philosopher, and one of the foremost metaphysicians of his day. Mr Kee was anxious for me to read the book, and insisted on me to do so whenever I was able to lay my hands on it. His copy was worn out, and he had not been able to get another, as he had frequently tried. So it turned out that one of the first books I looked for in the college library was Locke on the Human Understanding, an old book and out of print. In subsequent years when attending lectures, I found that one of the ablest lecturers did not seem as familiar with Locke as my old friend in his mountain home. Lock had become somewhat of a back number with his innate ideas, and a different theory was coming into vogue. The new theory was to cram the mind, and the more it should be crammed the more the education imparted. Now the tendency is beginning to show itself to work from within, and develop the mental faculties so that the mind is prepared to receive and make use of whatever it finds without that would be useful. With some qualifying conditions, Locke's theory is coming into use, and it may be thinkers will reach the position occupied by our old friend, 60 years ago, and claim honor and recognition for original research in educational affairs.

He had a passionate love for trees. He looked upon a tree as something of more real worth and use than gold or silver. If the forests were to be destroyed, his notion was that people would become like the traveler suffering from hunger and thirst on the desert, who noticed a well filled pouch not far ahead of him. Uttering a joyful exclamation, he hastened to pick it up. Upon opening it he found it filled with pearls of the most precious and valuable quality. such as queens only could afford to wear. The traveler threw it down and exclaimed: "Alas, I thought I was finding dates to quench my thirst and relieve my hunger."

He was a Jacksonian Democrat—first, last, and all the time. Were he alive now, with unchanged sentiments, Henry George would have had one friend in Pocahontas that he could have relied on through evil as well as good report.

Mr Kee claimed to be an Associate Reformed Presbyterian, commonly known as the Seceders or Covenanters. It was a blessing to our county to have such a person as Mr Kee identified with its history. I think this is a sentiment with which all will agree who remember something of his sterling character.

HENRY DILLEY,

Among the early settlers of our county, Henry Dilley deserves more than a passing notice. He was one of the four Dilley brothers, one of whom was the late Martin Dilley. It is believed the Dilleys came from

Maryland, and very probably of French descent.

Henry Dilley went over to John Sharp's, the early settler of Frost, often enough to persuade his daughter Margaret to have him for better or worse, and they were happily married and settled on Thorny Creek, and as long as Dilleys Mill will be known his name will not be forgotten. Mr Dilley never doubted the truth of the Bible—especially that place in Genesis where it speaks of the ground bringing forth "thorns and thistles." he had enough of these things to contend with on his Thorny Creek land, where he settled, opened up a home, and built a mill—one of the best of its kind at that day—and its successor keeps up a good reputation as Dilley's mill yet. Men may come and men may go, but the beautiful perennial stream, that was utilized by Henry Dilley, still goes on in its useful service for the benefit of his children's children, and a great many others, far and near.

Joseph Dilley, son of Henry Dilley, married Mary Ann, a daughter of the late Joseph Friel, on Greenbrier River, five miles above Marlinton, and near the mouth of Thorny Creek, and settled on a part of the homestead, where he yet lives.

Thomas Dilley married Peachy VanReenan, a native of Holland, and lived on Cummings Creek. He was a Confederate soldier.

Ralph Dilley married Mary Jane, daughter of William Moore, near Mount Zion, and settled on a section of the Moore homestead, at one of the head springs of Moore's Run, which debouches into Knapps Creek at Brown Moore's. Four daughters and one son composed their family.

Daniel Dilley married a daughter of the late Dr Addison Moore, near Edray, and migrated to Iowa.

William Dilley first married Mary Friel, daughter of Jeremiah Friel, the pioneer on the Greenbrier at the mouth of Thorny Creek, and settled in Huntersville as the village blacksmith, in which occupation his skill was very superior. His second marriage was with Elizabeth Baker. There were four children by this marriage. William Dilley's third marriage was with Ann Drepperd, and by this marriage there were five sons and three daughters.

John Dilley, son of Henry Dilley, was a mechanic of remarkable skill to be a self trained workman. He was honest and industrious, and it is believed by his friends that he sacrificed his health in his devotion to his useful calling through exposure. What he suffered it is hard for anyone to realize. His wife was Ellen Friel. These persons lived for years on Stony Creek. Their daughter Frances married Lieutenant Henry M. Poage. He was a gallant Confederate officer, and was killed near Warrenton, Virginia. Mrs Poage had died some time previously. They were survived by one daughter, who is now Mrs Sallie Woods Beery, of Rockingham County, Virginia. A Pocahontas camp of Confederate veterans has given to Lieutenant Poage the highest honor they can confer when they named their organization the Moffett Poage Camp, which has Marlinton for the place of rendezvous.

The name Dilley indicates a French origin, and although Martin Dilley claimed to be of German de-

scent, it does not necessarily follow that the family is
of pure German origin. A very important element of
the immigration to this country in the previous century
were the Huguenot French, who had refugeed from
France about or soon after 1685, to England, Holland,
and Germany, and thence to the New World, as it was
then so frequently called.

William Penn's colony had great attractions for the
Germans, and for many others besides. It is altogether possible, and quite probable, that there were Dilleys
(Dilles) from France among the exiles, and found their
way to Germany; and after living there some years,
thetr children, hearing of the advantages to be
had in America, came over along with the German
immigrants, and regarded themselves as such. As a
general thing, the Huguenot people were employed in
the shops and manufactures; but what was the loss of
France was the gain of continental countries and many
places in the United States, as the reader may readily
learn by reference to history.

For a long time, too, Lord Baltimore's Maryland
colony was really one of the best places for the early
immigrants, and a great many of the early settlers of
Maryland were attracted by the inducements he offered. But as "burnt children dread the fire," it is not
likely that very many of the French protestants should
be inclined to settle permanently in a Roman Catholic
colony, managed by an avowed Roman Catholic. To
Lord Baltimore's credit, however, let it be remembered that there was more of religious tolerance under his
administration than almost anywhere else in the civil-

ized world of that period. Some writers go so far as to say that Maryland was the birth place of religious toleration. The matter is an interesting one to inquire into.

JOHN SMITH.

This paper is designed to perpetuate the memory of two very deserving persons, who were among the first to open up a home on Stony Creen near its source, now known as the West Union neighborhood. John Smith was a native of Ireland. He came to this region a hundred and thirty years ago, from Pennsylvania, and upon becoming acquainted with the family of Levi Moore, the pioneer at Frost, he made love to Sally Moore, one of the daughters. Upon their marriage the two young people took a fancy to the large spring that gushes so copiously and beautifully from the rocky cliffs at the source of Stony Creek, and settled close by it and built up their home. The place is now occupied by the family of the late Captain William Cochran. Some particulars in regard to their sons and daughters have been already given in other biographic papers, that need not be repeated here in full. In addition, therefore, to what has been written the following fragmentary items of their history are recorded.

John Smith, Junior, married Fannie Cochran, daughter of the late John Cochran, near Marvin, and settled on the place now in possession of John Young, a great-grandson of John Smith, Senior, near Edray.

He afterwards moved to Roane County, and lived at the three forks of Reedy. He was a Union sympathizer, and was arrested by the Confederate military as such; but when it was ascertained that he was not a dangerous person, he was paroled on his honor, but died on his return home.

Andrew Smith's wife was Nancy Cackley, daughter of Levi Cackley, on Stamping Creek. After settling and living for a time at the old Stony Creek homestead, he moved to the State of Missouri.

Elizabeth Smith became Mrs Jacob Drennan. After living some years in Braxton County, they moved to Nicholas County, and located on Peter's Creek, fourteen miles west of Summersville, where members of their family yet reside.

Ann Smith was married to Captain William Young, and lived many years on the place near Hamlin Chapel now in possession of George C. Moore. She was a person of great industry, fine mental endowments, and a model homekeeper, and intelligently, sincerely pious. The writer remembers her and members of her family as cherished friends. Late in life she went west and died but a few years since at a very advanced age in the State of Iowa. The first wife of Captain James M. McNeill was one of her daughters. The late Colonel Samuel Young was her eldest son. Adam Young was another son. The only survivors of her family now in Pocahontas are her grandsons, John Young and Adam Young and their children.

Rebecca Smith was married to John Auldridge, and lived on Laurel Creek, a few miles from the old homestead, farther west. These worthy people reared an interesting and exemplary family, of whom special mention is made in the Auldridge memoirs.

Mrs Rebecca Auldridge died in 1899, over ninety years of age. Her last years were spent with her daughter, Mrs Nancy Newcomer, in the town of Ronceverte, and was hale and hearty up to the time of her death from extreme old age. Her late home was but a step or two from the Chesapeake and Ohio Railway on one side, and the other is at the edge of the Saint Lawrence boom, whence the logs are floated to the mills by the million. How different the surroundings of her youth and early life from those of her old age. A more marked contrast can scarcely be imagined. There is scarcely an hour, day or night, free from the thundering of the trains, fast or slow, and Mrs Auldridge seemed to regard them no more than she once regarded the rustle of the falling leaves around the old Laurel Run homestead, sixty miles away from the iron road.

Hannah Smith became the wife of Richard Auldridge, a brother of John Auldridge just mentioned. After living some years at the Smith homestead, they went to Braxton County. and were happily situated on Wolf Creek at the opening of the late sad war between the States. Mr Auldridge sympathized with the Southern Confederacy, and was killed. Both sons were in the Southern army. John Auldridge fell at the battle of Gettysburg. Allen Auldridge survived the war, witn an honorable record as a brave and faithful soldier. He sought a home in the State of Kansas,

taking his mother annd sister with him. Mrs Auldridge sleeps in her Kansas grave, while at last accounts
her son and daughter are keeping house and doing
well, as good dutiful children deserve.

Sally Smith was married to Robert Rodgers, and for
some years lived in Buckeye Cove, near Swago. Afterwards they settled in Nicholas County, West Virginia,
where Mrs Rodgers still lives, far advanced in years.

Martha Smith became Mrs Samuel Young. They
lived for a few years on a section of the old homestead
and finally moved to Logan County, Ohio, where their
descendants mostly have their present homes, and enjoy the fruits of honest labor and judicious management.

Thus we have been able to lay before our readers
some information in regard to these worthy persons
and their two sons and six daughters. In their day
their home was a place where the young people had
good times, as good times went in the pioneer era.
At log rollings, quiltings, wool picking, and flax pull-
ings the youngsters met, fell in love, and did much of
their courting. Sundays it would be preaching or all
day prayer meetings, when it was not deemed right
and proper to think and talk about anything but
Heaven and heavenly things. The grandest social
events would be the weddings, that occurred just as
fast as the young folks thought themselves old enough
to get married and go to themselves.

Mrs Smith survived her husband a good many years,
—and did her part well,—saw her children settled
in life. When the time came, folded her busy hands

in rest and quietly went to sleep. It is a comforting
reflection that here and there on the hillsides of our
beautiful land are planted immortal sleepers—like the
bodies of these worthy people—that will some day appear in all that is radiant and lovely. It is touching
to reflect how widely apart are the graves of their
children. Kansas, Ohio, Iowa, Missouri, and West
Virginia have graves where members of this family are
waiting for the coming of the Redeemer they learned
to know and love in the old paternal home on Stony
Creek.

WILLIAM YOUNG.

This sketch is designed to perpetuate the memory of
an early citizen of our county, whose influence was on
the side of morality and education.

Samuel Young, ancestor of the Youngs af Pocahontas, was a native of London. He came to America
about 1756, leaving his parents, John and Amy
Young, in England, and settled in Madison County,
Virginia. He afterwards lived some years on Knapps
Creek, Pocahontas County. He entered lands, and
then sold much of it to settlers for ginseng, deer skins,
and furs. This produce he took away to Winchester
er Fredericksburg, and exchanged for merchandise,
which he bartered or peddled, and thus acquired considerable wealth. When he became quite old, he visited his son Charles, in Kentucky, and never returned.

John Young, one of his sons, was born in Madison

County, February18, 1761. He volunteered in the
war of the Revolution, served his term of enlistment,
and then was drafted into the service.

About 1803 or 1804, he came to Anthony Creek, in
Greenbrier, and remained a few years. In the mean-
time he inherited considerable land on Swago Creek.
In 1809 he settled on Swago and opened up the
"Young Place," that commands such a beautiful pros-
pect from the sides of Rich Mountain.

John Young was married twice. His first wife was
Sarah Rogers, and during her life he lived in Madison
County. The names of her children were James, Eliz-
abeth, John, Jane, Samuel, and William. She died
July 6, 1806, leaving her youngest child William aged
four years.

John Young married Margaret Rogers, on Anthonys
Creek, in 1804. The names of her children were
Sarah Ann, Martha, and Andrew.

Her daughter, Mrs Martha Adkinson, was living in
1894, on the "Young Place," in her 78th year, and
the only survivor of one of the original pioneer families of our county. She had been blind for seven
years, with cataract, and most of her time was busily
occupied in knitting.

John Young died July 5, 1843, aged 82 years, 4
months, and 18 days. Captain William Young was
born in Madison County, May 1798, and was about 5
years old when his father moved to this region. His
youth was spent on the sides of Rich Mountain. His
first teachers were William Auldridge, Squire John
McNeill, and William McNeill. The school house was

on Rush Run, a mile or so from its confluence with
Swago Creek. In early manhood he entered John
McNulty's school, at the McNulty Place, near Marvin
Chapel. From this teacher he learned surveying.
which qualified him for the office he held for a number
of years. The text book used by Captain Young in
the study of surveying is yet in the possession of Capt.
William Cochran's family, whose first wife was Capt.
Young's sister Elizabeth. On its well filled title page
appears the following:

GEODÆSIA, or the Art of Surveying and Measuring
of Land made easy; showing by plain and Practical
Rules how to survey. Moreover, A more sure and
facile Way of Surveying by the Chain than has hitherto
been taught. As also how to lay out New Lands in
America or elsewhere, with Several other Things never
yet Published in our

Language.

By JOHN LOVE,

The Seventh Edition,

London, 1760.

In the address to the reader, the author says: What
would be more ridiculous than for me to praise an art
that all mankind know they can not live peaceably
without. It is near hand as ancient (no doubt on't) as
the world. For how could men set down to plant
without knowing some distinction and boundary of
their land. But (necessity being the mother of inven-
tion) we find the Egyptians, by reason of the Nile's
overflowing—which either washed away all their bound
marks, or covered them over with mud, brought this
measuring of land first into an art, and honoured much

the professors of it. The great usefulness, as well as
the pleasant and delightful study and wholesome exercise of which tempted so many to apply themselves
thereto, that at length in Egypt, as in the Bermudas,
every rustic could measure his own land.

On a fly leaf is this, in the handwriting of the young
student, now in the 20th year of his age:

> William Young, his book. Bought of
> Mr John McNulty, price six shillings.
> Aprile 16th, 1818, on Thursday.

Previously to him the following persons seemed to
have owned the book:

> Israel Hollowell, May 9, 1775
> John Goodrich, February 13, 1794
> Joseph Fisherton, January 30, 1795
> George Harrison, February 13, 1805
> Joseph McNulty.

This copy was bound in very substantial calf skin,
and when it became worn on the back edges by sixty
years service in so many hands, it was repaired by a
wide strip of dressed deer skin, sewed on by waxed
threads such as shoemakers use.

His tuition for two months was nine shillings, ($1.50)
—seventy-five cents per month.   Having learned surveying with Mr McNulty Captain Young taught school
a few months, and then repaired to Lewisburg, West
Virginia, where he studied grammer, taught by Dr
McElhenney, as a specialty, according to old Green-
leaf of bitter memory to grammar students of that

period. One study at a time, was the rule then. People have learned differently since. Upon his return from Lewisburg, Mr Young opened a school on Stony Creek, in the school house near George Baxters. His first grammar scholar was Samuel Waugh, brother of the late Rev John Waugh of revered memory. The school was taught by on the open or vocal plan, and Samuel Waugh did not object to the noise. Captain Young seems to have had the monopoly of grammar teaching on Stony Creek for many years.

Having completed his education, so advanced for his day, and under so many difficulties, his thoughts turned to settling himself in life. He was happily married to Miss Ann Smith, and built up a home on Stony Creek, and reared up a highly respectable family of sons and daughters.

He was the captain of the Stony Creek Company, Justice of the Peace, and was the second Surveyor of Pocahontas County, successor to Sampson Mathews.

He was a very quiet, exemplary person in youth, but did not unite with any church until somewhat advanced in life, when he became a member of the Methodist church.

He died of consumption, November 24, 1848, and his grave is in the Duffield grave yard, marked by a lettered stone. His widow and most of the children went west. Mrs Young was a person of uncommon force of character, and was much esteemed for her many virtues. She died in her far western home, 8th of May, 1891, aged 90 years.

Adam Young, one of the sons, married Susan Gay.

and their two sons, John and Adam, are about all of
Captain. Young's descendants—of his name—in the
county, with whose history he was so prominently
identified for so many years.

Colonel Samuel Young, whose memory was recently
honored by a large outpouring of the citizens at the
Sulphur Spring, Sunday, May 3, 1894,—according to
an appointment made forty years before, that if alive,
he would meet them there that day—was his second
son. He was a local preacher, and afterwards an officer in the Union army. He did not live to meet his
unique appointment, and among those who assembled
forty years after, there were eleven who were present
at the original meeting, which was a preaching service
in the open air, a large rock serving for a pulpit.

ADAM CURRY.

A generation since, one of the best known characters in West Highland, Virginia, was Captain Adam
Curry, a Revolutionary veteran. One of his grandsons, William Curry, is a well known citizen of Pocahontas County.

Captain Curry was a native of Scotland, and came
to America, and resided several years near Manasses
Junction. He was among the first to enlist in the war
of the Revolution, ond was chosen captain of his company, and participated in all the engagements in which
Virginia troops were engaged that followed Mercer
and Washington.

Soon after the war he gathered up the remnants of

his property and moved to Augusta County, locating in the Back Creek valley on property now owned by William Crummett in southwest Highland. He settled in the woods and raised a large family of sons and daughters. He was honest in his dealings, and was held in much esteem for his high sense of honor and patriotic impulses. It seems almost too strange to be believed that he would not accept a pension, offered him for his services as a brave and faithful officer in the Revolutionary struggle. He always declared that the service was its own reward. Instead of being a hardship, military service was the greatest pleasure of his life. He desired no better recompense than the fun he had, and the pleasure it gave him to see liberty secured for his invaded country. He was proverbially neat in dress and polished in his manners. To the close of his life, some forty or fifty years ago, he dressed in the colonial style—knee breeches, long stockings, and shoes with silver buckles.

He retained his habits of court life as to diet and sleeping as long as he lived. He died at the age of one hundred and five years, with but few signs of decrepitude visible. To the last he was erect as a young grenadier, cheerful in spirit, and mental faculties active apparently as ever. His remains are in the Matheny grave yard, near the Rehobeth Church, in the Back Valley, a few miles from his home.

A European traveler spent some time near Manasses, where Captain Curry lived before his removal to Highland. He speaks of meeting a party of gentlemen on a tavern porch: "No people could exceed these people in politeness. On my ascending the steps to the piazza every countenance seemed to say, 'This man has a double claim to our attention, for he is a stranger in the place.' In a moment there was room made for me to sit down, and every one who addressed me did it with a smile of conciliation. But no man asked me where I had come or whither I was going. A gentleman in every country is the same; and if good breeding consists in sentiment, it was found in the circle I had got into. The higher Virginians seemed to venerate themselves as men; and I am persuaded there was not one in company who would have felt embarrassed at being admitted to the presence and conversation of the greatest monarch on earth. There is a compound of virtue and vice in every human character; no man was ever yet faultless; but whatever may be advanced against Virginians, their good qualities will ever outweigh their defects, and when the effervescence of youth is abated—when reason asserts her empire— there is no man on earth who discovers more exalted sentiments, more contempt of baseness, more love of justice, more sensibility of feeling than a Virginian.''

Having lived for years in such society, we are prepared to believe all that has been written and told of Captain Adam Curry.

Late in the summer of 1861, some Confederate troops, commanded by Colonel William L. Jackson, were stationed at Huntersville, and used the Clerk's office for barracks. In the place of straw they scattered the office papers pell-mell on the floor and spread their blankets. It also became apparent the Federals

would soon enter the place, and so the court directed
their clerk, William Curry, to look out a safe place for
the county records.

In obedience to instructions, he secured the assistance of R. W. Hill, then a youth too young for military service, with a team. The clerk removed the
records to Joel Hill's residence, near Hillsboro, where
they remained until January, 1862. Deeming it necessary to seek a safer place, Mr Curry arranged for the
transportation of the records to Covington, via Lewisburg, young R. W. Hill teamster. For a time quarters were had in the upper rooms of William Scott's
store house, and afterwards for a few weeks room was
furnished in the county clerk's office.

September, 1853, on General Averill's approach to
Covington, Mr Curry carried the records to William
T. Clark's, eight miles north of Covington, and for
three weeks had them concealed in a rick of buckwheat
straw. The buckwheat patch was in the midst of a
forest and well hidden from view.

Matters became so threatening that arrangements
were made to made to move them into the mountains,
four miles east, to the residence of a Baptist minister,
absent as a soldier in the Confederate army, leaving
his home in the care of his wife and small girl as sole
occupants. He was assisted in this removal to the
lonely mountain refuge by Andy Daugherty, one of
Mr Clark's colored men. Andy afterwards became a
citizen of Pocahontas, and lived at Clover Lick. He
deserves recognition for his fidelity, because for two
years the safety of the records depended on his not

telling about them.

In June, 1865, after surrender at Appomattox, Mr Curry, assisted by John B. Kinnison, with a three horse team, carried the records back to Joel Hill's and in a month later placed them in a nearby house belonging to the Rev Mitchell D. Dunlap, where they remained until September, 1865. The first court after the war was held at Hillsboro, November, 1865, in the Methodist church; and from that time the records were kept in the old Academy building until June, 1866, when they were returned to Huntersville and placed in the residence of John Garvey, near the court house, and then after a few months were replaced in the office. Something more than five years intervened between the first removal and the final return of the records, and notwithstanding the risks encountered and the vicissitudes of war times, nothing was lost but an old process book of no intrinsic importance. This loss is believed to have occurred while the office was in use as Confederate barracks.

So far as known there is no other like instance of fidelity to official duty that surpasses the preservation of the Pocahontas County records. There were ten removals in all, from first to last, and when returned six months were spent in assorting and replacing the papers.

JOHN McLAUGHLIN.

For the past seventy-five or eighty years the Mc-Laughlin name has been a familiar one among our peo-

ple. For this reason the relationship so long identified
with our county history deserves special mention there
for. This relationship will be considered in groups as
it is so numerous and widely distributed and derived
from a varied though related ancestry.

John McLaughlin, the ancestor of several Pocahontas families of that name, was a native of Ireland, and
settled on Jackson's River, seven or eight miles below
Monterey, and was one of the pioneer settlers of that
vicinity previous to the Revolution. The lands he settled were lately in possession of his son, John Mc-
Laughlin, Jr.

His family consisted of six sons and five daughters.
In reference to these persons the following particulars
have been mainly learned from Mrs Morgan Grimes,
one of the descendants by the third or fourth remove.

Margaret became Mrs William Carpenter and lived
on Deer Creek, near Greenbank; Nancy was married
to John Carpenter and lived on Thomas Creek, near
Dunmore, where Peter Carpenter now lives; Jane became Mrs Alexander Benson and settled in Illinois;
Mary was married to John Beverage and lived on
Straight Creek, near Monterey; Susan became Mrs
Holcomb, and went to West Virginia; Abigail was
married to Thomas Galford and lived near Dunmore
on lands lately owned by J. H. Curry.

Major Daniel McLaughlin, upon his marriage with
Mary Carpenter, settled on Deer Creek, opening lands
now held by the Oliver Brothers. In reference to his
family the following particulars are in hand:

His son, the late David McLaughlin, married Jane

Wanless, daughter of William Wanless, on Back Alleghany, and settled on lands lately occupied by his sons Joseph and James; Abigail became Mrs A. Jackson Moore on Back Alleghany; Mary Elizabeth was married to George Sutton and lived near Greenbank; John M. McLaughlin married Mary Jane Moore, daughter of W. D. Moore on Elk. John was a Confederate soldier, taken prisoner and died at Camp Chase, Ohio; Margaret Jane was married to Morgan Grimes, and lives near Mt. Zion in the Hills.

Major Daniel McLaughlin was much respected. He was a very hard working man and almost wore himself out clearing lands. He was a major of militia and was a fine looking officer on the parades that came off annually.

Hugh McLaughlin, of John, the Irish immigrant, married Sally Grimes, daughter of Arthur, of Felix, the pioneer. He lived near Huntersville on lands now owned by Dr Patterson and others. J. A. McLaughlin, Mrs Mary Hogsett and Lieut. James Hickman McLaughlin, a Confederate officer who perished in the war, were his children. He was a popular and prominent citizen.

Samuel McLaughlin, another son of John, married a Miss Wright and lived on Jackson's River. There were two children. Mary Jane was married to Martin Sharp and lives on Little Back Creek, near Mt. Grove. H. P. McLaughlin married Alcinda Bird, daughter of the late George Bird, Valley Centre, Va. He lives on Brown Creek, near Huntersville. He was a Confederate soldier, 25th Virginia, Infantry.

Robert McLaughlin, another son of John the pioneer died in early manhood. He is reported to have been a young man of much promise.

James McLaughlin settled in Illinois soon after his marriage. His wife's name is not remembered. He was enthused by the gold excitement of 1849, and crossed the plains to California in search of wealth. He was in a measure successful. It may be said too, to his credit, he was not so very hard to satisfy, and so he returned to his family and settled in Missouri.

John McLaughlin, Junior, married Sally Hamilton, and spent his days at the homestead on Jacksons River. His children were Ewing, Ada, Sally, and Letcher.

John McLaughlin was widely known for his jovial ways and amusing expressions, and was also somewhat eccentric in his ideas. When about to be overcome by the infirmities of an advanced age, he pointed out a spot overlooking his dwelling that is well nigh inaccessible, and gave positive orders to have his body buried there. He seemed to abhor the idea of being trampled upon, and appeared to feel that his head would be secure from such indignity if he could have his grave in a spot almost impossible to reach, and so steep that erect posture would be impracticable. It was his boast that when he was alive he generally came out "on top," and so he seemed to wish to be on top when not alive.

His friends saw to it that his wishes should be complied with to the very letter. A more unique burial scene was never witnessed in that region. The pall-bearers on their knees and holding to the bushes and rocks with one hand and the coffin handles with the other, and the procession following on all fours, compose a scene the like of which may never be witnessed while the world stands Here an illustration of the ruling passion strong in death.

The second group of McLaughlin relationship trace their ancestry to two brothers and two sisters of that name who settled in Pocahontas early in the century. How near the relationship is, the writer has not the requisite information. William and John McLaughlin and their sisters Jennie and Nancy are the persons remembered as the ancestry of the second group.

William McLaughlin married Nancy Wylie, head of Jacksons River, and settled on Thomas Creek, near Dunmore,—his lands now held by his sons Hugh and Robert. Mrs McLaughlin died a few years since at a very advanced age, of a cancerous affection. She is remembered as a faithful and devoted nurse of her sick neighbors, and her services were held in high appreciation in times when there was no physician convenient. She and her neighbor Elizabeth McCutchan were sisters of charity in the best sense of the word. Sheep saffron was their main dependance in cases of measles. They were fully posted in the virtues of herb remedies.

In reference to William McLaughlin's family, we have the following details: His daughter Jane was married to John Hiner, second wife, and lives on Jacksons River.

Rachel became Mrs Jacob Beverage, and lives on

the Old Field Fork of Elk.

Elizabeth married James Townsend, and lived on Back Alleghany, near Driftwood.

Hugh McLaughlin married Nancy Ratliff, and lives on a section of the Thomas Creek homestead. Their children are Mrs Mary Alice Brooks, Mrs Lena Deputy, William Andrew Gatewood, Jacob Renick Cassell, Brown Letcher, Minnie Belle (lately deceased), Annie, Charles, and Lola.

Robert McLaughlin was married twice, and lives on a section of the homestead. His first marriage was with Minta Rusmisell. Her children were Nebraska, Melissa, Lovie, Christopher, Catherine, Bertha, Lawrence, Cameron and Russell. The second marriage was with Lydia Rusmisell. Her children are Elmer, Joseph and Annie. These ladies were cousins and were from near Moscow, Augusta County, Va.

Nancy McLaughlin, one of the ancestral sisters, became the wife of Jacob Cassell, senior, and lived on the Greenbrier at the Cassell Ford, four miles west of Greenbank.

Jennie McLaughlin, the other ancestral sister, was married to John Galford and lived near Glade Hill on property now owned by Frank Patterson.

John McLaughlin, one of the ancestral brothers, married Clarissa Gregory and settled on the place recently owned by the late Allan Galford, mouth of Deer Creek. Their children were John, James, Elizabeth and Nancy. Elizabeth was married to Harvey Ratcliffe and went to Roane county. Nancy became Mrs Henry Higgins and lived near Clover Lick; John

married Sydney Carpenter and settled on the homestead; James married a Miss Nottingham and migrated to the West.

Hugh McLaughlin was wounded during the war,
and suffers yet from the effects. Jacob McLaughlin
died in the war. He is remembered as one of the
noblest young men that was sacrificed in the cruel war.
His bravery and good moral character reflected great
honor upon his country and kindred.

An interesting letter has been placed in our hands,
from which we are permitted to extract such parts as
may be desired. It was written at Camp Bunker Hill,
Frederick County, Virginia, on the 1st of August,
1864, by Jacob C. McLaughlin to his cousin, Nannie
McLaughlin, a sister of H. P. McLaughlin, and is the
last he was ever known to write to her. He fell at the
battle of Cedar Creek, October 19, 1864.

The extracts illustrate what our young soldiers endured when true to their sense of duty to the cause.
He speaks of his mind preoccupied with memories and
thoughts of the passing summer's dreadful campaign:
"It is lamentable to look upon, for when we started
out this spring we had fifty men, now we have only
fifteen. The rest have been killed, wounded, and tak-
en prisoners. I tell you it looks discouraging to fight
under such circumstances; through throug the mercies
of God I have been one of the few that have been
spared, which I feel very thankful for and the kind
mercies bestowed on me."

"We have had a very hard time since we came to

the Valley. We had a fight at Lynchburg, at Liberty, and at Salem; and from there we did not follow old Hunter any farther. We then came to Lexington and Staunton and down the valley to Smithfield, and there we fought them again, and at Harpers Ferry; and from there we crossed the Potomac into Maryland, and fought them at Middletown, and the next day at Frederick City. And from there we went on to within sight of Washington City, and there we fought them two days. And when we retreated from there we had to fight them on our rear all the time until we crossed the Shenandoah River, and there we stopped and gave them a good whipping; and then came up to Winchester, and they whipped our division and then we went on up the valley to Strasburg and assembled all our forces together and marched back on them at Kernstown, three miles above Winchester, and gave them a whipping that has cooled them down a good deal. They had a large force—some 20,000—and we ran them back across the river into Maryland. Since that they have been more quiet, and we returned from the Potomac up to Bunker Hill, and there is no sign of them crossing the river after us, as yet. I am in hopes they may rest awhile, for the troops are very much exhausted from their fatiguing marches, for we have been marching and fighting since the 4th day of May, and I think that is long enough to give us some rest.

"I am sorry to inform you that both of your brothers are taken prisoners, and the whole 25th Regiment, excepting about fourteen, has been taken. Though we must expect to bear with many troubles in a war like this, you all ought to be thankful that they are prisoners, instead of being killed, as there have so many poor soldiers fallen this summer. I think a prisoner now is much better off than we poor men that have to march and fight so much. At least I know they are in less danger.

"You must excuse me for not not writing to you more frequent, though I have written to you once before since I got any letter from you. I would have written oftener, only it has been out of my power to do so, on account of our not stopping long enough for me to write—and we have had no conveyance for our letters half the time we have been here. Write soon and give me all the news, and think of the many pleasures that have been, and look forward that which is to come.

Yours with much love and due respect,

JACOB C. McLAUGHLIN.

HUGH McLAUGHLIN.

The third group of the McLaughlin relationship in our county are the descendants of Squire Hugh McLaughlin, late of Marlinton. His early life was spent in part on Jacksons River, Bath County. His wife was Nancy Gwinn, daughter of John Gwinn, Senior, and grand-daughter of John Bradshaw.

Squire Hugh McLaughlin and Hugh McLaughlin, late of Huntersville, were cousins and were intimately associated when they were young men. They were married about the same time, jointly leased a piece of land on Jacksons River, built a cabin and went to housekeeping. There was but one room. This they divided between them and kept separate establishments. Squire McLaughlin would often tell how an axe, maul, and wedge made up his original business capital, and how his housekeeping effects were carried by his young wife on a horse the day they went to themselves in their cabin home on leased land.

Upon the expiration of the lease, early in the twenties, Squire McLaughlin settled in the woods on Thomas Creek, and opened up lands now held by his son George H. McLaughlin.

Mr and Mrs McLaughlin were the parents of three sons and two daughters: William Jacob, John Calvin, George Henry, Elizabeth, and Margaret.

Margaret, a promising young girl, died suddenly.

Elizabeth became Mrs George Rowan, and lived on Roaring Creek, Randolph County, and finally located near the Hot Springs, where her family now lives. Mr Rowan was one of the builders of the Marlinton bridge. He was a Confederate soldier in the war from start to finish. His young wife refugeed from Roaring Creek soon after the battle of Rich Mountain, and with her two little children, one tied behind her and the other in her arms, made the journey from Roaring Creek to the Warm Springs alone on horse back.

William Jacob McLaughlin first married Sarah Gum from Meadow Dale, Highland County, and settled near Huntersville. One daughter, Nancy Jane, who died in early youth. His second marriage was with Susan Bible, daughter of Jacob Bible near Greenbank. In this family were two sons and two daughters. Elizabeth became Mrs John M. Lightner, lately of Abilene, Texas. Alice married Dennis W. Dever and they live near Frost. Mitchel D. McLaughlin married Emma K. Greaver, of Bath, and lives near Savannah Mills, in Greenbrier County. They have five children. Jacob Andrew McLaughlin married Sally Gibson, and lives at Brimfield, Indiana.

John C. McLaughlin married Isabella, daughter of Adam Lightner, of Highland County, and settled near Huntersville. When a youth going to school at Hillsboro, he was thrown from a horse and received injuries that disabled him for manual labor. He acquired a good education, taught school, wrote in the clerk's office, and was an expert business man much respected by his fellow citizens.

G. H. McLaughlin married Ruhamah Wiley; first lived near Dunmore, but now lives at Marlinton. He was a Confederate soldier. Their children are John, Edward, William, Clarence, Fred, Fannie, Mary, and Edith.

Squire Hugh McLaughlin was married the second time to Mrs Elizabeth Gum (nee Lightner), of Highland. There were two sons by this marriage.

Harper McLaughlin first married Caroline Cackley, and lived at Marlinton. Second marriage was with Etta Yeager, of Travelers Repose.

Andrew M. McLaughlin married Mary Price, and now resides near Lewisburg. He is a prosperous grazier and farmer, and a ruling Elder in the Presbyterian church. He was a Confederate soldier.

After residing a number of years near Dunmore, Squire McLaughlin located west of Huntersville where he prospered in business. Thence he removed to Marlins Bottom, where he died in 1870, aged 69 years. Squire McLaughlin was a prominent citizen—a member of the county court, a ruling Elder in the Presbyterian church. He acquired an immense landed estate—one

of the most valuable in the county. His influence was
largely in favor of economical industry, good morals,
and intelligent piety. His business sagacity was phenomenal, and he could see money where most others
could not see anything worth looking for.

About fifty years ago the county court refused to
license saloon keepers. The whole county was convulsed with the agitation that arose. At first Squire
McLaughlin strenuously objected to this action of the
court, as doing violence to personal liberty, and de-
priving the county of revenue. Whenever the matter
was discussed this thrilling Scripture was often repeated: "Woe unto him that giveth his neighbor drink;
that putteth thy bottle to him and makest him drunken
also, that thou mayest look on their nakedness."—
Hab. ii–16.

His conscience was touched, and he resolved to clear
himself of the fearful liability implied by doing anything to license vice and the giving of drink to neighbors, and let the revenue take care of itself, which it
could well do with a sober, prosperous citizenship to
depend on.

He was also much impressed with what was reported
to have passed between two saloonists. One was complaining to another how his business had fallen off.
The other remarked that at one time he noticed his
business was on the decline—the "old suckers" were
all going to the bone yard so fast, and he saw if "new
suchers" were not to be had he would have to quit the
business. He told every young man that he met that
he had laid in some of the nicest liquors that were ever

brought in, and that if he would come around he would give him a treat. The saloonist observed that after three or four drinks the youngsters would begin to buy and his business was on the rise quite satisfactorily. Thus he had found that a few dimes in treating meant dollars to him in selling.

Squire McLaughlin's services as a member of the court for eighteen years were of much use, and along with John Gay, Paul McNeel, and Isaac Moore—being themselves large tax payers—public affairs were managed on a judicious scale, and money, as a general thing, was laid out where the prospect seemed for the greatest good to the greatest number.

While these persons, and others like minded, were on the bench, the attorneys from a distance were in the habit of saying that the Pocahontas court was so hide bound and disagreeable that it was no use to try to do anything with it, or to make anything out of it at the expense of the people. Moreover, they complained the court kept the county too dry by refusing saloon privileges. Reasons for such objections to the Pocahontas county court we most devoutly hope may never cease to exist.

JOSEPH VARNER.

The ancestor of the Varner relationship in our county was Joseph Varner. He came from Pendleton county very early in the century and settled on the Crooked Branch of Elk, on property now in possession of William A. McAllister. Mr Varner's parents, it is be-

lieved, came from Germany to Pennsylvania, thence
to Pendleton, among the earliest settlers of that county.   The given names of these parents seemed to have
been forgotten.   The father lived to the age of 112
years and died in Pendleton.   The widowed mother
came to live with her son Joseph, on Elk, and died
there, and her remains were buried near the home.
Her reputed age was 114 years, the oldest person that
ever lived in this region.

Joseph Varner's wife was Susan Herold, sister of
Christopher Herold.   They were the parents of four
sons: John, Adam, Eli and Samuel.   Their daughters
were Elizabeth, Alice, Susan and Amanda.   The Varner sisters seemed to have been ladies by nature, and
were remarkable for their beauty, spriteliness, attractive manners and tidy housekeeping.

Elizabeth became Mrs John Holden, and lived many years at Huntersville.   During the war the family
refugeed to Rockbridge and never returned.   She died
near Lexington and is buried there in the cemetary not
far from the grave of Stonewall Jackson.

Alice Varner was married to Hiram Scott, for years
a well known and highlyrespected merchant at Frankford.   Mrs Captain Dolan, at Hinton, is her daughter.

Susan Varner became Mrs Thomas Call, for many
years a tailor at Huntersville.   Her family finally went
to Missouri.

Amanda, when about fourteen years of age, was sitting on a rock just in front of her cabin home one
Sabbath evening reading her testament.   The button-
pole of the roof fell upon her, killing her instantly.

The stone is still to be seen where this mournful event occurred. She is spoken of by the older people as such a beautiful girl, and so dutiful to her parents, and so capable and helpful in domestic affairs. She had been to Sunday school and prayer meeting in the morning.

In reference to Joseph Varner's sons we note the following particulars:

Adam married Caroline, daughter of William Gibson, Sr., so many years a merchant at Huntersville, and settled in Lewis county.

Samuel Varner was a merchant tailor, a business he learned of John Holden at Huntersville. He settled at Frankford.

Eli Varner was never married. He excelled as a mower. One season while mowing at his uncle's, Christopher Herold, on Douthard's Creek, a serious accident happened him. While grinding a scythe it was struck by the crank, and, turning in his hand, came near severing it at the wrist. The flow of blood was alarming, and it seemed that he would bleed to death in spite of all that was done to check the bleeding. Mrs Katie Herold, Peter Herold's wife, gets the credit of saving his life by checking the flow of blood with the use of certain words as a charm. It is believed the words are found in Ezekial xvi, 6. "And when I passed by thee and saw thee polluted in thine own blood, I said unto thee when thou wast in thy blood, Live! Yea, I said unto thee when thou wast in thy blood, Live!"

John Varner married Isabella Hannah, daughter of

David Hannah, a soldier of the war of 1812, and an early settler on Elk. They began in the woods and built up a prosperous home at Split Rock. There were five sons, David, John, Samuel, William and Benjamin. The five daughters were Margaret, who became Mrs Clinton Slanker; Mary. who was Mrs Robert Wilson, near Lexington; Virginia Susan, now Mrs William Snyder, of Iowa; Alice, Mrs John Stewart, Valley head; Jennie became Mrs Hamilton Snyder, Taylor county, Iowa.

Samuel married Ann Showalter, of Rockbridge, and lives near Linnwood; William married Mary Gibson, of William Gibson, and lives at the Gibson homestead; Benjamin married Ella Moore, daughter of Washington Moore, and lives in Iowa; John married Mary Moore, daughter of Washington Moore and lives near the homestead.

David Varner, the eldest of John Varner's sons, is remembered and spoken of by all who knew him as a very amiable and interesting young man. He died in the battle of the Wilderness, in May, at the time the Confederate lines were broken and General Edward Jonnson's command mainly taken prisoners of war. David Varner was in his place at the front with his face to the foe. He received the fatal shot near his heart, moved a little distance and fell upon his face and was dead before a comrade could reach him. In one of his letters to his sister, Mrs Slanker, he wrote in such a way as impress the idea that he had premonitions of the sad fate which awaited him. It was his earnest wish that if should fall, to be brought home and buried. Search was made for the body, but it could not be identified. The field had been burned over about the time he had had fallen and destroyed all traces of identity.

The writer had the pleasure of meeting Mrs Elizabeth Holden at Lexington, some years after the War. Her emotions overpowered her when she endeavored to tell me what had taken place since we last met in her pleasant home in Huntersville in 1861. I was told by others that she was one of the most regular attendants upon public worship and did more than her part in the benevolent work of the congregation, considering her broken health and reverses. She plied her needle with such industry that she lived nicely and had something to spare. It greatly pleased the writer to hear it remarked, "You must have good people in Pocahontas if Mrs Holden and ———— are fair specimens." What can be more worthy of aspiration than than to be a credit to the people among whom we happen to be reared. To be a credit to our families, our religion and our county is the highest aim that can stimulate true and useful endeavor.

WILLIAM SHARP.

It appears from such information as the compiler has been able to obtain, that this person was the pioneer settler of the Huntersville vicinity, and was the first to open up a permanent residence. Traces of the building he erected are yet visible near the new road around the mountain, a few rods from where the mountain road leaves the Dunmore and Huntersville road. Mr Sharp located here about 1773, and saw service as a scout and a soldier. It is believed he came here from Augusta County, and probably lived in the vicinity of Staunton. His wife's name was Mary Meeks. She was a very amiable person, lived to a great age, and died at the home of ner son, James Sharp, many years ago. In reference to their sons and daughter the following particulars have come to hand.

Nancy Sharp was married to Levi Moore, Junior.

Margaret Sharp was married to John Kelley and lived on Michels Mountain. Her children were William, John, Anthony, Nancy, Polly, Rachel, Jennie, and Margaret.

Nancy Kelley was married to Robert Sharp, son of James Sharp on Thorny Creek, and went to Iowa.

John Kelley was a Union soldier, and died on the Kanawha during the war.

Rachel Sharp, daughter of William Sharp, was married to Jonathan Griffin, and lived near the head of Stony Creek, on the farm now owned by Levi Gay. Here children were Abraham, Benoni, Jonathan, and Mrs Charles Ruckman.

Mary Sharp became the wife of Arthur Grimes, and settled in The Hills overlooking the head of Knapps Creek. In the Grimes memoirs special mention was made of all her children except one, Sally Grimes. She became the wife of the late Hugh McLaughlin, and lived near Huntersville, at the Bridge. One of her sons was Lieutenant James Hickman McLaughlin, who died in Winchester of a wound, during the war in 1864. He was on picket at the Rapidan River. He was of a very jovial disposition, and was joking the federal pickets and having his fun with them. By way of sport he stuck out his foot and in an instant his ankle was shattered by a minnie ball. He was taken to Winchester and was doing well, until one day the hospital was thronged with ladies bringing all sorts of nice things for the wounded soldiers. The Lieutenant indulged too freely for the good of his health, and died a victim of well meant sympathy and kindness. He was one of the few Confederates killed by kindness.

John Sharp, a son of William Sharp, upon his marriage with Sarah McCollam, settled on the farm near Verdant Valley, now occupied by his grandson, John Wesley Irvine.

William Sharp, Junior, was another son of the Huntersville pioneer, and settled Verdant Valley, and a numerous posterity is descended from them. Their children were James, William, Alexander, Jacob, Paul, John, Elizabeth, Jane, Mary, Rebecca, Anna, Ellen, Nancy, and Martha. He and his resolute young wife, Elizabeth Waddell, settled in the woods and built up a fine estate out of a forest noted for the tremendous size of its walnut, redoak, and sugar maple trees, and reared a worthy family highly respected for their industry and good citizenship.

James Sharp, late of Beaver Creek, was another of the sons of William Sharp, Senior. His wife was Ann Waddell, sister of Mrs William Sharp just mentioned. He opened up a home on Cummings Creek, a part of the Huntersville homestead. The property was recently owned by the late Joseph C. Loury. Upon disposing of his property to William Cackley, Mr Sharp located on Beaver Creek, on property known as the James Sharp place. He opened up an extensive area, and prospered in worldly affairs and reared a worthy family. Ehe names of his children were Mary, Rebecca, Margaret, Martha, Nancy, Ann, Rachel, Lucinda, William, Andrew, and James.

Mary was married to William Pyles.

Rebecca became Mrs James Lewis, and lived in the Levels. Mrs Ann Clark, at Hillsboro, is a daughter of Mrs Lewis. Mrs R. C. Shrader and the late Mrs Davis Kinnison are her daughters also.

Margaret Sharp was married to Jacob Civey, on Anthonys Creek. Martha Sharp was also married to a Mr Civey of the same locality. Nancy Sharp was married to Robert Ryder, and lived on Anthonys Creek.

Ann Sharp was married to Levi Cackley, Junior.

Rachel Sharp became Mrs Robert Gay, and lived on Beaver Creek at Beaver Creek Mills, lately in possession of Wallace Beard. Hamilton B. Gay, upper Elk; Sam Gay, Williams River, and Mrs William Jordan, on Elk, are her children. Lucinda Sharp was married to Jonathan Jordan, near Hillsboro; William married Susan, daughter of Solomon Bussard and settled in the West; Andrew married a Miss Bussard; James Sharp married Mary Byrnsides, on the Greenbrier east of Hillsboro, and settled at the old homestead. He died during the war, and Mrs Sharp went to Missouri where some of her family now reside. Mrs Hanson Mc-Laughlin, of Odessa, is her daughter.

James Sharp was a member of the court under the old arrangement, was high sheriff of the county, a conscentious member of the Presbyterian church, and was held in high esteem for his patriotism and strict, scrupulous integrity. The members of the court had much confidence in his judgment and he had great influence in framing decisions. He was much in the habit of hunting at the proper season, not only for the sport, but as a matter of business, for the proceeds were useful in bartering for family supplies for the comfort and sustenance of his household. While living at his first home on Cummings Creek he had a very sensational adventure on Buckley Mountain. It was growing late and it was near the time to set out for home. He was passing leisurely along when a panther suddenly mounted a log but a few yards in front of him. He shot the animal, but when the smoke cleared away another stood in the same place on the log. This performance was repeated nine times, when the hunter became panic stricken and flanked out for home. Some time during the night the remainder of the pack followed his trail to his house and kill d a yearling calf. Properly reinforced, Mr Sharp went back to the spot where he had fired nine times and there beheld what no hunter had seen before or since. Nine panthers, but they were good panthers now; every shot had told with fatal effect. It appears that there were seasons when these animals went in packs of fifteen or twenty, and this happened to be one of the times.

JAMES WAUGH, JR.

It is proposed in this chapter to give some particulars illustrating the family history of James Waugh, Jr. He was the eldest son of James Waugh, the Scotch-Irish emigrant, who was among the first to open land and build a home in The Hills. In these memoirs he will be spoken of as James Waugh the second. Early in life he married Rebecca McGuire, from Pennsylvania, whose name indicates Scotch ancestry, and settled on the Greenbrier where James Waugh the 3rd recently lived. In reference to his family we learn that Rachel was married to Frederick Fleming, Elizabeth was married to John Ratliffe and lived on Clover Creek; Nancy became Mrs Abraham Griffin and lived many years on Buckley Mountain, a few miles east of Buckeye. Mrs Claiborne McNeil, near Buckeye, is her daughter.

Jacob Waugh married Mary Brown daughter of Josiah Brown, near Indian Draft, and spent most of his married life in Upshur county. They were the parents of fifteen children. Only five lived to be grown. Jacob Waugh was a local Methodist minister of prominence. He was a very fine pensman and became clerk of the Upshur County Court, and occupied that responsible position for many years, and will be remembered as one of the best citizens in the history of Upshur county affairs.

James Waugh, the third of that name, married Sally Cochran, daughter of John Cochran, eldest of Thomas

Cochran, the progenitor of the Cochran relationship in Pocahontas county. He settled on the Greenbrier at the old homestead. His second wife was Hannah Lamb, from Highland County. In the sketch of Pocahontas County given in Hardesty's Encyclopedia the reader will find biographic details of James Waugh's personal history.

Morgan Waugh went to Kanawha County.

Allen Waugh went to Missouri and settled there.

Isabella Waugh became the wife of John Brock and settled in Kanawha County.

Marcus, the youngest son of James Waugh, married Susan Johnson, and settled on a farm adjoining the Waugh homestead higher up the river, a few miles east of Poages Lane.

Lorenza Waugh, a son of James the second, became a distinguished evangelist. From his autobiography, published in San Francisco, copies of which are in the possession of his friends in Pocahontas, we learn that he was born in 1808, at the home on the Greenbrier where his earlier years were spent. At the age of sixteen he was a teacher in Harrison County. He was a teacher in Mason County in 1831, entered the Methodist ministry in that year, and was junior preacher on the Guyandotte circuit. In 1833 he rode the Nicholas County circuit, and was transferred to the Ohio Conference in 1834. In 1835 he became a member of the Missouri Conference. On one of his Missouri circuits he met Miss Clarissa Jane Edsell, and they were married. It seems he first lost his heart in The Hills, but time makes up for such losses.

In 1837 Lorenza Waugh was an Indian missionary to the Shawnee nation. In 1840 he rode the Platte River circuit, now in Nebraska, and in 1848 he entered the Illinois Conference. In 1851 with his family he crossed the plains and settled in the Petaluma Valley, in California, where he resided until his death, in 1900.

SAMUEL WAUGH.

This paper is devoted to the memory of Samuel Waugh, one of the early settlers of The Hills, seven or eight miles north east of Huntersville. He was a son of James Waugh, Senior. His wife's name was Mary. This pioneer husband and wife opened up their home about 1774, on the place now held by John Shrader, one of their descendants by the third remove. Samuel Waugh, upon his marriage with Ann McGuire, settled at the old Waugh homestead. Their family consisted of nine sons and five daughters. Concerning these children the following fragmentary particulars have been collected.

Elizabeth Waugh was married to Caleb Knapp, and first settled in Greenbrier County. They afterwards lived awhile on Knapps Creek; thence settled on the Greenbrier, known as the Knapp place, where McCoy Malcomb now resides. Her daughter, Ann Knapp, was married to Richard B. Weir, and lives near Verdant Valley. Nancy Knapp married Henry Shrader; lived several years in Huntersville, where Mr Shrader operated a tannery, and finally settled on the Waugh

homestead. Mary Shrader, her daughter, was married
to the late William Fertig of Huntersville, lived some
years on Anthonys Creek, and now lives near Dilleys
Mill. Mr Fertig was a saddler by trade, then a merchant, was a member of the Pocahontas court, and
upon his removal to Greenbrier devoted his time to
farming. B. Franklin Shrader died in the war. R.
C. Shrader lives on part of the Waugh homestead, and
runs a farm and tannery successfully. His wife is a
daughter of the late James Lewis of the Levels. John
Shrader lives at the original homestead as mentioned.
His wife was a daughter of Nicholas Stulting.

Jacob Shrader married a daughter of David Kincaid
in Highland County, and lives near Dilleys Mill.
Luther Shrader married a sister of Jacob's wife, and
lived in Greenbrier. Ellen Susan Shrader became the
wife of Oscar Sharp, a local Methodist minister, and
lives at Frost. The names of the other members of
the Shrader family are Enoch, William, Charles, and
Margaret Ann.

Eleanor Knapp married Sampson Buzzard. Elizabeth Knapp married Peter Shrader. Margaret Knapp
married McCoy Malcomb: John and Thomas Malcomb
are her sons. Mrs W. B. Johnson is her daughter.

R. W. Knapp lived in Tucker County. A. J. Knapp
went to Missouri.

Rebecca Waugh married Andrew Moore, and for
some years lived near Frost, then at the head of Stony
Creek, and finally her family moved to Jackson county.

Rev John Waugh married Martha Moore, and settled on the Indian Draft, near Edray, where his son

John Waugh now lives. His son Samuel died in
youth, and was preparing for the ministry. Levi
Waugh, a Confederate veteran; Beverly Waugh, a
Union veteran; and John Waugh, lately deputy sheriff
of Pocahontas County, are his sons. Mrs Ewing
Johnson, near Marlinton, and Mrs Richard Mayse, of
Blue Ridge Springs, Va., are his daughters.

The Rev John Waugh is worthy of remembrance for
many reasons. He was a skillful worker in metals.
His specialty seemed to be the manufacture of hoes,
one of the most useful of implements in his time when
with many persons it was the main reliance in cultivating a crop and working a garden. He excelled also
in tempering axes—another implement of precious
value and essential use in preparing the land for culti-
vation. He taught school, and preferred the vocal
method, when all the pupils could con their lessons
audibly as well as recite them. He studiously improved his limited opportunities for mental improvement,
and became a well informed intelligent citizen, and
had his own well matured opinions about questions of
public interest. He was for many years a prominent
member of his church and a local preacher that seemed to have but little regard for what persons might say
about his discourse. He had a parable about throwing stones in the dark at certain things, and if there
was an outcry he knew that something was hit. He
died a few years ago, apparently in the full possession
of his faculties, at a very advanced age.

Samuel Waugh, Junior, moved to Missouri in early
manhood, and there—upon his marriage with a Mis-

souri lady, Mary Canterbury—he settled and we are favored with no further particulars.

Robert Waugh, remembered as a very bright and interesting young man, devoted himself to school-teaching. From exposure on damp ground he contracted a rheumatic affection that disabled him for manual labor. He was held in high reputation as a teacher, and some of his scholars yet speak of him with affection after a lapse of fifty years or more.

Robert Waugh seems to have been gifted with fine oratorical powers, for some of the older people tell me that they have never heard anything that could beat Robert Waugh speaking when he got warmed up on any subject. He died comparatively young at the old homestead, and never lived to realize his hopes and ambitions in this life. In his lonely grave amid the Hills a tongue is silent that may have enraptured listening audiences and secured for Robert an illustrious name.

William Waugh, another of Samuel Waugh's nine sons; married Martha, daughter of Josiah Brown, near Indian Draft. They were the parents of ten children. Upon leaving this place Mr Waugh settled in Upshur County, thence he went to Iowa, and afterwards to Missouri, where Mrs Waugh died many years ago. In 1894 Mr Waugh was struck by a passing train, not far from his home in Missouri, and died in forty minutes from the shock.

Alexander Waugh married Annie Cochran, of the Levels, and settled in Nicholas County.

Arthur Waugh, another of the nine sons, went in

early manhood to Kanawha, where he married Henrietta Boswell and settled.

Jacob Waugh married Sarah Ann Gay, youngest daughter of the late Samuel M. Gay, near Marlinton, and first lived at the Waugh homestead. Then he moved to Barbour County, and finally returned to Pocahontas and took charge of the Duffield mill, near Edray, where he died a few years since. This mill is now operated by his son, S. D. Waugh.

Beverly Waugh, the last to be mentioned of this remarkable list of sons of Samuel Waugh, married Martha Bradshaw, daughter of William Bradshaw, on Browns Creek. He lived many years on the place now occupied by Robert Shrader. He then moved to the Levels. Mrs Kenney Wade (first wife) and John E. Waugh were his children.

Mr Beverly Waugh was an estimable man. He led the Mount Zion class for sixteen years, and yielded the position to the regret of his christian brethren when it became necessary to change homes. He died of a cancerous affection but a few years since, and bore his dreadful sufferings with becoming resignation. He left an honorable reputation as a gentleman and a christian.

In reference to Samuel Waugh's other three daughters, we are able to furnish but the few particulars herewith given. Margaret Waugh was married to Samuel Martin, and lived first in Upshur County, and then moved to Iowa. Mary Ann Waugh became Mrs Reuben Buzzard and lived near Glade Hill a few years. Afterwards Mr Buzzard purchased Dilleys Mill, and lived there a considerable while, and finally emigrated to the far west.

Truly, our attention has been given to a family group whose history is suggestive and instructive. Samuel Waugh and Ann McGuire, his wife, imbued with the faith and energy so peculiar to the genuine Scotch-Irish, endured all that is implied in rearing a family of fourteen sons and daughters, and all living to be adults. The sons all lived to be grown, and not one was ever known to use tobacco or ardent spirits in any form. This seems scarcely credible, yet it is asserted to be a pleasing truth. Samuel Waugh was one of the original members of the old Mount Zion Church —one of the strongholds of its denomination for so many years. His history shows that in the face of pioneer hindrances and privations sons and daughters may be reared that may faithfully serve God and support their country in their day and generation.

JOSIAH BEARD.

So far as we have authentic information, the Beard relationship trace their ancestry to John Beard, the pioneer of Renicks Valley, Greenbrier County. He was of Scotch-Irish antecedents, his parents having migrated from the north of Ireland. While a young man he had his parental home in Augusta County, in the bounds of John Craig's congregation, and no doubt helped to build the old Stone Church and the forts spoken of elsewhere, and may have heard the very sermons Craig preached, opposing the people who were thinking of going back to Pennsylvania or over the Blue Ridge towards Williamsburg.

His valley home was in the vicinity of New Hope, and after attaining his majority he came to Greenbrier County, and commenced keeping bachelor's hall at the head of Renicks Valley, on lands now occupied by Abram Beard, a grandson. This was about 1770, and though unmarried, John Beard secured land, built a cabin, and cleared ground for cropping.

While living in this isolated manner, some Indians came along and liberally helped themselves to whatever they could find in the way of something to eat; and when they went on their way took the pioneer's gun, dog, and only horse.

It so occurred that Mr Beard was absent that day. It is thought he had gone over to Sinking Creek on a social visit to the Wallace family, old neighbors in Augusta, and whose coming to Greenbrier possibly had its influence with the young bachelor.

When young Beard returned and saw what liberties his visitors had taken in his absence, he looked up the trail and started in pursuit. Upon following the sign for some miles in the direction of Spring Creek, he heard the horse's bell. Guided by the sound he came upon two Indians in camp. They seemed to be very sick, and Mr Beard supposed it was from over eating raw bacon and johnny cake they had taken from his own larder. One appeared to be convulsed with paroxysms of nausea; the other was lying before the fire vigorously rubbing his belly with a piece of bacon, on homeopathic principles that like cures like.

Seeing his own gun near a tree and his own dog ly-i ng by it, he crawled near to get the gun, but the dog fiercely growled, and he was forced to withdraw quietly as he came, and leave the two sick Indians unmolested. He thereupon went to his horse, silenced the bell and succeeded in getting the animal away.

About this time, or soon after, Mr Beard seemed to realize there was nothing in single blessedness for him and he and Miss Janet Wallace were married by taking a trip to Staunton and making their wishes known to the rector of the imperial parish that extended from the the Blue Ridge to the Pacific ocean. In their pioneer home in Renicks Valley they reared a numerous family of sons and daughters, one of the sons being Josiah Beard, lately of Locust Creek. This paper will be mainly for the illustration of his personal and family history, as his name appears so prominently in our county history. Mr Beard was the first Clerk of the County after its organization and served in that capacity during the formative period of the county's history.

His wife, Rachel Cameron Poage, was the eldest daughter of Major William Poage, of Marlins Bottom. The names of their children are given in the paper relating to Jacob Warwick and his descendants.

He was an expert hunter, and found recreation in hunting deer upon the hills and ridges that make Huntersville scenery so picturesque. He killed scores of fine deer during his residence at the court house, and rarely went beyond the immediate vicinity in quest of game, unless it would be occasional visits to Marlins Bottom for a chase. It proved however that there were attractions to draw him there of a more pleasant and romantic nature.

He seemed to have his own ideas as to how he could best promote the interests of the county, and would sometimes carry them out. While residing at Locust Creek he set out one morning to attend court. On the way near his home he discovered fresh wolf signs. He hastened back, got his gun and called up the dogs, and sent Aaron, a colored servant, who was also a skilful hunter and a dead shot, to beat the laurel brake and drive out the wolves. Quite a number were killed and the pack retreated from the neighborhood so far back into the mountains as to give no further trouble.

In the meantime, court met and adjourned owing to the absence of the clerk. That official however was present next morning and explained the reasons of his absence, believing it would do the people more good to have the wolves killed and scattered than to hold court that day. Court could meet most any time, but it was not every day that such a good chance to kill wolves could be had.

He was a stanch friend of education, and was one of the first trustees of the Pocahontas Academy at Hillsboro, and one of its most faithful patrons and wise counselors. In business affairs he was successful, and in a quiet, judicious, industrious manner acquired a very extensive landed estate; the larger proportion of which is yet in the possession of his descendants.

His passion for hunting was strong to the last. Every fall he would get restless, and nothing but a hunt would quiet him. One of the last excursions to the mountains, though far advanced in age, he was the only one that killed a deer. On his return he would chaff his younger associates by telling all he met on the way that the young men had taken him along to kill their meat for them.

He retained remarkable bodily vigor to the age of four score and over; and his mental faculties were unimpaired to the last. Not many days before his final illness that closed his life, he felt it his duty to see the county surveyor on important business—as he believed it to be—and should be attended to without delay. He went from his home on Locust Creek to Mr Baxter's near Edray, about twenty miles distant, and returned —a cold, raw day it was, too. He overtaxed his endurance by the ride. He soon became sick, and peacefully passed from his long and useful life.

In his life was exemplified the highest type of the citizen—a pious, intelligent cultivator of the soil—the occupation for which the Creator saw fit in his wisdom to create the first man. It is the occupation now that feeds the world, and whatever hinders, depresses, or retards the farmers prosperity, threatens the worst evils that can befall our humanity.

DAVID JAMES.

David James, Senior, was one of the first settlers of the Droop neighborhood, in Lower Pocahontas. He was from Norfolk, Virginia. It is believed he came here soon after the Revolution, and located for awhile near the head of Trump Run, on property now owned by Richard Callison. He then lived some years at the

Rocky Turn, now known as the Irvine Place, where he built a mill. One of the stones is yet to be seen just below the road near where the mill stood.

From the Irvine place he moved on lands now occupied by George Cochran. The house is still standing and furnishes a correct idea of the kind of houses the pioneers lived in. It was here he passed the latter years of his life, and passed away at the age of 104 years. The name and parentage of his wife are not remembered. His family consisted of three daughters and two sons: Nellie, Martha, Sally, David and John.

Nellie James was married to Thomas Cochran, second wife, and lived near Marvin.

Martha was married to John Salisbury, and lived on Trump Run, and finally went west. This John Salisbury was a son of William Salisbury, a native of England, who opened the Salisbury settlement on Trump Run. William Salisbury's wife Mary was a native of Scotland. He lived to the age of 104 years, and is to be remembered as one of the pioneers of lower Pocahontas.

Sally became Mrs John Cutlip, who opened up an improvement on Droop Mountain, now in possession of the Renicks. Her children were David, Abram, John, George, Martha, and Elizabeth. The latter married David Kinnison and went to the west.

David James, Junior, married Catherine Parks and settled on Droop Mountain. They were the parents of these children: Mordecai, Jennie, Samuel, Elizabeth, John, Rebecca, Martha, and Mary.

Mordecai married Martha Tharp and went west.

The Tharps lived on the Joshua Kee place, near Marlinton.

Jennie became Mrs Jesse Cochran. Her marriage was attended by very romantic incidents, illustrating the fact that all may be well that ends well.

Samuel married Elizabeth Ewing, daughter of William Ewing, who lived on the Greenbrier, where Joseph Perkins now resides, and went west. William Ewing excelled as a maker of wooden mouldboards for plows, and had all he could do to meet the demand.

John married Nellie Cochran.

Rebecca became Mrs Emanual Barrett.

John James married Nellie, daughter of Thomas Cochran the pioneer, and settled on Droop, where Lincoln Cochran now lives, but finally went west. Their family consisted of three daughters and three sons: Jane, Eliza, Kate, David, William, and John.

Thus with the assistance of the venerable John Cochran, probably the oldest man living on the Pocahontas and Greenbrier border in 1897, and George Cochran, his relative and neighbor, the writer has been able to give something in illustrating the James family history. This paper will be concluded by recalling the fact that David James, Junior, lived to the age of 106 years, about the greatest age attained by any one of our Pocahontas citizens, concerning whom we have any authentic information. The cottage home still stands whence he departed for the unseen world, and his grave will be an object of interest in our local annals and should be carefully marked so as not to be forgotten.

David Cochran, a son of Thomas Cochran, by his second marriage with Nellie James, deserves mention from the fact that he was a veteran of the war of 1812. He had for his mess mates in the army William Salisbury, Jr., John McNeil, (known as Little John), and John R. Flemmens. He was in the affair at Craney Island, near Norfolk. While it is not certain, yet it is believed he served a tour under General Harrison in the west, as he frequently spoke of him. It is probable that he was in the battle of Tippecanoe. John Cochran; in 1898, was the only surviving member of the old soldier's family. He was 92 years of age November 2d of that year.

David Cochran, the veteran, suffered grievously the last three or four years of his life. He was treated by Mrs Diddle of Monroe County, for three years. She undertook to cure the case for forty dollars. Several visits were made. She was at his bedside when he died of hemorhage, caused by the cancer, in October 1831.

John Cochran has a vivid recollection of the Regimental Muster at Huntersville, in May, 1834. On returning from muster rather late in the evening, persons were racing their horses in a furious charge against imaginary British, on the Cummings Creek road, two miles from Huntersville. While not in the charge, Isaac Jordan's horse seemed to smell something of the make-believe battle, reared and plunged, throwing his rider and severely fracturing his thigh.

William Gibson, merchant and hotel keeper at Huntersville was sent for. After some delay, means were contrived to carry the injured and suffering man back to Huntersville, where they arrived after dark. Squire Gibson—though not a physician—took charge of the case, reduced the fracture and kept the patient at his house for three months. John Cochran was employed to nurse him, and staid by him all the while until he could be brought home.

John Cochran in his prime was a person of uncommon agility and muscular power. He was jovial in disposition and had a good word for everybody, and yet it was his misfortune to be in one of the fiercest personal combats that ever occurred in his neighborhood. With remarkable magnamity his opponent confessed himself in the fault, and ever after there was no more fighting for John Cochran. Trouble quit looking for him after that.

George Cochran lives in the old James house. He was a faithful Confederate soldier, and stands up for the Lost Cause with a fluent vim that is refreshing.

JOHN BURGESS.

Concurrently with the past century the name Burgess has been a familiar one in lower and middle Pocahontas. The progenitor of this family was John Burgess, Senior, a native of Ireland. He was a weaver by occupation, and settled near Albany, New York, where he diligently plied his vocation, some years previous to the Revolution. The name of his wife or her family is not remembered. There were two sons and four daughters.

Elizabeth Burgess became Mrs William Young.

Two of the daughters, names not remembered, married two brothers by the name of Kelley, and lived in New York State.

James Burgess became a preacher in the pale of the Congregational Church, and settled in Kentucky, among the pioneer ministers of that region.

John Burgess, Junior, married a Miss Kelley, of New York, and soon after the Revolution removed to Harrisonburg, Virginia. In his family were three sons and eight daughters, concerning whom we have the following details, furnished by David Burgess.

Mary Burgess married her cousin, James Young, and settled in Augusta County. Their son William Young was a soldier in the war of 1812, and died in service at Norfolk, Virginia.

Nancy was married to William Mayse, and settled at Millpoint, now Pocahontas county. He was among the first baksmiths to strike sparks from the anvil in that vicinity. William Mayse, a grandson, was a captain in the Civil War, and afterwards a government clerk in Washington, D. C.

Jane became Mrs Thomas Armstrong and lived near Churchville, Virginia.

Hampton Burgess went to Ohio in early manhood, married a Miss Smith and settled in that State.

Nathan Burgess married Martha Kinnison, of Charles Kinnison, the pioneer, and settled on lands now in sossession of the Payne family. He was a skillful gunsmith. Late in the 18th century and early in 19th, many of the older hunters were supplied by him

with rifles. Some of his rifles were used by riflemen
in military service. One of the best specimens of his
workmanship was made for the late William McNeil,
of Buckeye. When last heard of it was the property
of the late James Moore. It was reputed to be one of
the most accurate in aim and far reaching of mountain
rifles ever in the county. It would be well if it could
be gotten and deposited in the Museum of the West
Virginia Historical Society at Charleston.

John Burgess was born near Albany in 1778. He
was a mere youth when his father came to Harrisonburg. From Rockingham he came to the Levels about
1798. His first marriage was with Susan Casebolt and
lived near Millpoint. The children of the first marriage
were John, James, Archibald, Paul, Hannah and
Mary. Hannah became Mrs David McNair and lived
in Augusta. The first Mrs Burgess died about 1813.
Soon after her death John Burgess moved to the mountain farm, west of the head of Swago.

His second marriage was with Hannah McNair,
daughter of Daniel McNair, in the vicinity of Churchville. The McNairs were pioneers along with the
Boones, Millers, Moffetts, and McDowells, notable
familes in the Valley of Virginia during the pioneer
era. The McNairs were from Pennsylvania. The
children of the second marriage were David, Martha
and Elizabeth.

John Burgess was a carpenter by occupation. He did
the carpenter work on the dwelling occupied for many
years by the late George W. Poage, the ruins of which
are still to be seen near Preston Clarks beautiful resi-

dence. The Jordan Barn, near Hillsboro, was of his many jobs, and still stands in a good state of preservation. For a long series of years he made most of the coffins needed in Lower Pocahontas. He was drafted into military service during the war of 1812, but owing to the critical stage of his wife's health, he was permitted to put in a substitute, and remain with his family. He thus escaped the suffering privation which caused the death of many of our mountain people during the notable defense of Norfolk vicinity that was planned to shield Richmond from British invasion and depredation.

John Burgess, Junior, son of John Burgess, the immigrant, the immediate ancestor of the Pocahontas family, whose history is illustrated in part by this sketch, claimed to have been a Revolutionary soldier and served in the artillery, and was one of the first to enlist and the last to be disbanded of the New York Continental Troops. While we have in hand no positive information to this effect, yet there is much reason for believing that John Burgess was at the surrender of General Burgoyne.

As the reader will readily remember, very memorable events occurred not very far from where John Burgess, the immigrant, lived and reared his family. It is more than probable that his loom wove the blanket which his son used in the service, and some of the neighbor soldiers were clothed in material prepared by his industrious hands.

Thus closes one more brief chapter in the suggestive history of our Pocahontas People. Let it be our aim

not only to emulate, but to surpass what our ancestry
accomplished, and ever strive not only to keep but improve upon what has come to us from their self-sacri-
ficing toils and good names.

JOSEPH MOORE.

Joseph Moore, late of Anthonys Creek, was one of
the most widely known citizens of our county in his
day. His parents were William Moore and Margaret,
his wife. It is believed they came from Rockbridge
County about 1780. No known relationship is claimed with other branches of the Moores. They opened
up a home on the knoll just south of Preston Harper's,
on Knapps Creek, where a rivulet crosses the road.
Their house was just below the present road at that
point. It was here they lived and died. They were
buried on the east side of the creek, on the terrace
south of the tenant house now standing there. Persons
now living have seen their graves.

These pioneers were the parents of two sons and two
daughters: Joseph, John, Mary (Polly), and a daughter whose name seems to be lost to memory.

John Moore went to Kentucky.

Mary was the wife of Colonel John Baxter, who was
the first Colonel of the 127th Regiment, and was very
prominent in the organization of the county.

Joseph Moore was a soldier in the war of 1812.
During his service he met and married Hannah Cady,
in East Virginia. She was a native of Connecticut,
and was a school teacher, and is spoken of by the older

people as a sprightly person. Soon after his return, Joseph Moore settled on the homestead, building his house between Goelet's residence and the barn. He finally moved to Anthonys Creek.

Their family consisted of five daughters and three sons: Hannah, Sarah, Matilda, Margaret, Abigail, Daniel, Joseph, and Henry Harrison.

Sarah was married to Jackson Bussard, on Anthonys Creek. He was a Confederate soldier, and died in the battle of Dry Creek, near the White Sulphur. J. H. Buzzard, Assessor for Pocahontas, is her son.

Matilda became Mrs Elijah May, on Anthonys Creek. Her sons John and Calvin married Lizzie and Lillie, daughters of Register Moore, near Marlinton.

Margaret was married to Jacob Blizzard, of Greenbrier County, and went west.

Abigail became Mrs John Wade, on Anthonys Creek, and lived there.

Daniel was deputy sheriff under his father. He finally went to Missouri, and became a prominent citizen. He raised and commanded a company of volunteers for service in the Mexican War, and was with Colonel Doniphan in his famous expedition to New Mexico.

Joseph Moore, Junior, went to Braxton County.

Henry Moore married Martha Young, daughter of Captain William Young of Stony Creek, and is now living in Iowa.

Joseph Moore, Esq., was a very prominent citizen in county affairs. He was high sheriff, justice of the peace, and was very much sought after for drawing up deeds, articles of agreement, and writing wills. His judgment in matters of controversy seems to have been very correct, as but few suits brought contrary to his advice ever succeeded in the courts.

One of my earliest recollections of Squire Moore was when I was a half grown lad, attending school in Huntersville from home in Marlinton. My first lessons in grammar were conned during those morning and evening rides. One playtime I was at 'Governor' Haynes' Hotel on the corner now occupied by the McClintic property. Squire Moore, who had spent the forenoon in the clerk's office with the late Henry M. Moffett, was seen coming up the street very slowly. It was a hot day in summer, and he was in his shirtsleeves, with his vest unbuttoned and thrown open, and full saddle bags over his shoulder. Mr Haynes calls out: "Squire, you are taking things mighty slow, and move as if you had no business on hand and never had any."

In slow, measured tones the Squire observes, as if he had studied the matter very carefully: "Well, Governor, I have been around here long enough to find out there is no use in being in a hurry about anything except catching fleas."

The 'Governor' was inclined to take offense at this, but the Squire pointed significantly towards the refreshment counter, and in the clinking of glasses the flea trouble was forgotten.

It would require more time and space than is allotted to these memoirs to write out all that might come mind about this interesting man, so we will give only

one more reminiscence. In April, 1848, I spent a
rainy afternoon with Squire Moore in a school he was
teaching near Sunset, in the old Daugherty building.
He showed me a question in arithmetic that puzzled
him. He could find the answer called for but it would
not "prove out," and he could not be satisfied with
anything that would not "prove out."

We put our heads together and found a result that
would "prove out," so we both felt that we knew
more than the man who wrote the book,—that much
of it at least. We lingered after school was out, until
it was so near night that when I returned to William
Harper's the evening candle was already lighted and
placed on the supper table.

After proving out things in our ciphering consulta-
tion, we had a talk about the Bible and Christian religion. I was a Bible distributor at that time, as some
of the older people may remember. The habit the
Squire had of "proving out" things came into evidence
again: .

"William, you must excuse me if I talk a little plain
to you, for you may think strangely of the way I
sometimes talk. There are people who think I am an
infidel, because I sometimes make remarks they do
not agree with. I have studied a good deal about religion, and if you have as much sense as I think you
have, you will some day see these things as I do. I
always keep a Bible or Testament handy to me when
I am at home, and most always carry a Testament in
my saddle pockets when away on business.

"Now you must excuse me, William, when I say to

you that in my private opinion there can not be much
in the Christian religion if it puts its most earnest and
zealous professors to wearing out the knees of their
pants in religious services in the fall and winter, and
then lets them turn over and wear out the rest of their
breeches backsliding during the spring and summer.
Somehow, William, it does not prove out to suit my
notion what religion should be—provided there is such
a thing as religion anyway.''

I felt that Squire Moore was not disposed to discuss
personal piety seriously, and the subject was changed.
We never met again to compare opinions about any
matter. I learn from his friends, however, that during the closing years of his life he gave close attention
to his Bible. He has been seen sitting for hours in
the shade of an apple tree, with an open Bible on his
knee. It is my fervent hope that my aged friend was
able to 'prove out' that it is a ''faithful saying, worthy
of all acceptation, that Christ Jesus came into the
world to save sinners, even the greatest,'' and that he
was willing to take the sinner's place and receive the
sinner's salvation; at the same time praying: ''Cast
me not off in the time of old age, forsake me not when
my strength fails.''

ROBERT D. McCUTCHAN.

Among the citizens of our county deserving special
notice for industry, hospitality, and good influence on
society, Robert Dunlap McCutchan, late of Thomas
Creek, is to be remembered as one justly entitled to

such consideration. While he was not one of the
pioneers, he came to Pocahontas soon after the organization of the county, virtually settled in the woods,
and built up a home that was noted far and near for its
good cheer and lavish hospitality.

January 11, 1825, he married Elizabeth Youel Lockridge, near Goshen, Virginia, and settled on Thomas
Creek, in 1826. They were the parents of five sons
and four daughters. All of their children except two
preceded them to the grave. The eldest died in
infancy.

Samuel Hodge McCutchan was a Confederate soldier
and a member of Captain J. W. Marshall's company.
He was captured in 1863 and taken to Camp Chase,
and remained there until the close of the war. He
came home in broken health, and died of consumption
in 1869.

John Blain McCutchan was also a Confederate volunteer, and served in the same company. He married
soon after the war, Mrs Rachel Bird, daughter of
Jacob Bible, near Greenbank. He lately died. There
were four children: Iizzie, now Mrs F. M. Dilley;
Robert and Luther, twins, died young; and Margaret.

William Andrew Gatewood McCutchan went to
Georgia when twelve years of age, to be educated by
his uncle, Andrew Lockridge, a Presbyterian minister.
His health failed, and he returned home in his fifteenth
year. He soon after united with the church at Dunmore, and began studies for the ministry. He volunteered in the war. In the battle of Seven Pines he
went into action contrary to his captain's advice, feel-

ing it his duty to fight as long as he could handle his
musket, but being overcome by fatigue, he was ordered back to the rear, fell sick with pneumonia, and
never recovered.

Luther McCutchan died the first year of the war, in
his fifteenth year.

Christina Jane McCutchan married David Wetzel,
and lived in Lewisburg. Her children were William,
Sallie, Lizzie, and Lena. Sallie Wetzel married Newton Hartsook, and lived in Lewisburg. Lizzie became
Mrs Lake White, of White Sulphur. Lena married
Gordon Bright, and lived in Jtaunton. William Wetzel married Florence Ridgeway, of Monroe County,
and lives in Lewisburg.

Nancy Caroline McCutchan, an excellent young
lady, died in 1861.

Mary Martha McCutchan, when about verging into
womanhood, passed away from her earthly home.

Elizabeth Eleanor McCutchan married A. K. Dysard
and lives at Driftwood. Their children are Lawrence
and Mrs Bessie Beard.

Robert D. McCutchan was a ruling Elder in the
Presbyterian church for forty or fifty years. He was
born in 1803, and died after prolonged sufferings from
a cancerous affection, February 22, 1883.

Mrs Elizabeth Y. McCutchan was born in 1803, and
died July 2, 1878.

Mrs McCutchan, whose pet name was 'Aunt Betsy,'
was a typical Scotch-Irish matron, She was endowed
with the traits of character developed in her ancestry
by the civil and religious commotions that occurred in

the Scottish highlands and the historic parts of North
Ireland, to which reference has occasionally been made
in these notes. She was self reliant, kind hearted to a
fault, self possessed in all emergencies, diligent in
business, fervent in spirit, ever ready to weep with
those that wept, rejoicing with those that rejoiced, and
could hold more than her own if challenged on doctrinal points.

Mr McCutchan inherited the patient, plodding habits
of industry his ancestors acquired on the Scottish hills
that Robert Burns knew so well and disliked to practice so much. In a piny section of Pocahontas he
found lands that reminded him of the kind where his
own parents had toiled and made a bountiful living for
well nigh a century.

Far and near this family would attend religious worship, the weather be what it might. For years Greenbank and Huntersville, the first eight and the other
twelve miles away, were the nearest points of the
church service of their preference.

These pleasant people, so happy in their home relations, were not separated long. They and the most of
their children sleep in well cared for graves on a grassy
knoll overlooking the scenes where they passed their
quiet, useful lives for more than fifty years.

By his last will and testament Robert McCutchan
endowed Baxter Church with a fund of $500, Dr John
Ligon, Trustee. The annual interest to be for pastoral
support.

JOSEPH BROWN.

The Brown relationship trace their ancestry to Joseph Brown, whose wife was Hannah M'Afferty. They lived a few years in Bath County, on the Bull Pasture; thence removed and settled on lands now owned by the Mann family, near Edray. Some fruit trees and a fine spring indicate the spot where they lived. about three-fourths of a mile east of the Mann residence.

Mr Brown died a few years after settling here, but was survived by his widow for many years. She became suddenly blind, and remained so for twenty years. She spent her time in knitting, and taught many of her grand-daughters to knit. Among them was the late Mrs Thomas Nicholas. Mrs Nicholas would often tell how her grandmother would take her little hands into hers and put them through the motions until she could knit herself. A few years before her decease, Mrs Brown recovered her sight as quickly as she had lost it, and could count chickens and geese forty yards away.

The widow Brown's daughters Polly and Hannah lived and died at the old home.

Rachel Brown was married to William Brock, and settled on the homestead.

Ann Brown became the wife of Jeremiah Friel.

Elizabeth Brown married a Mr McGuire, and lived in Nicholas.

Joseph Brown, Senior, went to Nicholas County. His son Wesley Brown—a Confederate soldier—was at Edray during the great war between the States, and made himself known to his relatives.

John Brown was a soldier in the war of 1812, and never returned.

Josiah Brown, in whose memory this sketch is specially prepared, was the eldest of Joseph Brown's sons, and he married Jennie Waddell, near Millpoint. He was born June 22, 1777, his wife was born April 4th, 1771; married in 1799, and settled on the western section of the Brown homestead. They were the parents of seven daughters.

Eleanor Brown, born August 6, 1802, was married to Zechariah Barnett, from Lewis County, West Virginia. In reference to her family the following particulars are given: John Wesley and John Andrew Barnett died young, and Josiah Barnett. Sarah Jane Barnett was married to George McLaughlin, late of Driftwood. He was a Confederate soldier. Hannah Barnett married William Townsend. Martha Barnett, lately deceased. James, Thomas, Stephen, and Newton Barnett are well known citizens near Driftwood. The three first named were Confederate soldiers.

Hannah Brown was married to Jacob Arbaugh, who was from near Millpoint, and first settled on Sugartree Run, a part of the Brown homestead. Her children were Eliza Jane, Susannah Simms, Lauretta Frances, Nancy Caroline, John Allen, George Brown, James Marion, William Hanson, and Joseph Newton. John A. Arbaugh was a Confederate soldier, and died in 1861, at the Lockridge Spring, near Driscol. George and James passed through the war. George Arbaugh was in the 31st Regiment of Virginia Infantry.

Shortly after the war, Jacob Arbaugh moved to Jackson County, Missouri, which he jocularly referred to as his twentieth change of homes since his marriage.

Jennie Brown, born October 9, 1805, was married to John Friel, son of Jeremiah Friel the pioneer, and settled on a section of the Friel homestead on the Greenbrier River.

Ann Brown, born December 9, 1806, was married to James Courtney, and first settled on a part of the homestead. Their children were Andrew Jackson, Thomas, George Washington, Hanson, who died at the age of six years; Jane, who is now Mrs Adam Geiger; Julia, who is now Mrs James Rhea; and Hannah, who is now Mrs Godfrey Geiger. Andrew Courtney was a Confederate soldier, and died a prisoner of war at Fort Delaware. Thomas Courtney was also a Confederate soldier, survived the war, and now lives near Marlinton. George W. Courtney was a Confederate soldier, survived the war, but died near Buckeye in 1887.

Martha Brown, born February 14, 1808, was married to William Waugh, son of Samuel Waugh, the pioneer, and settled at the old home. Martha was known in her family as "daddy's boy," since she was constantly out of doors with her father. She could harness the teams, plough, or drive the sled, as occasion required. She was the mother of ten children: Davis, Zane, Robert, Enos, Ozias, William Clark, Jane Miriam, Mary Ann, and Almira. She died in Missouri, having lived awhile in Upshur County, West

Virginia, then in Iowa.

Miriam Brown was born August 6, 1810, was first married to James Walker Twyman, a native of Augusta County. Mr Twyman was a school teacher. They first settled on Elk, where they lived two or three years. The land he worked on Elk had been a part of David Hannah's. Mr Twyman put out a field of corn that grew finely and was very promising, but early in August there was a heavy frost; he became discouraged, gave up his land, and moved to Greenbrier River to land given them by Joseph Brown. Here he taught school; having the Friels, Moores, and Sharps for pupils. Mr Twyman had business in Huntersville the 17th of January, 1834, and on his return was drowned in Thorny Creek. The Greenbrier home was just above the "Bridger Place." Their daughter Mary Frances is now Mrs Otho W. Ruckman, on Indian Draft.

Mrs Twyman's second marriage was to the late Thomas Nicholas, on the Indian Draft, near Edray. Mr Nicholas was a skillful mechanic—a much respected and prosperous citizen.

Mary Brown was born April 13, 1812, and was married to Jacob Waugh, and lived in Buckhannon. She was the mother of fifteen children—five only lived to be grown. Her sons were Brown, Enoch, Homer, and John William. The daughter, Leah Waugh, was the third wife of the late Dr Pleasant Smith, of Edray.

The history of Josiah Brown was one of humble toil and self sacrifice for the good of his family. In the

course of his life he endured great personal suffering
and afflictions.   He was bitten twice by rattlesnakes
when in the ranges looking after his live stock.   Once
he was with his neighbor, William Sharp, who cared
for him and helped him home.   The second time he
was alone, and it is believed he saved his life by putting his lips to the punctures and sucking out the poison.   Finally, a strange sore appeared in the corner
of one of his eyes and spread over most of the right
side of his face.   Many believed this was the result of
the snake bites.   It caused him excruciating sufferings, that were greatly intensified by the efforts of
sympathizing, well meaning friends to cure him.

Sad and pathetic memories of his brother, John
Brown, seemed to be ever haunting his mind, and the
tears seemed to be ever ready to flow at the mention
of his name.   In the war of 1812 Josiah Brown was
drafted for service at Norfolk, Virginia.   John Brown
a younger brother, being unmarried, volunteered in
his brother's place and was accepted, and was ordered
to report for service at the Warm Springs.   John
seems to have been a very pious youth.   On the even-
sng before his departure for the seat of war, he came
over to his brother Josiah's to bid them all farewell
and have one more season of prayer and supplication.
Then as he went away over the fields he was heard
singing, "When I can read my title clear."   This was
the last ever seen or heard of him by his brother
Josiah's family, as he never came back from the war.

Truly, Josiah Brown's history is a sad and touching
one.   He now knows, no doubt, what Moses meant

when he prayed: "Make me glad according to the days wherein thou hast afflicted me and the years wherein I have seen evil."

WILLIAM AULDRIDGE.

William Auldridge, Senior, the ancestor and founder of the family relationship of that name in our county, was a native of England. His mother, who by her second marriage became Mrs John Johnson, a pioneer of Marlinton, lived to be more than one hundred years of age. His wife was Mary Cochran. Mr Auldridge built up a home at the Bridger Notch, and it is believed the old barn stood on the spot where one of the Bridger boys died. This place is now owned by William Auldridge, a grandson.

There were six sons and three daughters: Sarah, Elizabeth, Nancy, Thomas, William, John, Samuel, James, and Richard.

Thomas Auldridge, the eldest son, when in his prime was considered one of the strongest men physically in West Pocahontas. The first revelation of his strength was at a log rolling. The champion of the day attempted to take young Auldridge's handspike— which was a fancy article of its kind. The young athlete picked up both the champion and the disputed handspike and laid them on the log heap, with apparent ease.

Upon his marriage with Elizabeth Morrison, daughter of James Morrison, on Hills Creek, Thomas Auldridge leased lands now owned by John R. Poage near

Clover Lick, where he spent most of his working days. He then bought of Jacob Arbaugh and Captain William Young, near Indian Draft, and opened up the property now owned by his son, Thomas Auldridge. The sons of Thomas Auldridge, Senior, were James, William, Thomas, and the daughters were Sarah, Elizabeth, and Mary.

James Auldridge, the eldest son, first married Mary Ann Barlow, and settled on land now occupied by Nathan Barlow, and then moved to the home near Edray where he now resides. His children were Henry, Miriam, Elizabeth, Moffett, and George. He was sadly bereaved of his first family by the ravages of disease, one son George, alone was spared. James' second wife was Julia A. Duncan, a grand daughter of Colonel John Baxter. One daughter, Mary, now Mrs Lee Carter. George Auldridge, the survivor of the first family, married Huldah Cassel, and lives on the homestead near Edray.

William Auldridge married Elizabeth Moore, and settled on a part of the homestead. Their children were Malinda, Hanson, and Eliza.

Thomas Auldridge, Junior, married Catherine Moore and lived on the homestead. Two daughters, Mrs Margaret Hannah, on Bucks Run, and Mrs Ida McClure, who lives on a part of the old homestead.

Sarah Auldridge, daughter of Thomas Auldridge, Senior, married the late J. Harvey Curry, near Frost. Her life is believed to have been shortened by the exposure and exertion due to the burning of the home near Frost. Her son Ellis Curry married Miss Rock, and lives near Dunmore. William Curry went to Missouri. Mary Curry married Benjamin Arbogast, and lives near Greenbank. E nma Curry married William T. McClintic, and lives near Beverly. Bessie married J. K. B. Wooddell, and lives in Ritchie County.

Elizabeth Auldridge married Henry Moore and lives near Driftwood.

Mary Ann Auldridge married William Moore, of Elk. One daughter, Ann Moore, survives her.

William Auldridge, Junior, married Nancy Kellison and settled on the Greenbrier, two miles below the mouth of Swago. Their only child, Martha, married Geore Hill, son of Abram Hill of Hills Creek. While he was in service in 1861 at Valley Mountain he contracted the measles. He came home and his wife took down also with the same disease, and the two died within a week of each other, leaving a daughter, who is now Mrs Robert Shafer. William Auldridge's second wife was a Miss Shafer. Her son, James Edgar Auldridge, lives on the homestead.

John Auldridge married Rebecca Smith, who is particularly mention in the memoirs of John Smith, of Stony Creek.

Samuel Auldridge, son of William Auldridge the ancestor, married Miriam Barlow and settled at the Bridger Notch, finally on Greenbrier River near Stamping Creek. His children by the first marriage were William, John, and Mary Ann. Mary Ann died young. John was a Confederate soldier and was killed in battle. William lives at Millpoint.

Samuel Auldridge's second wife was Susan Grimes.

Mention is made of her family in the Grimes memoir.

James Auldridge was a tailor by occupation, worked awhile at Frankford, and then went to Missouri.

Richard Auldridge, youngest son of William the ancestor, married Hannah Smith, daughter of John Smith.

Sarah Auldridge married William McClure, and settled on the Greenbrier River, below Beaver Creek. Their children were James, Rachel, Mary, and Bessie. Rachel became Mrs Jacob Pyles; Mary, Mrs George Overholt, on Swago. Bessie died in her youth. James McClure was married three times: First wife, Miss McComb; second, Miss Pyles; and third, Miss Frances Adkinson. He lives on the homestead.

Elizabeth Auldridge married Jacob McNeil, and settled in Floyd County, Virginia.

Nancy Auldridge was married to the late Moore McNeil, on Swago.

Thus closes for the present the chronicles of this worthy man's family. The writer would make mention of the assistance given him by James Auldridge and his son George.

The venerable man whose history we have been tracing—as illustrated by his descendants—was a very estimable person. He was an ever busy, industrious, and exemplary citizen. His influence was ever for sincere piety, strict honesty, and quiet judicious attention to his own concerns. These same qualities characterize many of his worthy posterity. Early in his manhood he was greatly disabled bp a falling tree and was seriously crippled for life; and yet the work he

and his children accomplished in opening up abundant
homes, under difficulties, is truly remarkable and worthy of special appreciation.   He loved to hunt, and on
one occasion came near being killed by a panther from
which he escaped with difficulty.

Mr Auldridge, owing to his disabled condition, became a school teacher, and pursued that vocation for
years, and did much good in that line.   When he died
at an advanced age several years since, the common
remark was that one of our best old men had gone
from us.

CHRISTOPHER HEROLD.

Among the prosperous citizens of Pocahontas County in its early development, Christopher Herold deserves recognition of a special character.   He was of
pure German parentage—his immediate ancestry came
from the Fatherland, settling in Pennsylvania, thence
removing to Virginia.   Though he could not read
English, no one would have suspected it, so well posted he seemed to be in political matters and current
affairs.   His powers of memory were surprising, and
his business sagacity was equal to any of his contemporaries.   He was honest and enterprising.   He and
his sons accumulated an immense landed estate on Elk,
Douthards Creek, and other places, amounting to many
thousands acres.

Christopher Herold married Elizabeth Cook, of
Pendleton County, and soon after their marriage located on Back Creek, now known as the Thomas

Campbell place. From Back Creek, Highland County, he migrated to Douthards Creek, about seventy-six
years ago, and bought of Colonel John Baxter, and
settled on lands now held by Henry White and sons
and Henry Sharp, on Douthards Creek. On this place
Mr and Mrs Herold reared their family and passed the
residue of their lives. Their family consisted of seven
sons and three daughters: Susan, Jane, Elizabeth
Ann, Henry, Peter, Benjamin, Charles, Christopher,
Andrew, and Josiah.

Susan Herold was married to Philip Moyers, and
settled in Upshur County.

Jane was the wife of Captain John Buzzard, who
lived in Huntersville several years. He managed a
hotel, was Captain of the ''Light Horse'' company,
and finally moved to Missouri.

Elizabeth Ann married Samuel Hogsett, Junior, and
settled in Harrison County, where her family now live.
Mr Hogsett died, and she was afterwards married to
Mr Sapp.

Henry, the eldest of the pioneer's sons, married
Elizabeth Lockridge and settled at Driscol, and after
living there a number of years, moved to Nicholas
County. Their sons were Anderson, Washington, William, and Benjamin. Wise Herold, now living on
Knapps Creek, is a son of Washington. Henry Herold's daughter Elizabeth married a McClung, in Nicholas County; and another daughter Maria was married
to John McClintic at Frankford, W. Va.

Peter Herold married Catherine Snyder, of Highland; settled on the Red Lick branch of Elk, where he

died, and his family afterwards went to Missouri,
whither they had been preceded by Daniel Herold, a
son of Peter.

Benjamin Herold, a very prominent citizen in his
time, was married to Mary Boone of Franklin County,
and for several years lived at Driscol. He bought out
his brothers, Andrew and Josiah, and thereafter resided at the homestead. Finally he moved to Missouri.
Benjamin's sons were, Charles, Joseph, Peter, and the
daughters were Eugenia, Mary, and Lucy.

Christopher Herold's fourth son, Charles, died when
about grown.

His fifth son, Christopher, Junior, married Sally
Ann Hefner, daughter of Samuel Hefner of Anthonys
Creek, and lived on the homestead, where both died,
leaving a daughter, Sally Ann, who married Mr Wag-
goner of Webster County.

The sixth son, Andrew, married Maria Seybert,
dasghter of Joseph Seybert, and lived some years on
the old homestead, and then purchased near Frost,
where he now resides.

Andrews's family numbered nine sons and two
daughters: Mrs Ida Rebecca Moore, Myrta, Lanty W.,
Millard F., Joseph, died aged eight; Isaac Newton,
now in Missouri; John L., Edwin L., Horace F., in
Highland; Andrew Forrest and Pruyn Patterson, deceased.

The seventh son of Christopher Herold, Sr., Josiah
Herold, married Mary Ann Cleek, of Knapps Creek,
and located on Stony Creek, upon the farm occupied
by the family of the late James McClure. Deeming it

best to refugee during the war, he went to Mr Cleek's. There he was seized with diptheria in a malignant form, and he and his two little sons died.

To illustrate something of the privations endured by this worthy man and family in their efforts to make their way in the world, mention may be made of what occurred in the winter of 1840.

Andrew, then about grown, was sent to Elk to look after some cattle to be wintered there. A snow fell, early in the winter, between four and five feet in depth. The only chance to keep the cattle alive was to fell timber for browse. How to have this done was the problem that confronted the youth. Having procured the services of Joe Courtney, a man of stalwart form and needful pluck, they started for the browsing ground. Courtney went ahead, and the young man followed in his trail, snow up to the arm pits. They managed to cut what carried the cattle through.

In the meanwhile all communication between neighbors seemed cut off. Andrew's brother, Peter Herold had taken sick and died before he could hear of it. James Gibson, Senior, now living on Elk, managed to reach an eminence in hearing of the browsing party, and by the loudest tones he could command got Andrew to understand what had taken place. The funeral rites were performed under difficulties indescribable.

The winter finally passed away, and when Andrew returned home in the spring he was emaciated and changed in appearance almost beyond recognition by his neighbors.

When this venerated man---Christopher Herold---

died some years ago, he was verging ninety years.
He and his faithful wife sleep in the family burial
ground near their last home on earth, the scene of
much of their life's toils and mutual joys and sorrows.

DANIEL KERR.

Acknowledgements are due Samuel Sutton and Mrs
Harvey Curry, near Dunmore, for the following items
that may rescue from oblivion the memory of a very
worthy and useful pioneer of upper Pocahontas. This
was Daniel Kerr, who located soon after the Revolution on the upper end of the immense estate now owned by Uriah Hevener.

It seems very probable he came from Rockbridge
County. He established a mill, saw mill, and blacksmith shop on the Little Back Creek branch of Deer
Creek, and his place became a centre of industry for a
wide region.

He was married twice. The first wife was a Miss
Kirkpatrick, of Anthonys Creek. Their children were
Robert, John, William, Thomas, and James. Daniel
Kerr's second wife was a Miss McKamie, of Rock-
bridge, a very sprightly and attractive person. Her
children were David, Daniel, Nancy, Betsy and Mary.

He was a sincerely pious person, and the close of
his life was very touching. He had assemnled his
family for domestic worship. Upon finishing the
Scripture lesson he kneeled for prayer, and for a long
int erval he was silent. Upon going to him in that

position he was found to be speechless and helpless. Much of the time after this he appeared to take very little notice of what was going on, and seemed unable to recognize friends. One day there was a gleam of intelligence and he uttered these words: "Farewell to all," and then lapsed into silence, and not long thereafter died so gently he had been dead some minutes before the fact was realized.

Andy Hughes now lives on or near the site of the old Kerr home. Daniel's son, Robert Kerr, settled on a part of the old place, and finally moved west. John Kerr went to Augusta County, and lived there, and then moved to Missouri. William Kerr married a Miss Gillespie, and settled the place now occupied by Asbury Sheets. His family was composed of three sons and two daughters. These sons, Jacob, George, and Andrew now live in the vicinity of the old home place. Mary Ann, one of these daughters, married Henry Sheets. The other daughter, Rachel, married a Mr Armstrong, in Highland County.

Thomas Kerr, another son of the pioneer, married a Miss Foglesong, of Greenbrier, and settled where James Kerr now resides, near the road to the top of Alleghany. His family consisted of three sons and two daughters. The sons are Robert, George, and James. The daughters are Mrs Phœbe Phillips and Mrs Mary Wooddell. Robert has been quite a traveller over most of the western States and territories, and now owns valuable lands in upper Pocahontas.

Lieutenant Robert D. Kerr, a son of James Kerr, graduated with distinction from West Point, in 1898, being assigned to the engineer branch of the service. He was ordered to the Philippines, and died on board a troop ship, in August, 1898, and was buried in the Pacific Ocean.

Mary Kerr, of the pioneer family, became Mrs Warwick Wolfenberger. Her brother, James Kerr, lived in Greenbrier, not far from Lewisburg.

David W. Kerr, one of the younger members of Daniel Kerr's family, lived for years near Greenbank, and was a person of high reputation. He was a carpenter by trade, yet by diligent self improvement he rose to be a person of prominence as a member of the county court, Colonel of the Militia, ruling Elder in the church, faithful teacher in Sabbath schools, and leader in prayer meetings. His daughter Maggie became the wife of Rev J. C. Carson, a well known minister in West Virginia and Tennessee. Adolphus Kerr, M. D., of Millboro Depot, is his son, and his brother and mother reside there also.

Colonel Kerr's wife was Eliza Whitman, daughter of William Whitman, on Anthonys Creek. Mr Whitman was a native of Orange County, Goshen Township, New York. He was a remarkable person, and his influence was for good wherever he lived.

The blessing called down by the good old pioneer abide with his descendants to the third and fourth generation. "The mercy of the Lord is from everlasting to everlasting to those who remember his commandments to do them."

MICHAEL CLEEK.

The ancestor of the Cleek relationship in Pocahontas County was Michael Cleek, who was one of the earlier pioneers ty occupy the attrative portion of the Knapps Creek valley adjacent to Driscol, and came from Bath County. His wife was Margaret Henderson Crawford, whose father was from Lancaster, Pa., and lived in Bath County, near Windy Cove.

Michael Cleek opened the lands comprised in the Peter L. Cleek, William H. Cleek, and Benjamin F. Fleshman properties—the persons just named being his grandchildren. With the exception of two or three very small clearings, it was a primitive, densely unbroken forest of white pine and sugar maple. He built a log cabin on the site of the new stable, and some years subsequently reared a dwelling of hewn timber, now the old stable at Peter L. Cleek's. The late John Cleek, father of Peter and William, and who was the oldest of the family, could just remember when his parents settled here. They came out by the way of Little Back Creek, crossing the Alleghany Mountain opposite Harper's. His mother carried him in her lap, horseback, all the way from Windy Cove.

Michael Cleek's family consisted of three sons, John, William, and Jacob; and three daughters, Elizabeth, Barbara, and Violet.

Elizabeth married Jesse Hull, of Anthony's Creek. Their children were William Crawford, John, who died in the war; Jesse, Andrew, Mrs Margaret Mc-

Dermott, on Little Anthonys Creek; Mrs Eveline
Fleshman, Mrs Alcinda Stephenson, of Bath County;
and Mrs Charlotte Fertig, of Anthonys Creek.

Barbara and Violet, the other daughters of the
pioneer Michael Cleek, died in early childhood of the
"cold plague," and their brother Jacob died of the
same disease, aged eighteen years.

William Cleek never married, and spent most of his
life with his brother John. The attachment these
brothers had for each other was noticed and admired
by all their acquaintances. They never seemed so
well contented as when in each others company. His
wit and good humor was remarkable. If all his funny
harmless anecdotes could be recalled and written up,
the result would be a very humorous book indeed, and
nobody's feelings wounded thereby. He could be
fecetious without hurting any one's feelings—a gift
rarely possessed by humorists. He told most of his
jokes on himself.

It now remains to make further mention of John
Cleek, the eldest son of William Cleek's pioneer home.
He married Phœbe Ann Lightner, a daughter of Peter
Lightner.

John Cleek spent his life on the home farm. His
family consisted of three sons, Peter Lightner, William
Henderson, and Shelton Washington. The daughters
were Mary Ann, Caroline Elizabeth, Alcinda Susan,
Margaret Eveline, aad Eliza Martha.

Mary Ann was first married to Josiah Herold. She
was left a widow, and afterwards married William C.
Hull. Her daughters are Mrs Patterson Poage and

Mis Tokey Hull.

Caroline Elizabeth married the late Lanty Lockridge.

Alcinda Susan married Hugh Dever, and is now in Nebraska.

Margaret Eveline married Renick Ward, late of Randolph County, and lives in Colorado.

Shelton W. Cleek died in infancy.

William H. Cleek married Margaret Jane Fleshman. He died in 1899.

Peter L. Cleek married Effie May Amiss. The pleasant home occupied by them is near the original site, across the valley from the public road, and near the foot hills of the Alleghany. Formerly the main road passed by the old Cleek homestead, crossing and recrossing the valley for the convenience of the residents. Thus the traveler would cover a good many miles in making but little progress in direct distance, as matters were in former times.

THOMAS McNEIL,

The McNeil relationship on Swago trace their ancestry to Thomas McNeil, who came to Swago from Capon Valley, Frederick County, between 1768 and 1770. His parents, whose names can not be recalled, came from Scotland. Thomas McNeil's wife was Mary Ireson, from Franklin County, Virginia.

About 1770 Thomas McNeil entered three hundred acres of land and settled where Joseph Pennell now lives, and built the house occupied a few years since by the samily of the late William McNeil, one of his grandsons. His family of sons and daughters were widely scattered in the course of years, but wherever they went became useful citizens. His sons were Jonathan, Absolem, Enoch, and Gabriel, and the daughters were Naomi and Mary.

Naomi became Mrs Smith and Mary was married to William Ewing, and both went to Ohio,

Gabriel married Rebecca Stephenson and settled where Jonathan McNeil now lives, then moved to Jackson County, Ohio, where he became a well known citizen. From information furnished by one of his grand-daughters we learn that he was the first surveyor of his adopted county, and one of the most prominent of the pioneers. Gabriel McNeil was a civil engineer, machinist, chemist, botanist, farmer, physician, and preacher, and not a quack in any one, says a writer in the Jackson County paper, who had been on a visit to the neighborhood where Dr McNeil had lived.

Enoch McNeil married Jane Moore, and settled on what is now known as the "Enoch Place," a section of the original homestead, but finally moved to Jackson County, Ohio.

Absolem married Comfort Smith, and went West.

Jonathan, senior son of the pioneer Thomas McNeil, married Phoebe Moore, a daughter of Moses Moore, and settled at the Swago Mill, now held by Withrow McClintic. He appears to have been an enterprising person. Milling, weaving, fulling cloth and powder making were carried on under his supervision. Coverlets woven by one Jones are still to be found.— Mrs Phoebe McNeil survived her husband many years.

She was born February 13, 1774, and claims to have been 13 years of age at the time of the Drinnan raid. when James Baker and the Bridger boys were killed. The sons of Jonathan and Phoebe McNeil were John, William, Moore, and Preston. Preston, while a little boy three or four years of age, was drowned near the mouth of Dry Creek and his body was found some distance below, near the fording.

John McNeil married Rebecca McNeil, from Franklin Co., Va., and settled on Dry Creek at the place now occupied by his grandson, Charles McNeil. He was prominent in his church, the Methodist Episcopal; a member of the court, a faithful and competent school teacher, and possessed knowledge of medical remedies and at a time when physicians were no nearer than Frankford or the Warm Springs. His services freely given were of great comfort and relief to the suffering before regular attention could be had. Mrs Anna Moore, near Marlinton; the late Mrs Jane Kennison on Dry Creek; Mrs Naomi Dilley, near Dilleys Mill; the late Washington McNeil, on Buck's Run, where Joseph B. McNeil now lives; the late John McNeil, Jr., merchant at Hillsboro, were his children. There were other sons and daughters whose names are not in the writer's possession.

Moore McNeil first married Martha McNair, of Augusta county, and settled on Dry Creek, near the mouth. His second marriage was with Nancy Auldridge, daughter of William Auldridge, ancestor of the Auldridge connexion in our county. By this marriage there were two daughters and one son. Clark died in early manhood. Phoebe Ann was married to Reuben E. Overholt; Nancy Jane became Mrs W. H. Overholt.

William McNeil married Nancy Griffey, from Franklin county, Virginia, a daughter of a Swiss soldier who came over with the Marquis Lafayette, and remained to became a citizen of the United States. They settled on the Thomas McNeil homestead. He was a popular school teacher, and among the earliest of his profession in the present limits of our county. He taught a 12-months school at the Marony Place, and had among his scholars the late Martha Adkisson, Agnes Gay and Andrew Gay, brother and sister of the late John Gay. Martha Young boarded with her sister Mrs Elizabeth Cochran. The Gays boarded with Jonathan McNeil, at the Mill. The Buckleys went to this school also.— William McNeil died a lingering and painful death of cancer. The sons of William and Nancy McNeil were Jonathan, James, Claiborne, and Moore. The daughters were Jane, Elizabeth and Agnes.

Jane McNeil was married to John E. Adkisson, and settled on the head of Swago. She became the mother of a worthy family of sons and daughters, was much esteemed for her amiable character, and died a few years since greatly lamented.

Elizabeth was married to Solomon Cochran, son of Isaac Cochran on Droop Mountain, and settled in Harrison county, where she died but recently, after several years of widowhood, greatly missed by attached friends and children.

Jonathan McNeil married Angelina Adkisson,

daughter of the late Daniel Adkisson, at the head of Swago, and they settled on the old homestead near Buckeye, where he now resides. Mrs Aaron Kee and Mrs John Buckley are their daughters. Rev Asa McNeil, William, Daniel, Doc, Ulysses, Enoch, and the late McNeil were their sons.

Captain James McNeil, second son of William McNeil, the teacher, married Sarah Young, and settled on a section of the homestead, where he now lives. After her lamented decease, he lived in Nicholas County a number of years, employed in house joining. At the opening of the war between the States he enlisted in the Confederate service in a volunteer company at Summersville as a lieutenant. Upon the reorganization he was elected captain. He became a prisoner of war at the battle of Droop Mountain, and was kept at Fort Delaware a long and tedious time. His second marriage was with Mrs Fannie Perkins, and he came back to the old home near Buckeye. His son Douglas is employed as clerk in a government department at Washington. For years Captain McNeil has been disabled by rheumatic affection, but the worthy old veteran's heart is still warm with sympathy for the "lost cause."

Claiborne McNeil married Elizabeth Adkisson, and lives near Buckeye, on the place bequethed him by his relative, "Little John" McNeil. Their daughter Charlotte is the wife of Joseph Pennell, who lives on Dry Creek. Their sons were the late Joshua B. and D. T. McNeil, and Senator N. C. McNeil, of Marlinton. His second marriage was with Margaret Griffin.

Moore McNeil, the youngest son of William the teacher, became a preacher, and entered the itineracy under the auspices of the Methodist Protestant church, and traveled many years with marked success and acceptance in the counties of West Virginia bordering the Ohio River. His wife was Miss Eliza Jane Donaldson. At the present time he resides at Smithville, in Ritchie County. He is however still vigorous, and performs much ministerial service, in connexion with the duties laid upon him by the care of a large family and the management of extensive farming operations.

Thus we have traced the history of Thomas McNeil, the pioneer of Swago, as exemplified by brief allusions to those of his descendants whose names have been communicated to us. His name deserves honorable recognition for his courage in penetrating the danger-recesses of these forest wilds, at the time among the most exposed and dangerous points of the Indian frontier. He overcame difficulties and encouraged others to do the same, and showed how it was done. Then when this place came to be too narrow, his sons and daughters trained by him were fitted to make the best of the opportunities opened up on the Ohio frontier and were ready for them.

WILLIAM A. GUM.

The Gum relationship in Pocahontas consists of two groups, descendants of Jacob Gum and William A. Gum respectively. The group considered in this paper trace their ancestry to Willi̇om A. Gum, who left

Highland County (then Pendleton) in 1831, and located on the Redden place near Greenbank, now occupied by John Grogg. In 1841, Mr Gum moved to Back Alleghany and settled in the woods, and opened up lands now in the possession of his sons.

Mrs Gum was Elizabeth, daughter of James Higgins of Pendleton. They were the parents of one daughter and two sons: Margaret Elsie, James Henry, and Francis McBryde.

Margaret was first married to James A. Logan, and first settled on a section of the homestead. Her children were John Commodore, who died in 1861 while quite young, and Elizabeth, who became Mrs E. O. Moore, and lived on Deer Creek near Greenbank.

By her second marriage Mrs Logan became Mrs Gragg, and lives on Back Mountain near the homestead. It is her mother in law, Mrs Zebulon Gragg, who is believed to be the oldest person now living in the county.

James H. Gum fisrt married Sally Ann, daughter of Zebulon Gragg, and settled on a part of the homestead. His second marriage was with Tilda Hoover, daughter of Abel Hoover, near Gillespie. He was a Confederate soldier, attached to the 62d Regiment of mounted infantry, that formed a part of General Imboden's command.

Francis McBryde Gum first married Elizabeth Peck, from Lewis County, and settled on the homestead. There were two children by this marriage, James Floyd and Virginia Elizabeth, who are living near Montgomery City, Missouri. His second marriage was with Caroline Amanda, daughter of Ellis Houchin, whose wife was Comfort Slaven Higgins. The Houchin family was from east Virginia.

McBryde Gum was a Confederate soldier, and went out with the Greenbank company, known as Company G 31st Virginia Infantry. He volunteered in May, 1861, and served throughout the war, and as he was wounded three times he is to be remembered as a battle scarred veteran of that mysterious and strange war between the States.

Those who are familiar with the history of the 31st Virginia Infantry, need not be reminded that no regiment in the service of the Confederacy has a more interesting and honorable record, or more frequently posted in the "deadly imminent breach" or more relied on in dire emergencies.

Fortunately Mr Gum's wounds were slight and did not disable him for any length of time. The first wound was received in the bloody affair at Spottsylvania Court House. The second wound was inflicted at Liberty, Bedford County, when General Hunter was repulsed at Lynchburg. The third wound was received at the battle of Winchester. Instead of a wound, he had his mustache neatly and closely trimmed off by a minnie ball at the battle of Cold Harbor. Clippers might have done the trimming a little more in style, but not near so quickly.

He was twice a prisoner of war. He was captured the first time at Uriah Hevener's, in 1861, and paroled. The second time he was taken at his home on Back Mountain, in October, 1864. This time instead of being released on parole, he was taken to Clarksburg, where he suffered many privations, and had a "plague of a time of it." He blames the cook, however, for the most of the hardships attending his imprisonment. It seems that the cook was infected with the spirit of speculation that was so much in the air during war time, and saw a chance to realize some pocket money from the rations he drew at the commissary. While the cook would draw very liberal rations, he was excessively economical in feeding them out.

There were but two meals a day, breakfast and supper. For breakfast the bill of fare consisted of a slice of very light bread, about four fingers broad, half tin cup of weak coffee, and a slice of bacon two fingers broad and not much longer. Supper was served at 4 p. m., consisting uniformily of a tin cup of coffee and another small slice of bread, but no meat. It is but just to remark that all this was without the knowledge of the Federal officer in charge. An individual who had been in the Southern service was the cook, and took advantage of this opportunity to make a little something for himself. He had found out that Confederates were in the habit of living on little or nothing, and to feed such was just to his advantage. He would make a nice thing of it and they would not know the difference, and would think they had gotten all that would be allowed.

Thus with the cheerful assistance of McBryde Gum, the compiler of these sketches has had it in his power to illustrate the family history of William A. Gum, a worthy citizen of our county in his day. All who re-

member William A. Gum have a good word for him
as a neighbor, friend, and substantial, prosperous citizen. The way he came to have a middle name is a
little out of the usual order. When Dunkum & Co.
had a store at Dunmore, William Gum was a liberal
dealer. There was another William Gum from the
vicinity of Greenbank, and the merchant to note the
difference and not get their accounts mixed, called the
one from Back Mountain "William Alleghany" on his
books. In settling he had Mr Gum to sign his name
William A. Gum. From that circumstance he always
thus signed his name in business affairs and in correspondence, and so got his middle name Alleghany long
after he became a grown person. In studying the
origin of names, it is interesting to find that a large
number of names have originated from where persons
happened to live.

Forty-nine years ago, in August, the writer spent an
hour or two at his newly made home in the woods, and
ever since there has been a beautiful picture in his
mind of a truly contented man with his home and surroundings, endowed with the power of making himself
and all around him pleasant and cheerful.

JACOB GUM.

The second group of the Gum relationship are the
descendants of Jacob Gum, who came from what is
now Crabbottom, in Highland County, soon after the
war of 1812. Upon his marriage with Martha Houchin

he settled near Greenbank, on land now owned by C.
A. Lightner. A part of his wife's patrimony were two
colored girls, Delph and Daphne, and in their time
colored people were curiosities in this region. Upon
moving he settled on the place now held by Joseph
Beard.

Mr and Mrs Gum were the parents of seven sons
and four daughters. The girls were Mary, Margaret,
Nancy, and Nellie.

Mary married Randolph Powhatan Bouldin, a journeyman shoemaker.

Nancy married William Sutton, and lived on property lately occupied by Craig Ashford. Her children
were Robert, George, Sherman, Eldridge, Anna, now
Mrs Craig Ashford; Magnolia, and Mary.

Margaret Gum married Charles Mace and went to
Missouri.

Nellie was a lifelong invalid.

William M. Gum married Sallie Tallman, and lived
on Deer Creek. His children were George, Franklin,
Samuel, Milton, Lee, Martha Jane, now Mrs W. J.
Wooddell, of Addison; Caroline, who became Mrs Lafayette Burner; Ella, now Mrs Brown Trainer; Rebecca, now Mrs Lee Burner; Marietta, now Mrs Enos
Tallman; and Nancy, who died at the age of four years.

McBride Jackson Gum married Eliza Thomas, of
Harrisonburg, Va., and spent much of his married
life on Clover Creek. His family consisted of four
sons and two daughters: Brown, William, Filmore,
Woods, Agnes, and Caroline. McBride J. Gum was
a gallant Confederate soldier, and served most of his

time in Captain J. W. Marshall's company.

Jacob Gum, Junior, married Virginia Burke, and migrated to Ohio.

Charles Gum married Jane Hartman and migrated to Ohio. He was a blacksmith by occupation.

Gatewood Gum went to Ohio when a young single man and settled there.

Robert N. Gum married Anna Riley and resides on the old Cooper farm, two miles east of Greenbank. His sons are William, John, and Joseph. The daughters are Elizabeth, who became Mrs Harry Burner and went to Wyoming; Mrs Anna Cooper, and Blanche.

Robert N. Gum was a brave Confederate soldier in the 31st Virginia Infantry. On account of his coolness and self possession under fire he was frequently selected for ambulance service on the field in caring for the wounded. To be efficient for such a service requires more than ordinary nerve, and he was found to be well qualified for it. In times of peace he has become well known as a miller, and is now managing the Hevener Mill, on the North Branch of Deer Creek.

John E. Gum married Harriet Hudson, and lives on a section of the Bible place, two miles from Greenbank. He was a Confederate soldier in the 18th Virginia Cavalry, under Colonel W. L. Jackson, and acted well his part amid the sufferings and privations that soldiers had to endure on the outposts during the war.

From J. E. Gum the writer derived valuable aid for this sketch, as we sat on our horses one warm July morning, after a casual meeting in the public road.

The Pocahontas groups of the Gum relationship

trace their ancestry to the Highland families of that name. These Highland families have for their progenitors pioneers who are believed to be from western Maryland, and among the earlier settlers of Pendleton, possibly antedating the Revolution.

HENRY HARPER.

Among the persons whose industry, economical habits, and wise management of diversified useful industries did much for the development of our county, the name of Henry Harpe, Senior, is richly deserving of respectful notice. He was a native of Pendleton County, a son of Nicholas Harper, a native of Germany, who lived on the South Branch. Henry Harper's wife was Elizabeth Lightner, daughter of William Lightner, Senior, on Back Creek. For a few years after his marriage he lived on the Branch. About 1812, Nicholas Harper bought two hundred acres from Abram Duffield and Colonel John Baxter, on Knapps Creek, and on this purchase Henry settled.

The young settlers from Pendleton County found a few acres of cleared land. The thickets of thorn and crab apple and wild plums were almost impenetrable. The sheep, pigs, and calves had to be penned by the house to protect them from wolves and bears. By patient and persistent effort land was cleared and a home reared.

At his suggestion, William Civey, of Anthonys Creek, sunk a tan yard. Then Mr Harper established

a blacksmith shop and built the first tilt hammer in
this region. This shop was carried on under his own
personal supervision. Ralph Wanless, George Hevener of Pendleton County, the late Anthony Lightner of
Swago, and others, learned the trade with him, and
were all good blacksmiths. Mr Harper also reared a
flouring mill, which was operated by himself and son
Samuel chiefly. Father and son were smiths and millers and alternated in their work. William Gibson, late
of Huntersville, and Henry Harper were the contractors that built the Warm Springs and Huntersville
turnpike sixty-five years ago. Captain William Cochran, late of Stony Creek, was their principal foreman
and manager in construction. In the meantime the
farm was duly attended to and much land cleared for
grain and hay; additional lands bought and a splendid
estate became his.

He had a passion for hunting, which he indulged in
merely for recreation.

He died in 1859, aged 70 years. Mrs Harper followed her husband in 1876, aged 86 years.

In personal appearance Mr Harper was of medium
stature, somewhat stooped in the shoulders. His voice
was soft and flute like in tone, very quiet and retiring
in his manners and leisurely in his movements, and
yet his establishment was a busy hive of industry, and
all moved on like clockwork.

His family consisted of five sons and four daughters:
Elizabeth, Sally, Anna, and Susan. The sons were
Jacob, William, Samuel, Henry, and Nicholas, who
died at fourteen.

Jacob Harper married Lydia Civey, daughter of George Civey of Anthonys Creek, and settled on Meadow Creek, Greenbrier County, and finally mov.d to Monroe County, where his family yet resides.

William Harper married Elizabeth Civey, sister of Jacob's wife, and settled on the farm now held by William L. Harper, near Sunset. His last years were passed on Greenbrier River at the Friel place, where his son William now resides.

Samuel Harper married Malinda Moore, and lives on the old homestead, where he yet resides in the 87th year of his life. Their daughter Elizabeth Luena is the widowed wife of Rev James E. Moore. Sarah Ann married Washington Herold, near Frost. Matilda married Frances Dever. Their son, Preston Harper, married Lucretia Gum, daughter of Henry Gum, late of Frost. Frank Wilson Harper married Anna Gum, sister of Mrs Preston Harper. William Lightner Harper married Emma, daughter of George Hamilton, near Sunset.

Samuel Harper's second wife was Margaret Jane, daughter of John Gum, of Highland County. Her daughter, America, married R. D. Rimel, and Virginia, who died of diptheria at the age of five years.

Henry Harper, Junior, married Phœbe Sharp, and lived on the place now owned by Reddy Goulet, near Sunset. Their children were Peter and Rachel Ann. Peter died in early manhood. Rachel Ann married William Herold, of Nicholas County, where she now lives. Henry Harper, Junior, died of an accidental wound, inflicted while repairing a gate.

Elizabeth, eldest daughter of the pioneer, married the late James R. Poage, and lived first in the Levels, on land now held by Preston Clark, and then near Edray, where they both recently died. She was an invalid for seventeen years from rheumatic affection, most of the time too weak to help herself. Her husband for many years spent most of the days and all of the nights a patient and helpful watcher at her bedside. Her sons were J. R. Poage, Henry Poage, and William Poage. Their daughters: Elizabeth Poage, the first wife of Rev George P. Moore; Mary Poage, the wife of Amos Barlow; Sarah Ann Poage, the first wife of George Baxter, near Edray, and Amanda, first wife of Levi Waugh, on the old homestead.

Anna Harper was the first wife of A. Washington Moore, near Frost. Her daughter Sally married Zachariah Gum, son of the late Henry Gum. Her husband was killed by a falling limb, and she was left a widow with three small children. Mary Moore married John Varner at the Big Spring of Elk. Ella Moore married Benjamin Varner, and now lives in Iowa. Anna Moore is at home with her father, the venerable Washington Moore, near Frost. Newton Moore, Zane Moore, J. A. Moore, and Price Moore are his sons.

Sally Harper married James Malcomb and located in Nicholas County, where her family now reside, so far as known.

Susan Harper, the fourth daughter, married the late John D. McCarty, near Hillsboro. Their children were Ellis McCarty, the late Mrs G. H. Curry, and Della McCarty, who died a few years since.

Thus close for the present the notes on the Harper family. Something as to the improvements made under Henry Harper's supervision may be interesting.

The tannery shop was built by William Civey, son of George Civey, who built the grist mill. Robert Irvine and John Irvine built the saw mill, and the same parties put up the tilt hammer and shop. The residence near the road was built by John Irvine, and Chesley K. Moore erected the dwelling beyond the creek.

The mill stones first used in the Harper mill were made by Adam Sharatt, near Friel's, on the Greenbrier River. This person lived at the Sharatt place, three or four miles up the Greenbrier from Marlinton, where he had a mill. The first burrs were bought at John Bradshaw's sale, near Huntersville. These having been used for years, Mr Harper replaced them by burrs brought from Rockingham County, Virginia. The Bradshaw burrs are now in Highland County, taken there years ago by Mr Shultz. The Harper mill succeeded the Poage mill, owned by Peter Lightner. The rocks used by that mill are now on Cummings Creek, near Huntersville, taken there by the late Price McComb, and therefore must be among the oldest in the county—of their dimensions.

JOHN H. CONRAD.

This ancestor of the Conrad relationseip settled on the North Fork, just after the Revolution, on land

now occupied by Oscar L. Orndorf.   It was pree npted
land, and in the virgin forest.   It is believed that he
and his wife Elizabeth, whose family name not remembered, were from Maryland.   They were the parents
of three sons, Solomon, John, and David; and three
daughters, Mary, Nancy, and Sally.   Nancy and Sally
died in youth.   Mary became Mrs Charles Martin,
lived a short while near the Conrad homestead, and
then moved to the western part of this State.

John Conrad went to Ohio, married and settled
there.

David Conrad died young.

Solomon Conrad married Mary Hogsett Brown from
near Parnassus, Augusta County.   John Brown, her
father, claimed all the land by preemption from Par-
nassas to the head of Deer Creek, and it was from him
Harmon Conrad obtained his homestead.   Mr Brown
moved to Montgomery County, and it was there Solomon Conrad was married, and settled soon after on
the Conrad Homestead.   They were the parents of
three children, John, Margaret, and Mary Ann.

John married Huldah Sutton and settled on the east
section of the Deer Creek homestead.   Their children
were Charles, Emory, Marietta, and Alice.

Charles married Huldah Kerr, daughter of Jacob
Kerr, and settled on Deer Creek.   Emory married
Eliza Wooddell, and lived near Liberty Church.   Marietta became Mrs Wilson Pugh, and lived on the
homestead.   Alice became Mrs Milton Gum, and settled on the Deer Creek homestead.

Margaret, daughter of Solomon Conrad, became Addison Nottingham's first wife. Her surviving child, Amos, lives in Dakotah.

Mary Ann Conrad became Mrs William Orndorf, and lived on the homestead. William Orndorf was from Tennessee. He was a soldier in the Mexican War, going with a company from Memphis, led by Captain William L. Lacey. One of Lacey's lieutenants was the person who afterwards in the Civil War, in the battle on Alleghany Mountain, was a captain of Artillery, and was killed in that action. Mary Ann's children were Oscar, Margaret, Mollie, Esta, and Laura. Margaret became Mrs Samuel McAlpin, and settled at Cowen, Webster County. Mollie Orndorf became Mrs Schuyler Fitzgerald, and lives near Greenbank. Esta Orndorf married J. C. Crowley, and lives near Greenbank. Laura became Mrs Loring Kerr, and lives on the Alleghany. Oscar Conrad married Nebraska Gum, and lives on the Deer Creek homestead. Their children are Lela, Mamie, and Cassie.

Mrs Solomon Conrad was a lady of great piety and genteel deportment, and a model housekeeper. Solomon Conrad was one of the sterling citizens of the pioneer times. His experience in the war of 1812 was one of toil, danger, and lifelong sorrow.

Drafted as a soldier, he was marched to Norfolk,— over three hundred miles,—served his time faithfully, was honorably discharged, and walked back to his mountain home, infected with the deadly army fever, from which so few ever recovered of the mountaineers. He was just able to get home, and was at once prostrated. The joys of the soldier's return were in a little while changed to sadness. The entire family were seized with the fever, and David, Nancy, and Sally were borne to their graves very soon, one after the other. Long as Solomon Conrad lived the memories of that sad home coming seemed to over shadow his spirit, and imparted a tone of subdued sadness to his demeanor. In mature life he made a profession of his trust in Christ and lived devoutly, honestly, and consistently.

There is much reason for believing that Browns Mountain and Browns Creek derive their names from Solomon Conrad's father-in-law, John Brown, late of Montgomery County, elsewhere referred to.

MICHAEL DAUGHERTY.

Among the early permanent settlers of Knapps Creek, and a person of some prominence in county affairs was Michael Daugherty. He was a native of Ireland and came from Donegal, and settled here about 1770. The property he owned is now in possession of Peter L. Cleek, William L. Harper, and the Ruckman sisters Margaret and Nancy. Mrs Daugherty was Margaret McClintic, whose parents lived near Staunton, Virginia. They were the parents of seven children, four daughters and three sons.

Their daughter Martha became Mrs John Frame and lived in Nicholas County.

Isabella Daugherty was married to William Nicholas and lived on Douthards Creek. The late Thomas Nicholas, on the Indian Draft, was one of her sons.

Elizabeth Daugherty became Mrs Adam Sharatt and located on the Greenbrier three miles above Marlinton, where he built a mill, traces of which yet remain. The dam remained long after the mill went out of use and went to ruins. It was finally destroyed as a nuisance. A more substantial structure of the kind perhaps was never constructed anywhere in this region. Thence the Sharatts went to Jacksons River, near the head-waters.

Margaret Daugherty married William Ruckman and first lived in Highland, afterwards came to Knapps Creek to the old homestead. In reference to her family we have the following particulars:

Isabella Ruckman died at the age of fourteen years. Mary Ann Ruckman, a very sprightly, interesting person, was an invalid from her early youth, and died but a few years since. Two other daughters, Margaret and Nancy Ruckman, live on the homestead. Michael Daugherty Ruckman married Jane Minter, of Cumberland County, Virginia, and settled near Mingo, in Randolph County. Thomas Ruckman married Mary Minter, and settled in Cumberland County. Mrs Mattie Riggleman is his only surviving child. Samuel Ruckmau married Elizabeth Hall, near the Big Spring of Elk, and settled in Randolph County. Mrs Lula Swecker and her sister Ardelly Ruckman are her children. Jesse Ruckman died at the age of thirteen years.

In reference to the sons of Michael Daugherty, the pioneer, whose names were John, Samuel, and William, we have this information: John Daugherty went to Kansas soon after its admission into the Union, mar-

ried Margaret Clark, and settled in that State. Samuel
Daugherty died in early youth at the old home on Mill
Run. William Daugherty married a Miss Collins and
after living a few years on Knapps Creek, went to
Wythe County, Virginia. Wellington G. Ruckman,
who now lives near Sunset, is a great-grandson of Michael Daugherty.

It is believed that Michael Daugherty built the first
tub mill, propelled by water power, anywhere in this
whole region. The site was on Mill Run, near Sunset
and some traces of it yet remain. This mill seems to
have been patronized by all sections of upper Pocahontas, and had the reputation of being one of the best
of its kind.

It may be news to many of our esteemed readers
that there was a "real old Irish gentleman" among
those who endured the toils, privations, and perils that
were peculiar to the early occupancy of this region,
yet such appears to be the fact, as attested by authentic
tradition. He grew to manhood having the privileges
and advantages enjoyed by the sons of the Irish landed gentry. As far as possible he wished to have
aristocratic usages in his home on the frontier. He
was one of the few settlers that attended sales in Stan-
ton or Culpepper Courthouse, where the services of
passengers were put up at auction in order to secure
the charges for transportation from foreign ports. If
a passenger could pay all charges himself and show a
receipt for the same, it became his patent of nobility
in the new world; but if he could not, it seems he
could not make good his claim to be one of "the qual-

ity,'' some of us people used to hear so much talked
about. In those old times when Michael Daugherty
was living, if a person could pay his own way across
the ocean, and hire or purchase the services of such as
were less fortunate, then he was one of "the quality."
As he was able to do both, then Michael Daugherty
was one of the first of the new fledged nobility that
occupied the Knapps Creek region.

With the notions peculiar to the Irish gentry, their
young people felt it was essential to their comfort to
have servants come and go at their bidding. Such a
domestic arrangement was a pleasant shade in summer
and a good warm fire in winter. The tradition is that
Michael Daugherty was one of the first to enjoy the
shade alluded to and the winter fires.

It is believed by his descendants that his father had
designed his son Michael for the Catholic priesthood,
and with a view to this had given him special educational advantages. Before receiving holy orders, the
father died. It appears that in arranging the affairs
pertaining to the settlement of the estate, in some way
a serious disagreement arose between Michael and his
step mother, and he thereupon received a portion of
the goods allotted him and he came to America, and
seems to have been lost sight of the Donegal Daugher-
tys. It is believed with good reason that could Michael Daugherty's descent have been shown to the satisfaction of the Irish Court of Claims, that his West Virginia heirs would have come in for a handsome share
of the ancestral legacies.

TIMOTHY McCARTY.

The progenitor of the McCarty connexion, and one of the earliest pioneers in our county, was Timothy McCarty, a native of Ireland. He settled on Knapps Creek previously to the Revolution, and was a soldier in that memorable war for independance. He could speak from experience that hard was the contest for liberty and the struggle for independance. With his humble hand he helped to make the history that forms one of the most instructive chapters in the annals of human endeavors for life, liberty, and the pursuit of happiness.

His first marriage was with Nancy Honeyman, and settled on lands now in the possession of Wilson Rider and the Gibson brothers near Frost; thence moved to Browns Mountain and opened up the property now in the possession of Amos Barlow.

By the first marriage there were seven sons: Daniel, Preston, Justin, James, Thomas,—the names of the other two not remembered. All of these sons were soldiers in the war of 1812, and but one ever returned to Pocahontas—Daniel McCarty—to live. The rest either perished in the war, or went to Tennessee or Kentucky.

Timothy McCarty's second marriage was with Jane Waugh, sister of Samuel Waugh of the Hills, whose memoirs appear elsewhere. By this marriage there were thirteen children. The names of but eight are in hand: Eli, Reuben, Samuel, Jacob, Nancy, Jane,

Martha, and Sally.

Nancy was married to Robert McClary, a saddler at Millpoint, and finally went to Ohio.

Jane became Mrs Harvey Casebolt, and after living awhile at the head of Locust Creek, went to one of the western counties of the State.

Sally was married to Ezekiel Boggs, in Greenbrier.

Eli married Margaret Moore, and lived most of his married life on the place lately occupied by John Simmons, head of Stony Creek. His daughter Jane was married to John Simmons. Robert, Amanda, Margaret, Calvin, Milton, Warwick, and Nancy are their children.

Reuben McCarty lived and died unmarried.

Samuel Waugh McCarty married Phœbe Moore, a daughter of "Pennsylvania" John Moore. Their children were James, George, Margaret, William, Elizabeth, and Peter. In reference to Samuel McCarty's family the following particulars are available.

James McCarty went to Ohio, married Mary Hadden, and thence went to Minnesota. His second marriage was with Melissa Overly.

George McCarty, a Union soldier, 3d West Virginia Cavalry, Company I, was killed at the battle of Winchester under Sheridan.

William McCarty, a Union soldier, 10th West Virginia Regiment, Company A, died at home, in 1861.

Margaret McCarty was married to James Curry, and they went to Kansas.

Elizabeth McCarty, a life long invalid, but an industrious, useful person, died a few years since at the old homestead.

Peter McCarty was a Union veteran, 3d West Virginia Cavalry, Company I. He married Elizabeth Araminta Hill, daughter of Aaron Hill on Hills Creek, and resides on the homestead near Dilleys Mill. The names of their children are James William, Leanna Frances, Amos Hedrick, Albert Granville, Carrie Virginia, and Mary Price.

Jacob McCarty, son of Timothy McCarty, was a member of the West Virginia legislature in the reconstructive period. His first marriage was with Annie Boggs of Greenbrier, and lived on Droop Mountain. There were six children by this marriage: Samuel, Elizabeth, Mahala, Melissa, Julia, and Franklin. The second marriage was with Hannah Brock, of Droop Mountain. George and Fanny are the children by this marriage. George McCarty lives on the homestead on Droop Mountain, overlooking the Hillsboro charming landscape.

Miss Susie McCarty and her brothers, James H. and Thomas, teachers in the public schools, are the grandchildren of Jacob McCarty. Their parents Samuel and Eliaabeth McCarty of Bruffeys Creek.

Jacob McCarty, Esq., as already intimated was prominent in the political affairs of our county, soon after the war between the States. He seems to have been quite ready at repartee. Soon after his return from Wheeling, some one undertook to guy him in this fashion:

"Well, Jake, you have been to the legislature and found out what a fool you are."

"Yes," rejoined Mr McCarty, "and that is more than you can say for yourself."

Daniel McCarty was the only one of the seven sons of Timothy McCarty that went to the war of 1812, and returned to Pocahontas permanently. His wife was Elizabeth, daughter of "Pennsylvania" John Moore, and they lived on Browns Mountain. Their children were George, John David, Margaret, Louisa, and Jane.

George McCarty married Eliza Herold, and settled where Sheldon Moore now lives. The names of their children were Andrew, Lanty, Catherine, Ella, and Lillie.

John David McCarty married Susan Harper and lived near Hillsboro. Their children were Ellis, the late Mrs Julia Curry, Sherman, who was drowned in a tan vat; Martha and Della, who died young.

Margaret McCarty was married to Jeremiah Dilley, and lived near Mount Tabor.

Louisa became Mrs Warwick Jackson.

Jane was married to Henry Tomlinson and settled in Iowa.

Daniel McCarty when in service was in the company commanded by Captain William Cackley, living at the time at Millpoint. He was greatly attached to his captain, and seemed never to tire in rehearsing the deeds of kindness and careful attention performed by his greatly esteemed captain.

Among his war stories the old soldier seemed to take great delight in telling how the turkeys would make him run into camp, when he would be foraging for something fresh to eat for his messmates. In explaining how this could be for a soldier brave as he claimed himself to have been, Daniel would wink one eye, fix his tobacco, and study awhile, and if it happened to be in a refreshment room, he would have to have a nip of thirty cent Kerrs Creek whiskey.

When ready he would tell how he would bait fish-hooks with grains of corn, and then throw the line where the turkeys could see it, and when one would take the bait it would start right for him, and he would break for the camp, and the old gobbler would never stop or let him alone until it was knocked on the head. Then it was his time to tackle the brave old critter and fix him for a turkey roast, for giving him such a scare and hard race.

When it was insinuated that it took him a very long time to tell nothing much at last, his rejoinder would come quick as a flash: When there is nothing much to talk to it takes time to say nothing much, as the Preacher tells us.

We have thus traced as well as we could the family history of Timothy McCarty, with such assistance as Mrs Margaret Simmons and James H. McCarty were able to render. The narrative is brought down within the memory and observation of the living. Some future biographer of the McCarty connection should collect material for correction and expansion at a later day.

Timothy McCarty was one of those who stood faithful in the struggle for American independence. He is one of the few Revolutionary veterans buried in our mountain land.

JACOB CASSELL.

Jacob Cassell, ancestor of the numerous relationship of that name, was a native of Pendleton. In early manhood he came to Bath, where he married Nancy McLaughlin, a sister of Squire Hugh McLaughlin, late of Marlinton. After living several years in Bath, he bought out Mr Deaver, on Greenbrier River, three miles west of Greenbank, now known as the Cassell fording. Here he settled and became a wellknown citizen of our county, about seventy years ago. His family were two daughters and five sons: William, Jacob, John, Samuel, James, Nancy and Jane.

William married Matilda Wanless, and settled on Back Alleghany where he spent the remainder of his life—he was eigthy-two years old when he died. He was married twice. The first children were Nancy Jane and George. The daughter became Mrs Henry Barlow and lives near Edray. George was a Confederate soldier and died of wounds during the war. William Cassell's second marriage was with Nancy Collins. By this marriage there were seven children. Mary Catherine became Mrs Thomas Beverage; Martha Ellen was married to Robert Sutton, a prominent teacher of schools; William, Jr., married India Sutton and settled on the homestead; Louisa was married to John Cassell and lives near the old home; Charles married Annie Geiger and lives at Huttonsville. Sarah Ann died aged 13 years; George went to Texas and after many adventures on cattle ranches was drowned.

Jacob Cassell's son, Jacob, married Nancy Sharp, daughter of the late William Snarp, near Verdant Valley, and settled in Illinois.

John, third son of Jacob Cassell, married Sally Curry and went to the far West.

Samuel Cassell, the fourth son, married Eliza Valentine Tomlinson, of Augusta county, near Staunton, Virginia, and lived for a while on the Greenbrier homestead, then settled on Back Alleghany on lands now held by his son, Jacob Cassell. Samuel's daughter married Harvey Hevener, and lived on the Greenbrier. four miles, above the old homestead; Jacob married Clara Sutton, daughter of the late Samuel Sutton, and settled on Back Alleghany; Mary Ann married Cyrus Tallman and settled on Back Alleghany; Alice married John Wooddell and settled near Travelers Repose; Margaret Jane married George Baxter, near Edray. It is to this member of the Cassell family that the writer is mainly indebted for assistance in preparing this paper. Rachel married Zechariah Swink and lives on Back Alleghany; Hannah married George Wanless and lived on the old Wanless homestead; Huldah became Mrs George Auldridge and lives near Edray.

James Cassell, son of Samuel, married Margaret Ann Swink, of Rockbridge county, Virginia, and settled on the Greenbrier homestead. His son John married Louisa Cassell and settled on Back Alleghany; Samuel married Martha Hevener and lives on the Greenbrier, near the old Cassell home; James married Sarah Shinneberry, and lives on Back Alleghany;

Thomas married Lydia Galford and settled on Back Alleghany; Ella married Henry Kessler and lives in the same neighborhood. Nancy Jane married Benjamin Collins, a Minister of the German Baptist church; Rachel Ann married Amos Gillespie, justice of the peace and a prominent teacher in the public schools, and lives at Cass.

Nancy Cassel, daughter of Jacob Cassell the ancestor, married Allen Galford, and lived on the Greenbrier near the mouth of Deer Creek.

Jane Cassell, the other daughter of Jacob Cassel, married Jacob Wilfong, and when last heard from they were in Minnesota. Their children were Jacob and Margaret Jane.

Jacob Cassell, Senior, the founder of the Cassell family in upper Pocahontas, was a person of remarkable muscular strength and agility. He was passionately industrious, and even in extreme old age never satisfied without something useful to do. He and his family have done very much in developing that part of the county where he resided. In his attire he was very neat and particular, and a perfect gentleman in his deportment. His personal influence and example were for fair dealing, strict integrity, and pure morals. He lived to be ninety-two years of age. Mrs Cassell died several years before her husband. Her death was occasioned by nasal hemorrhage, brought on by over-exertion in crossing a very high rail fence.

With the assistance of a grand-daughter of these venerated persons, the compiler has been able to prepare this memorial of two very worthy people, richly deserving of lasting and grateful remembrance for the part they and their descendants have performed in rescuing from a rugged and remote forest wilderness and laboriously developing one of the more really prosperous sections of our great county.

JOHN COLLINS.

For nearly a hundred years the name Collins has been a familiar one among our people. The progenitor was John Collins, a native of Ireland. He found his way from Pennsylvania to Pendleton county, where he met and married Barbara Full. He first settled on the Dunwoody place, near Meadow Dale, in Highland. About the year 1800 he moved to what is now Pocahontas county, and settled on the Greenbrier on lands now held by William H. Collins, and built up a home. There had been some improvements begun by former settlers, but so little that to all intents and purposes he settled in the woods. Mr and Mrs Collins were the parents of four sons and four daughters: John, James, Lewis and Charles; Barbara, Susannah, Mary and Elizabeth.

Barbara went west; it is believed to Ohio; Susannah became Mrs George Nottingham and lived in Athens county, Ohio; Elizabeth became Mrs William Queen, and went toMarion county, Ohio.

In reference to the sons of John Collins, we learn that John was a dealer in horses, and upon going to Richmond with a drove he was never heard of afterwards. The probability seems to be that he was killed and robbed in the Blue Ridge.

James went to Lawrence county, Ohio, married Henrietta daughter of Judge Davidson, settled seven miles below Ironton, and reared a large family. He was a prosperous prominent citizen.

Lewis was facetiously called the "monarch of all he surveyed," being regarded by common consent the strongest, most athletic and largest man in the county. He excelled as a ditcher, fence builder and mower. He belted many large tracts of land, and cleared many fields. He was noted for his good temper and jovial disposition. He never was known to provoke any one and, stange to say, he had more pugilistic knockouts than any one person of his times. He finally went to Nicholas county where he met and married Sally Boles and then settled in Upshur county. His children were James, Charles, Elizabeth Margaret, and Mary. James married Mary Leonard, went to California and engaged in the lumber business; Elizabeth became Mrs Sampson Jordan; Charles never married, and Margaret remained unmarried and kept house for her brother at the old homestead.

Charles Collins, of John the ancestral emigrant, married Mary McCarty, on Brown's Mountain, and settled on Back Mountain where Jacob Shinneberry lives. They were the parents of six sons and three daughters, concerning whom the following particulars are given: Martha became Mrs John Conaway and lived in Upshur county; Susannah lived at home with her brothers William and Benjamin: Nancy married William Cassell, and lived on Back Mountain; John married Martha Moore, of Pennsylvania John, in the Hills, and settled in Upshur county. His second marriage was with Widow Nancy McFarland, at Lumberport, Braxton county. Benjamin married Margaret Shinneberry and settled on Back Mountain near McLaughlin Chapel. Their children were Peter, Charles and Emma, who became John Shinneberry's first wife. Andrew married Martha Boggs, of Braxton, lived awhile in Pocahontas, and then moved to Upshur. Their children were Mary, who became Mrs Lawrence Fitzgerald; and Alice who became Mrs John Reed.

William Hutcheson Collins first married Sallie Varner, and located at the Greenbrier homestead. In reference to the first family these items are given:

Benjamin Collins is a minister in the German Baptist Church. He married Nancy Jane Cassell and lives on the Greenbrier homestead.

James Solomon is at home.

John Riley married Birdie Hoover, and lives in Upshur.

William Hunter married Vernie Hoover, and lives on Leatherbark Creek.

Andrew Morgan married Luella May Gragg, and settled near Travelers Repose.

Samuel and Susan died in youth.

Mary Elizabeth became Mrs Amos Nottingham, and lives at Beech Flats, on the Greenbrier.

Amanda Catherine first married William Hoover, on Back Mountain. Her second marriage was with Lytle Green Jackson, and lives at Wetumpka, Ala.

Her last marriage was the result of an advertisement and exchange of photographs.

The second wife of William Collins was Caroline Gragg, daughter of Zebulon Gragg. The children of this marriage are Effie Alice, Joanna Susan, Lewis, and Adam.

W. H. Collins was a Confederate soldier from 1862 to 1865. He first belonged to Company G, 31st Virginia Infantry, and after the seven days fight around Richmond was released from service under the rule of not enlisting over 35 years of age. When this was revoked he joined Captain William L. McNeel's cavalry.

Sally Joice, daughter of Charles Collins, never married, and was a confirmed invalid.

Charles Collins married Barbara Varner, of Highland County, and lived on Top of Alleghany. He was a Confederate soldier.

Samuel Collins first married Margaret Hayes and lived in Upshur County. One son, John William, became charmed with a show, left home and lived a life of adventure. His second marriage was with Celia Weimer, of Lewis County. They had two children, Samuel and Amanda. Amanda became the wife of Rev Queen, a minister in the M. P. Church, and lives in Pennsylvania. Samuel Collins was a Union soldier in the 10th West Virginia Infantry.

With the assistance of the venerable William H. Collins, the writer has been able to illustrate in part the domestic history of a family that has done a great deal in subduing our primitive forests, and prepared the way for many families to live in comfort now.

JOHN WEBB.

John Webb, the subject of this biographic article is a character about whom it may be said, as was said about Melchizedek, he was without father or mother—so far as any biographical purpose can be served. His Irish brogue and his habit of saying not foolish things and never doing anything very wisely, tended to corroborate what he always averred—that he was of Irish nativity. He had the papers showing that he was an honorably discharged soldier of the Revolution, and as a pensioner received ninety-six dollars a year. How he ever came to Pocahontas is simply conjectural, but from the fact he chose his place of rest near Mount Zion, he must have had some acquaintance with parties that may have been in the army when he was.

This Revolutionary veteran, though he exposed his life for independence, never owned any land and never married. Yet he wanted a home of his own, a place where he could lay his head and feel at home, which was very commendable in him. He received permission of William Moore, son of Pennsylvania John Moore, to use without rent as much land as he might want for a cabin, garden, and "truck patch." He built himself a cozy cabin, and opened up two or three acres, where he produced corn, vegetables, and poultry. On this he subsisted, with the assistance of his pension and such wages as he could earn in harvesting and haying for the farmers on Knapps Creek. This spot was on the place recently owned by Ralph Dilley, and now in the possession of William Moore.

One of John Webb's favorite places to work in hay-making and harvest was at Isaac Moore's. At this period making hay was a long, tedious industry. One morning quite early as the hands gathered in the meadow when Webb, to use his own expression, came up missing, it was surmised that he had worn off his "wire edge" on the hot sun the day before, and was about to give it up for the time being, and so the hands went to work, Between nine and ten o'clock they heard his jovial brogue in the direction of the apple cellar, and upon looking in that course Webb's head was seen, "red as a beet," peering over the comb of the cellar roof. He inquired in the most impassioned manner whether any one would like to have a "dhrink ave cither." It seems Webb knew where to look for the lost "wire edge," and had indulged his thirst until he was so much exhilerated as to climb the roof with nimble feet and willing hands, and from his lofty perch invite others to share with his jovial comforts that he had been finding for the past hours in "dhrinks ave cither."

This Revolutionary veteran had one of his arms very curiously tattooed between the wrist and elbow with the initials of his name and emblematic characters like anchors and arrows, whose significance was not known. This was done while he was in the army, and several other soldiers were tattooed at the same time. The chemicals used disabled them so much that a regimental order was issued prohibiting the practice. Tattooing seems to have been a fad among soldiers and sailors. If anything should happen, their personality might be identified and assistance obtained from some guild or fraternity. At least, this was the supposition. He never disclosed to any one what the characters symbolized. The initials of course could speak for themselves. It is commonly believed now that he served with the troops from Augusta County under General Mathews.

In the later years of his life John Webb was very piously inclined and was demonstrative of his religious emotions, and was long remembered as the life of many "good meetings" at old Mount Zion, Frost, and elsewhere. He would frequently have "the jerks," which was such a feature in the revival services so common at the time. As long as he lived he would always have a spasmodic jerk as he repeated the "amen," even when asking a blessing on his meals.

This phenomenon, that characterized the religious services of most of the denominations a hundred years ago in Kentucky, Tennessee, and Virginia; has been attentively considered by mental experts as one of the curiosities of the emotional faculty of the human race. What surprises them in their investigations is to find some of the most pronounced examples of its influence among the Mohammedan Dervishes in the East, and in the West it seems to have been the most striking feature in the Indian Ghost Dances but a few years since. The Dervishes furiously deny the existence of the Holy Ghost as a fiction of Christianity; and American Indians have never so much as heard that there is a Holy Ghost. Max Nordau, a Jewish scientist thinks he has found the explanation to be a disease of the nervous system that is so highly infectious as to sweep the whole round of humanity at recurring periods.

John Webb remained in his bachelor home until he became disabled by the infirmities of advanced age. Then it was the late Martin Dilley, of revered memory took charge of the old veteran; He built a very comfortable cabin for his use in the yard near his own dwelling, and cared for him until the old soldier "fought his last battle" on the borders of the unseen world. This building is standing yet. His grave is in the Dilley Grave yard, on the line between the Andrew Dilley and John Dilley lands.

WILLIAM BAXTER.

Among the worthy citizens of our county deserving of special mention was William Baxter, near Edray, W. Va. He was born on Little Back Creek, in 1808. He was the eldest son of Colonel John Baxter, whose name appears prominently in the early history of Pocahontas County. His mother was Mrs Mary Moore Baxter, a sister of Joseph Moore of Anthonys Creek. She was a very industrious and careful housekeeper, and diligently trained her children in habits of industry and economy.

At an early age his parents moved to Pocahontas County, and resided a good many years at the Sulphur Spring. Being the eldest son, he worked hard in assisting to support the family, consisting of four sons and three daughters. His sisters were Mrs Jane

Moore, wife of the late John Moore near Marlinton; Mrs Martha Duncan, wife of Henry Duncan, head of Stony Creek; and Mrs Sarah Duncan, wife of William Duncan, near Edray,

Mrs Baxter and three sons, Joseph, John, and George, finally located in Braxton County, where she died a few years thereafter. John died, too, soon after the removal to their new home. Joseph was a Federal soldier, and died of wounds in Kanawha County. George was a Confederate soldier, and died a prisoner of war somewhere in the State of New York.

From early boyhood William Baxter manifested great fondness for reading, and he improved his available opportunities very studiously. His father owned the largest and most select library then in the county, and William read most of the books. At an early day he began teaching, and was one of the most popular teachers of his day. In 1840 he purchased land sold for taxes by the late Jacob Arbogast, as commissioner, and built up a home on property now owned by his son George Baxter, County Surveyor.

This land was a section of the Philips Survey, dated 1795, and the papers call for twenty thousand acres. This famous survey began at the McCollam place, extended beyond Beaver Dam, thence on to Williams River, and from there came ont on Elk at the mouth of Crooked Fork, thence passed on towards Greenbrier River at a point near Verdant Valley, thence along the lines of Drennan, Gay, and others to and up Stony Creek near the old Salt well, and thence to the beginning.

His wife was Elizabeth Barlow, daughter of John Barlow. By industry and economy this worthy couple opened up a pleasant home in the primitive forest and reared their family very respectably indeed. George, Samuel, and William Baxter, near Edray, and Mrs Mary Moore, near Marlinton, are their surviving children.

For many years William Baxter, Senior, served as justice of the peace and member of the Pocahontas court. He was a skillful amanuensis, and did a great deal of work in that line, framing business papers, as articles of agreement, conveyances, deeds, and wills. His opinions were much relied upon as to the right or wrong of questions that would occasionally arise between neighbors, and frequently matters were quietly adjusted that otherwise might have led to tedious court proceedings, and much disagreeable personal animosities.

This model citizen was moreover regular and atten-tive in his attendance upon all religious services within his reach, but did not avow his trust in a personal Savior until advanced in life.

He died September, 1881, aged about 73 years. In two or three weeks thereafter his faithful wife also passed away, thus lovely and pleasant in their lives, and in death not long divided. At this day there are many to rise up and call them blessed.

THOMAS COCHRAN.

Among the persons who have been identified with our county history, the Cochran relationship claim recognition. For more than a hundred years the name has been a familiar one. The Pocahontas Cochrans are the descendants of Thomas Cochran, senior, a native of Ireland, one of three brothers who came over together. One of these brothers settled in Augusta and his descendants are highly respected in that county. Another of these Cochrans went to Kentucky, it is belived. Thomas Cochran, the subject of this sketch, married a Miss MacKemie, near Parnassus, in Augusta county, and settled on the Rankin place on the Greenbrier, near the mouth of Locust Creek. Thence he moved to the place now held by Mathews Ruckman. The relationship is so widely extended that it is only possible to trace his descendants to a degree where the present generation can take up the line and complete it.

By the first marriage there were two sons and three daughters. One daughter, name not known, became Mrs William Caraway and lived on Muddy Creek, Greenbrier county; Nancy became Mrs Masters and went to Ohio; Mary was married to William Auldridge.

John Cochran married Elizabeth (Betsy) James, daughter of David James, senior at the end of Droop Mountain, and settled near Marvin, on property recently occupied by the late Michael Scales. There were four sons and four daughters. David James married a

Miss Corby, in Augusta, and went to Clay county, which his son William represented in the legislature a few years since; Thomas married Miss Skeene and lived near Marvin. Their children were Franklin, America, Eliza and Harriet, now Mrs T. C. Wooddell. John had two other sons, John and William, about whom we have no information.

As to the. daughters, Margaret (Peggy) became Mrs Jacob Shue; Sally became Mrs James Waugh, late of Verdant Valley; Fannie became Mrs John Smith, on Stoney Creek; and Elizabeth.

Thomas Cochran, jr., son of the pioneer, married Mary Salisbury, settled on the side of Droop Mounttain, near Locust, and finally went West. Their children were Gordon, Robert, William, Richard, Deemie and Sabrie—two daughters and four sons.

Thomas Cochran's, the pioneer, second marriage was with Nellie James, daughter of David James, senior, already mentioned. The fruit of this marriage was seven sons and four daughters, viz: William, Samuel, Isaac, David, Solomon, James, Jesse, Rebecca, Mary and Nellie.

Rebecca's first marriage was with William Salisbury on Droop Mountain. By her second marriage she became Mrs John Burner, and lived in Ohio; Mary was married to William Cochran; Nellie was married to John James and went to Ohio. Her children were Jane, Eliza, Kate, William, David and John James.

Samuel went to Ohio.

Isaac Cochran married Jennie Salisbury, daughter of William Salisbury, who lived near where Richard

Callison now lives. His children were Elisha, Solomon Salisbury, Lewis Presley, Jackson, Bruffey, Margaret, and Sarah-

David, son of Thomas Cochran, married Sarah Salisbury, and lived near Droop Mountain. His children were John, William, Andrew, Biddie, Susan and Mary. Biddie became Mrs Gabriel Underwood; Susan, Mrs Joseph Rodgers, late of Swago; and Nellie was the first wife of the late Anthony Lightner; John first married Miss Hanna, of Greenbrier; second wife was Sally Smith; Andrew Cochran married Miss Rachel Lewis and lived on Sinking Creek.

Solomon Cochran, of Thomas, the pioneer, married Biddie Salisbury. Their children were Sally and Rebecca, Porter William and George. Salley died in youth; Rebecca became Mrs Bruffey Cochran; William married Almira Cochran, in Braxton county, and went to Illinois; George Cochran married Nancy, daughter of John Cochran, and lives at the end of Droop Mountain.

James Cochran married Nancy Hannah, and lived at the end of Droop. Their family six daughters and four sons: David, William, Joseph, James, Elizabeth, Jennie, Nellie, Eveline, Mary, and Rachel.

Jesse Cochran married Jane James and settled on the end of Droop, on property owned by his son, David J. Cochran. Their children were David James, Thomas, Samuel, Clark, and George Brown.

David married Hannah Duffield, and lives on the homestead.

Thomas settled on the homestead upon his marriage

with Nancy Stearns.

Clark married Sally Underwood daughter of Gabriel Underwood, and lives on the James homestead.

William Cochran, son of Thomas the progenitor, first married Jane Young, near Swago. Her children were Washtngton and Elizabeth. Washington Cochran married Phœbe Mace, of Mingo, and settled on Stony Creek. Himself, wife, and son John, aged 7, all died during the war.

Elizabeth Cochran married George Young. Mr Young died in Richmond during the war. His sons, William and Washington, live in Iowa. Mrs Young became Mrs Bruffey Cochran, went to Iowa, where she recently died.

Captain William Cochran's second marriage was with Melinda Moore. Her children William Cochran, Junior, and Mrs Catherine Sharp.

Captain Cochran was a busy man of affairs, noted as a skillful blacksmith, and built the first tilt hammer on Swago. He was captain of the Stony Creek militia, superintended the construction of the Warm Springs and Huntersville turnpike, and was superintendent of the Lewisburg and Marlins Bottom road. The Captain also took much interest in church affairs as a prominent layman of the Methodist Protestant Church.

The James and Salisbury families, elsewhere mentioned as early settlers of Droop Mountain, have been virtually absorbed by the Cochrans. The James boys went to Ohio, and the Salisbury men settled in Braxton and other places in West Virginia, and some went finally to Ohio.

The writer in closing this paper would gratefully recognize the assistance of David J. Cochran, that was so helpful in collecting the particulars, and so cheerfully given by him, although suffering at the time severely from rheumatic and other troubles, that seemed to be wearing his useful life away.

ABRAM BURNER.

Abram Burner, the progenitor of the Burner relationship in our county, was from the lower Valley, probably Shenandoah Countyr Soon after his marriage with Mary Hull; of Highland County, he settled on the Upper Tract, early in the century. Their children were Mary, Elizabeth, George, Jacob, Adam, Henry, and Daniel.

Mary Burner became Mrs George Grimes and lived near Mount Zion, in the Hills.

Elizabeth Burner was married to Hon John Grimes, and lived in the Little Levels on the lands now owned by the county for an infirmary.

Jacob Burner married Keziah Stump, and settled in the western part of the State.

Adam burner married Margaret Gillespie, one of Jacob Gillespie's nine daughters at Greenbank, and settled in upper Pocahontas.

Daniel Burner married Jennie Gillespie, sister to Margaret. Daniel Burner was drowned near Peter Yeager's in a deep eddy, during harvest, and left one son, Joshua Burner.

Henry Burner met his death by drowning in the

east fork of Greenbrier.

George Burner, eldest son of Abram the pioneer, after his marriage with Sally, daughter of Andrew Warwick, settled on part of the Burner homestead where the road crosses the east prong of the Greenbrier. Their children were Andrew, Enoch, Allen, Lafayette, Lee, Charles, Nancy, who became Mrs William Wooddell; and Isabella, now Mrs Lanty Slaven.

Enoch Burner married Rachel Ann Tallman, and settled in Missouri.

Lafayette Burner first married Nannie Wooddell and lived on the upper Greenbrier. Second marriage with Caroline Gum.

Lee Burner married Rebecca Gum, daughter of William Gum and a sister to Caroline just named, and lived on the Upper Tract.

Allen Burner first married Elizabeth Price, daughter of James A. Price, of Marlins Bottom, and settled at Greenbank. George Burner, of Minneapolis, is her son. Allen Burner's second marriage was with Virginia Clark, of Parnassus, Augusta County, and he now resides at Cass. Lula and Emma Burner, well known teachers are her daughters.

Charles Burner married Elizabeth Beard of Greenbank, and lived on the Burner homestead.

Hon. George Burner was a prominent citizen from the organization of the county. As noticed elsewhere he was one of the first members of the county court. He represented the county several terms in the Virginia Legislature, and was a Jacksonian Democrat in his political proclivities, and strange to say one of the original Pocahontas secessionists. so intense his devotion to State rights had become.

His second marriage was with Margaret Poage, daughter of George W. Poage, of the Little Levels.

ANDREW WARWICK.

One of the best known names in our pionee. annals was that of the Warwicks.   John Warwick; the ancestor of the Greenbank branch of the connexion, was of English descent.   It is believed he came to upper Pocahontas previously to the Revolution, and opened up a settlement on Deer Creek, at the place now in the possession of Peter H. Warwick and John R. Warwick.   Mrs Warwick, whose given name can not be certainly recalled, was a member of the Martin family in the Valley of Virginia.

John Warwick seems to have been a person of great enterprise, and braved the dangers of pioneer life with more than ordinary courage and devotion to duty. He had a fort raised upon his premises, to which himself and nelghbors would resort when threatened by Indian incursions or raids Being so near to Clover Lick, whose facilities for hunting and fishing were so much prized by the Indians, its erection seems to have been very exasperating to them, and were very troublesome to the settlers living in reach of the Warwick fort.

The only Indian Major Jacob Warwick was ever certain of killing was shot from a tree not far from this fort. The warrior had climbed the tree to reconoitre the fort, and it is more than probable that the death of the scout interfered with the Indian plans and intentions of attack.

In reference to John Warwick's children we have the following particulars: Their names were William, John, Andrew, Elizabeth—of whom special mention was made in the Slaven sketches: Mary, who was probaly the first lady teacher of schools in our county; Margaret, who became Mrs James Gay and went west; Ann, who became Mrs Ingram and lived in Ohio.

As the Warwick relationship is so extended, it will be treated in groups in these biographic notes. In this paper the descendants of Andrew Warwick will be mainly considered and their history illustrated, concluding with a fragmentary reference.

Andrew Warwick went to Richlands, in Greenbrier, for a wife and married Elizabeth Craig, and then opened up a home on Deer Creek. This property is now occupied by Major J. C. Arbogast. Their children were Jane, who was married to James Wooddell, near Greenbank; Margaret became Mas Samuel Sutton, first wife; Nancy was married to Jacob Hartman, north of Greenbank, and went to the far west. Her children were Sarah Lucretia, Virginia, William; and James. Mary Warwick became the second wife of Isaac Hartman, and lived on property now held by Joseph Riley. Elizabeth Warwick was kicked in the face by a horse about the time she was grown to womanhood, and lingered for years in great suffering and finally died of the injury. Sally Warwick became Mrs George Burner, of Travelers Repose. Anna Warwick was married to Rev Henry Arbogast, and lived near Gladehill.

Jacob Warwick, son of Andrew Warwick, married Elizabeth Hull, of Virginia, and settled on the Deer Creek homestead; moved thence to Indiana, and finally to Missouri. His children were Mathew Patton, Amos, Andrew Jackson, William Craig, Caroline, who became Mrs George Tallman; and Rachel, who was the youngest. They all went with their parents to the western states.

This paper will be closed by a fragmentary reference to John Warwick, of John the elder.

In the winter of 1861 there was an officer with the Ohio troops in the Cheat Mountain garrison by the name of Warwick. The writer has been informed that he claimed descent from the Pocahontas Warwicks, and made some inquiry concerning the Warwick relationship.

The tradition is that John Warwick. Junior, married Margaret Poage of Augusta County. It is believed James Poage, her father, lived awhile on Knapps Creek, and afterwards moved to Kentucky.

Upon his marriage John Warwick, Junior, settled on the lower end of the farm now owned by Captain G. W. Siple. Parties yet living remember seeing traces of the cabin he had built and dwelt in. He remained here but a short time however, and moved to Ohio about 1790.

There were three little boys, one of them named John- The Union officer claimed to be a descendant of a John Warwick from West Virginia, a grandson, and was a son, doubtless, of one of those little boys that went to Ohio with their parents from their cabin home on Deer Creek. This Federal officer became a member of Congress, and achieved a national reputation by defeating William McKinley in a Congressional contest. Many no doubt will readily recall this interesting event in the history of Ohio politics.

WILLIAM WARWICK.

The group of the Warwick relationship treated of in this paper includes the descendants of William Warwick, son of John Warwick, the early pioneer.

Like his brother Andrew, William Warwick lost his heart in the Richlands of Greenbrier, and married Nancy Craig, a sister of Mrs Andrew Warwick. They settled on Deer Creek, where Peter H. Warwick now lives, and were the parents of three children : Robert Craig, Elizabeth. who became Mrs Benjamin Tallman; Margaret, who became Mrs John Hull, and lived on the head of Jacksons River.

Robert Craig Warwick, the only son, at one time crossed the Alleghany to pay his sister a visit. One result of the visit was that he and Esther Hull were soon married, and the happy young people settled on the Deer Creek homestead. They were the parents of three sons and six daughters. In reference to their children the following items are recorded:

Catherine Hidy Warwick is now Mrs William Bird. Her children Elvira Louisa, now Mrs William McClune, near Millpoint; Robert Craig Bird, at Clifton Forge; John Henry Bird, Covington; George Newton

Bird, Clifton Forge; William Lee Bird, Roanoke City,
Virginia. Her husband, Major W. W. Bird, was a
Confederate officer. He had command of Company
K, 52d Virginia Regiment in the battle of McDowell,
and was in charge of a regiment of reserves in the bat-
tle of New Hope. He was near General William
Jones when he fell in that engagement, and received
his last orders just a few minutes before his death.
He was named for William Wallace, a renowned hero
in Scottish history.

Nancy Jane Warwick is now Mrs Jacob Lightner of
Highland, Virginia. Her children were John Adam,
now in the west; Robert, on Back Creek; William C.
died in youth; Jacob Brown, on Back Creek; Peter H.
lives in Greenbrier; James Cameron, a lawyer at the
Warm Springs, Va.; Mrs Malcena Catherine Cleek, on
Jacksons River; Mrs Virginia Rachel Wallace, of
Highland; Mrs Mary Etta Gum, of Meadow Dale, Va.

Sarah Elizabeth Warwick married Daniel Matheny,
and lives at Valley Centre. Her children Esther Ann,
Melissa, and Robert Matheny.

Margaret Ann Warwick became Mrs Nelson Pray.
Her family was quite a large one, but only one survives, Ella, who is now Mrs John Riley and lives in
one of the western counties. One of Mrs Pray's
daughters, Regina, received fatal injuries in a railway
collision.

Hannah Rebecca Warwick was married to Captain
George Siple, a Confederate officer, 31st Virginia Infantry, and lives on Deer Creek in sight of the Warwick homestead. Her children were Nancy Jane, now

Mrs Pierce Wooddell at Greenbank; Anna, Mrs William Jackson, at Dunmore; Mary Catherine, now Mrs Bernard McElwee at Dunmore; Clara Belle, William, and Joseph Siple.

Louisa Susan Warwick was married to Eli Seybert, settled near Mt. Grove, Va., then went west. But one of her children survives, Mary Amaret, now Mrs Morgan Matheny, Top of Alleghany.

William Fechtig Warwick was named for a pioneer Methodist preacher. He married Anthea Pray, and lives near Mt. Grove, Va. His children Paul, Pray, Robert, Nelson, Peter Hull, George Craig, Charles, Amelia, who became Mrs George Dilley, and is now Mrs Hopkins Wanless near Mount Tabor; Amanda Gabrielle, now Mrs John Landes, near Mt. Grove; Sally, and Louise Catherine. Three of the sons, Peter, Robert, and Nelson, went to Kansas.

Peter Hull Warwick married Caroline Matheny, and settled on the Deer Creek home place. The children were Jesse, Otis, Forrest, and Elbert. By the death of Cecil, in 1896, at Cowen, Webster County, his mother's heart was so broken that she did not survive him very long.

John Robert Warwick married Jennie Cleek, daughter of the late John Cleek of Bath County, and lives on a section of the Deer Creek homestead. Their children are Mary and Nancy. Lieutenant Warwick was a Confederate officer, 31st Virginia Infantry, and served as a commissioner of the Pocahontas Court.

Elizabeth Warwick became Mrs Benjamin Tallman, and lived on the property now held by Captain Siple.

Her children were William, James, Robert, John,
Cyrus, and Nancy. Nancy became Mrs Benjamin
Tallman and lives in Illinois.

Margaret Warwick was married to John Hull, on
Jacksons River. Her children were William Hull,
who was one of the California forty-niners, and has
not been heard of since; Robert, Andrew, Nora, Nancy Jane, who bechme the wife of Colonel Peter H.
Kincaid, in Crabbottom; Margaret, who is now Mrs
Christopher Wallace, of Williamsville; Irene Esther,
the first wife of James Fleisher, of Meadow Dale.

This relationship has furnished our citizenship with
good citizens, brave soldiers, industrious tillers of the
soil, and good homekeepers, and deserves honorable
mention in the short and simple annals of our own
Pocahontas people.

JAMES CALLISON.

The Callisons of Locust have a claim for special
recognition in our biographical sketches as one of the
oldest families of southern Pocahontas. Members of
that relationship have done a great deal in developing
their section, and have shown what can be done with
our soil in our climate by well applied energy and industry. The progenitor of this relationship, so far as
it is traceable, was James Callison, Senior. This person and his wife Elizabeth were natives of Ireland,
but, as the name indicates, were of English origin.
No doubt the Callisons were among the families that
King James the First encouraged to settle in the north

of Ireland.

Late in the eighteenth century it appears that James Callison went from Greenbrier County to Granger County, Tennessee, and made a permanent settlement and reared his family. The sons of James Callison the imigrant and Elizabeth his wife were James, Anthony, Isaac, Jesse, Samuel, and Elisha. Their daughters were Rebecca, Abigail, Mary, Nancy, and Ruth. In reference to the whereabouts of most of these sons and daughters but little has come to our notice.

Isaac Callison settled in the Meadows of southwest Greenbrier, where some of his descendants now live.

Colonel Elisha Callison, another son of the emigrant and pioneer, married Margaret Bright, daughter of David Bright, of Greenbrier, and lived on the noted Callison homestead near Lewisburg.

About 1782, James Callison, another son of the pioneer emigrant, came from Tennessee to Locust, now lower Pocahontas, and settled on a tract of 164 acres, preempted some years previously by his father. Soon after locating on Trump Run, Mr Callison took a great fancy to Miss Susan Edmiston, the charming daughter of James Edmiston, Senior, who was then living on the farm now owned by George Callison, a grandson of the lovely woman just referred to. James Callison and Susan Edmiston his wife were the parents of five sons and two daughters, concerning whom we are able to give the following pa.ticulars:

. William Callison married Hannah Ray, and settled in Nicholas County.

Isaac Callison married Nancy Jordan, lived awhile in Nicholas County, and afterwards returned to Pocahontas.

James Callison married Rebecca Gillilan, daughter of John Gillilan, and settled in Missouri.

Josiah Callison married Nancy Hill. They spent their days at the old homestead, and were the happy parents of five sons and three daughters. We give the following particulars in reference to their family:

James Callison married Ellen Alkire, of Lewis County, and settled in Greenbrier, where he died in 1885. His widow and two children now live in the State of Kansas.

Thomas F. Callison has been married twice. His first wife was Minta Myles, of Greenbrier County, and his second marriage was with Jane Myles, a cousin, and he now lives near Locust.

William Callison, recently deceased, married Fannie Whiting, daughter of Ebenezer Whiting, on the summit of Droop Mountain, and lived on Locust creek a mile or so from its source. Locust Creek springs from the base of Droop Mountain a full sized creek, receiving but little volume from visible tributaries on its course to the Greenbrier.

George Callison's wife was Miss Mandie McNeel, and his residence is at Hillsboro, on the place occupied so long by the late Colonel John Hill.

Richard Callison married Fannie Beard, daughter of Charles W. Beard, near Hillsboro, and he lives on the old Trump Run homestead, near Locust.

All of these sons are among the more prosperous

citizens of lower Pocahontas. They are devoted to farming and raising live stock, thus contributing very much to the substantial prosperity of our county.

Martha Callison, daughter of Josiah Callison, was married to James K. Bright.

Mary Callison was married to Lorenza Reger, and their residence is in Roane County.

Jemima Callison became Mrs Jesse Bright, near Frankford, in Greenbrier. She died in 1886.

The other branch of the Callison relationship in our county is represented by the descendants of Anthony Callison, a son of James Callison, the imigrant from Ireland. Anthony Callison was reared in Tennessee, and soon after coming to Virginia he lost his heart in Greenbrier County, and he and Abigail McClung were married and settled on lands adjoining the possessions of his brother James. These persons were the parents of six sons and four daughters.

Abram Callison married Frankie Blair, from North Carolina, a sister of the late Major William Blair near Hillsboro, and after living a few years in Pocahontas went to North Carolina.

Joseph Callison married Elizabeth Bright, of Greenbrier.

Isaac Callison married Hulda Hickman, in Bath County, and moved to Indiana.

Anthony Callison, Junior, was married to Martha Hill, and settled in Indiana.

Israel Callison married Mary Bright, sister of Joseph's wife, lived many years on the old homestead, and finally moved to Illinois.

Elisha Callison located in the Meadows of west Greenbrier.

Margaret Callison, daughter of Anthony and Abigail Callison, became Mrs William Burnsides and went to Indiana to seek a home.

Elizabeth Callison married Jonathan Jordan, and they lived on Cooks Dry Run, the place lately occupied by Peter Clark, deceased. It was here she died. Her twin sons, John and Anthony, also died.

Abigail Callison became the wife of James Gay, and they settled in Indiana.

Julia Callison, the youngest daughter, married when she was just past fifteen the late Colonel Woods Poage. The writer will ever cherish the memory of Mrs Julia Poage as one of the kindest friends of his boyhood.

The writer has thus far been enabled to make a brief contribution to the history of the Callison relationship, which deserves an important place in the annals of our county. It makes him feel sad to think that the kind friend (Mrs Nancy Callison) who so patiently furnished him the information, without which this paper could not have been written, is not here to receive the thanks that are so justly due her. It looks now like it was a special providence that permitted us to meet at the time when we did, an.. is so regarded by the compiler. Her bright and pleasant way of recalling the reminiscences of friends and acquaintances was something like which one can not expect to witness very often now, as so few are left to rehearse the story of that past which was once a living present to them.

These people whose lives make up the past, whose

history so few survive to repeat, sowed in tears, in privations, and hardships what we who now live are reaping in a joyful harvest. What they sowed in tears we the living may reap with grateful joy, if we have proper appreciation of what they did and suffered in their day and generation. Let us not forget that the frugality, industry, and careful attention to duties that enabled them to secure this goodly heritage, is all important for us to observe and imitate in order to keep it from slipping away and vanishing from our reach.

Like busy bees the pioneer people all over our country tried to improve every shining hour, and turn to some good account every opportunity in sight, no matter how hard it may have seemed. It has been well said that those who look only for easy places, will finally round up in the hardest places and have no way to get out except by death.

WILLIAM EDMISTON.

William Edmiston, in whose memory this biographic paper has been prepared, was one of the early settlers of the lower Levels. He seems to have been born and reared in upper Greenbrier, near Falling Spring, and his ancestry came from Augusta County. His wife was Rebecca Walkup, from the Falling Spring vicinity, where there are families of the name now residing. She was a sister of the late John Walkup, of Falling Spring, a greatly respected citizen and exemplary Christian man. One of her sisters was the wife of Samuel Beard, who was a brother of Josiah Beard, and his home was in Renicks Valley.

Upon his marriage with Rebecca Walkup, Mr Edmiston settled a few miles south of Hillsboro. Their family consisted of one son, James Edmiston, and four daughters, Rebecca, Jennie, Mattie, and Margaret.

James Edmiston married Margaret Woods, of Nicholas County- He settled on Cooks Dry Run, at the "Sinks," which is now known as the Peter Clark place. The names of James Edmiston's children known to the writer were Samuel, William, Christopher, and Rebecca. This daughter Rebecca became the wife of Jackson Edmiston, son of Andrew Edmiston, a brother of William Edmiston.

About 1840 James Edmiston sold his possessions to the late Andrew Johnson and migrated to Iowa, where many of his descendants now live.

Rebecca Edmiston became the second wife of Jonathan Jordan.

Jennie Edmiston was married to Isaac Hill. Upon his decease she and her family removed to the State of Iowa.

Martha Edmiston married George Hill, and settled on Hills Creek and spent her life there.

Margaret, the fourth daughter of William Edmiston, was married to George McCoy, moved to Cedar County, Iowa, and were among the first settlers of their vicinity, and grew up with the development of that renowned county. William McCoy, their son, could not forget the girl he left behind, but returned to .Pocahontas and married Elizabeth Grimes, daughter of the late Hon John Grimos.

These few particulars illustrating something of the family history of these good people have been laid before our readers with the assistance of the late Mrs Nancy Callison and the venerable James McCollam. The writer has some remembrance of these persons personally, but not very distinct as to any important impressions.

Mr Edmiston and the late Samuel Davies Poage were congenial friends and attached Christian brethren though of different persuasions and rather strenuous in their respective doctrinal views. This indicated that their hearts were imbued with a pious fervor that got the better of their mere intellectual doctrinal notions. They agreed to disagree, and not mar their Christain fellowship with vain wrangling about their respective creeds and formalities.

Mr Edmiston's piety was of the highly emotional, demonstrative type, and for years his emotions seemed to be the first to kindle and burn with the holy fervor that makes religious services so interesting to many persons. His Christian character was above reproach, and all regarded him as sincere. He was looked up to as a master Christian, and had it not been for the somewhat counteracting influence exerted by Nathaniel Kinnison, a silent, calm Israelite indeed in whom there was no guile, the impression might have been that no one could expect to be a model Christian like Mr Edmiston without his zeal and demonstrative fervor

Such might have been the impression, but when the

characters of Nathaniel Kinnison and Davies Poage were considered, the impression prevailed there were different ways in which people could be warm hearted, genuine Christains, and so there was mutual respect and lovely Christian fellowship.

For many years Mr Edmiston was a pillar in the M. E. Church, and the secret of his influence was his lovely Christain deportment. Nathaniel Kinnison was also a pillar in the M. E. Church, but his piety was that developed in the calm retreat, the silent shade, that seemed to him by God's bounty made for those who worship God—so suitable for personal prayer and praise to the unseen though ever present one.

When far advanced in life Mr Edmiston vacated his old pleasant home amid the gently rolling lands and pleasant groves for a home on Hills Creek, and his last days were spent amid the inviting scenes that surround the place where Daniel Peck now lives.

The writer feels grateful that he ever knew this good old man, even to a slight extent, and may the time never come when the presence of persons of like Christian fervor, generous, liberal, fraternal impulses cease to exist, for should such a dire calamity befall the county then envy, strife, confusion, and many evil works will be tolerated—all in the name too and for the sake of religion.

JOHN YEAGER, SENIOR.

For well nigh a hundred years the Yeager name has been a familiar one. The Reager relationship derive their name from John Yeager, an imigrant from Pennsylvania, reared near Lancaster City. From the most authentic information available for these notes, he first located in Crabbottom. Upon his marriage with Anise Hull, a granddaughter of Peter Hull, one of the original settlers of the Crabbottom section, they settled at Travelers Repose, where Peter D. Yeager now resides.

In reference to John Yeager's family the following particulars have been obligingly furnished by the Hon H. A. Yeager, one of his well known descendants.

John Yeager, Junior, went to the far west, and settled finally in Illinois; and his descendants are scattered widely over the great Northwest.

Jacob Yeager married Sarah Hidy, of Crabbottom, and thereupon he settled on what is known as Camp Alleghany. In his time he ranked among the most extensive land owners in that whole region. His claims comprised many thousand acres, embracing the 'Dutch Settlement' and other tracts contiguous. His sons were John, Joel, Jacob Brook, and the daughters were Jane, Elizabeth, Anna, Caroline, Margaret, Catherine, Christine, and Serena. In reference to his daughters the following particulars are in hand.

Jane became Mrs Joel Vest, and lived in Iowa.

Elizabeth was married to Colonel John Bonnett, and lived in Lewis County. Her sons Jefferson and Asbury Bonnett are prominent citizens. Sarah Ann Bonnet became Mrs Wasley Crookman and lives at Cowen. Serena Catherine Bonnett became Mrs Eber Post, and lives near Hackers Creek, in Lewis County. Caroline became Mrs Rhinehart.

Margaret married John Arbogast and lived near Glade Hill.

Caroline was William J. Wooddell's first wife, and lived at Greenbank.

Anna first married Warwick Arbogast and settled near the homestead at Camp Alleghany. He and two children died of camp fever in 1861. Her second marriage was with John Luzadder, and lives near Tollgate, Ritchie County, and is the mother of a large family.

Catherine was married to Robert Willis, and lived in Indiana. There were three daughters: Virginia married a Mr Britt, who was a mining expert at Frisco Colorado. Josephine married Dr Simms. Laura became Mrs Carroll.

Christine became Mrs Jonathan Siron, and lived near McDowell, in Highland. Her children were Joel, lately deceased: Milton, in Upshur County; Margaret, now Mrs Malcomb, in Highland; and Christine, who became Mrs William Wooddell and lives on the Siron homestead.

Serena was first married to John Claiborne, of Lexington, Virginia. Her children were James, who died in Arizona, and John, who lives at St. Joseph, Mo. John Claiborne was a Confederate soldier and died in service. Serena Yeager's second marriage was with William Wilfong, of Gilmer County, and is the mother of three sons by this marriage.

Joel Yeager married Rebecca Pray, of Highland County, and settled in Indiana. There are three sons, Newton, Luther, and Clinton. One is a lawyer, another a doctor, and the third a prosperous farmer.

Jacob Brook Yeager married Margaret McDaniel, at McDowell, in 1856, and settled in Indiana at South Whitney, where he still lives. Two sons and a daughter. His son Charles recently visted Pocahontas.

John Yeager, the third, settled at the homestead.

Andrew Yeager, another son of John Yeager the pioneer, married Elizabeth Dilley, and settled on the homestead. Two sons, Peter and Martin, and one daughter, Ella, who died at the age of 15 years of diptheria, one of the first cases to appear in our whole county. In 1861 Andrew Yeager refugeed to Highland, where he and his son Martin died of camp fever. His property was burned in the absence of the family. The battle of Camp Bartow was fought here in 1861.

Peter Dilley, the only surviving child of Andrew Yeager, married Margaret Bible, daughter of Jacob Bible, and rebuilt the pioneer homestead. The following particulars about his family are in hand: Charles Andrew married Allie Arbogast, and lives at Marlinton; William Jacob married Grace Hull; Etta became Mrs Harper McLaughlin of Bath County; Alcena is now Mrs Charles Pritchard, of Dunmore; Alice was married to Henry Flenner, and lives near the homestead; Gertrude is at home with her parents.

Peter D. Yeager now resides at Travelers Repose, the pioneer homestead, which he in a large measure restored from the terrible devastation of war. He was a Confederate soldier, became a prisoner and spent a long time at Camp Chase. He was not released until July, 1865.

John Yeager, the pioneer, seems to have been a

person of great physical endurance, a noted hunter, and an industrious, laborious farmer. One of the incidents coming to us by tradition, illustrating what manner of man he was, is related in the Arbogast sketches. A panther had been driven by dogs up a very lofty, densely branched hemlock, at night. A torch of pine was prepared, and the fearless, agile man ascended the tree, torch in hand, until he could locate the game. Upon doing this he laid the torch on two limbs and descended until he could reach the flintlock rifle, carefully primed and charged. He then returned to his torch and by its light shot the panther.

JOHN YEAGER, JUNIOR.

The relationship bearing the Yeager name is at present mainly represented in our county by the descendants of John Yeager, of the third remove from the pioneer John Yeager. Hence this paper will be mainly devoted to the home history of his descendants.

John Yeager's wife was Margaret Arbogast, granddaughter of Adam Arbogast, the pioneer of the east branch of the Greenbrier. Soon after his marriage he settled on the homestead, now known as Camp Alleghany. The sons were William Asbury, Henry Arbogast, Brown McLauren, Paul McNeel, and Jacob Reese. The daughters Eliza Ann, Fannie Elizabeth, Sarah Jane, who died aged 13 years; Eveline Medora, Leah Alice, and Emma Mildred.

Eliza Ann became Mrs A. M. V. Arbogast and lives on the east branch of the Greenbrier, near the northern limits of the county.   Her home is widely known.

Fannie Elizabeth is now Mrs James D. Kerr, and lives at the Kerr homestead on Salisburys Creek.

Eveline Medora was married to Josiah O. Beard, and now lives near Greenbank. Her children are Irbie, Leslie, Arthur, Brown, Monroe, Blanche, Bertie, Bertha, Ruby, Nellie Bly, and Margie. Monroe and Blanche are twins, also Bertie and Bertha.   Mr and Mrs Beard had their home on the upper Greenbrier.   Blanche died of membranous croup, in her father's absence, and the house being isolated by deep water, the mother could get no assistance from the neighbors on that sad day.   In a field near the present home Arthur was caught in a shower.   He first sheltered under a wagon, but as it leaked so much he ran to a neighboring tree and was instantly killed by lightning.   His brother Irby was near and saw it all.

Leah Alice and her brother Jacob Reese died of diptheria.   They were among tne first victims of this drehd malady in our whole county, so far as there is any record.

Emma Mildred first married Michael O. Beard, and settled in Texas.   He died at Fort Worth, Texas. Mrs Beard's second marriage was with W. P. Ledbetter, of Georgia.   She then settled in the Indian Territory, at Ardmore, where she died a few years since. Her children, Clyde Yeager Beard and Veva Ledbetter, are in the motherly care of her sister Mrs Eliza A. Arbogast.

Emma Mildred Yeager had a passion for learning, and was very popular in society and greatly esteemed for her attractive character.   She had about completed

the course of study at Winchester for a literary degree
with marked distinction.   Had it not been for circumstances over which the brilliant young student had no
control, she would have been the first lady from our
county to be thus honored.

William Asbury Yeager was a Confederate soldier
in the 31st Virginia Regiment, and was killed at
Hatcher's Run, Feb. 6, 1865.   He was in the battle
of Winchester, September 19, 1864, and when the engagement was over seventeen bullet holes were found
in his clothing, but he did not get a scratch.   The impression preuails among those who remember him that
he was in all the engagements with the 31st, unless it
was at Gettysburg, at which time he was in a Staunton
hospital.   He had but one furlough during the war.

Henry A. Yeager married Luverta Beard, of Greenbrier County, and settled at Camp Alleghany.   His
children were Eula Joe, recently deceased, who was
the wife of Dr J. M. Cunningham, of Marlinton;
Maud Leps, named for Rev J. C. Leps, the chaplain
of the 31st Virginia Regiment, now Mrs R. C. Mc-
Candlish, cashier of the Pocahontas Bank; Sallie
Glenn, now Mrs S. B. Scott, of Marlinton; Walter H.
lives in Cheyenne, and is a clerk in the emyloy of the
Union Pacific Railway.   His wife was Mabel Tupper.
William Edgar Yeager died while holding the position
of paymaster's clerk at Washington.   At the same
time he pursued a course of medical studies, and had
about finished with credit half of the four years prescribed course when his health failed.   He died Nov.
26, 1896.   Paris Dameron Yeager spent some years

at Cheyenne, Wyoming, in the service of the Pacific Express Company and the Continental Oil Company.

Hon H. A. Yeager was a Confederate soldier in the 31st Virginia Regiment, and was in all the engagements except when disabled by wounds. He has represented his county in the legislature, and was special agent of the National Land Office during the first Cleveland administration, and was stationed at Cheyenne, Wyoming. He was among the first to boom Marlinton.

Brown McLaurin Yeager married Harriet Elizabeth Arbogast, and they live at Marlinton. Their children are J. Walker Yeager and Lewis A. Yeager, lawyers; Dr John M. Yeager, Sterling, Bruce, and Paul McGraw, and the daughters are Daisy, now Mrs W. B. Sharp; Texie, Brownie, and Goldie. Mr Yeager is local manager for the Pocahontas Development Company. He has surveyed many thousand acres of land in Pocahontas and has served as commissioner of school lands.

Paul McNeel Yeager married Huldah Arbogast and lives on the pioneer homestead opened up by Adam Arbogast. His children are Pearl, Lucy, Mamie, Jewell, Frederick, and Clinton. He has a great reputation as a hunter. His portrait in hunting garb and a sketch of his exploits have appeared in one of the hunting journals.

John Yeager, the third, was a person of more than ordinary endowments. By a patient course of studies, mainly self directed, pursued at times when he could get an hour's leisure from manual labor, he became qualified for the duties of a surveyor. He was deputy surveyor for a number of years, associated with Sampson L. Mathews, who was the first surveyor of Pocahontas County. He was in subsequent years associated with Colonel Paul McNeel and George Edmiston in searching for vacant lands, and under their direction made entries comprising acres that even now have a fabulous sound in our ears—as to their extent and numbers.

When Colonel Rust, of the 3d Arkansas Regiment, became acquainted with Mr Yeager he was so favorably impressed by his intelligence and experience as to select him for the perilous duty of reconoitering the Federal fortifications on the summit of Cheat Mountain. The Colonel left his encampment in the most secret way possible, and with John Yeager as pilot and solitary companion, approached the Federal encampment unobserved and succeeded in passing into and throughout the garrison, made careful observations of the character and position of the defence, and withdrew without arousing suspicion as to the purpose of their presence in the camp. With the knowledge thus obtained, Colonel Rust planned the assault he soon after attempted to make, but owing to high water and other obstacles, time was lost, and the Federal officers were thus enabled to learn what was going on, and they made preparations accordingly. When this became apparent to Colonel Rust he withdrew without making the assault, as had been so skillfully planned at the extreme personal risk of himself and his trusted guide, John Yeager.

A few months after this perilous adventure John Yeager died, December, 1861, aged 48 years. When the battle of Alleghany was fought in that same month the balls seemed to fall like hail upon the roof, but none of the inmates were touched.

ABRAM DUFFIELD.

The first cottage prayer meeting the writer remembers was at the home of Abram Duffield. Early one Sabbath in May, the writer's parents with their four children came to the Duffield home to attend the meeting that had been announced. No one had yet arrived when we reached the place. Upon entering the porch voices were heard within as if persons were engaged in reading or prayer. Standing by the door and listening we found that it was the venerable Abram Duffield reading to his invalid wife the account given by Saint Mathew of our Redeemer's temptation in the wilderness. He was reading at the moment where it is written: ''He shall give His angels charge concerning thee and in their hands shall they bear thee up, lest at any time thou dash thy foot against a stone.'' Then she remarked: ''Oh, that is so good; how encouraging it is for poor me.'' Finally the venerable man resumed and then prayed after reading. ''Then the Devil leaveth him, and behold angels came and ministered unto him. Then again the same one observed: ''Oh, how good to hear that our Lord gained the victory. How safe it makes one feel to have him for our Saviour who is so loved by the angels.'' There seemed to be mutual rejoicing over the Redeemer's victory, and if the benefits of this victory had been for these two old people alone, their satisfaction could not have been, seemingly, more real. When silence intervened we knocked at the door and were told to come in. There were the two old people, and no one else, in the room. It was not long, however, before quite a number assembled, and the cottage prayer meeting was quite a spirited one-

Abram Duffield is believed to have come from the lower Valley, during the Revolution or soon after, and at the time referred to was living on the farm now occupied by Newton Duffield. The venerable Mrs Duffield was Hannah Moore, daughter of Moses Moore, the well known pioneer.

From Mrs Catherine Kellison, on the Dry Branch of Swago, we gathered the following particulars.

Andrew Duffield was the eldest son of Abram Duffield's family. He married Jane Moore, daughter of Robert Moore, Senior. In reference to Andrew Duffield's family, we learn that Robert M. Duffield lives in Jackson County, West Virginia. William Duffield, a Union soldier, died during the war at the home of Jacob Waugh in Barbour County. Andrew Duffield, Junior, died of fever at the age of sixteen years. Rebecca Jane Duffield is now deceased. Eliza Duffield became the wife of Captain Walton Allen of Clover Creek, who was a well known scout in the late war between the States. Catherine Duffield was married to Clark Kellison, near Buckeye, a Union soldier under Sheridan. He was also on detached service on the western plains after the war in the U. S. Cavalry. He received his discharge just in time to escape the Custer massacre.

John Duffield, son of Abram, the pioneer, married Rebecca Sharp, daughter of John Sharp, Senior. Mr Duffield settled at the Mill property on Stony Creek, but his later years were spent on the farm where his father Abram had lived and died. His sons were Hamilton, Wesley, Newton—who lives on the old homestead;—Emory, and McKendree in Colorado. Andrew, a bright and beautiful little boy, the pet and pride of the household, was at play on the porch. His mother was busily sewing just inside the door, not six feet away. Wondering what was keeping Andrew so quiet, she turned to the door and found him dead— strangled by the crupper of her saddle. The shock was such that she never fully recovered from the effects, though she lived for more than fifty years afterwards.

Sarah Jane Duffield became the wife of Joseph Moore, son of the late Addison Moore.

Nancy Ellen Duffield was married to the late Marcellus Ratliff, and now lives on a portion of the old homestead near Green hill school house.

William Duffield, son of Abram and Hannah Duffield, married Hannah Brock, daughter of Thomas Brock. He settled near the Sulphur Spring. The property is at present occupied by William Gay, whose wife, Martha Gay, is a daughter of William Duffield. Mr Gay was a Union soldier, and had remarkable adventures while escaping from the army below Richmond, and making his way with five or six others through East Virginia, the Valley, the mountains of Bath and Pocahontas back to Stony Creek.

Caroline Duffield was married to George Auldridge. They are living in Iowa, having the comforts of a prosperous home.

Hannah Duffield was married to David Cochran and lives at the end of Droop Mountain.

One of William Duffield's daughters died in early youth of what was called the "cold plague," but judging from reported symptoms it would be called now "congestive chills."

This hard working man, William Duffield, finally met his death by a tree falling upon him which he was chopping for browse. The snow was quite deep, and when the family became uneasy that he did not come to dinner, Rebecca, the eldest of the family, went to see what was the reason. She found him dead under the tree, buried in the snow. She told what had happened, and other members sf the family hastened to the neighboring homes for assistance. Rebecca went back and chopped the large tree in two, and had the log rolled away before any one had time to get there, and was holding her poor dead father's head in her arms. Rebecca now resides in Kansas, and is reported to be living in very comfortable circumstances.

Mary Duffield became the wife of Alexander Moore and went to the west.

The writer cherishes very tender recollections of John Duffield, the honest and faithful miller, whom he met so frequently at mill when a mere youth. A few

months before the venerable man's death we met after
a separation of more than thirty years. It was at a
sacramental service, and during the recess we met and
conversed for some time. He feelingly expressed the
pleasure it gave him to meet once more in this life.
From what I can learn this was about the last time my
venerable friend ever put to his lips the visible cup of
salvation.

WILLIAM WANLESS.

For more than a hundred years the Wanless name
has been a familiar one in our region of country. According to tradition vaguely entertained, Ralph and
Stephen Wanless, natives of England, came to Virginia and settled on the Wanless place, near Mount Tabor
school house, in the "Hills," five miles north of Huntersville. One of Ralph's sons was William Wanless,
who married Nancy Wilson, from near Fort Defiance,
Virginia. She was a sister of the wife of Isaac Moore,
Senior, of Knapps Creek. They settled on Back Alleghany, and were the parents of nine daughters and
seven sons. The daughters were Rachel, Jane, Eliza,
Martha, Nancy Ann, Margaret who died aged 7 years,
Mary died aged 15 years, Melinda who was drowned
when a young woman in Leatherbark Creek, and Matilda. The sons were James, Andrew, Nelson, Ralph,
Allen, and two unnamed who died in infancy.

Rachel, the eldest daughter, married the late John
Logan, and settled in Randolph County, lived awhile
in Barbour County, and finally located on Alleghany.

Mr Logan was a very estimable citizen, a ruling elder in the Presbyterian church, and a very skillful cabinet maker, and an upright person in his dealings. In reference to the Logan family these particulars are given: Nancy Jane Logan is on Back Alleghany. Eliza Ann Logan became Mrs Enos Curry, and lives near the homestead. Mary Elizabeth Logan was married to John Curtis, and settled on Back Alleghany. Rebecca Logan married James Galford, and lives on Back Alleghany. Ina Josephine Logan was married to Samuel Renick Hogsett and lives on Browns creek. Preston Logan died at the age of seven, and William Logan when three years old.

Jane Wanless was married to the late David McLaughlin near Driftwood.

Eliza Wanless was married to the late Chesley K. K. Moore, of Dunmore, and now lives on Alleghany.

Martha became Mrs Henry Nottingham.

Nancy Ann married P. Nicholas and moved to Minnesota, where she now lives.

Matilda Wanless was married to William Cassell, on Greenbrier River, a few miles east of Greenbank.

The Rev James Wanless, a brother of William Wanless, was in his day widely known as a minister of the M. E. Church, and in the last years of his life was in the pale of the M. P. Church. Early in life he married Miss Elizabeth Sharp, daughter of John Sharp, Senior, one of the original settlers near Frost, and settled on Thorny Creek at the place owned at this time by Newton Fertig. Sometime in the twenties James Wanless cleared considerable land. His brother Ste-

phen was a blacksmith, and lived on Back Creek near
the Irvine Brick House. While trying to shoe a re-
fractory herse belonging to Squire John Hamilton,
about sixty years ago, he was instantly killed. His
sons were John F., William, and James. Rev James
Wanless adopted the three nephews and reared them
to manhood. In the meantime he prospered financially, and bought from James Sharp the property now
occupied by John F. Wanless. In connexion with his
farming enterprises, James Wanless operated two mills
and prospered enough to accumulate a very respectable
competency for those times.

James Wanless was a zealous local preacher, and
rarely ever spent a silent Sabbath. He seemed to have
had great admiration for John the Baptist as a model
backwoods preacher. It was evidently his belief that
it was his duty to lift up a voice in the Pocahontas wilderness against the vanities of the times. His spirit
would be deeply stirred by the advent of a new fashion
and then he would look up Mathew xi. 8 for his text:
"But what went ye out for to see? A man clothed in
soft raiment? Behold they that wear soft clothing are
in king's houses."

While commenting on the wearing of soft raiment
then the preacher would assign to the fashions and the
vices their portion in due season, as he thought it was
needed. "Now just consider what I say, my brethren
and hearers. How would John the Baptist have looked in a swallow tailed coat, pointed toed shoes, pipe,
whiskey bottle, and stovepipe hat, et cetera!" The
devout people felt it would have been out of the ques-

tion for John to have been fond of such things, and many of the younger people from their talk evidently thought that to be in the fashion was to make a long step in a downward career.

While it is hard to suppress our smiles, still it must be acknowledged that when it was felt to be a Christian duty to be plain and economical, it saved a vast deal of needless expenditure, and to rear a family and furnish a passable home was not the heavy, perplexing business it is now.

Ralph Wanless, Junior, first married Anna Poage, daughter of G. W. Poage of the Levels. After living in Huntersville several years as thr village blacksmith, he located on the homestead at Mount Tabor. Their children were George Poage, Hopkins, Milum, Samuel, and Margaret.

John Wanless married Elizabeth Bridger, and settled in Lewis County. Mrs Wanless was noted for her skill in nursing the sick. and her services were in demand far and near. Sick people had so much confidence in her that they seemed to think there was no danger of dying if Mrs Wanless could be had in time.

Most all the Wanless brothers were industrious and skillful workers in iron, acquired from their father, who seems to have been a genius in that line of industry, so useful to the people in pioneer and later times. When Ralph Wanless and his sons wrought at the anvil and caused the primitive forests to ring with their strong and resonant striking of hammers and sledges, their business was of essential importance. In their times most of the implements used in clearing lands, cultivating the ground, and building houses were made at home. In the pioneer shops, and for years subsequently were forged axes, hoes, shovel plows, bull-tongues, coulters, brush hooks, seng hoes, mattocks, broad axes, frows, grubbing hoes, pot hooks and pot hangers, kettle bales, log chains, double trees, single trees, door hinges and latches, and other articles.

> Toiling, rejoicing, sorrowing,
>   Onward through life he goes,
> Each morning sees some task begun,
>   Each evening sees its close—
> Something attempted, something done
>   Has earned a night's repose.
>
> Thanks, thanks to thee, my worthy friend,
>   For the lesson thou hast taught :
> Thus at the flaming forge of life
>   Our fortunes must be wrought,
> Thus on the sounding anvil shaped
>   Each burning deed and thought.
>   —The Village Blacksmith.

WALTER DRINNON.

Among the pioneer settlers of the Edray district the Drinnons are believed to have been among the very first. From what the venerable James McCollam, a grandson of Lawrence Drinnon, remembers there were three brothers, Charles, Lawrence, and Thomas, sons of Walter Drinnon from Ireland. It is more than probable they came here about the time John McNeel

and the Kinnison brothers had made their settlement
in the Levels, for they came from the same county
and neighborhood.

Lawrence Drinnon settled on the Greenbrier above
the mouth of Stony Creek. His wife was a member
of the Day family, referred to in the Kinnison paper,
but her name is not remembered. Their children were
James, Charles, John, Susan, and Sally.

Susan married John Boggs, and lived for years in
the Meadows of Greenbrier. Mr Boggs was engaged
for a long time with Charles McClung, a noted Greenbrier grazier and stock dealer, and prospered in business. From Greenbrier he went to Putnam County,
entered 16,000 acres of land, and founded the notable
Boggs settlement by situating his sons and daughters
around him.

Sally Drinnon became Mrs William McCollam, and
lived on Bucks Mountain.

John Drinnon married his cousin Elizabeth, daughter of Thomas Drinnon, the Edray pioneer, and opened up the property lately owned by Thomas Auldridge,
Senior. His sons were Thomas, Lawrence, James,
and John. Thomas Drinnon married Rebecca Grimes
and lived in Huntersville, keeping jail and shoemak-
ing. Finally he went to Harrison County. Two of
his sons were with the Union cavalry engaged in the
battle of Droop Mountain. Lawrence Drinnon married Bettie Ratliff, and moved to Roane County.
James Drinnon went to Nicholas County. John Drinnon went to Clay County, and was a teacher of schools
in Clay and Nicholas counties.

John Drinnon, of Lawrence, was a soldier in the war of 1812, and was in camp near Norfolk. One damp day he was out on dress parade, rather too early after an attack of measles, took a relapse and died soon after.

At that time the late William Gay, Senior, was a youth living at Josiah Brown's. He had been to mill on Knapps Creek and was returning home after sundown, and it was getting dusk as he came near the place where the gate opens leading to Thomas Auldridge's present residence. The way to Browns went up the crest of the ridge on the side of which are the traces of the John Drinnon residence yet to be seen. The horse suddenly stopped, and the mill boy looked to see what it was, and there in a fence corner he saw John Drinnon, wrapped in a blanket, and seemed to be taking his rest, but before he could speak to him the horse started off at headlong speed, and he could not check him up before reaching Brown's. He told the family he had seen John Drinnon on his way home, and now they would hear news from the war. Upon going to Drinnon's however it was found that he had not come in, and when they looked for him he could not be found.

The whole matter remained a mystery until David Cochran and John R. Flemmens returned bringing the news of Drinnon's death. Upon comparing the time of nis decease with the time Gay saw the apparition at the side of the road, there was a striking coincidence.

Thomas Drinnon, brother of Lawrence the pioneer, settled at Edray. After him Drinnon's Ridge is nam-

ed, and so he has a monument as enduring as the everlasting hills. He made the first opening where the
village of Edray now stands and owned much of the
land that comprise the attractive farm homes that present such a charming scene when viewed from the 'big
turn' on the mountain road, whence is unfolded some
of the most picturesqe mountain scenery in our county.
Near where his house stood had been a favorite camping place for Indians, and many stone relics in later
years have been found in the fields thereabouts. A
fine, bold spring is one of the features of the place,
near William Sharp's present residence. Thomas
Drinnon's home was broken up by Indians and his
wife carried away prisoner and cruelly murdered on
Elk Mountain, several miles from her home. The
names of his sons were Jacob, William, and James.

Jacob Drinnon married Elizabeth, daughter of John
Smith, on Stoney Creek, and settled in Nicholas county. William Drinnon lived in Nicholas county.

James Drinnan settled in Muskingum county, Ohio.
He seems to have been deeply interested in legends
concerning silver on Elk Mountain, at a locality called
Hickory Ridge. It is belived he returned from Ohio
and spent quite a while in efforts to identify the place,
but was not able to make the find he was after.

Charles Drinnon, believed to have been a younger
brother of Thomas and Lawrence was in Indian captivity for several years. When redeemed and brought
home he frequently complained of it, as if he was sorry to leave his captors so attached he seemed to have
become to Indian usages, manners and customs. It is

hinted too that there might have been an attractive
young squaw in the question, a daughter of some tribal
chief, but we will leave this for what it may be worth
as a romantic confecture.   At any rate he seemed sick
about something and he always had a good word for
the Indian friends of his youth.   One of the nice and
pleasant things about Indian habits in his estimation
was that his old friends make their fires, took the good
of them and were never in a hurry about their business
of any kind.   His name is perpetuated by a field now
owned by Anderson Barlow.   The legend is that this
field was cleared by Charles Drinnon, and was probably the first opening on Hazel Ridge.   It is now designated as the "Charley Field."

The compilor has recently learned from a very authentic source some particulars which he hopes the reader may notice and correct a statement elsewhere made
about Mr Baker, who was killed by an Indian, being
named James and a school teacher.   His name was
Henry Baker and he was doing a job of clearing for
Lawrence Drinnon.   Richard Hill was employed in
raising the house a story higher and putting on a new
roof.   Patrick Slator was the school teacher and one
of his pupils was the late Mrs Sally McCollam.   Lawrence Drinnon had recently set out some apple trees
he had carried from Hardy county.   Early in the morning of Baker's death some one was seen among these
trees and it was supposed to be Slator pulling up the
weeds and grass, it turned out however to be an Indian warrior.   Soon as night came after the shooting

of Baker, Nathan, a colored servant belonging to
Lawrence Drinnon, was sent across the river into Marlin Mountain, crossing Knapps Creek at Leydon Bottom, then following Buckley Mountain, came to
Greenbrier at Stephen Cave Run, and thence went to
the fort at Millpoint, located where Isaac McNeel's
residence now stands.

ROBERT MOORE.

Robert Moore was a son of Moses Moore, the distinguished pioneer. He was born May 27, 1772, and
was reared on Knapps Creek. His wife was Rebecca
McCollam, of Brown's Mountain, near Driscol. After
living a number of years on the Greenbrier at the
Bridger place, he moved to Edray on the Drennon
opening. They were the parents of five sons, Isaac,
Robert, Andrew, James, William, and one daughter,
Jane, who became Mrs Andrew Duffield and lived at
the head of Stoney Creek, now owned by the Delaney family who recently moved into our county.

Isaac Moore married Catherine Gillilan and settled
at Edray where S. B. Moore lives. In their family
were three sons and five daughters. Mary Ann became Mrs Amos Barlow, first wife; Rebecca became
Mrs David Hannah; Elizabeth is Mrs Bryson Hannah,
near Frost; Eveline became Mrs Paul Sharp; Julia is
now Mrs William Sharp.

Allen Taylor Moore married Mary Catherine Gay,
daughter of the late Robert Gay and Mrs Bettie Gay.

He lives near Edray. His children are John Kenney, Evansville, Indiana; Robert, in Butte City, Montana; Georgia Miami, who was the late Mrs Isaac Sharp; Alwilda Nebraska, now Mrs John Young; and Lula Elizabeth, now Mrs Davis Barlow.

William Rives Moore married Ruth Gay, and lived near Edray. He was a person greatly respected. His sympathies were with the Union adherents, and he died at Wheeling during the war, after many vicissitudes.

Samuel Bryson Moore married Ann Sharp and lives on the Edray homestead, and is a farmer and merchant. Mrs Effie Barlow and Mrs Flora Gay are his daughters.

Andrew Moore fell from a tree near the sugar camp at the Bridger place in early youth, and was instantly killed.

William Moore, upon attaining his majority, went to Ohio, where he rose to eminence as a physician and became widely known as a preaching elder in the Church of the Disciples.

James R. Moore, upon his marriage with Mrs Jane Funkhouser, of Rockbridge County, lived some years on part of the homestead. He thence moved to Braxton County. His children were Porterfield, Ephraim, and Mary Ellen. The latest information the friends have of his sons they were arranging for a trapping and hunting excursion to the Rocky Mountains. They had previously hunted a great deal in the Williams River wilds and were quite successful. The mantle of their eminent ancestor, Moses Moore, seems to have fallen on them.

Robert Moore, Junior, married Eliza Bruffey, a grand-daughter of Richard Hill, the pioneer. After living on the Edray homestead many years he moved to Iowa. His sons are Franklin, Moses, and George.

Franklin D. Moore married Sallie Young, and resides at Fort Scott, Kansas.

Moses C. Moore married Susan Livermore, and after a brief residence at Edray, moved to Kansas. He is a telegraph operator. Mrs Moore is a teacher.

George P. Moore first married Lizzie Poage, and settled on a section of the Edray homestead. His second marriage was with Mrs Ruth Moore. He is a local elder in the pale of the M. E. Church, a successful merchant and grazier, proficient as a mechanic, Coroner of the county, and has been commissioner of the court, and President of the Pocahontas Bank.

The property owned by Robert Moore was first opened by Thomas Drinnon, and is one of the earliest settlements in this regions. The Drinnon tract must have included thousands of acres. The quality of the land is of the best, much of it spontaneously sodding in bluegrass when timber is belted. Parties who know are rather reticent as to the precise spot occupied by the Drinnon cabin home, since surveying parties have been so anxious to locate it. It will be remembered that Thomas Drinnon's home was broken up and some of his family killed and carried into captivity by the Indians.

When Robert Moore took possession but a few acres were cleared. He and his sons made extensive im-

provements of a very substantial character. He erected a commodious two story brick building, the first
and only building of its kind in the vicinity. The site
is very near William Sharp's residence, and much of
the brick was used in the new building. A field just
beyond William Sharp's in the direction of Elk is
thought to have been one of the first to be cultivated.

It is more than likely that the first time Robert
Moore ever set foot on lands some day to be his own,
was when he came from the east with his father and
others in pursuit of French surveyors and their Indian
guides. An Indian was killed and a Frenchman
wounded near where the two prongs of the Indian
Draft converge. It has not been so many years since
human remains were unearthed near that place. It is
the impression of some, too, that it was the dispersion
of this exploring party that originated the legends of
hidden treasures in two or three localities of our county, some near Millpoint others near Marlinton.

Robert Moore was the worthy son of a worthy father. Everybody had confidence in "Uncle Bobby,"
and when he went hence to be no more, genuine tears
embalmed the memory of the kind, honest, and brave
old settler.

ISAAC MOORE.

One of the sacred duties resting on the living is to
preserve memories of worthy citizens now deceased,
and heed the lessons illustrated, that may stimulate
and encourage useful endeavors to have similar aims

in our own lives.

> "For as the light
> Not only serves to show but render us
> Mutually profitable; so our lives,
> In acts exemplary, not only win
> Ourselves good names, but do to others give
> Matter for virtuous deeds by which we live."

The aim of this article is to perform such a service with reference to Squire Isaac Moore, whose name appears in the first records of our county, and was associated with its history for forty years.

He was born March 2, 1800, at the "Bridger place" four or five miles east of Edray. He grew up familiar with many of the privations of pioneer life, but was happily exempt from the risks and perils that were such features of the times a few years previously from Indian raids.

The surroundings of his home were picturesque: the river with its rapid waters of crystal purity, the overhanging hills that bordered the wooded valley where the log home stood, made a scene that would attract notice anywhere. It was only one place among hundreds to be found in a vast expansive region to which Homer's famous line about Ithaca would apply:

> "A rough wild nurse land, whose crops were men."

Here Mr Moore lived snd toiled until early manhood. The greatest sorrow of his young life was when he saw his brother Andrew buried. He was killed by falling from a tree near the sugar camp, while members of the family were stirring off a kettle of sugar. In 1820 Robert Moore, his father, moved his family to Edray and built near the noted Drinnon Spring. Soon after this change Isaac Moore married Miss Catherine Gilliland, daughter of Squire John Gilliland, whose residence was on top of the mountain overlooking Millpoint.

The young people soon settled in the woods near the old home. Not a tree was cut before Mr Moore began to clear out a place for a house, garden, and grain patch. Three times a day the young wife would go to the Drinnon spring, nearly a mile away, to attend the milking, churning, and getting things for table use.

Mr Moore was fond of books and was anxious to become a good scholar. He diligently improved his opportunities, and with such assistance as he received from an old field school teacher he mastered what was called the three "R's"—Rithmetic, Reading, and Riting. Fortunately for him Colonel John Baxter, a near neighbor, had what is believed to have been the largest and best collection of books in the county, probably as many as one hundred volumes—history, travel, fiction, and poetry. He had the use of these books at will, and thus his taste for reading was in a measure gratified until he could procure ample reading elsewhere.

For a good many winters young Moore taught school in a house near the present residence of George Baxter. It was of the pioneer style, built of unhewn logs, chinked and daubed, roofed with boards, kept in place by press poles, one end taken up by the chimney of sticks and clay. A window extended the entire length of one side, lighted with greased paper, a substitute for glass.

The Barlows, Moores, Baxters, Duncans, Smiths, and Duffields were the chief patrons of the school during the years of his service. To promote order and discipline the young teacher cut a haw switch of portentious length and placed it in view of the whole school, and for a time the effect appeared salutary. One day, however, just as play time was over and the scholars were gathering in, the teacher was arranging a backlog, and while in a stooping position one of the scholars took down the switch and dealt the teacher a stinging blow across the shoulder and side of the head. He skipped out of the door and ran at the top of his speed through the woods with the teacher in hot pursuit. In about a half mile the fugitive was overtaken, and the first impulse was to punish him by wearing out the switch. The recreant scholar seemed so sorry and plead so piteously that the teacher relented and agreed to let him off that time. He became a good boy and gave no more trouble.

At the first term of the Pocahontas Court Mr Moore was appointed a captain of the 127th Regiment of Virginia Militia. He served as magistrate for many years, and was high Sheriff when his time came as senior member of the court. He was one of the main business agents of his neighborhood in drawing up wills, deeds, writings, and articles of agreement, in all which he excelled. Important changes in the public roads suggested by him were made, and new roads were projected. At his request a largely attended meeting was held to consider reforms in the schools. So much was he interested in educational affairs that at this meeting a Board of Education was organized to supervise the schools in the Edray district, and have them taught by such teachers as were examined and approved by the Board. He led a spirited controversy in the effort to have silent schools in place of the noisy vocal schools. His point was carried and silent schools became the rule. This occurred about the year 1846.

In politics Mr Moore was a Henry Clay Whig. Among his last votes, perhaps his very last, he cast for the ordnance of secession. During the summer and fall of 1861 Edray swarmed with soldiers on the march or in the camp. Mr Moore contracted camp fever late in the season. About the time he had convalesced enough to move about, he was seized by measles of a malignant type, from which he died December, 5, 1861, in the 62d year of his age.

Some years previously he avowed his faith in Christ. Until lately the writer of this tribute had a letter written to him while at College by Mr Moore, giving information of the great change that had come over his mind, and of his new desires and heavenly hopes. In that letter, too, he expressed a regret that he had not borne the cross from his youth, and permitted so many years to pass away unmindful of his duty to Christ as an open follower. He was a conscientious person from his youth to old age. He had the substance, if not the form. To the writer and many others his name is precious, and will be for years to come.

His memory long will live alone
In all their hearts as mournful light,
That broods above the fallen sun
And dwells in heaven half the night.

WILLIAM MOORE.

This paper is devoted to the memory of William Moore, the youngest of Moses Moore's sons. It is believed by some that the plaee of his birth, (which occurred September 18, 1784,) was near the McClintic Mill on Swago. The locality was indicated quite recently by some apple trees of great age. His youth and early manhood were passed on Knapps Creek. After his marriage to Christine Dods, of Rockbridge County. he lived for a time near Timber Ridge in that county, and then settled permanently on Hazef Ridge, on lands now owned by Lee Carter and Anderson Barlow, between one and two miles west of Edray. Their family consisted of three sons and two daughters: James Elliot, Addison, Alexander, Margaret and Jane.

Margaret Moore was married to Colonel John W. Ruckman, and lived near Millpoint.

Jennie Moore married Captain William D. Hefner. Captain Hefner was a millwright by occupation. After living in Pocahontas some years he located in Fayette County. He was a gallant Confederate officer, an effective scout, and finally lost his life in the battle of Lewisburg, along with his eldest son Franklin. Mrs Hefner now lives in Kansas. Pathetic memories arise in the mind as we think of the father and son falling side by side, mingling their blood in death on the gory ground, and then dust to dust in one honored grave.

Alexander Moore first married Mary Bradshaw, near Huntersville, and settled on the homestead. His second marriage was with Mary Duffield, and finally went to Kansas. The names of his children: Lee, Moffett, Florence, Susie, Mary Winters, Frankie, and Elliot.

Addison Moore, after his marriage with Elizabeth Hannah on Elk, settled on Hazel Ridge, where he lived many years- went to Iowa, then returned, and died at an advanced age at the home of his son, William Allen Moore, at Huttonsville a few years since.

Addison Moore seemed to have been a born physician. He acquired by reading and experimenting considerable medical skill, and rendered much valuable service to afflicted friends and neighbors.

James E. Moore was married three times. His first wife was Margaret Sutton. Her children were Davis, who died in Iowa; John Sutton, a prominent teacher of schools in Pocahontas County; Enoch H., a merchant; Bryson, Confederate soldier, slain at Gettysburg; Rachel, wife of the late M. A. Friel; Martha, first wife of Andrew Taylor, and lived on Laurel Creek; and Agnes, now Mrs Rufus Wheeler of the Baltimore Conference.

Second wife was Mary Burr. Her only son, Wallace, was drowned at Ronceverte a few years since.

Third wife was Luemma, daughter of Samuel Harper on Knapps Creek. Her daughter Ella, now Mrs Marion White; Birdie, wife of Rev W. H. Ballengee of the Baltimore Conference. Lloyd Moore married

Ressie Bird, and lives in Lynchburg, Va. Frank Moore married Annie Cleek and lives near Millpoint. Lee Moore married Lizzie Hicks, of Bath, and lives at the Millpoint homstead.

Rev James E. Moore was a busy man of affairs. He taught school in many places at intervals for fifty or sixty years, was a local Methodist preacher nearly as long, a laborious farmer, and was Commissioner of the Revenue. He is remembered by the old soldiers that went out to Grafton with Captain Andrew McNeel's cavalry and Captain D. A. Stofer's "Pocahontas Rescues," for the farewell address that he delivered at John Varner's, near Split Rock, one Sabbath morning. This scene connected with the departure of these troops for the most advanced and exposed post of the Confederate frontier, ready to do and dare, was full of interest. By the next Sabbath these troops were at Grafton with their "tin cups and pocket knives," ready to do and dare in the nearest north and most exposed of all Confederate positions.

General William Skeene also made an address in response to Mr Moore's, and some of his words are yet fresh in the memories of aged men. In his most impassioned and eloquent manner General Skeene exclaimed: "If you will attend to the ballot boxes we will attend to the cartridge boxes, and we will return to enjoy the blessings of liberty amid these green hills, bringing our laurels with us."

The few persons now remaining that remember William Moore—"Uncle Billy" as he was called by every body—speak of him as the kindest of persons to every one. He and Mrs Moore built up a very attractive home and reared a nice family. This home became widely known for open handed hospitality.

Mrs Moore, old "Aunt Teenie," as she was so familiarly called by the neighbors, was one of the most helpful and benevolent of persons in seasons of sickness or bereavement. She spared no pains day or night at all seasons, in vernal showers, in summer's heat, in autumn storms, or wintry snows, Aunt Tenie's skillful hand would be one of the first to bring relief when pain and anguish furrowed a neighbor's brow, or where the death angel was heard knocking at the door of some one's life. Her religious proclivities were decidedly and very positively presbyterian.

While not a member of the church, William Moore's walk and conversation exemplified all the visible traits of genuine Christian principle. In a religious meeting in the old Hamlin Chapel, some years before his decease, he was invited by the class leader, the late John R. Duffield, to testify what he thought of the Christian religion. William Moore arose in that solemn and dignified manner for which he was rather remarkable, and stated that he had been a praying person for fifty years, and had conscientiously tried to live with a conscience void of offence toward God and man and, moreover, it was his heart's desire hereafter to live in all good conscience toward the same. This testimony is remembered as one of the most to the purpose ever heard in that venerable place of worship.

When Aaron Moore, on the Greenbrier, his brother, was nearing his end, William Moore paid him what proved his final visit. His kind heart was so touched at seeing his aged brother so near death that before leaving he kneeled at the bed side and poured out his full heart in prayer and fraternal intercession for his aged dying brother. They then parted to meet no more alive. A more impressive scene is hard to imagine.

Mrs Moore's death was occasioned by a cancerous affection. Mr Moore survived her a few years.

These esteemed persons, so lovely and pleasant in their lives, lived to a great age. They have quietly gone from us, and are now—with so many others—at rest in the Duffield burying ground. This is a place that should be carefully and sacredly cared for as Gods Acre, planted with so much precious, immortal seed, that will some day appear springing up to the praise and glory of our Redeemer's blood.

JAMES COOPER.

During most of the 19th century the Cooper name has been familiar in our region. James Cooper, the progenitor of the Cooper relationship, was a native of Augusta County, and was reared in the Mossy Creek section of that great County. Having married Nancy Agnes Wooddell, he came over with the Wooddells, very early in the settlement of the upper section of our county, and opened up property now owned by Robert N. Gum, near Greenbank, then known as the Piney Woods. They were the parents of four sons and six daughters.

Elizabeth Cooper became Mrs Woods, and settled at Greenhill, Highland County.

Margaret became Mrs Enoch Hill and lived in Ritchie County. Her daughter Harriet became Mrs Fling, and lived at Flag, Ohio. Nannie became another Mrs Fling, and lived in Ritchie County.

Jane Cooper became Mrs Andrew Kerr and lived near Dunmore. Her daughter Nannie became Mrs Washington Hoover; Anne, now Mrs Raymer Davis, near Greenbank; Caroline, now Mrs Gatewood Sutton, at Durbin. Her son William Kerr in Pocahontas, and John Kerr lives in Lewis County.

Lucinda Cooper became Mrs John Alexander Gillespie, late of Greenbank. Her children were Taylor, Amos, and Wise, the three sons. Her daughters were Nancy, who became Mrs George Beverage; Rachel, now Mrs Henry Sheets, near Dunmore; Margaret now Mrs John L. Hudson, near Louise, Mary now Mrs George Sheets, and Martha.

Nancy and Melinda are the names of James Coopers other two daughters. Thomas Cooper died in youth.

John T. Cooper married in Marion County. He was a popular physician. He resided a number of years in Parkersburg and then at Claysville, where he died in 1878. His daughter Flora teaches school in Parkersburg. His son James a foreman in machine shops at Parkersburg and other points. Another son Arthur is a Presbyterian minister in Illinois, and there are three children deceased.

Dr Cooper read medicine with the late Dr Strather, of the Warm Springs. He was prominent in church circles, being a ruling elder in a Parkersburg Presbyterian congregation.

James Harvey Cooper married Julia Ann Whitman, of Greenbrier County. They were the parents of five sons and three daughters. The daughters were Agnes who died in 1861, Julia Ann, and Rebecca. In reference to the sons we have this remarkable but sad record. They were all Confederate soldiers. Robert died in the war. James lost an arm in battle. John and Charles were each severely wounded, and George was killed in 1864 in battle near Fishers Hill.

Joseph W. Cooper married Rachel Tallman Sutton, and lived near Greenbank. They were the parents of four sons and one daughter: Rachel, George Clark, James Amos, John William, and Charles Calvin. In 1863 in the course of three weeks the dipthiretic scourge removed the mother, her daughter and three sons by death.

J. W. Cooper's second marriage was with Harriet Wade of Bath County. She lived about one year.

His third marriage was with Mary Arbogast, near Glade Hill. Snowden, Walter, and Vivian were the children of this marriage.

The writer would hereby cheerfully acknowledge the thanks due George C. Cooper for assistance rendered by him on the wayside, July 1, 1901, when we casually met near Marvin Chapel and took notes under an apple tree, the thermometer 96 degrees. Without the data given by this grandson of the venerable pioneer this sketch could not have been prepared and the name of a most worthy pioneer would have been overlooked.

James Cooper's name appears in the organization of the county as one of the constables appointed. He served the public as magistrate, assessor, and teacher of schools. He was regarded with high esteem for his honest and elevated character in social and business relations. He was a prominent member of the Liberty Church in the early history of that historic congregation, and his influence was ever for good morals, intelligence, and refinement of manners, himself being a fine specimen of what is termed "a gentleman of the old school," and was noted for his polite and gracious manners, correct and entertaining conversational powers.

ALEXANDER WADDELL.

One of the pioneers of our county from whom quite a number of our people trace their descent was Alexander Waddell. He was of Scotch-Irish descent and was among the earliest settlers in the neighborhood of Marvin Chapel. His wife was a Miss Rouss. He came from Augusta County before the Revolution, but in what year is not certainly known. He came out to examine the country, and looked over the Levels and the lands beyond Buckeye and around Sewall's Cave, and selected the place so long known as the Waddell Place, where the public road reaches the highest point on the mountain in passing from Buckeye to Millpoint. When he first explored the Levels all was mainly vacant or unclaimed, and he might have entered the greater part of it. He concluded it was too level and glady, and so he preferred the lands north of Millpoint where he could be high enough to keep in the dry.

Their daughter, Martha, married the late John Barlow, of Edray, mentioned elsewhere.

Elizabeth Waddell married William Sharp, near Edray.

Ann Waddell married Squire James Sharp of Beaver Creek. Each of these sons-in-law of the early pioneer are specially mentioned in this book as men of prominence in the affairs of the county.

Mary Waddell married Squire John Gillilan, near Millpoint. This large family moved to Missouri, where their numerous descendants have their prosperous homes.

Jennie Waddell married Josiah Brown, near Edray.

Miriam Waddell was married to John Thompson and moved to Ohio.

The Waddell sons were John, William, and Alexander. To give his sons a chance to have their homes near him, the venerable pioneer concluded to move to Ohio and settled near Gallipolis. These sons all died in Ohio, and their history is not much known to their friends in West Virginia.

Mr Waddell seems to have been a fervently pious person. It was his intense desire to live one hundred years, and he made this desire for longevity a matter of special prayer. He died in Ohio at the age of one hundred and two years, thus receiving a full measure and more of borrowed time. With long life God satisfied him, and showed him his salvation.

The history of his life shows he had paid good attention to Bible reading where it is written in the thirty-fourth Psalm: ''What man is he that desireth life and loveth many days that he may see good? Keep thy tongue from evil and thy lips from speaking guile; depart from evil and do good; seek peace and pursue it.''

This Psalm was a great favorite with our pious pioneer people, to give them consolation in their times of danger and distress.

RICHARD HUDSON.

The Hudson family trace their ancestry to Richard Hudson, whose wife was Elizabeth Redden. They came from Augusta County early in the century, and settled in the woods on the head waters of Sitlingtons Creek, on lands now held by their grandsons, Warwick B. and John L. Hudson. This land was purchased from a Mr Armstrong. A small opening had been made by one Posten previously. Mr and Mrs Hudson were the parents of seven daughters and three sons.

Sally and Polly Hudson went to Ohio and married and settled in that State.

Keziah Hudson, of whom the writer has no definite information, more than that she was named after one of Job's daughters.

Rachel Hudson married Dysard and lived in Barbour County.

Matilda married Thomas Humphries and lived in Barbour County.

Naomi became Mrs Samuel Mathews, and lived in Randolph County. M. G. Mathews, deceased, a teacher and superintendent of Pocahontas schools, Charles Mathews and Captain J. W. Mathews, of Alvon, West Virginia, are her sons.

Nancy Hudson first married John Seybert, of Highland County. Her second marriage was with Andrew Lockridge, of Bath County.

Thomas Hudson went to Missouri, and married and settled there.

Madison Hudson went to Maryland in his youth, and married and reared a large family. He prospered in business, and was a citizen of prominence in neighborhood and county affairs.

Elijah Hudson married Margaret Deaver, daughter of James and Sally Deaver, who are believed to have been the first settlers on Back Alleghany. They went to housekeeping on the home place, and were the parents of five daughters and eight sons: Jackson, Thomas, William, Warwick, Bird, Davis, Dallas, Paul McNeel, John Letcher, Sarah, Harriet, Laura, Nancy Jane, and Susan. In reference to the daughters we learn the following particulars.

Sarah died in early youth.

Harriet became Mrs John E. Gum, and lives near Greenbank. Her children are Dolly Bell, now Mrs Robert Ralston, in Highland. Nebraska is Mrs Oscar Orndorf; Margaret is at home. Charles went to Wisconsin. William located in Colorado, and was with a party of engineers when he lost his life. Warwick operates a lumber train in Upshur County.

Laura married Madison Humphries, and lives near Philippi.

Nancy Jane became Mrs Levi Beverage, and lived on Clover Creek, and was the mother of five sons and six daughters.

Susan is now Mrs Uriah Bird, and lives at Marlinton, and is the mother of seven daughters and a son.

In reference to Elijah Hudson's sons the following particulars are in hand:

William Hudson was a Union soldier, and settled in Missouri, where he married Maggie Palmer. They were the parents of four sons and one daughter. Their son Frank is in business in Oklahoma. William Hudson is an eminent physician and banker. He has prospered greatly in business, and lives at Union Star, De Kalb County, Missouri.

Paul McNeel Hudson also went to Missouri, and married Eliza Livingstone. They are both dead, and are survived by their daughter Mary.

Davis Hudson, a Union soldier, settled in the west.

Dallas Hudson, a gallant Confederate soldier, 31st Virginia Infantry, died in battle at Port Republic.

Warwick Bird Hudson married Nancy Galford, and lives on a part of the homestead. Their children are William Frank, Mary Roxanna, Jesse Arden, and Rachel Cornelia Margaret. W. B. Hudson was a Confederate lieutenant, 31st Virginia Infantry, and served in the war from start to finish.

John Letcher Hudson married Margaret Virginia Gillespie, a daughter of the late John Gillespie, and resides at the old homestead on Sitlington's Creek. They are the parents of six sons and six daughters: Marion Conner, Henry Harper, David Warden, Ed-

ward Arbuckle, Luther Gilbert, William McNeel,
Ethel Grace, Hattie Jane, Laura Mattie, Clara Margie,
Lucy Elizabeth, and Minnie Ruth.

Kindly assisted by Mrs Virginia Hudson, the writer
has thus been enabled to illustrate in a measure the
history of one of the oldest of Pocahontas families. It
will be noticed that Elijah Hudson's decendants are
the main representatives of the relationship now in our
county. For this reason and others special mention is
due his memory.

Elijah Hudson, Esq., represented Pocahontas in the
Virginia Legislature, was a member of the Pocahontas
Court, and transacted a great deal of neighborhood
business, writing wills, deeds of conveyance, and articles of agreement. He was endowed with natural
abilities of a high order, and he persistently made the
most of his limited opportunities for mental improvement. During his life he taught many terms in the
Old Field school house for the benefit of his neighbors
and his own family.

He was a speaker of more than ordinary fluency.
The writer heard him on but one occasion, in 1844.
His manner was instructive and logical. The tones of
his voice were soft, and his enunciation was so perfect
that not a word need be mistaken. His aim seemed
to be to convince and instruct rather than to be amusing. It is the impression of some that he never crack-
ed a joke in his life while making a political address.
He seemed to take it for granted that everybody was
sensible like himself, and liked to hear sensible speaking when the welfare of the country was in question.

He had a large pair of saddle bags about full of books, political pamphlets, and clippings from the newspapers, to which he would frequently refer to illustrate and enforce the points he made. Taken altogether, the effort was statesmanlike, and much above the political harangue so much in vogue at the time. He was a Jacksonian Democrat.

He died after much intense suffering March 4, 1881, aged about 80 years. Mrs Hudson survived her husband until December 31, 1889, when she too passed away, aged about 83 years.

Late in life Mr Hudson became a member of the Liberty Church. He witnessed a very satisfactory, intelligent profession of his faith in the atoning blood of Christ. The older people tell us that one of the most solemn scenes they ever saw at the old Libelty church was when Elijah Hudson arose in the presence of the congregation, and with a contrite spirit assumed his Christian vows before taking his place at the communion table, to take the cup of salvation and call upon his Lord and Redeemer.

JOHN SUTTON, SR.

July 27, 1894, was the last time the writer met the late John Sutton, Junior, whose painful death by a cancerous affction was mourned by a large circle of attached friends. Much of the morning was occupied in family reminiscence. His father, John Sutton the senior, was a native of Westmoreland County, and hence was neighbor of the Washington family. His home was on the Potomac not far from Mount Vernon. For some years John Sutton, Senior, was manager for Jacob Warwick at the Dunmore farm, late in the last century. Finally he bought land and settled where his son, John Sutton, Junior, lived. Mrs Sutton was Rachel Gillispie, daughter of Jacob Gillispie, who owned nearly all the land in sight of Greenbank looking north and east. Mrs Jacob Gillispie was Rebecca Berry, a half sister of Mary Vance Warwick, the widow Berry having married Mr Vance, who lived at Mountain Grove. Jacob Gillispie's family consisted of nine daughters and six sons.

John Sutton, Senior, paid a visit to his old home on the Potomac where it is said to be twelve miles across. His friends seemed astonished when he told them he had seen the head spring and drank of its water on Laurel Fork, near what is known as the Wilfong Settlement.

JAMES TALLMAN.

Among the names identified with our county's history that of Tallman has figured prominently for more than a hundred years, and while there are scores of our citizens with Tallman blood in their veins, yet the name is borne by but few anymore; as so many have moved away to other counties and western States.

The Tallman relationship trace their ancestry to James Tallman, who was a native of Augusta County. His first marriage was with Nancy Crawford, of that county, and soon afterwards settled on property west

of Greenbank, now held by Joseph Beard, the heirs of
Adam Arbogast, and Dr Moomau. This must have
been before the Revolution, as all the probabilities
point to that conclusion. There were in the first family three sons and two daughters: Rachel, Rebecca,
Benjamin, William, and Boone.

Rachel was married to Peter Hull, of Highland, who
was a son of Adam Hull.

Rebecca was married to Reuben Slaven.

Benjamin Tallman married Elizabeth Warwick, and
settled on property now owned by Captain Siple. The
names of his children William, James, Robert, John,
Cyrus, and Nancy, who became Mrs Benjamin Tallman (son of Boone) and lives in Illinois.

Benjamin Tallman was a colonel of the 127th regiment, a member of the court, represented the county
in the Virginia House of Delegates, and was for many
years a ruling elder in the Liberty Presbyterian
church, and a justice of the peace.

William Tallman married Jane Bradshaw, and settled on a section of the Tallman homestead. It was
their son James Tallman who was the successor of
Henry Moffett in the clerkship of Pocahontas courts.

Boone Tallman, the third son of the early settler,
went to the Levels often enough to win the affections
of Mary Poage, daughter of George W. Poage. Their
children were George, James, Benjamin, who met his
death by drowning, and Rachel Ann, who became Mrs
Enoch Burner.

In reference to the second marriage of James Tallman, Senior, we learn that his second wife was

Jemima Gillispie.   Their children were Jane, Nancy,
Margaret, Sally, Samuel, and James.

Jane Tallman became Mrs William Arbogast and
settled at Greenbank on the estate now owned by Dr
Moomau.   Their   children were William, James,
George, Alcinda, who married Isaac Moore, near
Dunmore, Margaret, who became Mrs David Maupin,
first marriage, and Mrs Thomas Maupin, second marriage, a much esteemed lady—lately deceased.   It was
her son Harvey Maupin whose tragic death occurred
near Marlinton in 1898, while sliding logs.   Nannie
Arbogast the youngest, became Mrs Dr J. P. Moomau
and lives near Greenbank on the homestead.   E. S.
Moomau, pharmacist at Lewisburg, Dr L. H. Moomau
at Greenbank, James Moomau, Mary, now Mrs Dr C.
L. Austin, Misses Flora, Lillian. Boone, Lucy, and
Frederick are their children.   Dr Moomau is a physician of more than forty years standing, and a prominent citizen of affairs.   He has represented the county
in the Legislature of West Virginia.

Nancy Tallman became Mrs Brannon and lived in
Lewis County.   Margaret Tallman became Mrs Goff,
and also lived in Lewis County.

Sally Tallman was married to William Gum, and
settled on Deer Creek.

The Tallman relationship has been long and conspicuously identified with the development and improvement of important communities.   They were a
people who aspired to be first in everything that promoted the improvement and elevation of their neighbors and themselves, and their influence has been

deeply impressed upon many characters. Though the name has well nigh ceased to be heard among us, yet the writer is pleased to believe that the spirit of James Tallman, the early settler, is yet moving about among scores of our families.

DAVID L. RUCKMAN.

Fifty years ago one of the most active men in lower Pocahontas was David Little Ruckman, Constable of the Levels District. He was tall and wiry in person, quick and nervous in his movements, and usually rode in a rapid trot. He always meant business, and when he went to collect a debt the money or property had to be in evidence. Were an arrest to be made he nearly always found the person that was wanted. His home was in the cove near Marvin, and is now occupied by his grandson, Mathews Ruckman.

Full particulars of his ancestry are given in another chapter. David L. Ruckman was born on Back creek. He had three brothers who lived to be grown. Samuel Ruckman, whose son Colonel David V. Ruckman is widely known in our county. John Ruckman went to Ohio. James Ruckman settled in Illinois. He had also these sisters: Fannie, who married John Gum. She was the mother of Mrs Samuel Harper, on Knapps Creek, and Mrs Martha Ginger, whose son George W. Ginger now resides in Huntersville, the village blacksmith. Mr Ginger, her husband, was killed during the war. Mary Ann Ruckman went with her brother John to Ohio.

David L. Ruckman came to Pocahontas in 1832 and located at the place already pointed out. He married Priscilla Wade, daughter of Otho Wade of Highland. She was a very superior person in all the relations of life. She died in 1860. Her husband died in 1841, thirteen years after their removal to Pocahontas from their home in lower Highland.

Charles Ruckman, their eldest son, was born in Highland County. He was devoted to books and became one of the best scholars of his time. He taught school and transacted business for his father. He married Maggie Griffin, daughter of Jonathan Griffin, on Stony Creek. In the latter years of his life he became a rheumatic invalid, but in spite of pain and suffering tried to be useful to the last. He moved to Ohio, and was survived by a son and daughter, Julia Ann and Leonidas.

The second son Samuel, died at the age of 15 years.

The third son was John Wade, lately living on the old homestead near Marvin. He was born in Highland, 1824, and was eight years old when the family moved to this county. He married Margaret Ann Moore. Their son Mathews married Margaret Hogsett, daughter of Josiah T. Hogsett, and lives at the homestead. Many years since Colonel Ruckman lost his hearing. Some time before his death one of his eyes was seriously affected. Before he was overtaken by these afflictions none seemed to have better prospects for wealth and advancement and social prominence.

James Watts Ruckman was another member of David L. Ruckman's family. He first married Caroline

Bruffey, daughter of Patrick Bruffey, near Greenbank. By this marriage there was one son, William Wallace Ruckman, who now resides near Millpoint, whose wife was Miss Lizzie Patton. James W. Ruckman's second wife was Caroline Arbogast, near Greenbank. Her sons were Renick and Otho Ruckman. Otho lives near Buffalo Mountain, beyond Greenbank. Renick Ruckman is a prosperous citizen on the homestead. Her daughter, Nancy Priscilla Ruckman, is now Mrs Winfield Slaven, near Millpoint.

In the war between the States James W. Ruckman was a Confederate soldier, and belonged to Captain W. L. McNeel's company. While on a scout near Edray in 1864, he was captured and sent to Fort Deleware. Thence he was sent to Richmond for exchange, and died before leaving the city.

Otho Wade Ruckman first married a Miss McClung, of Nicholas County. Her daughter became the second wife of Levi Waugh, near Edray. His second wife was Mary Frances Twyman, near Edray.

Clarissa Ruckman, eldest daughter of David L. Ruckman, married Peter Overholt, and is now dead.

Mary Ruckman married Jacob Cackley, whom she survives, and she resides on Stamping Creek with her nephew Wallace.

Catherine Ruckman married Peter McNeel. She is dead, but is survived by her daughter, Mrs John S. Moore.

David Ruckman, Junior, the youngest of David L. Ruckman's sons, was a Confederate soldier. He first belonged to Captain Smith's command in Greenbrier

County. For a good while his company was assigned to General Loring's body guard. Finally it was attached to a cavalry battallion and ordered to Tennessee. He was mortally wounded near Morristown, Tennesse, and died in a few days thereafter.

Thus closes the narrative for the present. Characters have passed under our notice that illustrate what may be achieved by persons who diligently make use of their opportunities. These persons were patriotic, industrious, and endowed with good minds, and have left their impress upon their community that makes for good morals, conservative citizenship, and intellectual improvement.

ISAIAH CURRY.

Not long after the war of 1812 Isaiah Curry, a native of Rockbridge County, located on Back Alleghany, at the place now owned by Zechariah Swink. Mrs Curry was Abigail Hall of Virginia. These worthy persons are the ancestors of the Curry relationship on Back Mountain. Late in life they moved to Lewis County. Their family consisted of four sons and four daughters: William, James, John, Robert, Sally, Elizabeth, Anna, and Margaret.

William Curry was a stone mason, and a very swift workman. His wife was Nancy Lytton, of Rockbridge, and after his marriage they settled in Lewis County,

James, when about grown, was killed by a falling tree while browsing cattle near home. Robert Curry and Isaac Hayse were near him at the time, likewise employed.

John Curry married Virginia Wanless and settled on Back Allegnany.   During the war he was taken prisoner and kept until peace was ratified and the prisoners released.   He then located in Barbour County.

Robert Curry married Elizabeth Swink, of Rockbridge, and lived on Back Mountain.   In reference to his family the following particulars are available:

His son James was a Confederate soldier, and was among the last soldiers killed at Appomattox in 1865.

Enos married Miss Logan, a daughter of the late John Logan, and lives on Back Alleghany.

Nancy was married to Samuel Hevener, and lives on Back Alleghany.

Charlotte became Mrs Brown Gum and lives in Randolph.

Venie became Mrs Jacob Cassell, and lives on Back Alleghany.

Charles married a Miss Burner, and lives on the homestead.

Robert Curry was an elder of the German Baptist Church.   He died in 1881, meeting his death by drowning while attempting to ford the Leatherbark.

In regard to the daughters of Isaiah Curry, the ancestor, the following illustrative items are in hand:

Sally married James Cassell and settled in the far west.   Elizabeth was married to James Jones, and settled in Harrison County.   Anna became Mrs Isaac Hayse, and located in Barbour County.   Margaret became Thomas Galford's first wife.

Thus with the assistance of Mrs L. A. Hefner, on Swago, (a grand-daughter of Isaiah Curry), the writer has been able to record what has been done in illustrating the history of this family relationship.

Isaiah Curry possessed many good traits of character, and he was a fair specimen of the genuine Scotch-Irish people. His remote ancestors were among the people that suffered for their religious views in the north of Ireland, and came to the Valley of Virginia seeking a place to worship, unmolested by civil and religious tyranny.

A predominant trait in this man's character was his plain, common sense views of profane language. To start with, in his home training his mother and father had their son to notice that in the ten commandments cursing and swearing were forbidden along with murder, licentiousness, and theft. He could not bear the idea of being classified with the murderer, the immoral and the dishonest, in the sight of Him who has the power of life and death, and who is to dispense the final rewards and penalties. Hence his speech was pure, and he deplored profanity in others.

As a matter of course Mr Curry's opportunities for observation were not very wide, but still his ideas were impressive, and who is prepared to prove them incorrect? So far as it was his misfortune to hear profanity, he observed that profane persons were of two kinds: There were some profane people who were without good advantages in early life and through companionship with tough, half civilized people acquired profane habits of speech. They may have in after years become ashamed of the habit and honestly tried to overcome it, but in a state of fret, worry, or sudden excitement have forgotten themselves for the time being. Simon Peter was probably one of this kind, and when confronted by a servant girl about his identity began to "curse and to swear," and thus betrayed the character of his early associations. To Simon's lasting credit be it remembered that he upon reflection became so utterly disgusted with himself that he went out and wept bitterly.

It was Mr Curry's misfortune, and the disagreeable misfortune of society in his day, to have observed that there was another class of profane people. Their profanity was the outcome of their coarse, sacriligious characters or dispositions, and were thus to be regarded as moral monstrosities or mental monstrosities, or mental degenerates.

Trained as he had been, this is the way he felt and talked about "cussing," and who can demonstrate where he was mistaken in his views?

ROBERT BEALE.

About the year 1827 Robert Beale, of Botetourt County, Virginia, settled on Elk, a half mile southeast of the place where Mary's Chapel now stands. A bed of tansy near the roadside marks the spot where the residence stood. The house was built of hewn timbers and floored with plank sawn with the whip saw by hand, and was considered an excellent building at that time.   His wife was Mary Vance Poage, daughter of Major William Poage and Nancy Warwick Poage, whose home was at Marlins Bottom.   She was a lady of most excellent qualities of mind and heart.   These worthy young people soon built up an attractive home in the forest, and they seemed fully contented with their surroundings.   The neighborhood was called the Old Field Fork of Elk.

Mr Beale was very energetic and industrious, and while he owned servants, he worked with his own hands as laboriously as the humblest.   It was believed he contracted his fatal illness at a log rolling.

The Sabbath days were mostly spent in prayer meetings and Sabbath school services with the families of David Gibson, David Hannah, and Joseph Hannah, their near neighbors, and for the most part held in his own dwelling.   Ministers of the gospel made his home their place of preaching.   Dr McElhenney, Revs Kerr, William G. Campbell, pioneers of the Presbyterians in his region, officiated at his residence, and pleasant, profitable meetings were the result.

In personal appearance Mr Beale was fine looking, his manners were those of a cultivated Christian gentleman.   He was sincerely and intelligently pious and had he lived there is no estimating the influence he might have had all over our county, for he had come to stay and make this particular place his home for life. His ideal of a home such as he desired was to have ample pastures, with flocks of sheep and herds of cattle and horses, live removed from the extravagance and allurements of society life, so termed, have books and papers and be on pleasant terms with kind and honest neighbors. His aims were rapidly materializing in this picturesque region, famed for its bluegrass, fertile heavily timbered mountains, pure streams, cool, crystal springs, and quiet sheltered dales. His was the sagacity to perceive that for all the elements of true, happy prosperity for new beginners, no place could excel Elk as it then was. Therefore it was a real mysterious providence that a person so much needed in our county, and in such a sense the right man in the place after his own heart, with success just in reach, should be stricken with insidious disease, slowly pine away and at last die. His death occurred in 1833. On an eminence overlooking his home, where he frequently passed Sabbath evenings in summer with his wife and little daughter, his grave was made, and he now waits for the Redeemer to come, as he has promised to do to those who love his appearing.

SAMPSON L. MATHEWS.

Among the citizens of prominence in the early history of Pocahontas County was Sampson Lockhart Mathews, the first county surveyor. His grandfather was Sampson Mathews, one of the early residents of Staunton, whose wife was a Miss Lockhart, hence the name borne by members of the family connexion. She had a sister married to a Mr Nelson, and another married to a Mr Clark. Thus the Montgomerys and the Mathews became related.

The subject of this sketch was the second son of Sampson Mathews, Junior, and Mary Warwick, daughter of Jacob and Mary Warwick, of Clover Lick. Early in life he manifested an intense desire for an education, and his wishes were gratified. Much of the time he passed in studies he was under the care of Dr John McElhenny, who established and for so many years conducted the renowned Lewisburg Academy.

Upon reaching his majority in 1821, young Mathews and his father, who had become a widower, moved to the farm on Swago now owned by Mrs Mary McClintic, his only daughter. Father and son lived in this manner for several years.

In 1825 young Mathews was married to Miss Nancy Edgar, daughter of Thomas Edgar and Ann Matthews, whose farm afterwards became the site now occupied by the town of Ronceverte. Mrs Edgar was the daughter of Archie Mathews, whose residence is now known as the Alexander farm, three miles from Lewisburg.

He continued his residence on the Swago farm until 1834. In the meantime he received his appointment as County Surveyor. In a letter written by the Hon J. Howe Peyton, in his time one of the most eminent members of the Staunton bar, mention is made of the first sessions of the Pocahontas Court, and of the appointment of Mr Mathews. This letter is to be found in Mr Peyton's biography, an interesting volume recently prepared and published by his son, Col. J. T. Peyton of Staunton.

Soon after their marriage Mr and Mrs Mathews gathered a Sabbath school in their home. Mrs McCollam sent her children, Isaac, Ruth, and James. William McNeil sent Jonathan, Claiborne, Jane, and Elizabeth and Joshua Buckley was one of the scholars also. Mr Mathews would read a chapter and offer prayer. Mrs Mathews did most of the teaching. The exercises would open at ten o'clock, and have a recess at noon. In the yard was an arbor formed by a luxuriant hop vine. Under its shade the children would sit and enjoy their luncheon, brought from their homes. After recess the school would meet and continue two or three hours. The summers of 1826 and 1827 were occupied in this useful service.

In 1834 Mr Mathews purchased property in Millpoint from Valentine Cackley and James Cackley, and resided there the remainder of his life.

In his religious sentiments he was a Presbyterian from conviction, and for years was the sole representative of the New School branch. These schools have consolidated since the time of his death on terms of mutual respect and Christian confidence, and hence the wisdom of his position has been vindicated by results.

He was in declining health for quite a while, and awaited his decease with a calmness and self possession that was the wonder of many and the admiration of others. His arrangements were calmly made, his instructions were given, and his requests were expressed as if all was a matter of course.

He died September 23, 1854, and was buried in a place selected by himself. It commands a lovely prospect in the midst of a landscape famed for beautiful vistas.

JOHN JORDAN.

John Jordan, the ancestor of the relationship of that name in Lower Pocahontas, was a very worthy native of Ireland. By occupation he was a tailor, and when he once met a fellow member of the craft after a prolonged separation his friend was very demonstrative in the pleasure the meeting afforded him. In his joyful exhilaration, as a special manifestation of his delight, he struck his friend Jordan on the back of his hand with a side blow of his own. This friendly lick was so powerful as to inflict a bruise so serious in its effects as to necessitate amputation of the arm just below the elbow. Nevertheless he learned to use a hoe or an axe to a good purpose in after life.

Mr Jordan came to this region as a traveling merchant, dealing in Irish linens and other portable merchandise. He was a "hard money" man in his financial preferences, and converted all paper money he received into silver and gold. Miss Miriam McNeel, daughter of John McNeel, the Levels pioneer, found out in some way that the young merchant had about a half bushel of coin, and it seemed to occur to her mind that if a person disabled as he was could make that much money, he could certainly take good care of her. To the surprise of her friends that a nice sensible girl as she was should fancy a cripple, she did not discourage the attentions of the hustling young Irishman, and they were happily married.

At that period of our local history a young man's recommendation was his ability to clear land, split rails, and grub, but to marry a cripple in store clothes was not to be thought of.

After their marriage Mr Jordan continued to prosper in making a living, and purchased some servants to wait on the girl that had made such a surprising venture as to marry him. He settled on the Millstone Run, between Hillsboro and Locust, opening up a property now in possession of Isaac McNeel, whose wife Miriam Nannie Beard is a grand-daughter of the pioneer merchant. There were five sons and three daughters: John, Jonathan, Isaac, Abram, Franklin, Jane, Nancy, and Martha.

John Jordan, Junior, married Martha Burnsides on the Greenbrier in view of the homestead, and settled near Hillsboro, where they spent the remainder of their lives. Their children were Christopher, Jonathan, Mary, Miriam, Nancy, and Jemima. Christopher married Elizabeth Wallace, daughter of Benjamin Wallace of Bath County, but long a resident of Pocahontas. Jonathan married Lucinda, daughter of James Sharp, on Beaver Creek. He was a Confederate soldier, and died at home while on a furlough from the army. Mary became Mrs Jacob McNeel, and lived on the McNeel homestead. John Henry and Samuel her sons. Miriam married Aaron Hill and settled on Hills Creek. Nancy became Mrs George Hill and died a few years since at Falling Spring, Greenbrier County. Jemima was married to Captain Samuel Gilmore, and lives in Highland County.

Jonathan Jordan, son of the pioneer, first married Elizabeth Callison, daughter of· Anthony Callison at Locust. Her twin sons John and Anthony died young. Jonathan's second wife was Rebecca Edmiston. They settled on Dry Run, the place now in possession of Sherman Clark. The children of the second marriage were Elizabeth, Rebecca, Miriam, William and James.

Isaac Jordan, another son of the pioneer, married Mary Callison, daughter of James Callison on Trump Run, and settled just west of Hillsboro at the spring now owned by J. K. Bright. He afterwards moved to Davis County, Missouri. Isaac Jordan's second marriage was with the widow of Captain William Renick, Lafayette County, Missouri. He became a prominent citizen in his adopted State, was commissioner of the revenue and justice of the peace. His daughter Elizabeth became Mrs Samuel Beard, son of Josiah Beard of Locust, and they resided in Missouri near Odessa. Mr Beard died recently.

Abram Jordan married Jane Edmiston, daughter of the late Andrew Edmiston, near Locust. She was a sister of the distinguished judge Mathew Edmiston of Weston. Abram lived a few years on the old Jordan homestead, and afterwards migrated to Saline County, Missouri. Nancy and Lydia were his daughters. Nancy became Mrs Faulkner, and Lydia was married to William Renick, from Greenbrier County. Mr Renick was an extensive dealer in live stock, and was partner in trade with Levi Gay during his sojourn in Missouri.

Franklin Jordan married Martha Edmiston, and

went to Missouri. After her decease he married Mrs Ballenger, from Ashland, Ky.

Jane Jordan, eldest daughter of the pioneer, was married to the late Major William Blair, and lived near Hillsboro. Her sons were Morgan, Claiborne, Doctor Franklin, Colbert, and John, who died during the war. Morgan Blair married Ann Gay, daughter of George Gay, and settled in Iowa. Claiborne Blair married Lavinia Bruffey and went west.

Mrs Jane Blair's daughters were Frankie Blair, who was married to the late Isaac Clutter, and lived on Briar Knob, head of Hills Creek. Miriam Blair was married to William Hill, and settled in Iowa. Elizabeth Blair became Mrs John G. Beard, and lives on the Blair homestead near Hillsboro. Martha Blair was first married to Peter Clark, and after his decease she became Mrs Abram Beard, and lived in Renick's Valley, where she died not long since.

Nancy Jordan, the second of pioneer Jordan's daughters, was first married to Isaac Callison and went west. Her son, James B. Callison, lives at Jamesport, Mo. Her daughter Miriam was married to William Walkup, from Greenbrier County, and lived in Missouri, where she died. Mrs Walkup's son is a Presbyterian minister. Mrs Nancy Callison's second marriage was with the late George Edmiston near Locust, lived awhile on the old Andrew Edmiston homestead, and finally went to Missouri.

Martha, the youngest of the Jordan sisters, was married to the late Joseph Beard of Hillsboro. For several years they lived on Spring Creek in Greenbrier,

and then resided in Hillsboro. Her son John Jordan
Beard married Minerva Edmiston. Their daughter
Mollie became Mrs C. F. Moore. Harry Beard, one
of their sons, is a physician in Lewisburg, and J. Fred
Beard lives at Huntersville.

Lieutenant J. J. Beard was a gallant Confederate
officer. He was severely wounded and greatly disabled by wounds received in battle in the lower valley.
He served for two terms as clerk of both the circuit
and county courts of Pocahontas. His death occurred
in 1898.

Margaret Jane Beard, her eldest daughter, was married to Captain William L. McNeel. Mrs George Callison, Mrs J. Thrasher, Misses Mary, Pauline, and
Maggie McNeel are her daughters. Joseph McNeel
and the late Henry McNeel are her sons.

Miriam Nancy, Mrs Martha Beard's youngest
daughter, was married to Isaac McNeel, at Millpoint,
where they now dwell. Their son Thomas Summers
is Prosecuting Attorney for Pocahontas County, and
Harvey Winters McNeel is a physician at Hillsboro.
Lanty McNeel is at home, and Mary Gold their only
daughter.

Mrs Martha Beard died quite recently, over eighty
years of age. Some time before her death she was
disabled by a fall that prevented her from walking for
the remainder of her life.

Thus far we have been able to record something in
memory of a very worthy and rather remarkable person. If the reader has derived any pleasure from this
sketch his thanks are largely due James McCollam and

the late Mrs Nancy Callison, upon whose retentive
memories the writer has drawn for most of the particulars here given.

John Jordan, the pioneer, was one of the original
ruling elders of the Oak Grove Presbyterian church.
His house was open to Methodist and Presbyterian
ministers without any apparent discrimination, and for
years was one of the main preaching places for Methodist ministers. He donated the site for the Methodist
church near his residence. This church was destroyed
by fire about sixty years ago. In its time this was the
most comfortable building of the kind in Pocahontas in
possession of that sect. In his death Mr Jordan was
greatly mourned, for many felt they had been bereaved of a true and useful friend. He was buried near
the ruins of the Millstone Run Church, and his grave
seems to have been nicely cared for. A neatly carved
stone (the handiwork of the late John Bruffey) marks
the place where a good man rests in hope. His life's
duty is done, and with tears of genuine affection he
was tenderly laid under the trees, planted by the unseen hand of the God he served.

JOHN BRADSHAW.

In his day and generation one of the most conspicuous citizens of our county was John Bradshaw, Esq.,
of Huntersville. His residence was on ths site now
occupied by the "Lightner House" belonging to Amos
Barlow. John Bradshaw was a native of England.
Bradshaw is a historic name in England—as readers of

English history readily remember—and so is the name Herold.

About 1760 two brothers, James and John Bradshaw came to America. James Bradshaw went to Kentucky to reside. John Bradshaw remained in Augusta County, Virginia, and married Miss Nancy McKamie, in the vicinity of Parnassus, and soon afterwards settled on the Bullpasture River, ten or eleven miles below McDowell, on property at this time owned by Franklin Bradshaw and the family of the late John Bradshaw, County Surveyor. Here he resided a number of years, and then early in the last century came to Huntersville. His family consisted of four sons and four daughters: Nancy, Elizabeth, Margaret, Jane, James, John, Thomas, and William.

James Bradshaw married Isabella Stevens of Greenbrier County, and settled on the old homestead. John and Franklin Bradshaw, well known citizens of Highland County, were his sons. Mrs Eveline Byrd, near Falling Spring, Greenbrier County, was a daughter. Captain R. H. Bradshaw, a gallant soldier who fell in the battle of Port Republic, was a grandson, and James Bradshaw of McDowell is also a grandson of James Bradshaw.

John Bradshaw married Nancy Stevens, sister of Mrs Isabella Bradshaw, and settled in the Big Valley between the Bullpasture and Jacksons River, on what is now known as the Porter Place, and afterwards went to Missouri. These ladies were the daughters of Robert Stevens, who owned the famous ferry at Fort Spring over the Greenbrier.

Thomas Bradshaw married Nancy Williams on Anthonys Creek, and settled on Browns Creek, three
miles from Huntersville, on property now held by C.
L. Moore. He exchanged farms with his brother William, and moved to the Bradshaw place near Millpoint
now owned by Isaac McNeel. He was a botanical
physician of the Thompsonian School, and had all of
Pocahontas County for his practice. Lobelia and
"No. 6" were the main remedies employed, along
with hot baths and bleeding. Dr Bradshaw died at an
advanced age in Huntersville in 1862. His family
first moved to Webster County, and then to Missouri.

William Bradshaw was a soldier of the war of 1812.
His wife was Jane Elliot Hickman, daughter of William Hickman on Back Creek, who was the ancestor
of the Hickman relationship in Bath. William Hickman's wife was Mary Elliot, and one of her sisters was
the wife of Moses Moore, and hence the name Elliot
or Ellet so frequently used in the Moore connexion.
William Bradshaw first settled near Millpoint, where
he lived several years. Then upon exchanging places
with his brother Thomas he moved to Browns Creek,
where he reared his family. He operated a carding
machine along with his farm. The machine stood near
the Dunmore road about where the Sheldon Moore
road turns off. The bales of rolls were fastened with
black thorns, which were gathered by boys for a small
consideartionr Mr Bradshaw finally moved to Lewis
County, where he died a few years since at an advanced age. As was intimated, he was a soldier of
the war of 1812, and was a very good man in all the

relations of life, and reared a highly respectable family
of eight daughters and one son.

Nancy Makamie Bradshaw married Isaac Hartman,
near Greenbank. Mary Jane married Alexander
Moore, on Stony Creek. Senilda Eiler married Washington Nottingham, of Gladehill. Huldah Hickman
became the wife of John A. McLaughlin, near Huntersville. Martha Ann was married to the late Beverly Waugh, near Hillsboro. Matilda Margaret was
married to the late Nicholas Linger, of Lewis County,
where she now resides. Rebecca Frances, a very promising person, died in early youth. Rachel Hannah,
the pride of the family, died at six years of age. William James married Mary Ellen Watson, in Lewis
County, and settled there.

Nancy Bradshaw, daughter of the Huntersville
pioneer, married Levi Cackley, and lived on Stamping
Creek, near Millpoint.

Margaret Bradshaw, the second daughter, was married to the late John Gwin, on Jacksons River. Her
daughter Nancy was the first wife of Squire Hugh Mc-
Laughlin, late of Marlinton. Her son David Gwin
married Eliza Stevenson, on Jacksons River. Another
son, John Gwin, Junior, married Miss Gillespie, and
lived near the Hot Springs. B. Austin Gwin is her
grandson. Jane Gwin, her daughter, married a Mr
Starr, an Englishman, and lived at Winchester. Elizabeth Gwin married a Mr Givens on Jacksons River.

Elizabeth Bradshaw, daughter of the pioneer, was
the first wife of the late Samuel Hogsett, who came
from Augusta County, and was a relative of the Mak-

amies. He was a well known citizen, a member of
the old county court, and was in every sense of the
word a justice ef the peace. He was over six feet in
height and large in proportion, and feared the face of
no living man. On public days his presence and
strong arms spoiled many a fight. Mr Hogsett lived
on the farm now owned and occupied by Hon William
Curry. Their children were John, who married Leah
Cackley, Nancy, who became Mrs McAtee, William
Perry, Josiah Thomas, Samuel, Margaret, Mary,
Eliza, and Elizabeth.

Jane Bradshaw, fourth daughter of the pioneer, was
married to William Tallman of Greenbank, and lived
at the old home. Her son Colonel James Tallman was
a protege of Henry M. Moffett, and was clerk of the
two courts of Pocahontas for many years, and Colonel
of the 127th Regiment of Virginia Militia. He is remembered as one of the mest popular and promising
young citizens of his times, and his sad and early
death was sincerely lamented by the entire county.

Mrs Tallman's second marriage was to Thomas Gammon. William, John, Franklin, Cyrus, and Martha
were her children by this second marriage. William
Tallman Gammon married Elizabeth Slaven, and located at Huntersville, and became a prominent citizen,
merchant, member of the court, promoted from captain
to colonel of the militia, and was a ruling elder in the
Presbyterian church. Martha Jane Gammon first married Amos Campbell, son of Thomas Campbell, Highland County, Virginia. Her second marriage was with
the Rev J. W. Canter, of the Methodist church.

Thus far we have it in our power to tell our readers
something of one of the most noted men in the early
history of our county, aided by his granddaughter Mrs
Huldah McLaughlin.   Mr Bradshaw owned the lands
new held by William Curry, Amos Barlow, that recently held by the late William J. McLaughlin, the
site of Huntersville, and from the James Sharp property on Browns Creek to Dilleys Mill.   He donated
and deeded the site for the public buildings of Pocahontas County, without reservation.   In a lottery venture he drew a prize of ten thousand dollars, which
made him one of the money kings of his times.

In appearance his personality was striking, large
and portly and scrupulously neat in his dress.   He
used a crutch that was profusely ornamented with silver mountings.   His manners were those of an elegant
gentleman of the old school.

About the time of Tarleton's raid to Charlottesville,
he was drafted into the service.   Late Saturday evening the notice was served on him to be ready for duty
Monday morning.   His young wife was equal to the
emergency.   She cooked, washed, cried, and prayed
all day Sunday and had him ready for the war early
Monday morning, and by night he was in Staunton on
his march to Yorktown, where he said he fought in
blood "shoe-mouth deep."

He died suddenly in 1837,   His grave is marked by
the wild cherry tree in the old Huntersville cemetery,
that is said to be growing directly over his grave.

JOHN GAY.

Hon. John Gay, but lately of Marlinton, a citizen of marked prominence in the affairs of our county for forty or fifty years, deserves special mention in local annals. He was born May 26, 1804, on the place now occupied by his son, Levi Gay. His parents were Robert Gay and Hannah Moore, who were among the pioneers of our county as early as 1770.

John Gay was married in Huntersville June 24, 1834, to Margaret B. Clark. She was born in Cecil County, Maryland, June 19, 1810. The whole of their married life was spent on the home farm. Their family consisted of eight children, four sons and four daughters.

Samuel M. Gay lives near Edray, at the head of the Indian Draft, a prosperous citizen. He was a Confederate soldier attached to the 31st Virginia Infantry, one of the most distinguished regiments in Lee's army. He was wounded at the battle of Strasburg, Virginia.

Levi Gay resides on the home place near Marlinton, and is a widely known citizen. He was also a Confederate soldier in the 31st Infantry, and was wounded at Spottsylvania Courthouse. .

Edward lives with his brother Levi. James died in infancy not more than a year old. Hannah died in 1862, a grown young lady. Harriet died in 1861.

Susan first married Adam Young. Her sons John Young and Adam Young are citizens of Pocahontas.

Upon her second marriage she became Mrs D. A. Peck, and resides on Hills Creek.

Ann Maria became Mrs Jacob Moore and iived on upper Elk, a few miles from Edray.

Sallie Hamilton died in 1857, four years of age.

By common consent this family was regarded one of the very interesting and pleasant families of the community, and as neighbors not to be excelled.

For twenty-eight years Mr Gay was a justice of the peace, deputy sheriff, and high sheriff and captain of the Stony Creek company, State militia. He served three or four terms in the Virginia House of Delegates 1839 and 1844. It was during one of his terms of service the charter for the Staunton and Parkersburg road was issued and its construction undertaken. The road was located by Engineer Crozet.

For many of the qualities that prepare for useful citizenship Mr Gay was justly distinguished. A solid conservative mind, judicious management of his business affairs, and a high sense of personal honor. He seemed to realize that that public office is a public trust, and that the peoples money should be used as carefully as his own, and expended where it was likely to yield the most serviceable returns.

In person and manners he was a model type of the Scotch-Irish, a stock of people that get the credit of being the first to move in the contest for American Independence. He lived to the age of eighty-five, and carried his years so well that up to his final sickness his intellect seemed clear as it ever was, and but slight indications of bodily decrepitude were discernable.

In politics he was a Jacksonian democrat. "Old Hickory" never had a more loyal admirer and adherent, or Thomas Ritchie of the Richmond Enquirer, a more attentive reader.

For a number of years he was a professing Christian, and his end was peaceful and hopeful. He and his devoted wife were not long separated in their decease, which occurred but a few years since. He died October 30, 1890. Mrs Gay was a very superior person, and the writer cherishes her kindness to him as among the most pleasant memories of his early life. Beauty is vain and favor deceitful, but a woman that feareth the Lord, she shall be praised.

She survived her noble husband but a few fleeting months. Her decease was sudden but very safe. Their bodies repose in the Gibson grave yard, and their graves indicated by beautiful monuments placed there by their dutiful children.

WILLIAM POAGE.

The Poage relationship claims a place in the annals of our county, and some attention will be given to them in this sketch.

The Poages are of pure Scotch-Irish ancestry. The line of descent can be traced to two brothers, Robert and John Poage, who "proved their importation at their own charges," at Orange Courthouse, 1740. The Pocahontas Poages are the descendants of Robert Poage, who settled between Staunton and Fort Defiance, and was among the first to occupy that attractive portion of the famous Valley of Virginia. His wife was Elizabeth Preston, whose family settled in the vicinity of Waynesboro with the pioneers about 1740. Their son John married Mary Blair and settled near the Poage homestead in Augusta County.

William Poage, one of John Poage's sons, married Margaret Davies and settled in the Little Levels about 1782, at the place where Charles W. Beard now resides. Mrs Poage died in 1843, aged 98 years. Their children were William, George Washington, Moses Hoge, Samuel Davies, and Elizabeth.

William Poage, Junior, married the widow Nancy Gatewood, a daughter of Major Jacob Warwick, and lived at Marlin's Bottom. Their daughter Rachel was married to Josiah Beard, of Locust.

Mary Vance Poage was married first to Robert Beale, and settled on Elk, where he died, leaving one daughter, Margaret Elizabeth Beale. There was another child that died at the age of a few months. When it was buried the father walked around the grave and then looking upward with his tearful eyes said: "Our God in heaven only knows who will be the next to be buried here; it may be myself." Four weeks from that day he too was carried there and buried.

Mrs Mary Beale was married the second time, to Henry M. Moffett, clerk of the county, and lived first at Huntersville, and then at the Levels. Margaret Beale, her eldest daughter, became the wife of Dr G. B. Moffett. Their sons Robert and James Moffett live in St. Louis and Chicago, employed in the Standard Oil business. Sally Moffett became Mrs Alexander

McChesney, late of Charleston, W. Va.   Martha Moffett is now Mrs Hall, of Philippi, Barbour County. Mary Evelina was the late Mrs William P. Thompson, of New York.   Rachel Moffett is now Mrs Robert McChesney, of Lewisburg.   George H. Moffett became a lawyer, speaker of the West Virginia legislature, and distinguished editor.   He resides at Parkersburg.

Colonel William Woods Poage, son of Major William Poage, married Julia Callison of Locust, and settled on the homestead, finally moved to Poages Lane, where his sons John Robert and Quincy W. Poage now reside.

Margaret Davies Poage was married to the late Jas. A. Price.

Moses Hoge Poage, son of William Poage, the Levels settler, married Martha McDannald, of Windy Cove, Bath County, and settled on the place now held by Alvin Clark.   Their sons and daughters were William, Franklin, Cyrus, Davis, Elizabeth, who became Mrs George Van Eman, a Presbyterian minister; and Mary Poage, who became Mrs Hanna.   Late in life Moses Poage emigrated to Missouri.

George Washington Poage married Miss Rankin and settled on the place now occupied by Preston Clark.   The children of the first marriage were William, who was killed by a falling tree; Rankin, who married Nancy Wolfenbarger, and settled where the late Rev M. D. Dunlap resided. He finally went west. James R. Poage, late of Edray.   Mrs Ann Wanless, wife of Ralph Wanless in the Hills.   Mrs Elizabeth Burner second wife of the late George Burner of Travelers Repose.

George W. Poage's second wife was Elizabeth Beard, sister of Josiah Beard. The children of the second family were George Washington Poage, Jr., Samuel Davies Poage, John B. Poage, and Elizabeth Poage, who became Mrs William P. Hill.

George W. Poage was a person of fine appearance, and his resemblance to the portraits of Washington— of whom he was a namesake—was frequently remarked upon. An evergreen prayer meeting was conducted at his house on silent Sabbaths. He loved to "wail with judicious care" the hymns and tunes that were sung by the Covenanting ancestry in Scotland. While there was much singing and much reading and much praying, but few things were sung, read, and prayed, and so the minds of the worshippers were concentrated on the few things needful—the forgiveness of sins through the blood of Jesus, a new heart and a right spirit. Advanced in years, Mr Poage went west with his family and settled in Missouri.

Samuel Davies Poage, youngest son of William Poage, Senior, married Miss Rebecca Arbuckle, of Lewisburg, sister of Captain Charles Arbuckle of Texas and lived at the old homestead. He had been educated for the Presbyterian ministry, but declined the exercise of its duties through a morbid sense of unworthiness, unfitness for assuming duties so sacred and responsible as he regarded Ministerial vows demanded. He was a faithful helper in the prayer meetings led by his brother George Poage. While attending school taught by Rev Joseph Brown at the Brick Church, the

writer boarded in Mr Poage's family. He has heard
him in secret prayer in his private room long after
midnight, such were his devotional habits. It matter-
ed not how cold the night might be, Mr Poage would
spend hours in that room in secret devotions, and
oftentimes he would come out with his features all
radiant with ecstatic emotion.

Elizabeth Poage, daughter of William Poage, Sr.,
became the wife of Colonel John Hill, son of Richard
Hill, so often mentioned in these biographic notes as
a pioneer and scout.

Colonel Hill, late in life, felt it his duty to remove
west. It was one of the most mournful episodes that
ever occurred in the social history of the Levels when
Moses Poage, George Poage, and Colonel Hill set out
for the west with their families in order to seek new
homes in their old age. The most of these persons located in Davies County, Missouri, and many of their
descendants are in that State, which has been to so
large extent occupied by Virginia people as to be regarded as a new Virginia.

William Poage, Senior, was a Presbyterian ruling
elder, and virtually the founder of the Oak Grove
church. Some of the first meetings conducted by
Presbyterian ministers in this region were at his house.
When the pulpit would be vacant years at a time there
would be religious meetings at his home or the homes
of his sons, who were also elders.

Visiting friends from Kentucky brought with them
the revival spirit that has rendered the early history of
Kentucky so famous, and it broke out in the Levels in

1801. Parties in Augusta heard of it, and came over to see and hear what it all meant.

The pastor of the Old Stone Church, Rev William Wilson, a relative of the Poages, and fifteen or twenty of the young people, also relatives, came over together. They became imbued with the spirit of the moment, and went back singing and praying as they traveled along. The effect upon the home people in the valley as they rode up singing and praying was overwhelming, and from that point—the Old Stone church —the revival influence went all over the State, whereever there were Presbyterian congregations, and the results are visible at the present time. So it appears that a great matter was kindled by a little watch fire that had been kindled in the old Poage homestead.

WILLIAM SHARP.

One of the most substantial and prosperous citizens of our county in its formative period was the late William Sharp, near Verdant Valley. He was the son of William Sharp, Senior, who settled near Huntersville. He had scarcely attained his majority when he and Elizabeth Waddell were married at Alexander Waddell's. This worthy couple at once settled in the woods and opened up a fine estate out of a forest noted for the tremendous size of its walnut, red oak, and sugar maple trees, and reared a worthy family. In reference to their sons and daughters the following particulars have been mainly learned from his daughter, Mrs Martha Dilley, near Dilleys Mill.

James Sharp, the eldest son, married Althea Martin and lived on Browns Creek, on the farm now owned by Amos Barlow. His son William died at home. Hanson died in Camp Chase, Ohio. George died a prisoner of war. His daughter Elizabeth married Thomas Logan, in Randolph County, and Sarah Sharp has her home with her sister.

William Sharp, Junior, married Rachel Dilley, and settled near Linnwood. His sons Harmon, Silas, and Hugh are well known citizens. Bernard fell mortally wounded at Duncan's Lane. Henry was wounded near William Gibson's on Elk, and died of his wounds. Luther was shot near his father's home by a scouting party. All three of these sons were Union soldiers. Mary Ella, the only daughter, died at the age of six years.

Alexander Sharp married Mary Dilley, and settled on a section of the old homestead. His only child is Mrs Hannah Johnson. A. D. Williams his grandson

Jacob Warwick Sharp married Elizabeth McNeel, and lived on the homestead. His son William married Julia Moore, and lives at Edray. Their daughter Lura is Mrs Dr J. W. Price. Paul married Eveline Moore, and lives on the Greenbrier River at the Bridger place. Isaac lives near Edray. Giles lives on the homestead. Jacob, junior, died in childhood. Elizabeth married J. R Poage, and Catherine married Quincy W. Poage. Francis married A. N. Barlow, and lives on a section of the homestead. Ann became Mrs S. B. Moore. Jacob W. Sharp died but recently much lamented by a very large circle of friends and relatives.

John Sharp married Sally Johnson, daughter of the late William Johnson on the Greenbrier, and lives near Marlinton. His sons are Henry, Hugh, Ewing, James, and David. Mary is Mrs Frank Dilley, Nancy is Mrs Ervine Wilfong, Martha is Mrs James Wilfong, Susan is Mrs Amzi Ervine.

Elizabeth Sharp married Hugh McLaughlin, at Huntersville, and has recently died aged nearly a hundred years.

Jane Sharp married James Hanson and settled in Galla County, Ohio. Her children were William, John, Lydia, Elizabeth, and Catherine.

Mary Sharp married David Gibson and settled on Elk, where Robert Gibson now lives.

Rebecca Sharp married Wm. D. Moore, and settled on the Crooked Branch of Elk, on the place now owned by her son Jacob S. Moore. Her children were Mary Jane, who married John McLaughlin, son of Major Daniel McLaughlin, and settled beyond Greenbank. Elizabeth married Joseph C. Gay, and lives on Elk Mountain near the old home. Mr Gay was a noted Confederate scout and is a prosperous citizen. Matthias Moore married Jennie Mays, and lives in Botetourt County, Virginia. C. L. Moore married Mary Martha McLaughlin. Jacob Moore married Harriet Gay, lately deceased. Nancy Moore married Jonas Simmons, and lived at Mingo, Randolph County.

Anna Sharp married Alexander Stalnaker, and settled in Randolph County. Her daughter Mary married Bryson Hamilton of that county.

Ellen Sharp married Warwick Stalnaker, of Randolph County. Her daughter Lizzie became Mrs Dr David Gibson of the same vicinity.

Nancy Sharp married Jacob Cassell, from Back Alleghany, and are living at Woodstock, Illinois.

Martha Sharp, youngest daughter of the pioneer, married Andrew Dilley and settled on Thorny Creek.

Thus far the writer has been able to furnish some historical items that illustrate the family history of two very estimable persons. As related elsewhere, these people were the intimate friends of Jacob Warwick and his wife. Mr Sharp lived to a very advanced age, having survived his wife many years. He lived to see his children married and settled. His appearance was venerable, and nature had done very much for him in the way of natural endowments of mind and vigor of body.

He first saw the young person he married at Thomas Drinnon's, near Edray, where she spent a week or two spinning flax. While she was there a preacher happened to come along, (believed to have been Bishop Asbury). Mr Drinnon drummed up a congregation. and among those present was a young and bashful youth with a new coonskin cap that he seemed to set a great deal of store by. Miss Waddell seemed to think it was very funny, and when she went home made some remark about the ugly, funny looking young man she had seen at the meeting. The mother remonstrated and said: "Oh Betsy, don't talk so; that young chap will be to see you yet, first thing you know."

Sure enough he did slip in, and found Betsy not exactly "robed and ready" either. She had just finished and hung out "a wash," and by way of a restful change was performing on her spinning wheel, in short petticoat, chemise, and bare footed. Having shown him a chair, she resumed her performance at the wheel and as he meant business and time was precious, matters were pretty well arranged by midnight.

These young people thus being all the world to each other and not afraid to work, their cabin home was an earthly paradise. A fine estate was opened up, a worthy family was reared, and the way prepared for many worthy families to have a local habitation and name in a goodly land. The influence of these good people was in the interest of untiring industry, honest dealing, generous hospitality, and patriotic citizenship.

MARTIN DILLEY.

Among the well known citizens of our county from the twenties to the forties was Martin Dilley. It is believed he was from Maryland and of Quaker descent. His wife was Hannah Moore, daughter of Pennsylvania John Moore, the pioneer. He located near Dilleys Mill where his son the late Andrew Dilley lived. Here he settled in the virgin forest and rescued from the wilderness quite a large estate and accumulated an ample competency. His home was known far and near where a bountiful hospitality was dispensed, a cordial welcome awaited friends and strangers alike. In reference to his family the following particulars have been gleaned from the reminiscences of some of his surviving friends.

His son John Dilley married Isabel (Ibbie) Dilley, daughter of Henry Dilley, a brother of Martin. John Dilley's daughter Margaret married Samuel Sutton near Greenbank, where she now resides. Jeremiah Dilley, son of John, married Margaret McCarty, daughter of Daniel McCarty. Clayton Dilley married Mary Moore, daughter of James Moore. Clark Dilley a Union soldier, married Margaret Arbogast, daughter of Rev Henry Arbogast, who was slain during the war between Frost and Glade Hill.

John Dilley's second marriage was with Naomi Mc-Neil, daughter of John McNeil, of Swago. The children by the second marriage were as follows: Hannah Jane married Wesley Irvine and lives near Verdant Valley. George married Amelia Warwick. He died in Lewis county. His widow married Hopkins Wanless and now lives near Dilleys Mill. Register Dilley lives in Iowa. Wilson Dilley married Margaret Rush and lives on Brown's Mountain. Fletcher Dilley married Nancy Hannah, on Elk, and lives near West Union. Kenney Dilley is a journeyman printer and founded the Pocahontas Herald at Huntersville in 1893. Davis Dilley at home. Summers married Amanda McLaughlin and died near Frankford recently. Peter married Georgia Hamilton and lives on Knapp's Creek. Rebecca became Mrs Gratton S. Weiford and lives on the old homestead.

Elizabeth Dilley, daughter of Martin Dilley, marrid Peter Yeager, and lived at Travelers Repose where Peter Yeager, her son now lives. Her other children were Martin and Ella.

Ann married William Sharp and lived on Thorny Creek where Lindsey Sharp now lives.

Martha married William Cleek, of Bath county, Virginia, and lived near Windy Cove. Her sons were William and Charles. Her daughter Ann Cleek married George Simpson. Sarah Cleek married William Simpson, and both lived in Bath.

Rachel Dilley married William Sharp, junior, and lived near the Big Spring of Elk. Her daughter Ella died at the age of six years. Her sons Bernard, Henry and Luther were Union soldiers and died of wounds received during the war. Hugh, Silas and Harmon are well known and prosperous citizens, living on and near the homestead.

Mary Dilley married Alexander Sharp, near Verdant Valley, and lived on a part of the William Sharp homestead. Her only child is Mrs Hannah Johnson.

Andrew Dilley, Martin Dilley's second son, married Martha Sharp, youngest daughter of William Sharp, senior, and settled on the homestead. His family consisted of two sons and a daughter, Hanson, Amos and Elizabeth, who died aged two years.

Amos J. Dilley married Araminta, daughter of Ralph Dilley, near Mt Zion in the Hills, and settled on Thorny Creek. Their children were Missouri Francis, now Mrs George A. Fertig; William Andrew; Noah Patterson; Howard Dennis, lately deceased; Uriah Hevener; Elizabeth Martha; Virgie May; Ernest, and Everett Amos.

Hanson Dilley married Caroline Stalnaker and settled at Dilley's Mill of which he is the present owner.

John Dilley and Andrew Dilley were worthy sons of their very worthy father, Martin Dilley. In his day Martin Dilley was one of the most widely known of Pocahontas citizens, and his presence and character reflected credit upon the citizenship of the county in the estimation of those coming from abroad. He was of that type of citizenship of which any county might be considered fortunate to possess. As a member of society Martin Dilley was worthy of high esteem because of his energy, industry, attention to business, honest economical thrift, and exemplary morals. He owned a family of slaves to whom he was very indulgent and lenient. For many years on public occasions at Huntersville—musters, superior courts and presidential elections—"Dilley's George" was usually one of the most conspicuous figures in the crowd as the vender of ginger cakes, apples and cider. He would be dressed "fine as a preacher," very dignified in his manners and would count the cakes and deal out the cider as if it made no difference to him whether you wanted it or not. He put on very sanctimonious airs trying to look and act like the preachers, and the imitation of tone, look and gesture was quite a success. The articles he vended were the admiration of the whole county, and the prosaic old colored man found it remunerative, and all was owing to the indulgence of his benevolent master.

Some years before his decease, Martin Dilley was waylaid, fired upon and severely wounded at the bend of the road a mile or so east of Driscol. The event startled the whole county, and was one of the most pathetic and tragical scenes ever transacted in our county.

Mr Dilley deserves to be remembered as one of the more substantial and useful citizens of his generation. He should be held in high esteem for what he accomplished in developing his part of our county, for he demonstrated that a rich reward awaited the diligent worker, and that an ample competence could be secured by such in spite of natural obstacles of dense forests rugged soil and seemingly capricious climate.

A chilly, rainy evening in April, 1847, the writer spent under the roof of this good old man and shared the comforts so profusely provided. And he will ever remember how impressively the venerable man stood up, repeated and sang a hymn. Then he had us to kneel and he the "priest and father" led in the family devotions preliminary to retiring for the night's repose. Such are the homes whence true peace and prosperity come forth to bless our people at large. May there be many such.

WILLIAM NOTTINGHAM.

For more than a hundred years Nottingham has been a familiar name in our part of West Virginia. The ancestor of the Nottingham relationship was William Nottingham, Senior, a native of England. His wife, whose name cannot be recalled, was of Irish descent. Soon after the Revolution these persons settled in what is now Pocahontas on land at present owned by Uriah Hevener and the heirs of the late Washington Nottingham. Their family consisted of five sons and a daughter. Their names were William, Sampson, James, Jacob, George and Elizabeth. James Nottingham migrated to Tennessee. Sampson Nottingham settled on the upper part of the home place. Jacob Nottingham settled on part of the Glade Hill farm, then went to Braxton County. George Nottingham settled, it is believed, in Lewis County.

William Nottingham, Junior, married Mary Arbogast, daughter of Adam Arbogast, and settled on the farm now held by the family of the late Adam Nottingham. In reference to his family the following particulars have been furnished us by his son, Harvey Nottingham.

Margaret Nottingham married James Moore in the Hills. Mary Moore, her daughter, married Clayton Dilley. She was the mother of A. L. Dilley and F. M. Dilley. A. L. Dilley is remembered as one of the founders of the Pocahontas Herald. William Moore, a son of James and Margaret Moore, was in the Confederate service, and is numbered with the unknown dead.

Mahala Nottingham married Captain John McElwee lately of the Hot Springs, Va. Her sons, Divers McElwee of Driscol, Bernard McElwee of Dunmore, and Burton McElwee of Greenbank, are well known citizens of our county.

Jennie Nottingham married William Tallman, and moved to Upshur County.

Hessie Nottingham married James C. Moore, near Dilleys Mill. Mr Moore was killed in battle, June, 1864, near New Hope, Va.

Mary Nottingham never married, and died many years since.

Addison Nottingham, son of William Nottingham, Jr., has been twice married. His first marriage was with Miss Margaret Conrad, daughter of Solomon Conrad, near Greenbank. His second wife was Miss Elizabeth Herron, near Frost. He settled in the unbroken forest with his young family on the place where he now lives, and by patience and perseverence, with the blessings of Providence, he has prospered.

Harvey Nottingham, another son of William Nottingham, Jr., married Miss Caroline Swink, whose parents came from the Valley of Virginia in her early youth. He settled on a section of the home farm where he now resides, near Glade Hill. He began in the woods, and in the course of a few years, after much industrious toil, these persons have gathered about them the comforts of a charming home on the hill-side facing the rising sun. The two brothers, Harvey and Addison, live on adjoining farms, and here one can find an illustration of what may be realized by prudence and industry in the way of a comfortable competency.

William Nottingham, son of William Nottingham, Jr. went west.

Washington Nottingham, son of William, Jr., married Miss Senilda Bradshaw, daughter of the late William Bradshaw, on Browns Creek. She was a granddaughter of John Bradshaw, Esq., the founder Hunt-tersville, and a first cousin of the celebrated Bishop William Taylor, who claims to have preached all around the world, and has led a hundred thousand souls to the cross, according to the best of his knowledge and belief.

Hon. Adam Nottingham, son of William, Jr., married Miss Henrietta Philips, near Travelers Repose, and lived on the Glade Hill homestead opened up by his father. At an early age he was thrown upon his own resources by his own choice. His natural endowments were of a high order, and he studiously improved whatever opportunities came to hand: For several years he taught school, afterwards became deputy-sheriff, and then sheriff, and he also served as magistrate several terms. He represented Pocahontas in the house of delegates in the Virginia Legislature at Richmond, Va. He was an influential political leader and was a strenuous Jacksonian Democrat.

Mr Nottingham has been dead but a few years. His widow and several sons and daughters survive him, some of them still at the old home, while others have gone out, some far as Texas and the far west.

SAMUEL WHITING.

Samuel Whiting was a native of Sussex County, England, where he was born May 18, 1776. His wife was Sarah Lancaster, and was four years younger.

After a long, tedious voyage of three or four months Mr Whiting and his young family landed at New York in 1823, where he remained for a year or two. Thence he came to Virginia in what what is now Gilmer county. From Gilmer county to Jacksons River in Bath county, thence to Elk near the Big Spring, where Mrs Whiting died unexpectedly in her chair.

They were the parents of three sons and two daughters: Samuel, Robert, Ebenezer, Mercy, and Mary. Mercy became Mrs Varner; Mary was first Mrs Sleathe then Mrs Massenger. Both sisters settled and lived in Gilmer County. Two of the sons, Samuel and Robert, settled and lived in Gilmer County, where their descendants now live and are reported to be very estimable people. Samuel Whiting, Junior, was born in 1811, and died in 1858.

Upon his second marriage with Jennie Hannah, daughter of Dr David Hannah, on Locust Creek, Samuel Whiting, Senior, settled in the woods on Droop Mountain, on property now owned by his grandson, George W. Whiting. Here he lived many years, opened up a fine improvement with the assistance of his son Ebenezer, who was the staff of his declining years, a kind, devoted son. These persons, father and son, were skillful masons, plasterers, and brick layers. Some of their work yet remains in the Renick mansion in Renicks Valley, and the old chimney at Alvin Clark's. It is reported that the mortar they used would adhere so tenaciously that sometimes the stone had to be chipped or the brick would break in removing it. The smooth finish they would give to the plastering was sometimes looked upon as phenomenal in their times, and people tell us they have seen nothing to excell it in our times, with all the modern improvements.

Samuel Whiting was a devout Wesleyan Methodist, and died strong in the faith giving glory to God, and was placed where he wished to sleep and wait for the dawn to break upon the golden shore. The writer never saw him but once, and that was in January more than fifty years ago. I was trying to find the "short cut" from Locust to Renick's Valley which led by the Whiting home. Upon calling at the fence to make inquiries Mr Whiting appeared. His presence was impressive, and is vividly remembered to this day, and the writer seems to see and hear him now as he gave his directions in slow and solemn words. There were several places where paths deviated and where there were crossings. "When you come to these keep straight on, turn neither to the right or to the left." I kept my eye on the western sun, moved towards it, and though there were numerous deviations and crossings, by keeping the words in mind, "turn neither to the right hand or left," I did not make a single miss, and by twilight I was amid the charming surroundings of one of the most pleasant of homes.

Many a time since that venerable presence has seemed to stand before me, leaning on his staff, looking towards the setting sun, and admonishing the traveler to "turn not to the right hand or to the left." Many times have I moralized on these words, and reflected how many deviations and mistakes we might avoid by keeping the setting sun of our lives in mind, and turn neither the right hand or the left, and finally when the sun went down find a place of rest in the valley intervening our journey's end.

The reader will please pardon this digression, and we will return and finish up what was begun.

Ebenezer Whiting married Sally McMillion, head of Spring Creek, and lived at the homestead on Droop Mountain. In reference to his sons and daughters the following particulars have been kindly furnished by his daughter, Laura Frances.

Rachel Ann became Mrs James Schisler, and lives at the noted "Big Spring," head of Renicks Valley.

Margaret Jane became Mrs Peter Hill, and lives at Jacox, and is the mother of five sons and three daughters: Lena, Mary, Anna, Wllson, Sherman, George, Ernest, and Simon.

Mary Elizabeth was married to Luther Blair, and went to Lamposas, Texas. Her children were Neva, Myra, and Mary.

Sarah Caroline was married to Rev Joseph S. Wickline, and now lives in Delaware.

Susan Virginia became Mrs Alexander Knight, and lived on Sinking Creek in west Greenbrier. Her children were Thomas, Minnie, and Emma.

John Sherman Whiting died aged nine months.

George William Whiting married Elizabeth Bruffey and settled at the homestead. Mr Whiting now lives at Falling Spring, in Greenbrier. His children are Mabel, Bessie, Grace, Floy, Harry, Thomas, Milton, and Earle.

Laura Frances became Mrs William H. Callison and lives near Locust. Her children are Quincy, Thomas, James, and Ima.

It was the writer's privilege to be somewhat acquainted with Ebenezer Whiting. In April, 1848, the writer was distributing Bibles and Testaments, and spent a night at the Whiting home. Somehow he let his tongue wag rather freely, and Mrs Whiting humored matters by appearing very much amused. Mr Whiting appeared to be very solemn and groaned in spirit while the rest would be in smiles. While the visitor tried to be funny and thought he would get Mr Whiting to feel better, he found out by bed time that there was no fun about it. When it was time to "get ready for bed," Mr Whiting snuffed the candle and took down the Bible, and for some time was turning the leaves and seemed much troubled in spirit from his sighs and suppressed groanings and solemn features. At last he found the chapter he wanted and began reading fifth of Ephesians:

Be ye followers of God as dear children.

And walk in love, as Christ also hath loved us, and hath given himself for us an offering and a sacrifice to God for a sweet smelling savor.

But fornication, and all uncleanness, and covetousness, let it not be once named among you, as becometh saints.

Neither filthiness, nor foolish talking, nor jesting, which are not convenient, but rather giving of thanks.

He read the whole chapter, but he read the verses named in a much louder tone than the rest of the chapter. He then prayed long and very feelingly that the meditations of all hearts and the words of all mouths might be acceptable in the sight of Him who is our strength and redeemer.

Worship over, such a solemn stillness pervaded the atmosphere that Mrs Whiting became very sleepy and withdrew with the little children. The features of the man of the house relaxed into a smile when I proposed to retire, and he showed me where to sleep. I felt somewhat mortified, and was sure that he had lost all respect for me as a pious youth.

Much to my surprise the next morning he handed me the Bible and requested "a word of prayer," before breakfast. As well as I can remember the sixth chapter of Galatians was about the first that fell under my eye, and this was read:

Brethren, if a man be overtaken in a fault, ye that are spiritual restore such a one in a spirit of meekness, considering thyself lest thou also be tempted.

Bear ye one anothers burdens and so fulfill the law of Christ.

For if a man think himself to be something when he is nothing he deceiveth himself.

But let every man prove his own work, and then shall he have rejoicing in himself alone and not in another. For every man shall bear his own burden.

Worship over, breakfast was served, pleasant words of farewell were exchanged, and pressing invitation to return came from the hearts of both as well as their lips, and their names are in the book of my remembrance as good people trying to walk in "all the commandments and ordinances of the Lord blameless."

Ebenezer Whiting was born in England, September 4, 1817, and died at the Droop Mountain home May 31, 1869. It was a gloom giving day when attached friends, neighbors, and children placed him lovingly and tenderly in his secluded mountain grave.

JAMES RODGERS,

Among the worthy industrious persons whose arduous toils and severe privations helped to make our county what it is, deserving of respectful mention was the late James Rodgers, Senior. He was a native of Madison County, born February 13, 1789. His first marriage was with a Miss Jackson of Madison County. The issue of this marriage was seven children. The sons were Robert, whose wife was a daughter of John Smith, one of the pioneers of Stony Creek, Joseph, and Drury. The daughters were Sarah, Elizabeth, Mary, and Tabitha. Respecting these children we have virtually no particulars in hand.

James Rodgers came to Pocahontas in 1824 and settled in the woods on Lewis Ridge, at a spot overlooking the Buckeye Cove. Thus he and his family became identified with the county almost from its organization.

His second marriage was with Nellie Lewis, of the Little Levels, a grand daughter of Alexander Waddell, whose descendants are so numerously represented by prosperous and influential citizens in our county at this time. By the second marriage there were six children:

Margaret, who became Henry Adkisson's first wife. Rebecca, who became Mrs Fillren. William Rodgers married Polly Fleming, daughter of the late James Fleming of Swago, and settled on part of the Fleming homestead near Buckeye, where his widow and two daughters now reside. He was a Union pensioner for service in the Union army. Chesley Rodgers married Mrs Sally Morrison and settled near Jacox. John Rodgers married a Miss Harter.

James L. Rodgers, Junior, was married twice. The first wife was Eliza Burgess. There were ten children in the first family: Justice N. C. Rodgers of Buckeye; the late Mrs Hannah Wade; G. W. Rodgers on Beaver Dam; Davis Rodgers, deceased; John H. Rodgers, also dead; Maggie became Mrs William Adkisson of Buckeye; Eliza became Mrs Olie Auldridge and lives at Hillsboro, Mary, and Alvin W. near Buckeye. .

By the second marriage with Mrs Mary Kellison there was a son Lewis, who is now dead, and a daughter Laura.

Thus the writer has endeavored to present the available information concerning this worthy old citizen and his family, aided by his grandson, A. W. Rodgers.

In his time James Rodgers had the reputation of being one of the most industrious of working men. He tried to train his sons and daughters to habits of industry and strict economy. Soon as they became old enough for service they went from home and found ready employment as field hands and house keepers. This venerable man was a zealous and devoted adherent of the Methodist Protestant church. He was one of the first members in the Buckeye society, and probably one of the first in the county. His prayers and experience talks were in good language, interspersed with allusions to the parables and quotations of the promises. All this indicated that in early, impressible youth he must have been familiar with persons of more than ordinary culture, such as Madison County was distinguished for. In his speech he had the tone and style that characterized the old Virginia gentry, as the writer learned to know in subsequent years from actual acquaintance with east Virginians.

The writer cherishes the memory of this old citizen with feelings of much respect, as the two often toiled in the meadows and harvest fields side by side in his boyhood. He remembers being often impressed by the pathos and fervency of the old man's occasional prayers in the morning worship. This was something which was never omitted in the old Marlinton home.

The belief of the older people was that "prayer and provender hinder no man," and so time was always found for prayer, as well as for breakfast and supper.

Some of his expressions still linger in memory after more than fifty years. One was an allusion to the grapes of Eschol as typical of the richness of the promised land. His idea was that God would give his humble praying people here while on the pilgrimage a cluster now and then from the heavenly vine so as to refresh and encourage them to put forth their earnest, faithful efforts to go up and receive possession of the heavenly land. This allusion was utilized as suggestive of a sermon prepared and preached by the writer thirty years ago. May we meet and see for ourselves the blessed land in all its richness and glorious beauty, and especially the vine from which the clusters were gathered that cheered and encouraged him.

REUBEN BUSSARD.

Reuben Bussard, the progenitor of the Bussards, was the son of an emigrant from Germany, who settled at an early day near Lancaster, Penn. Upon his marriage with a Miss Sicafoose, in Pendleton County, he settled on lands now in possession of his descendants near Glade Hill, or rather between Glade Hill and Frost. These early settlers were the parents of five sons and four daughters, as we learned from Morgan Grimes, Esq., near Mount Zion. Susan, Fannie, Hester, and Martha were their daughters. The sons were Eli, Solomon, Henry, Reuben, and Sampson.

Fannie Bussard was married to Benjamin Bussard and lived in Greenbrier County.

Hester Bussard became Mrs Henry Grimes and lived in the Hills.

Martha Bussard was married to Charles Grimes, and lived in the Hills near Mount Zion.

Eli Bussard married Margaret Moore and settled on a part of the home place, now occupied by his son Armenius. In reference to their family the following particulars are given:

Arminius Bussard married Frances Kelley and settled near Glade Hill. He was a Union soldier, a member of Company D, 10th West Virginia Infantry.

Morgan Bussard married Rhoda Simms, daughter of John Sims from Pendleton County. Their children are Sherman, Ellis, Perry Lee, Cora, now Mrs William Shinneberry near Driftwood, and Alcinda, who was married to Embry Shinneberry near Clover Lick.

Peter Bussard, son of Eli, married Nancy Moore, a sister of Eli Bussard's wife, and lived near Glade Hill where John Lindsay now resides. The daughter Sarah was married to John Lindsay. Virginia was married to John Philips, of Barbour County. He was a Union soldier, 6th West Virginia Infantry, and was killed in the affair at Bulltown, Braxton County. Martha became Mrs Hedrick and lived in Preston County, but now lives at Grafton. Mr Hedrick was a Union Soldier.

Perry Bussard belonged to Company I, 3d West Virginia Cavalry, and died in a Maryland hospital in the early spring of 1864.

Laura and Phœbe were the names of Eli Bussard's daughters.

Solomon Bussard, son of Reuben, married Rachel Grimes and settled on a section of the homestead. Their children were Wesley, who married Miss Matheny of Highland, and settled in the Big Valley. Jesse Allen lived in Highland. Susan married William Sharp and went west. Mary was married to David Kincaid and settled in Highland County, at Bolar Springs.

Henry Bussard married Mary Hannah and lived on Cummings Creek near Huntersville. Their daughter

Sally became Mrs J. B. Pyles, Susan Mrs Tillotson Auldridge, and Asbury married Miss Burnsides and went west.

Henry Bussard's second marriage was with a Miss Perkins. Of the two sons of this marriage, Moses lost his life eight or ten years since near Millboro by the overturning of a wagon he was in charge of. George is a carpenter and lives on Cummings Creek.

Reuben Bussard, Junior, married Mary Ann Waugh daughter of Samuel Waugh in the Hills, and after living some years at Dilleys Mill, went to Iowa. The names of their children are Arthelia, Rachel, Samuel, and Adolphus. Samuel Bussard is a prominent physician in Lucas County, Iowa.

Sampson Bussard was another son of the pioneer. His wife was Eleanor Knapp, daughter of Caleb Knapp, and he settled on the place purchased of Solomon Bussard. Their children were Cornelius, Cronin, Mildred, and Jerusha. Mildred was married to Abram Shinneberry, and lives near Clover Lick. Jerusha became Mrs Isaac Shinneberry and lives near Glade Hill.

Where Reuben Bussard the ancestor made a selection for a permanent settlement was far from being an inviting spot in pioneer days. His idea seems to have been that though the lands were deemed of little value, yet these glades and marshes could be made into valuable meadows. The mountains around afforded good range for stock for much of the year, and by blending the facilities for ranges and meadows, live stock could be handled to good purpose. By making moderate gains and saving what would come in hand, he saw there was a living in reach of the hands of the diligent. Were Reuben Bussard now to revisit the scene of his pioneer toil and privations, he would see more than realized the highest expectations he may have ever cherished in reference to the development of this sequestered vale amid the mountains, where he selected a place for his permanent habitation.

Moreover it turned out that this vicinity was well adapted to fruit raising. A supply of good fruit adds very much to the comfort of a home, and the time will come when such land, heretofore deemed of comparatively little value, will be greatly prized for its fruit producing qualities. There is plausible reason for believing that the largest apple tree in Pocahontas County, and it may be even in West Virginia, may be seen near the place where Reuben Bussard built his frontier home. It measures three feet and six inches in diameter. The branches were about forty feet long. Seventy-five bushels have been gathered from this tree at one time.

From what we can gather from Reuben Bussard's personality, he seems to have been a man that pondered Agur's prayer to a good purpose: ''Two things have I required of Thee, deny me them not before I die. Remove far from me vanity and lies; give me neither poverty nor riches; feed me with food convenient for me. Lest I be full and deny Thee, and say who is the Lord; or lest I be poor and steal and take the name of my God in vain.''—Proverbs xxx. 7–9.

DAVID BRIGHT.

Owing to numerous family affiliations in our county, some particulars in regard to the Bright connexion in Greenbrier are interesting to our readers.

David Bright came from Pennsylvania and was one of the pioneers of upper Greenbrier, and located on place now occupied by Andrew Brinkley and sons near Frankford. David's wife was a Miss Grant, also of Pennsylvania. Their sons were Michael, Jesse, David and George. There were two daughters, one of whom was named Mary.

Jesse Bright married Margaret Hamptenstall, and settled on the homestead and reared the family that has so many relations in Pocahontas County. His daughter Margaret was married to Joseph Callison, and went to Illinois. Mary Bright was married to Israel Callison, lived awhile in Pocahontas, then went to Illinois; and was still living at last accounts (in 1897.)

Rachel Bright became the wife of the late Joseph Levisay, near Frankford. Her son, G. W. Levisay, married Maggie Beard, youngest daughter of the late Josiah Beard of Locust, and located at Frankford, where he farms and merchandises. Josephine Levisay became Mrs Preston Clark of the Levels. Mary Levisay became Mrs F. I. Bell, and lives near Savannah Mills. Samuel Brown Levisay was one of the victims of the fearful boiler explosion that occurred in 1896 near Frankford. Jesse A., Letitia, Louella, and Elizabeth are the names of Mrs Levisay's other children.

Jesse Bright, Junior, married Margaret Pinnell and resides in Lewisburg.

Margaret Bright, daughter of Jesse Bright, Senior, became the wife of the late John Levisay, who settled near Frankford, where he lately died. Her eldest daughter, Mary Margaret, is the wife of Rev D. S. Sydenstricker, D. D., the pastor of the Oak Grove Presbyterian Church. Sabina Levisay was married to John Rodgers, and moved to Gallipolis, Ohio. Jesse Levisay married Miss Addie Johnson and migrated to Illinois. Cornelia Levisay was married to W. Henry Wallace, and lives on Sinking Creek. John Brown Levisay married Minnie Johnson and resides on a portton of the old homestead. Lillian Levisay was married to Dr James A. Larue and now resides at Pulaski, Tenn. James W., Virginia, and Louisa Levisay live on the homestead.

Francis Bright was married to James Ludington and went to Illinois.

Samuel Bright married Miss Mary Pollock.

Julia Bright was married to Allan S. Levisay, and lived near Frankford. Mr and Mrs Levisay have for a few years lived near Marlinton with their daughter, Mrs Levi Gay. Their son John Granville Levisay married Emma Robinson and lives near Frankford.

David Bright married Elizabeth Price.

Sarah Bright married William Cassidy and settled in Fayette County.

George Bright married Harriet Bowen and moved to Missouri. His second wife was a Miss Steenberger of Missouri.

Abram Bright married Margaret Bowen. Abram's second wife was a lady from Richmond, Va. His third wife was Miss Nickel, of Monroe, and fourth was Miss Swisher, now of Gallipolis, Ohio.

The ladies that were the first wives of George and Abram Bright just mentioned were sisters, and daughters of James Bowen, who lived at the mouth of Spring Creek. Mr Bowen was a person of great business ability and promoted a number of useful industrial enterprises. He built a grist mill, carding machine, saw mill, and oil mill on the property now held by Newton Mann.

This about exhausts all the information in the compiler's possession that illustrates the relationship these good people sustain to the citizenship of our county.

The writer feelingly cherishes the memory of Jesse Bright, Senior, about whose large and interesting family these biographic notes have been prepared. The last time he ever saw this venerable man was on a Sabbath morning in the spring of 1857, on the way to church. As I was passing from Mr John Levisay's to Frankford, near where the cemetery now is, I heard a singular noise, and on turning around saw that someone's horse had stumbled and thrown the rider. On going back it was found to be Mr Jesse Bright. In the meantime his daughter, Mrs Margaret Levisay, with her husband and two daughters, Mary and Jennie, had come up with him. Mr Bright was led to a fence corner where he remained a little while, apparently not much hurt, but thought it best to return home. It is said he never felt the same after the contusion he suffered from the falling of his faithful old grey horse that had carried him so safely and pleasantly for many years. From the noise made the animal fell heavily, and the wonder is the rider escaped instant death.

The compiler of this sketch is mainly indebted to Mr Washington Levisay for the information given here, taken from memory or gathered by him from the reminiscences of elderly friends.

SAMUEL PRICE.

What is relied upon as authentic tradition is to the effect that the progenitor of the Price relationship in Greenbrier. Botetourt, Craig, Monroe, and Pocahontas counties was one Samuel Price, who was among the earlier settlers of Augusta County in the vicinity of New Hope. He was it is believed a native of Wales but had lived in Maryland before coming to Virginia. So far as known his family consisted of three sons, Thomas, Jacob, and Samuel. All three were Revolutionary soldiers and Indian fighters.

Samuel Price, Junior, settled in Greenbrier County, near Savanna Mills, on preempted lands, a part of which is now in the possession of Washington Price, a descendant of the fourth remove. Samuel Price's first wife was Margaret Black, of Albemarle County, and her childred were Samuel (third), William, Jacob, James, Sally, who became Mrs Michael Bright; Mrs Thomas Beard and Mrs Jacob Walkup. The names of Mrs Beard and Mrs Walkup are not known to the compiler. The second marriage of Samuel Price, Jr., was with another Miss Margaret Black, of Augusta County, and a relative of the former wife. Her children were John, whose son Washington has just been named, a daughter who became Mrs Archibald Mc-Clintic and went west; Margaret, who became Mrs Hemptonstall. She was the mother of the late Jesse Bright, near Frankfort, W. Va.

Jacob Price, son of Samuel the progenitor, married Winneford Tillery, and lived in the Big Levels on property lately occupied by Frank Bell. Their children were James (born 1780), John, Samuel, William, Jacob, Abraham, George, Isaac Austin, Margaret Colvert, who became Mrs Cochenour, west Greenbrier.

Jacob Price, Junior, married Mary B. Cox and settled near Organ Cave in the Irish Corner. Rev Addison H. Price, a widely known and useful Presbyterian minister, was one of his sons. J. M. Price, Mayor of Ronceverte, was his youngest son.

Jacob Price, Junior, was a veteran of the war of 1812, a soldier under General William Henry Harrison at Tippecanoe and the battle of the Thames. He was born November 1, 1790, and died July 28, 1887, aged 96 years. He had sons in the war between the States, and grandsons in the war of 1898.

Through the painstaking care of William P. Campbell, of Monterey, Hon. J. M. Price, of Ronceverte, the late Mrs Sarah Price, of Organ Cave, Anne W. Scott, of Craig City, Va., and others, the writer has in hand biographic material enough to make a considerable book. The contents, however, would be of special interest only to the relationship and the numerous families connected by intermarriage distributed so numerously throughout southern West Virginia and Missouri. But as a very small element of the Price relationship has been identified with the citizenship of our county, what remains of this article will be devoted to some biographic particulars illustrating the family history of Thomas Price, one of the three sons of Samuel Price the Welshman.

The name Price is a blending of two Welsh words, 'ap' and 'reese.' Ap means son, and reese means a stout or strong man. Then ap-reese would be the son of the strong man, and Price is a short way of saying ap-reese.

The Pocahontas branch of the relationship are the descendants of Thomas Price, whose home was on Howard Creek, Craig County, seven miles east of the Sweet Springs, at the base of Seven Mile or Middle Mountain.

Thomas Price had some knowledge of medicine and surgery. One of his books on medicine, bearing his name and the date 1790 is in the possession of Dr J. W. Price, of Marlinton, one of his descendants.

His first wife was Elizabeth Taylor, whose parents were Scottish immigrants. They were the parents of seven daughters and one son. Mary became Mrs William Scott. Sally became Mrs Littlepage. Elizabeth became Mrs Holstoin. Margaret became Mrs Bennett. Sophia became Mrs Jacob Price. Rebecca became Mrs John Hank, of Monroe County. John Hank was a brother of Jehu Hank, the noted singing evangelist of former years. Agnes Price became Mrs William A.

Mastin, proprietor of the "Mastin Hotel" at White Sulphur Springs, in its time one of the most noted in the mountains. John William Price, the only son of the first family, was never married. He was a surgeon on board of a ship in the war of 1812, stationed near Norfolk, and died on board the ship, and so far as is known to the contrary may have been buried at sea.

Thomas Price's second marriage was with Margaret, the eldest daughter of John Beard of Renicks Valley, who with his wife were among the pioneers of that part of Greenbrier County. There were two sons and two daughters in the second family: James Atlee, Thompson, Virginia and Medora.

In reference to the Beards we have learned these additional items. Thomas Beard, the ancestor of persons of that name in Augusta, Greenbrier, and Pocahontas Counties, with his brother Edwin came from Scotland with the Scotch-Irish. Edwin went to Georgia, while Thomas settled in Augusta County, along with the earliest settlers, near what is now known as the New Hope vicinity. His family consisted of two sons, John and Thomas, Junior. The daughters were Rosa, who became Mrs Colonel James Kincaid, near Lewisburg. Elizabeth, who became Mrs John Poage, who lived awhile on Knapps Creek, Pocahontas County. The other five daughters, whose names are not known to us, married in Augusta County, whence four of them and their families migrated to Kentucky.

Thomas Beard, Junior, had no family.

John Beard, the Renick's Valley pioneer, reared a family of five sons and six daughters: Margaret, who became Mrs Thomas Price; Mrs Jane Armstrong; Mrs Agnes Walkup, Mrs Sabina Walkup, Elizabeth, who became Mrs George W. Poage of the Levels, and one whose name is not remembered. The sons were Samuel, Thomas (third), Josiah, Jesse, and William.

As Josiah Beard was a lifelong and prominent citizen of our county, his history is of special interest and has been referred to in other places. His wife was Rachel Poage. Mrs Grace Clark Price, the wife of one of the publishers of this book, is one of his granddaughters.

Josiah Beard was a person of fine mind, had a good education, which he improved upon by reading and reflection. Though gentle in his manners, he had a pronounced will of his own, being endowed with physical and moral courage to a marked degree, a rare combination. His practical wisdom and spotless integrity gave weight to his opinions. The tenor of his life was peaceful, and his influence was for good morals and intelligent piety, and there is but one instance where his temper seems to have gotten the better of his discretion. This was while a prisoner in the hands of federal soldiers towards the close of the war. At the time referred to he was past seventy years of age, and some taunts and jeers were made at his expense. The aged prisoner flared up, reminding his captors that he was old and unarmed, but if they would put down their guns, "pick out a dozen men, and come at him one at a time he would show them a thing or two."

Thompson Price, son of Thomas Price, Junior, died when about grown in Botetourt County.

James A. Price, married Margaret Davies Poage, settled at Marlins Bottom. Particulars are given of his family in the memoirs of Jacob Warwick. They died in 1874 and are buried near their Marlinton home. They were people who had but few advantages in their youth, compared to what is to be enjoyed now by their posterity. Both were righteous before God, and to the best of their knowledge tried to walk in the commandments and ordinances of the Lord, aiming to walk humbly, loving mercy and acting justly.

> "Our boast is not that we deduce our birth
> From loins enthroned and rulers of the earth:
> But higher far our proud pretensions rise,
> Children of parents passed into the skies."

Medora Sabina Beard Price was married on Powell Hill, near Marlinton, May 14, 1834, to William Hamilton, of Bath County. They were the parents of seven daughters and three sons: Virginia Agnes, Sue Margaretta, Alice M., Mary Sophia, John William, Ellen Frances, Rose L., Eugenia Gatewood, Charles Atlee, and Paul Price. After a residence of several years on Back Creek near Mountain Grove, Mr Hamilton moved to Texas, in 1855, Blanco County, where he became sheriff, and had many narrow escapes from the Comache Indians, who went on the war path while he was in office. He was born in 1811, and died at Blanco City, Texas, July 4, 1894. Mrs Hamilton had died at the same city November 10, 1882.

Paul Price Kelley, one of the sons, became a U. S. soldier in 1865, served in Montana against the Nez Perces, developed heart disease, was honorably discharged, and returned to Blanco City, where he died September 24, 1892.

Walter P. Campbell, of Monterey, Va., and his sisters Lillie and Virginia, widely known in our county as popular teachers, are grandchildren of William Hamilton. Their parents Mr and Mrs Austin Campbell, live in Hinton.

The eldest daughter of the second family group was Virginia Agnes Price, who became Mrs Nathaniel Kelley, of Monroe County. They were the parents of four children: William, Samuel Henry, Catherine, and Medora. Upon the death of her husband she came to Pocahontas to live with her mother Mrs Thomas Price. Their home was the Abram Sybert place, two miles east of Hillsboro. By over exertion one wash day, Mrs Kelley was stricken by a very malignant attack of brain fever, of which she died in about two weeks. At the close of the burial services, Samuel Henry approached Mrs Elizabeth Miller and said he wanted to go home with her. The kind lady took him to her home and for years cared for him with a motherly kindness truly and affectionately bestowed. This occurred in 1839. The three others remained for some years with their grandmother. They attended school at the Academy and made a good beginning in their educational course.

About the time Samuel Henry Kelley became grown he went to California, in 1848. So far as can be learned it appears that he opened a store near Los Angeles and appeared to be doing well. One night, in 1861, his store was broken into by Mexican bandits. In the effort to repulse them he was slain, his goods carried off, and the building burned.

William Scott Kelley, the eldest of the family, was born in 1827. He attended school several sessions and made fine progress under the instructions or Messrs Brown and Dunlap, eminent teachers in their day. He also went to California in his early manhood, but did not remain very long. For some years he led a roving life in the west, and seems to have become pretty well known from Cincinnatti to New Orleans as a sporting man. Finally he decided to study medicine and was graduated in fine standing, in 1858, by Newton's Clinical Institute at Cincinnatti, Ohio. Soon after he located in Buchannon County, Missouri, where he married Miss Nellie Curle, daughter of Clayton Curle of Kentucky.

Dr Kelley rapidly advanced in his profession, had a fine patronage, and stood high as a skillful practitioner. He was an enthusiastic Confederate, and was among the first to enlist at the opening of the war between the States. He was appointed Surgeon General on the recommendation of General Sterling Price, commander of the Missouri Confederate forces. Dr Kelley was in all the battles with the Missouri troops during the first year of the war. He died of typhoid-pneumonia December 11, 1861, and was buried at midnight in his garden.

Dr Kelley was survived by his wife and daughter

Willie. After residing a few years in Missouri, Mrs
Kelley returned to Kentucky and remained there until
1875. Miss Willie Kelley was a teacher, and in 1883
was married to George L. Rector, of Nashville, Ark.,
manager of the Rector Store Company. They were
the parents of seven children: William Henry, Nellie,
Lillian Augusta, Jesse Nathaniel, George, Lenora,
and John Carlisle.

In thinking of William S. Kelley, who is remembered by many persons in Pocahontas, it is pleasant to be
able to say that he was known in Missouri as a person
of pure life, and in his family circle the gentleness of
his nature was beautifully developed. The care and
attention he gave his sisters should be remembered and
was rewarded in a very remarkable manner, as our
readers will learn.

Catherine Kelley finished her education at the school
taught by Miss Maria Richards, at Warm Springs, Va.
She was enabled to do this by her brother William's
assistance in good part. She met Dr William N. Snodgrass at Fincastle, Va., and they were married in
1856. He graduated from the medical department of
the University of New York in 1851. Soon after their
marriage they settled in Jefferson City, Mo., where he
became recognized as an able physician. He espoused
the Confederate cause and was a surgeon in General
Price's command, and was in the battles of Carthage,
Wilsons Creek, and Missouri. He was with the Missouri troops until within a few months before the war
closed. Owing to his broken health he was obliged to
leave the service, and went to his father's home in

Jackson County, Texas, whither he had previously sent
his wife and two sons.   His health was never restored,
and Dr Snodgrass died in November, 1865.

After the death of her husband, Mrs Snodgrass and
her two children lived for a time at Walnut Hill, Ark.,
and afterwards at Rocky Comfort, Ark.   Her son
Newton was born in 1857, and died in 1875 on Red
River, whither he had gone on business.   We are informed that he was a youth of fine character and marked business ability.   The other, William Edward, was
born in 1859.   In 1884 he married Miss Louella Rhea
and is now living in Little Rock, in business with M.
Cohn, a leading clothier of the city.

October, 1877, Mrs Kate Snodgrass married her
second husband, W. C. Sybert, a prosperous merchant
of Nashville, Ark., and lived there until · her decease
in 1889.   She is spoken of as a noble Christian woman, a devout member of the Episcopal church.   Mr
Sybert died May 16, 1881.

Medora Virginia, Mrs Nathaniel Kelley's youngest
daughter, was left an orphan at the tender age of two
or three years.   She remained with her grandmother
Price until she was about eight years old.   After her
grandmother's death she lived with her aunt Madora
Hamilton until her brother William Kelley had her
placed in a school taught by the Misses Daingerfield,
near the Hot Springs.   She afterwards entered Hol-
lins Institute, whence she graduated with great credit
in 1858.   While on a visit to her sister in Jefferson
City, Mo., she met and married Dr Charles T. Hart,
of Georgia, her brother William's partner in the prac-

tice of medicine. Dr Hart was the son of a wealthy planter, who spared no pains in the education of his son. Dr Hart graduated from the same Cincinnatti medical institute and in the same class with Dr W. S. Kelley. He had previously obtained diplomas from two other medical schools. Dr Hart was a surgeon in the Confederate service. He establshed a hospital at Lewinsville, Ark., for wounded Confederates. After the war he was Professor of Medicine in a New York school, and proprietor of a popular drug, whose discovery he claimed. His health was broken by exposure during the war, and he died in August, 1868, and buried in Greenwood cemetery. Dr Hart's ancestors came over with William Penn.

After his death Mrs Hart went to Rocky Comfort, Ark., to be near her sister Kate. On October, 16, 1872, she married Dr W. H. Hawkins, of North Carolina, a graduate of a Philadelphia medical college.

In January, 1882, Dr Hawkins moved to Texarkana, where he died September 7, 1887. Dr Hawkins stood high in his profession, was at one time president of the Arkansas Medical Association, a brigade surgeon in the war, a public spirited citizen, a genial, courteous, Christian gentleman. Mrs Medora Hawkins died March 17, 1888.

Lillian Hart was born in 1861, near Saint Joseph, Mo. In 1877 she married George Reid, a merchant of Rocky Comfort. After living there several years, they moved in 1884 to De Kalb, Ark., and from thence to Texarkana in 1888. They have two children, Charles William, born in 1880, and a daughter.

Kate Knox Hawkins, Medora's second daughter, was born at Rocky Comfort, July 23, 1873. At the age of 14 she was bereaved of her parents within a few months. January 3, 1894, she married E. W. Stewart, a merchant, and settled in Texarkana. They have one daughter.

Thomas Price, son of Samuel Price the Welsh immigrant, was a veteran of the Revolution, and was in General Lincoln's command when surrendered at Charleston, South Carolina, and thereupon became a prisoner of war. He and a comrade managed to elude the sentries at day break while the change of guards was going on. They hid in a briar patch and waited for night to come. It was a day of much suspense and anxiety. Some British soldiers while driving in a fresh cow with her calf come very near running over them as they hugged the ground. A British soldier approached the patch later in the day and seemed to look right at them, but he turned away, and from that on they expected to have a squad to surround and capture them. Much to their relief he never came back, and soon it was night and they, guided by the pole star, set out for home and liberty.

At one stage of their journey, when about famished, they happened about daylight on the camp of a negro fugitive trying to make his way to the British. He was soundly sleeping, and when they waked him he jumped up and ran for dear life. They found inexpressible enjoyment in the ash cake raked from the coals and the piece of bacon found in his wallet, and

and resumed their journey with new strength and hope. From that time on it was easy to find all that was needed for their sustenance and refreshment until they were at home again.

THE BRIDGER BOYS.

John and James Bridger were slain by Indians during the last raid made by Indians in what is now Pocahontas County. They were in the party that came to the relief of the Drinnon family on the Greenbrier River, nearly a mile above the mouth of Stony Creek. Henry Baker was killed while he and Richard Hill were going to the river to wash and prepare for breakfast. Nathan, a colored man belonging to Lawrence Drinnon, notified the settlers in the Levels. A party came on and on their return the Moore and the Waddell families joined them. The Bridger brothers and Nathan left the main party and took across to the near way through the Notch, while the rest passed around by the Waddell's.

Indians were concealed at a place where a clump of lynn saplings were growing out of the decaying stump of a tree that had been cut down for sugar troughs. Two shots were fired in quick succession. John fell mortally wounded. The other, being untouched, ran on through the "notch," closely pursued by an Indian. Just at the foot of the mountain was a straight path

through which the young man was running when the
Indian paused and shot him in the back. The mark
of the Indian's heel was seen where he halted to deliver the fatal discharge.

Nathan had stopped to fasten his moccasins, and
was thus out of reach. He scolded the Indians for
hurting the boys, and escaped unhurt. The rest of the
company were at the Waddell place when the heard
the shooting.

Shortly after the shooting, loud whoops were heard
near the Notch. These seemed answered by whoops
on the Gillilan Mountain, and then were whoopings
heard near the head of Stamping Creek, as if the savage bands were signaling to that the settlers were on
the move and danger was threatening, sor soon all became silent and nothing more was . seen or heard of
them in the vicinity. By the time the refugees reached the fort, on the hill now occupied by Isaac McNeel's
residence. all danger was over.

Arrangements were quickly made to bring in the
slain. John Cochran had brought a "half sled" to
the fort and an old, gentle horse. The sled was taken
to where Jim Bridger lay weltering in his blood, and
and remained there until John was carried down from
the Notch, and thus they were borne to the fort and a
grave prepared for them on the knoll overlooking
Millpoint.

Old Mother Jordan, who lived when a young person where Mathew John McNeel now lives, remembered how Jim Bridger was fixing himself up like he was
going to a wedding while the men were getting ready

to go to the relief of the Drinnons. He wanted to borrow her silver shoe buckles, and she objected: "Jim, you had better not take my shoe buckles, for the Indians might get you and I will never see my buckles any more."

Aunt Phœbe McNeel and Mrs Sally McCollam, daughter of Larry Drennan, remembered with emotion long as they lived how the heart broken father of the Bridger boys put his arms around the necks of his slain sons ere they were put into the one grave. His sleeves were all bloody, and when the men gently forced him away from his dead, and he lay upon the ground resting his head on one arm and wiping his tears with the bloody sleeve of the other, it looked so pitiful.

This should always be remembered as a consecrated spot, being made sacred by the tears of a father wept over sons cruelly slain, incidental to the perils and hardships of the early settlement of Pocahontas.

II.

THE MAYSE FAMILY.

In 1765 the Indians raided the Mayse home in Bath County, a few miles from Bath Alum. Joseph Mayse, aged 13 years, his mother, an unknown white girl and Mrs Sloan and her infant were taken prisoners.

About five or six miles from the Mayse residence the party halted on the top of a high ridge by a large rock to rest awhile. The Indian leader, an old man, sat on this rock. Around his shoulders hung a bear's intestine filled with cornmeal mush. This he would squeeze out and eat for his lunch. Thence the Indians proceeded on a bee line westward over the Warm Springs Mountain, and on the evening of the first day camped on Muddy Run, about five miles north east of the Warm Springs.

On the second day they crossed Jacksons River near Warwickton, Back Creek Mountain, and camped near the mouth of Little Back Creek, now Mountain Grove. The boy prisoner, Joseph Mayse, was placed to sleep between two warriors. He was made very uncomfortable by a large root of the tree under which they had lain down to sleep. His sufferings becoming too painful to endure, he took one of the Indians by the hand and placed it on the source of his misery. He understood the trouble and made the other lie over and give young prisoner a softer place to sleep.

The third day they crossed the Alleghany and camped about half way between Marlinton and Huntersville. Early on the fourth day, just after crossing the Greenbrier River at the Island ford, the Indians and their prisoners were overtaken by a pursuing party. The young prisoner was on a pack horse, and it becoming frightened when the skirmish opened, ran off and became entangled in some grape vines. The boy was pulled off into a thicket of nettles. The Indians were so closely pressed they had not time to turn and kill the boy. The Indians were pursued some distance up Stony Creek and Indian Draft, but could not be overtaken. On their return the pursuing party picked up the young prisoner, still in the nettles near the fording, and took him back to the settlement. The late George Mayse, Esq., of the Warm Springs, was a son of this prisoner. The infant had been dashed to death against a tree on the first approach of the pursuers. It was buried near the crossing of the Marlin Run in Marlinton.

Eight or nine years after his captivity Joseph Mayse was a soldier in the battle of Point Pleasant, and was severely wounded. Forty-six years afterwards his wounded leg was amputated above the knee, by Dr Charles Lewis, who came all the way from Lynchburg and remained with his patient six weeks. Joseph Mayse served as magistrate between forty-five and fifty

years, and was twice high sheriff. His memory was
considered as reliable as an "official record." His
health was such he was never known to take a dose of
medicine, and never knew what whiskey and coffee
taste like. He died "serene and calm," in April,
1840, in the 89th year of his age.

Mrs Mayse, Mrs Sloan, and the nameless white
girl, were taken to the Indian towns near Chilicothe,
about 275 miles from Marlinton, by the route taken
by their captors. From Chilicothe they made their
way towards Detroit. By the aid of friendly Indians
they received directions, and finally reached Pennsylvania and thence home, after an absence of about fifteen months.

When her son was wounded at Point Pleasant, October 11, 1774, and she heard where he was, she went
with a led horse two hundred and fifteen miles and
brought him home early in November.

MAJOR ANDREW CROUCH.

May 5, 1857, the writer paid a visit to the late Major Andrew Crouch, at the time regarded the oldest person in Tygart's Valley. He lived near the mouth of Elkwater, Randolph County. Among the interesting items he gave us was one in reference to a land title.

Near the old Huttonsville brick church one James Warwick built a pole cabin and cleared a potato patch, in virtue of which he claimed the whole bottom contiguous. John and William White, two brothers, asserted their claim to the same land. It was finally decided to settle the dispute by a fair fight, fist and skull. Mr Warwick, being a small man, proposed to Joseph Crouch—or rather to his father—to exchange lands with him. He did so, and moved on to the tract. The Whites came on soon after to drive him away. After some wrangling it was finally agreed upon to settle the dispute by a fight, provided Andrew Crouch would accept the challenge, Joseph Crouch being somewhat deficient in pluck.

The ground was chosen for the contest, and John

White was sent to inform Andrew Crouch of the arrangement. He accepted the challenge and defeated
William White. The title was settled, and the parties
were very friendly ever afterwards.

William White would frequently visit the home of
Andrew Crouch, Senior, and the Major had a vivid remembrance of the impression White's appearance made
upon his youthful mind as he walked the floor, he was
so very tall and portly.

John White fell in the battle of Point Pleasant, and
William White was killed by Indians in what is now
Upshur County.

———

In the visit to Major Andrew Crouch, May 5, 1857,
this aged man related a reminiscence of his boyhood.

When he was about six years of age his father took
him to the corn field, and while the father worked the
little boy sat on the fence. One of his uncles came up
in great haste, bringing the news that Lewis Canaan
and three children had just been killed by Indians.
The two Crouches hurried their families to the home
of James Warwick, not far from where the old brick
church stood. In their hurry the Crouch brothers and
Warwick seized their guns to go to the help of the
families exposed to the Indians farther up the river,
they neglected to barricade the fort, and so the little
boy and two little girls went out to the branch, and
while the boy was washing the blood from his face,
caused by his nose bleeding, the little girls became
frightened, and without saying anything, ran back into

the fort and left him alone. When his bleeding stopped he went back and found the fort barricaded. The
Crouch brothers had been met by some persons from
the lower fort, took them along, and so their wives
and children were left to themselves at Warwick's to
make the best of their perilous situation.

When the boy Andrew Crouch came to the fort he
heard his aunt in a loud voice giving orders as if there
were quite a number of men in the fort, when in fact
the force consisted of three white women and one colored man and wife, and some little children.   An Indian climbed the roof of one of the fort buildings after
nightfall and set it on fire. The colored man put it
out. Then the stable was fired. The black man said
they should not burn his horse. He went out and carefully approached the place. Seeing an Indian by the
light he shot at him, and let the horses out and returned in safety to the fort. He dared the Indians to
come on, and as there seemed to be not more than two
or three that showed themselves, it seems they were
not disposed to storm the loud but little garrison.

When the barn burned down and all became dark,
the colored woman insisted on leaving the fort and
giving the alarm lower down. She was allowed to do
so, and the next day the men came up and moved all
farther down, and then the little boy with eight or
ten others went to bury the slain Lewis Canaan and
his three children. He says no one wept nor did any
seem afraid while the burial was going on.

After the funeral the men, seeing no signs of Indians, believed they had withdrawn, and so they dis-

banded. But late in the evening one Indian killed a man named Frank Riffle, near where the brick church stood, and burned two houses not far away belonging to James Lackey.

Major Crouch remembered seeing Lackey not very long after the battle of Point Pleasant. He could show the rock on which Lackey sat and sung a war song, then very popular among the mountaineers in commemoration of that eventful struggle.

In subsequent years James Warwick moved to Ohio, and rewarded his faithful negro with his freedom for his gallantry in saving the fort and the property. This Mr Warwick was the ancestor of the Ohio Congressman who represented the McKinley district a few years since.

IV.

CAPTURE OF THOMAS WILSON.

About 1750 John Wilson and Bowyer Miller located on Jacksons River, in what is now Highland County, Va. Mr Wilson settled at the mouth of Peak or Stony Run, while Miller located at Wilsonville, farther up. During Braddock's war Mr Miller refugeed to Tinkling Spring, and finally across the Blue Ridge. leaving land, house, and property uncared for.

About 1756 Mr Wilson refugeed near Greenville. taking his movable property with him, but finding it impossible to get subsistence, sent his horses and cattle back and employed some one to do the ranging and salting. We hear nothing more of him. In a year or two his family ventured to return and took up their abode on the east bank of the river, some two hundred yards perhaps below the crossing leading to the Bolar Spring. The Indians then raided their home about the year 1760.

This John Wilson, the pioneer, was the grandfather of the the late William Wilson, whose daughters Charlotte and Susan married Adam and Washington Stephenson, citizens of Highland County.

The morning of the raid John Wilson, one of the sons, had gone to Fort Lewis on the Cowpasture to invite hands to assist in raising the house recently occupied by Mrs Washington Stephenson. In the meanwhile Mrs Wilson and her daughters Barbara and Susan were very busy in preparations for the raising, and were cooking and washing on the east bank of the river near the cabin. Thomas Wilson, a younger son, was at the mill grinding the needed corn meal. The mill stood near the crossing of the Warm Run leading to the residence of the late David Stephenson.

Upon John's return late in the evening as he came in sight of home he was fired upon by Indians. One ball passed under his arm pit and tore the fringe off his hunting shirt. Mounted on a fleet horse he turned instantly to return to the fort whence he had just come and was soon out of sight of the Indians. While going at full speed through the gap a limb knocked his hat off. He stopped and picked it up at the peril of his life. This person was the father of the William Wilson already mentioned, and of the late Mrs Esther Bolar near the Warm Springs.

Upon reaching the fort he told what had happened and begged for assistance at once. None were willing to venture that night. The captain then ordered a draft for a detachment. It was very late in the night before the detail reached the summit of Jack Mountain overlooking the valley. It was dark, no light save that of the summer stars, and in the valley this light was obscured by a dense fog. With sad forebodings they began the descent into the darkness of the ravine beneath, through which they were to grope their way, and where their young guide had been fired on and pursued by the wily enemy. They cautiously moved down the mountain, quietly passed through the gap— all on foot except their guide John Wilson. At the gap he dismounted, hung up his saddle and bridle, and turned the jaded horse out to graze in the woods. He also advised his friends to leave the path, cross the Warm Run, and pass down the right bank by a circuitous way to the mill to see whether it was running or not. "If it be running," says John Wilson," "it is a bad sign, for then I know the Indians have surprised Brother Tom and killed him, because they would not know how to stop the mill. But if it is not running there is some hope, for he may have seen the Indians, stopped the mill and made his escape, for I know no Indian can catch him by running."

The mill was found to be silent. Young Wilson entered it quietly and found everything in place, and the newly ground sack of meal was at the chest, securely tied. Taking hope from this, the rescuing party crossed the river just above the mouth of the Warm Run, and passed over the bottom to the knoll on which the church stands, and thence moved with the greatest caution in the direction of the dwelling on the opposite side of the river.

Upon reaching the camp just opposite the cabin, John Wilson advised the men to remain there until he could wade over and find out what had happened. If all was well he could call them over, but if the cabin had been destroyed or occupied by the Indians he would return and determine on what would be best to do. When he approached the dwelling he found the doors heavily barricaded, but through a well known crevice he discovered the family was yet there. Thereupon he gave the signal, and his friends hastened over in all the transports of exulting joy, so great was their relief from the long and powerful suspense they had been in for so many hours.

The mother and her daughter Barbara had been wounded by the clubs or tomahawks of the Indians, but not fatally injured, Susan had escaped unhurt. It was found that none but Tom Wilson was missing. The last thing known of him he was at the mill. Upon going to the mill early in the morning, the party found his track, and that he had been running. This they followed until they found where Tom had stepped on a stick, had fallen, been overtaken and captured. The Indians were trailed from that point across the river to the bluff near the residence of the late Michael Wise. Thence they went southwest to a point about a mile below where the church now stands. There they remained some time, as the signs indicated. From that point they were traced back to Peak's Run, up which they went.

Tom's sister Susan took the lead in all this search for Tom. She was well nigh frantic with grief. At frequent times she would cry out as she went in advance of the party by fifteen or twenty yards: "Here are my poor brother's tracks."

Upon reaching the top of Back Creek Mountain, it was thought best to go no further, as fourteen men could do nothing with so many savages as the signs indicated. It was with great difficulty that Susan could be prevailed on to return. For years nothing was heard of Tom. He died of fever soon after his capture. We hear nothing of John Wilson, the father, as he does not appear to have been at home.

The writer is indebted to the late John Cleek, Esq., for the material for this and other sketches.

———

Information was received concerning Tom Wilson in the following manner.

David Kincaid, who had been one of the fourteen rescuers, went with an expedition sent to treat with the Indians at Fort Pitt concerning the ransom of prisoners. A treaty was made and a day appointed for giving up all in captivity. That day passed away and no prisoners were brought in as agreed. It looked suspicious, and that night every precaution against surprise was taken, lest the Indians should prove hostile and treacherous, but nothing occurred as feared.

The next day was nearly spent, when late in the evening a little girl ten years of age was brought in. She could speak nothing but Indian dialect, and could tell nothing about herself. Mr Kincaid's wife and three children had been taken prisoners about the time Tom Wilson was taken. He remembered one of the children had lost a thumb. Upon examination it was found as he had stated, and the recognition of father and child was of the most touching character. The next evening Mrs Kincaid was brought in, whereupon husband, wife, and the only surviving child were reunited.

Mrs Kincaid could tell all about that which had happened to Tom Wilson. He had just finished his task at the mill, and was on the way to the house, when he discovered the Indians, who were coming down the east bank of the river. Wishing to take him alive they headed him off, and he took up the river and was caught. They wished also not to alarm the women at work near the dwelling, nor the men at work on the west bank near where the new house was to be reared, getting in the logs and hewing them.

Tom and the other prisoners were taken to a place some distance away. They were securely bound and left in the charge of an old Indian, while the rest should return and capture the parties already referred to. In this they failed, and all escaped to the house, though some were slightly wounded by the tomahawks thrown at them. The doors were barricaded, and the Indians repulsed without taking any captives.

John Wilson having made his escape on horseback, the Indians supposed he would soon return with men from the fort, and so they did not press the seige, but started immediately for their towns and were miles away ere John returned.

Thomas did not survive his captivity very long.

John Wilson said he had great difficulty in persuading the family to give up the house raising and go to the fort until it was certain all danger for the time being was over. John also reports that among the wounded, besides his mother and sister Barbara, was

an Irish weaver whose name is forgotten.   At the time
the attack was made he was weaving in an out house.
During the melee an Indian came upon him and drew
his gun.   The Irishman fell forward on his face just
as the trigger was pulled, the ball inflicting a wound
on his hip.

When the relief party came in the night, and the
question was asked "is anybody killed?" the Irishman
quickly responded: "An faith, there is nobody killed
but meself !"

The writer is also under obligatiovs to Squire John
Cleek for the following items:

A fight occurred between the whites and Indians at
Cunningham's fields, near Harpers, head of Kerr's
Creek.   The Indians are reported by tradition to have
carried their dead to the summit of the mountain and
buried them under the stones now found near the roadside on the way from Rockbridge Alum to Lexington.

The first settlement on the Bullpasture River, in
Highland, was made near the Blue Spring, known as
the Locrkidge farm, by the Hicklins and Estills.   The
Grahams and Carlyles the next farms higher up the
river.   Pullin, a native of Ireland, settled above Car-
lysle.   A good many of these settlers sold out and
moved to Kentucky, and some of them prospered
greatly in their western homes.

V.

BATTLE NEAR CRAB BOTTOM.

The writer received the following items of history from the late William McClintic, Esq., of Bath County. This gentleman was a prominent citizen, and accepted most of the important county offices in the gift of his fellow citizens, and he had a passion for history. He has a grandson living in our county. Dr F. T. McCllntic, who ranks high as a physician.

Mr McClintic says that when the Indians gained their victory near the mouth of Falling Spring Run, in Alleghany, 1768, they were so elated that one hundred and eighty warriors pressed on as far as Kerr's Creek, where some persons were slain and others taken prisoners. On their return they crossed the Warm Springs Mountain near the springs, and camped close by the springs. The next day they camped on Back Creek, near the place where John Gwin resided a few years since, eight or ten miles above Mountain Grove.

As soon as possible, three companies under Captains Lewis, Dickinson, and Christie started in pursuit. Christie's company was from near Waynesboro. The Indians were followed to the north fork of the South

Branch of the Potomac. The scouts discovered the
encampment not far from Harper's Mill. Strange.to
say the Indians seemed to be heedless of danger.
Some were dressing deer skins, mending or making
moccasins, some cooking and hunting and fishing.

The scouts having made their report, it was debated
whether the attack be made at once or wait until night.
It seemed most likely that the Indian scouts might get
on the trail of the whites before night and hence be
warned of their danger, and it was concluded best to
attack them without delay.

The three companies were to be deployed in such a
manner as to invest the camp and to begin the attack
simultaneously. Major Vance was sent forward to a
point overlooking the encampment, with instructions
that if the Indians showed any signs of having discovered the approach of the whites to signify it by firing a
gun. Lewis and Dickinson had nearly reached the
points they wished in order to open the attack, but
Christie had not quite reached his position, when the
signal was heard. Lewis and Dickinson rushed in.
Unfortunately, Christie's men set up a tremenduous
yelling and began to rush toward the scene of action.
The Indians, with much presence of mind, retreated
in the direction where there was no noise, and what
happened to be the course most favorable for their escape, so they succeeded in making good their retreat
with but a slight loss of life. One warrior came into
camp after a short lull, and dodged from tree to tree,
escaping the shots discharged and the stones and tomahawks thrown at him until he reached his gun, and

then he darted off, apparently unharmed.

Blame was attached to Major Vance for being in too much of a hurry in giving the signal for the attack, but he and his companions made what was decided to be a good excuse. Major Vance said they happened on two Indians, one leading a horse and the other holding a buck upon it, and they were coming in a direction by which they would unavoidably be discovered, so it was thought better to shoot them than be discovered, and the Indians in camp have timely warning of the approach of the pursuers.

All the plunder of any value found in the camp, horses, blankets, guns, knives, pots, and kettles, were taken to Waynesboro and about twelve hundred dollars realized by their sale.

LACKEY'S SONG.

On page 567 reference is made to one Lackey singing the "Shawnee Battle Song," commemorative of the battle of Point Pleasant. As a matter of curiosity the words are herewith reproduced.

> Let us mind the tenth day of October,
>   'Seventy-four, which caused woe,
> The Indian savages they did cover
>   The pleasant banks of the Ohio.

> The battle beginning in the morning,
>   Throughout the day it lasted sore
> Until the evening shades were returning down
>   Upon the banks of the Ohio.

Judgment proceeds to execution,
 Let fame throughout all dangers go,
Our heroes fought with resolution,
 Upon the banks of the Ohio.

Seven score lay dead and wounded
 Of champions that did face the foe,
By which the heathen were confounded
 Upon the banks of the Ohio.

Colonel Lewis and some noble Captains
 Did down to death like Uriah go:
Alas ! their heads wound up in napkins,
 Upon the banks of the Ohio.

Kings lamented their mighty fallen
 Upon the mountains of Gilboa,
And now we mourn for brave Hugh Allen,
 Far from the banks of the Ohio.

Oh bless the mighty King of Heaven
 For all his wondrous works below:
Who hath to us the victory given
 Upon the banks of the Ohio.

V.

"MAD ANN."

March 22, 1858, it was the writer's pleasure to visit
Mrs Smith, the aged mother of the late William Smith,
who resided five and a half miles north of Covington,
on Jackson's River. She had been well acquainted
with "Mad Ann," and related some recollections of
this noted character of pioneer history.

She was of English birth, and claimed to have hail-
ed from Liverpool. Her first husband was a Mr Trotter, who was drowned in Jacksons River near the residence of the late Squire Alexander McClintic. The
water was quite shallow, but being in a state of intoxi-
cation he perished in the ripples, leaving a widow and
two sons, William and John. William Trotter, in
1858, was living at Point Pleasant.

Mrs Trotter lived awhile as one of the nearest neighbors of the Smith family. Her property was a little
rude log hut, three acres of arable land, two cows, two
pigs, and a horse. Before her reason became impair-
ed she was a person of fine sense, and was much better
educated than the generality of females at her day.
As to her moral reputation in later life, she was not on

a par with Cæsar's wife—above suspicion. Yet she
paid her debts, would not steal, or seek revenge for
any insult in stealthy ways.

She made frequent journeys to Point Pleasant to
carry powder and lead.for the use of the troops stationed there to check Indian incursions. She became
very erratic in later life, her mind becoming unsettled
by grief over the death of one Baily, supposed to have
been killed by the Indians. In person she was quite
small, and after her mental troubles preferred to wear
man's attire. She rode "Liverpool," a black, blaze-
faced pony, and carried her rifle and shot pouch. She
chewed tobacco, drank liquor, and thought it very becoming to use profane language.

She was regarded as perfectly harmless, unless irri-
tated. Then she would shoot just as quickly as the
triggers would work. On her last visit to Alleghany
she went into camp and remained most of the summer,
and the neighbors furnished her with with provisions
cheerfully and plentifully. Mrs Smith's husband having lost his horses by water murrain, hired "Liverpool" to plow corn; paid well for his use, put him in
good order, and so poor Ann had a good fat horse to
ride back to Ohio when her visit ended in the fall, and
she soon after died.

Only one incident occurred to mar the pleasure of
her last visit. One night some mischievous persons
out coon hunting molested her camp by throwing
stones. She was soon out after them with her rifle,
and it was with difficulty they escaped by flight and
concealment. They were thus made to know how it

feels to be hunted themselves, and quiet prevailed after that.

She had a great many marvelous tales of adventure with the Indians to relate, but Mrs Smith thought they were mostly fanciful. The one she would tell the oftenest was that when pursued by the Indians she took refuge in a swamp, and by lying in the water all night made her pursuers lose her trail, and they could not track her the next day. Mrs Smith thought the following to be a true occurrence:

A man, to annoy "Mad Ann" and to amuse himself and others to see how she would talk, weep, and rave, told her that one of her sons was dead. As was expected, she was greatly distressed and was very demonstrative in her expressions of grief, until she heard it was all in fun. When she met the young man afterwards she reminded him of the cruel jest, and told him in a most solemn manner that he would be the first to die in his neighborhood. What she foretold actually occurred the following summer, almost a year afterwards. It was a striking coincidence, to say the least.

She died in Kanawha, aged, as was supposed, one hundred and five years. The Hon. Virgil Lewis has prepared an interesting sketch of this remarkable person, and her fame is assured as long as the history of pioneer adventure has interested readers, and that will be as long as the State of West Virginia has a local habitation and a name.

VI

UNION AND CONFEDERATE SOLDIERS.

In response to our request for the names of Union and Confederate soldiers, the following are all that have come to hand, furnished by H. P. McLaughlin, Beverly Waugh, and A. L. Gatewood.

Company I 25th Reg. Virginia Infantry, C. S. V.

D. A. Stofer, Captain.
J. H. McLaughlin, 1st Lieutenant.

Angus, Timolean
Alderman, Andy C.
Akers, James H.
Arbogast, Daniel
Boon, B. B.
Burr, George
Burr, Frederick
Burr, William
Bradley, James
Corbett, Mustoe H.
Cleek, Peter L.
Cash, George H.
Carpenter, William H.
Cole, William

Johnson, Joe
Lyons, Enos
Moore, Levi
McGlaughlin, H. P.
Maher, Patrick
Moore, Michael
Mitche, Sylvester
Mathews, J. W.
Moriarty, Pat
Piles, John
Piles, William L.
Pence, J. W.
Robey, Walter H.
Swadly, James

Eagan, Charles
Ervine, William H.
Friel, M. A.
Grandfield, John
Griffin, M. P.
Grimes, Peter
Gammon, William
Gammon, C. S.
Hannah, Robert
Hannah, Joseph
Helmick, George A.
Henson, William H.
Hogsett, William R.
Herold, C. B.
Herold, B. F.
Haines, J. B.
Hamilton, A. G.
Jordan, Joseph J.

Slaven, W. W.
Seebert, Lanty S.
Sivey, Cain H.
Shannon, James
Shannon, Miehael
Smith, Louis
Simmons, C. A.
Shrader, B. F.
Varner, David A.
Weaver, C. W.
Weaver, R. L.
Ware, Eugene
Ware, George
Ware, William T.
Ware, Benjamin
Willihan, Michael
Willihan, Pat
Waugh, Levi

This company was engaged in the following battles : Philippi, McDowell, Winchester, Cross Keys, Port Republic, Seven days fight around Richmond, Slaughter Mountain, Second Manassas, Bristow Station, Sharpsburg, Fredericksburg, Second Winchester, Gettysburg, Mine Run, and Wilderness. In the latter the 25th Regiment was captured. Seventeen men of Company I were in the capture. They were first taken to Point Lookout, Md., thence to Elmira, N. Y. Eleven of the seventeen lived through the war, the others died prisoners.

———

Twenty men enlisted in Company I, 3d West Virginia Cavalry, U. S. A., viz:

John Kelly, Perry Buzzard, W. H. Sims, C. O. W.
Sharp, Peter H. Grimes, Sargeants; Frank Grimes,
Abraham Sharp, C. N. Kelley, J. B. Hannah, Corpo-
rals; Beverly Waugh, Lieutenant. Privates Zane B.
Grimes, D. K. Sims, Calvin Kelley, J. H. Duncan,
Wesley Barlow, Alfred D. Gay, George W. McCarty,
Clark Grimes, W. A. Kelley, John W. Tyler.

Then there were Union soldiers from this county in
other regiments, viz: Andrew Wanless, Nelson Wanless, John Curry, Thomas Akers, William Cutlip, Jeremiah Sharp, Armenius Buzzard, Clark Kellison, Andrew Kellison, James Kee, William Duffield, William
Duncan, Joseph Moore, David Moore, Milton Sharp,
Brown Arbogast, George Arbogast, James E. Johnson
Clark Dilley, John Slaton, John F. Wanless, Peter
McCarty.

———

When the Levels Cavalry under Captain Andrew G.
McNeel, 1861, were disbanded, many of its members
joined the Bath Cavalry under Captain Archie Rich-
ards. April 25, 1862, this company was formed into
two companies, "F" and "G," and was known as the
Bath Squadron, attached to the 11th Virginia Cavalry.
Dr A. G. McChesney was Captain of Company F. A.
C. L. Gatewood, 1st Sergeant, and Edwin S. Beard,
2d Sergeant. The following persons from Pocahontas
were members of this company : Moffett Beard, W.
W. Beard, John G. Beard, John J. Beard, James
Burnside, James Callison, Clark Cochran, George B.
Cochran, Andrew Edmiston, Richard Edmiston, Mat-

thew Edmiston, John L. Kennison, Davis Kennison, D. B. McElwee, B. D. McElwee, John McCarty, A. G. McNeel, G. H. Moffett.

Foxhall A. Daingerfield was captain of Company G. John Andrew Warwick 2d lieutenant by brevet. Andrew G. Price, James Friel, James W. Warwick, Jr., and George Young were members of the company when organized.

Quite a number of our citizens were soldiers in Captain William L. McNeel's and Captain Jacob W. Marshall's companies of mounted infantry, and in Captain J. C. Arbogast's Greenbank company, 31st Virginia Infantry, but the compiler has been unable to secure requisite information respecting them.

VIII.

HUNTERSVILLE—THE FIRST COUNTY SEAT.

For a number of years previous to the organization of the county, in 1821, Huntersville had been a public place, as merchants and tradesmen from the east would arrange to meet the hunters here and barter goods for the proceeds of the chase. It was suggested by some that Smithville would be an appropriate name for the county seat, for apparent historical reasons. The present name Huntersville, however, was strenuously insisted upon by John Bradshaw and his friends, as a special compliment to the hunters that swarmed there during the trading season, and to whose presence and patronage the place owed very much for its prosperous development.

It was for a long while after the organization of the county that Huntersville retained precedence as the principal trading place for the entire county. The largest stores were usually here. Many people would come every month to the courts, and once a year the "Big Muster" would bring out all subject to military duty between the ages of 18 and 45, and many others besides. During the superior courts and the big musters, quite a number of persons from the eastern counties would be here to sell hats, saddles, harness, stone ware, tobacco, thirty cent whiskey, and other commodities too numerous to specify. The stores and bar rooms would do a rushing business, and the horse and cattle market would sometimes be very lively. Take it altogether, Huntersville was by common consent regarded as a little place with large ways. It was no uncommon thing for Huntersville merchants to realize three or four hundred per cent on dry goods, and not much less on groceries, during the period from 1822 to 1845. When the Huntersville and Warm Springs turnpike was made, and the Parkersburg road penetrated upper Pocahontas, then stores of importance opened at Greenbank and Millpoint and in rapid succession at other points until mercantile operations have come to what they are now.

A very disastrous fire occurred in the winter of 1852 by which the most of the business part of the village was consumed to ashes. The Craig residence, two stores, and a hotel, comprising a range of buildings extending from the Presbyterian church to the corner opposite the court house. At the time there lived on Browns Mountain one of Napoleon Bonaparte's veterans who had fought in the battle of Waterloo, named Frederick Burr. He came down to view the smoking ruins and on his return he was met by a person who inquired: "Well, Mr Burr, how does Huntersville look now?" In his solemn way he replied: "It looks like a coat with nothing but the tails left."

During the war Huntersville was burned by Federal

troops sent in from the garrison at Beverly, to prevent it being a Confederate depot for military supplies.

When peace was restored between the States, Huntersville recuperated rapidly. Flourishing stores were carried on by Amos Barlow, J. C. Loury & Son, and Loury & Doyle. The farms were reinclosed, improved methods of agriculture adopted, and at this time presents a more attractive appearance than at any time in all its previous history.

The more notable days in the history of Huntersville and of the county citizenship, were the trainings and the general muster that would follow. For several years after the organization of the 127th Regiment the Brigade Inspector was Major John Alexander, of Lexington. He would bring his drummer and fifer with him, two likely colored men uniformed in scarlet like British soldiers, and were the admiration and envy of all the colored people. Some of the black boys would say that they desired no better heaven than be musicians and wear such red clothes.

When the militia regulations were modified, the colonel of the regiment would train the officers for about three consecutive days before the regimental muster. These were usually seasons of much social hilarity, and the saloons reaped lucrative returns. The musters came off in May, jutt after corn planting. More animated scenes were never witnessed in our county, as the throngs passed into Huntersville from all sections.

About 11 o'clock the long roll of the drum was heard. The colonel and his staff appeared at the head of the street, and paraded the street preceded by fife

and drum. On their return the colonel instructed the
adjutant to have the regiment formed. The colonel
and staff would then disappear and retire to headquarters.

In the meantime the loud orders of the captains
were heard for their men to fall into ranks, and when
formed the adjutant placed them in position and then
reported to the colonel that all was in readiness. The
colonel and staff reappeared at the head of the regiment. Three beautiful silken flags were put in charge
of the color guard. The rear rank of the regiment fell
back a few paces in open order. A procession, formed of the colonel's staff and color guard, preceded by
the band, reviewed the regiment, stationed the flags,
and returned to the head of the regiment.

In stentorian tones the order was given to close
ranks and form a column of twos, and soon the whole
regiment would be on the march to a neighboring field
selected for the evolutions. The field just west of the
town was frequently selected, and the one back of the
court house was sometimes used. Two or three hours
would be passed in the evolutions. The bugle would
sound the retreat, the drum and fife take up "Bonaparte's Retreat from Moscow," and the whole column
would prepare to leave the field and fall back on Huntersville in slow and regular order. Having formed in
open order on the street the colonel and staff, preceded
by the music, had another procession to collect the
flags. The color guard was led to the head of the column, the colonel dismounted, received the flags one
by one, and each was saluted by the roll of the drum.

and placed away for safe keeping.

After this the regiment was disbanded, and then came the funny scenes that would require a graphic pen to describe with due justice. Cakes, beer, and something stronger were now in profuse requisition. The sun would sometimes go down leaving a large crowd enjoying the hilarity of the occasion, seemingly sorry that muster day did not last a week at least. "Tomorrow is Sunday, and there is no use in being in a hurry to get home. Let us go it while we have a chance," were some of the communications that were quite a strain to good morals.

Among the distinguished citizens of the county who were colonels of this regiment appear the names of John Baxter, Benjamin Tallman, John Hill, Paul Mc- Neel, D. W. Kerr, James Tallman, W. T. Gammon, James T. Lockridge. David W. Kerr yet lives, and is the only survivor.

The next notable days were the superior court terms when lawyers and judges from abroad would be present and hold the courts with great dignity, being out of reach of the voters and asked nobody any favors. Their decisions were above suspicion, and but few cases were ever appealed. Such as were appealed never amounted to anything very encouraging.

The circuit judges, in the order named, were Judge Taylor, of Lexington, J. J. Allen, of Fincastle, Judge Johnson, also of Fincastle, who died while attending court in Huntersville. Judge Harrison, of Union, Judges Holt and McWhorter, of Lewisburg, and Judge Campbell, of Union.

The clerks of Pocahontas have been John Baxter, pro tem., Josiah Beard, H. M. Moffett, James Tallman, General William Skeen, William Curry, Robert Gay, and John J. Beard. The foregoing held both of the offices at the same time. A few years since the offices were divided, and J. H. Patterson became circuit clerk, and S. L. Brown county clerk. During the war William Curry was clerk, and his adventures and success in preserving the records will be long remembered, as one of the most notable instances of official fidelity in the history of the State.

The responsible office of Commonwealth's Attorney has been held by Johnston Reynolds, of Lewisburg, W. H. Terrell, of Warm Springs, D. A. Stofer, R. S. Turk, and L. M. McClintic.

The attorneys who have plead at the Huntersville Bar include such names as the following, besides those already mentioned: J. Howe Peyton, General Samuel C. Blackburn, George Mayse, Andrew Dameron, Captain R. F. Dennis, J. C. Woodson, Matthew Edmiston, F. J. Snyder, Judge Seig, C. P. Jones, L. H. and J. W. Stephenson, William McAllister, Judge Baily, Governor Samuel Price, Dr Rucker, J. W. Arbuckle, T. H. Dennis, J. T. McAllister, J. A. Preston

The resident attorneys have been T. A. Bradford, D. A. Stofer. William Skeen, H. S. Rucker, R. S. Turk, C. Osborne, C. F. Moore, N. C. McNeil, W. A. Bratton, L. M. McClintic, Andrew Price.

The physicians who have been located at Huntersville were Dr Sexton, Dr McClelland, Dr Porterfield Wallace from Rockbridge, and Dr Payne of Waynes-

boro. Dr Payne claimed to be sufficiently proficient
in fifteen trades and occupations to make a living by
any one, if required to do so. So far as known, Dr
George B. Moffett was the first graduate in medicine
to locate in Huntersville. He came in 1843. Since
then the Scott brothers, Howard & Archie, Dr Matt
Wallace, Dr H. M. Patterson, Dr J. M. Hamilton,
and Dr S. P. Patterson have been resident physicians.
The last named is the present resident physician.

For many years a thriving business was carried on
in the harness and saddlery business. First by John
Haines, who employed three or four hands. After
him William Fertig, who employed as many, and
handsome returns were realized by both. The business
is now in the hands of William Grose & Son.

Before the peripatetic children of Israel brought
ready made clothing in our county, tailoring was a
good business at Huntersville. Messrs Campbell and
John and James Holden turned out a great deal of
work. Three or four hands would be busy much of
the time, especially in the fall and early winter, or
when there were weddings in prospect. Weddings
also gave the saddlers a goodly share of business. It
was considered in good form for the bride to have a
new outfit, horse, saddle, and bridle. The groom
would not think he had much of a chance for success
if he did not do his courting and visiting on a new saddle and bridle, all made at Huntersville.

For a long while blacksmithing was an excellent
business, as there was so much horse shoeing and
wagon repairing to do for the teamsters, and so few

shops of any pretensions anywhere near. Finley's shop stood at the intersection of the Cummings Creek and Marlinton roads. Three or four hands seemed to have all they could do. No traces of it now remain.

Jack Tidd, a man of herculean strength and physical proportions, carried on the work in a large shop that stood in the corner now occupied by H. S. Rucker's law office. Jack Tidd was succeeded by William Dilley, whose skill as an artisan was thought to be rather remarkable. The business is now in the hands of G. W. Ginger.

For a long series of years, however, nothing seemed more flourishing that the hostelry business in conjunction with salooning. One of the principal hotels, and where the colonels usually had their headquarters, was located about where the Loury store house now stands. It was conducted by J. Williams, John Bussard, John Holden, Porterfield Wallace, I. C. Carpenter, and E. Campbell in succession, but was burned in the great fire of 1852. The other hotel was managed by William Gibson, John Haines, and Davis Hamilton in succession, but was burned during the war by the federal troops. About the year 1848 license for salooning was refused by the court, which course has been uniformally sustained from that day to this.

In regard to educational interests, Huntersville has had some good schools. About the year 1841 a chartered Academy was built near the place now occupied by Dr Patterson's residence. The names of the teachers, as now remembered, were J. C. Humphries, from Greenville, Augusta County, A. Crawford, of Browns-

burg, Va., Rev T. P. W. Magruder, from Maryland,
J. Woods Price, and a Professor Miller, from Pennsylvania.

To Huntersville is due the distinction of being the
first place in Pocahontas where a Sunday school was
held throughout the year. In the year 1839, Rev J.
M. Harris, a young minister in broken health, was advised to come to the mountains as a relief for bronchial
troubles. He was a native of Pennsylvania, and in
his preparation for the ministry he was a student of
such brilliant promise that he was called to do his first
preaching by a church in New Orleans. His charge
has since become the foremost Presbyterian church in
the city, and achieved a national reputation under the
ministry of Dr Palmer.

For a time it looked as if Mr Harris were destined
to be a pulpit star of the first magnitude. Nervous
prostration disabled him, and he resorted to the Virginia mountains as his forlorn hope for health. In a
few weeks after reaching Huntersville he opened
school, and also gathered a Sabbath school. His school
room was in a building near where the Methodist
church now stands, and was in after years used by Dr
Matt Wallace as a physician's office. After a sojourn
at Huntersville for a year or two, his health improved
y good deal. It was in his room at Holden's Hotel
the writer saw what a Greek Testament and Hebrew
Bible looked like, and came to the conclusion that it
would require something more than human to be able
to make any sense out of books printed with something that looked more like grammatical bug tracks

and systematic fly specks than printed words.

When Mr Harris left Huntersville he went to Hampshire County. There he married a lady of considerable wealth, and lived for many years in an isolated mountain home, where it was high and dry. He had a fine library, the leading newspapers, reviews, and magazines, and kept well informed as to what was going on in the world. He tried to do good when opportunities permitted, though expecting any year might be his last. Mr Harris was in early life the peer of Summerfield, and both entered the ministry about the same time. Summerfield's career was brief, but brilliant and famous. Harris by coming to the mountains had a career that was long, but useful and happy.

The first published notice of preaching services at Huntersville occurs in the diary of the Rev S. B. Witt, a Baptist minister. He spent a year or two in pioneer preaching in Pocahontas, Bath, and Greenbrier Counties, about 1823–24. During the time of his first visit to Huntersville there was a dancing school in progress. The dancing master very politely suspended when time for preaching came, and took his scholars to hear the seamon. Soon as the preaching was over the class reassembled and finished the lesson at a later hour. Here is an extract from Dr Witt's diary :

SEPTEMBER 18, 1824—Preached to-day at Huntersville to a considerable congregation. At this place there is a dancing school just commencing, and as soon as the meeting was over the greater part of the congregation returned to the ball room and commenced

dancing. Oh, that I may be the honored instrument
in the hands of the Almighty of bringing them to the .
knowledge of the truth.

Dr Witt became a noted minister in Prince Edward
County, and gathered a church of seven or eight hundred members on Sandy River. The writer while a
student at the seminary heard Dr Witt preach the memorial sermon of a wealthy citizen, who committed
suicide on his wife's grave a short time after her death.
The writer led the singing of the hymns. After the
service we made Dr Witt's acquaintance. The venerable man had not forgotten about the dance, and mentioned the Poages and Callisons as persons he well remembered. Dr Witt was quite independent, even
wealthy, and spent his old age in a charming country
home in the limits of the grand congregation he had
gathered in a pastorate of nearly thirty years duration.
S. B. Witth, Jr., a Richmond lawyer, is his son.

For many years religious services were held in the
courthouse. Then when the academy was built in 1842
it was used as a place of worship by Methodists of all
branches, Episcopalians, and Presbyterians. The
Presbyterian church afterwards became the place where
all denominations generally worshipped. This building was erected about the year 1855. It was used for
barracks during the war and was much defaced.

In the early summer of 1865 the Rev M. D. Dunlap
and W. T. Price were engaged in the first sacramental
meeting held after the war. A detachment of federal
troops from Buckhannon passed through the town, rode

around the church, looked in at the broken windows, examined the horses with critical eyes, and religious services were going on all the while without even pausing. Sermon and sacramental services over, Mr Dunlap, who had rode in from the country that morning and hitched his horse near the church, went to get his horse and found that it had been taken away as a "branded horse." During Averill's retreat through the Levels this horse was abandoned as worn out. Mr Dunlap had taken it up and put it in good condition. The venerable preacher had to return to his home at Hillsboro on a borrowed horse.

Ten or eleven years since the Methodist church was built on its present site, and so for the present the town is well provided with churches.

Five or six years ago the Masonic fraternity of Pocahontas County, represented by the Huntersville Lodge, needed a lodge room. Arrangements mutually satisfactory were made with the trusteeship of the Presbyterian church, and the building was enlarged and renovated in very attractive style. The inception and completion of this arrangement is largely due to James H. Doyle.

Nature seems to have marked Huntersville and vicinity as designed for something of more than ordinary importance. The locality is approachable from the four quarters of the earth by valleys converging here. The beauty of the scenery everywhere displayed is something phenomenal, in the view of all who have eyes to appreciate whatever is picturesque in mountains, forest and streams. The air is pure and exhilarating. Mineral waters abound in profusion, chalybeate, alum, and sulphur. The most remarkable, however, are the arsenious-lithia fountains that bubble up in the Curry Meadow, in volume sufficient to meet the needs of a world of health seeking people requiring the benefits of lithia remedies.

IX.

AVERILL'S RETREAT.

In December, 1863, General Averill's army suddenly appeared on the crest of the river ridge opposite
Hillsboro, and covered the face of the country by
straggling along routes parallel with the county roads.
It was the army that a few weeks before had been victorious at Droop Mountain. Now cold, wet and starving the men were in headlong, disorganized retreat.
They appeared so suddenly that the men who were at
home had no opportunity to escape and were taken
prisoners, and the women had no time to conceal their
scanty household stores. At one place the house was
ransacked, but a large quantity of maple sugar was not
found. It was under a lounge, and the lady of the
house had three girls calling. They sat on the lounge
and spreading their skirts concealed effectively the
treasured sugar.

The soldiers were practically starving. At one place
they eagerly consumed all the scraps of rancid fat that
had been set aside for soap grease. At another place
some Dutch soldiers drank and ate from the swill tub.
A woman whose husband was in the Confederate army

saw her slender supply of bacon carried away by a private soldier. An officer riding up, she appealed to him for protection. He ordered the man to leave the bacon. The soldier replied, "You be ———!" The officer immediately fired upon the soldier, who dropped the stolen meat and ran.

The men who were at home were nearly all taken. A large number of these prisoners were kept in the old Academy in Hillsboro, and the guards who were placed over them slept the sleep of utter exhaustion. A bold movement on the part of the pursuing Confederates would have captured the whole force. Not until the town of Edray was reached and news of immediate reinforcements from Beverly, did the men of Averill's command see any peace or comfort. The retreat was made from Salem to Beverly, four hundred miles, in sixteen days and in the worst weather.

The information from which this sketch is written is gathered from various sources, and we can not personally vouch for its correctness, and it is very apt to be criticised by those who were actors in these scenes. But that is the general fate of war literature. Let an old soldier write of the war, and men who have served with him will have a different version of it. It will not be until the memory of man runneth not to the contrary that a true history of the great war will be written.

General William Woods Averill was born in Cameron, N. Y., in 1832. He was graduated at West Point in 1855, and until 1857 served in the garrison at Carlisle, Pa. He then went to the frontier in the Indian

wars, where he was wounded.   At the battle of Bull
Run he was first lieutenant of a company of mounted
riflemen.   He was made colonel of the 3d Pennsylvania Cavalry later in 1861.   His most notable
achievements were his campaign in Virginia and his
notable retreat in December, 1863, whereby he extri-
cated his army of five thousand men from the heart of
the Confederacy, was his most brilliant exploit.   He
attained the rank of Major General, and resigned at
the close of the war.   He was afterwards president of
a manufacturing company.   His campaign in this section made his name famous.

The "fourth separate brigade" was created March
28, 1863, and the command given to General Roberts,
who fixed his headquarters at Weston.   It included the
all the eastern section of West Virginia, in which section were numerous Confederate sympathizers, there
being probably more Confederate than Union people.
This was the "bushwhacking" section of the country,
there being so many deadly rifle shots, and both sides
engaged in this species of unlawful warfare.   Regular
soldiers would at times practice it.

A staid old man (a Union soldier who has made his
fortune in the west) told the writer :   "Three of us lay
up on the hill-side just west of the Marlinton bridge
on a scout.   We saw a man in Confederate uniform
ride up to the end of the bridge, stop his horse and
look through.   We all cocked our guns and took aim,
but we thought it might be a neighbor and held our
fire.   He turned and I saw it was an uncle of yours.
I have always been glad we waited.   He never knew

how near he came to being shot."

This state of things General Roberts intended to put
down, by driving the Confederates out.   Jones, Jackson, and Imboden made a raid on him, and all abandoned the country to pillage, and Roberts was soon in
disgrace at Washington.

May 18, 1863, Averill superseded him.   His orders
were to find Roberts and relieve him of his command,
protect the country between the line of the Baltimore
& Ohio and Kanawha River, and guard the passes in
Cheat Mountain.   At this time he was about thirty
years old.   He tried to clear the country of Confederates between Pendleton and Greenbrier.

In August he destroyed saltpetre works near Franklin.   He passed through Monterey, and instead of
proceeding against Staunton as Imboden expected, he
came to Huntersville, where he dispersed small de-
tachments of Confederates, capturing some arms and
stores.   A few days later he met a force of 2500 Confederates under General Jones at Rocky Gap, near the
White Sulphur, and after fighting a day and a night
was utterly routed.   This was a hot fight.   The can-
nonading was heard in Pocahontas by people who
could not imagine what forces were engaged.   Captain
Von Koenig was killed in this battle by his own men,
and two reasons are given.   The one is that he had
struck several of his men recently, and the other that
he was killed by men who thought it was Averill.
The Union forces retreated to Beverly, reaching there
August 31.

On Averill's next appearance in the county the   battle of Droop Mountain was fought. The Confederates fell back from Huntersville to the Levels without making a stand, but there was continual skirmishing. These Confederates were under the command of Colonel William P. Thompson, who married a Miss Moffett of this county, and who after the war became a great railway magnate of New York. The Confederate forces numbered 4000, and were under the command of Major Echols. They took their stand on the top of Droop Mountain, where the turnpike crosses. From the front it seemed impregnable. Some four or five miles distant in the Levels, Averill's 5000 men pitched their tents. From the heights of Droop Mountain the Confederate soldiers could almost see what the enemy was cooking for supper. Averill waited a day for reinforcements which did not arrive. Echols was reinforced. November 6th Averill began the battle. He sent Colonel Moore with 1000 men west to flank, while he made a show of an attack on the front and made a fent of passing to the east of the enemy down the old road around the end of Droop Mountain where the Greenbrier passes through.

The flanking detachment made a curve of nine miles and fell upon the Confederates to the west. As soon as Averill detected the confusion incident to an attack in an unexpected quarter, he hurried his men up the mountain, and on their arriving at the top the Confederate forces scattered. It moves the old Confederates to smiles to this day to think how well they ran that day after the field was lost.

It was here that Colonel Cochran of Virginia made

his famous escape.   He was, apparently, in the power
of a squad of Union soldiers but escaped.   When asked why he had not surrendered, he said: "If they had
said, 'Colonel, surrender!' I would have done so; but
they yelled, 'Stop, you ——— red-headed son of a
gun!' and I would not accommodate any man who used
such language to me."

Averill went as far south as Lewisburg, and then
went to the northern part of the State in Hampshire
County.   He was notified that he must make a raid
to Salem, Virginia, and destroy the Virginia & Tennessee Railroad.   This was sending him with a small
force into a country which the Confederates held in
undisputed possession.   His route lay through Petersburg, Franklin, Monterey, Mt. Grove, Callahans,
Sweet Sulphur Springs, and New Castle to Salem.
Colonel Moore with a considerable force advanced
through Pocahontas County.   The march began December 8th.   It was a hurry call and the horses were
not all shod, and this work had to be finished on the
road.   Averill reached Salem just as a train load of
soldiers were arriving to defend the place.   His artillery forced the train to back out of the place, and he
destroyed the railroad, cut the telegraph wires, and destroyed the stores.   The track was torn up for sixteen
miles, five bridges burned, 100,000 bushels of shelled
corn, 10,000 bushels of wheat, 2000 barrels of flour,
1000 sacks of salt, 100 wagons, and much other valuable property was destroyed.   Six hours were spent in
this work.   Having completed this work, his next
business was to get out of a death trap.   Averill was

hemmed in by forces under Fitzhugh Lee, Jackson, Early, and Echols, and a terrible rain setting in every stream was flooded. It was one of the memorable freshets of this section.

His object was to cross into West Virginia, striking Monroe, Greenbrier, or Pocahontas county. The first brush with the Confederates on the retreat was within eight miles of the James River Bridge, on the Fincastle and Covington turnpike. The Confederates raced for the bridge, crossed it first, but did not have time to burn it. He raced them to the next bridge, five miles farther, and the same thing happened. At the second bridge before he could get cross, Jackson's force was upon him, and Averill held the bridge at a loss of 124 men. General Early sent a formal request for his surrender, to which Averill made no reply. He crossed the Alleghanies, and so one morning when the weather was bitte.ly cold and the Greenbrier greatly swollen, he put his command across it and swarmed into the Levels, before the inhabitants knew there were any soldiers about. It is to be doubted if there was ever a more wretched lot of soldiers.

They were in perfect agony as they approached the Marlinton Bridge, where a road from the east joins the State road running north and south on which they were traveling. We have heard men who were carried along as prisoners say that when they passed tne point where Marlinton is now built without being intercepted their spsrits rose and they seemed to be immediately relieved from all fears of being captured. At Edray they camped, and so worn were they that the setinels

could not keep awake.   It is said that a hundred men
could have taken the whose army.   They were ready
to drop with fatigue, and their powder was wet.   The
government recognized this as a briiliant achievement,
though their escape was due to pure luck, the Confederates taking the wrong roads.   The United States presented each of Averill's men with a suit of clothes and
a pair of shoes to take the place of those worn out on
the march.

X.

FROM THE COUNTY RECORDS.

At April Term, 1826, two gentlemen were indicted for horse racing on the public road.

Against another for retailing spiritous liquors by the small measures without a license therefor.

A list of the rates fixed for ordinaries: Whiskey by the half pint 12½c, French brandy half pint 25c, rum per gill 25c, apple brandy 12½c, peach brandy 18¾c, wines 25c, diet by the meal 25c, grain by the gallon 12½c, hay for 24 hours 12½c, lodging 12c.

The crop of old wolf scalps for 1825–6 amounted to twenty-one at $5 each.

James Brindly is allowed $7 for traveling to Lewisburg for stovepipes.

Surveyors of the county roads were allowed 6½ cents for each day necessarily employed: William Brock, 62½c for 10 days; James Waugh 25c for 4 days, etc.

June, 1827 a levy of $49 was laid and John Bradshaw and Samuel Hogsett commissioners were appointed to let out the erection of the public stocks and pillory.

The court seems to have the power to license preachers and gentlemen to celebrate the rites of matrimony by taking a bond of $1500.

Everyone has heard of Major Jacob Warwick's famous servant Ben who accompanied him on all his warring, hunting and surveying trips, and to whom his master granted his freedom. At the August court the following order was entered in reference to his life and character:

"Ben, a man of color, who is entitled to his freedom under the last will and testament of Jacob Warwick, deceased, bearing date on the 7th day of March, 1818, of record in the Clerk's Office of this county. This day motioned the court, (the commonwealth's attorney being present) for permission to remain in this county: whereupon, it is the opinion of the court, that the said Ben be permitted ro remain and reside for his general good conduct and also for acts of extraordinary merit, it appearing to their satisfaction that the said Ben hath given reasonable notice of this motion.

"The acts of extraordinary merit, upon which the order of the court is founded, are the following:

"It appearing from the evidence of Mr Robert Gay that at an early period when the county of Bath (now Pocahontas) was invaded by the Indians, he protected with fidelity the possessions of his master, and assisted in defending the inhabitants from the tomahawk and scalping knife.

"In addition to this public service it appears from the evidence of Messrs Waugh and P. Bruffey that he rendered most essential service to his master in saving his life on divers occasions.

"Upon these meritorious acts the court grounded their order."

March 1828, William Brock, prisoner for debt, confessed the amount of his debts, $30, and all parties consenting, he took the benifit of the act for the relief of insolvent debtors, which consisted of his giving up a schedule of all his property, and the sheriff is directed to release him from custody when he shall have delivered the property named in the schedule.

April, 1828—The county is laid off into three districts. The upper end as low down as Sitlingtons Creek, then down to the mouth of Beaver Lick Creek, then to the lower end of the county.

June Term, 1829—County levy $341.37½. Six hundred and eighty-one tithables at 50 cents each. Wolf scalps, eleven old ones at $8 each, and four young ones at $4 each—$104, or nearly one third of the expenses of the county. The wolves seemed to have taken up the greater part of the page space in the early history of our county, and to have taken a very large part of the revenue. That the citizens had these destructive creatures on the run is apparent from the records. The price upon their heads rises by stages—$4 $6, $8, $10, $12,—and finally reaches the princely sum of $15, at which price two were proved in 1855. About that time a number of old fox scalps were proved at $1 each. From 1829 up, the young wolf scalp was worth half as much as an old one would bring from the public.

September court an appraisement bill was filed which contained an item which has passed out of such lists forever: ''To two black women, Delph and Daftie, $71.00.'' These must have been very old slaves, or of little value from some other cause.

In another appraisement bill filed at the October Court is a list of slaves: One black man named Bill willed to be sold, $200; one black woman named Nancy, $250; one black girl named Eveline, $75; one black man named Aaron, $300r one black man named Lewis, $150; one black boy named Peter, $275, one black girl Rachel, $100; one black child Charlotte $40.

In this appraisement bill sheep are rated at $1 a head, cows $10, four year old steers $10, horses $35 to $45.

The Messinbird negroes were liberated by their master, Henry Messinbird, who settled on the mountain overlooking the Levels, and to whom he left his property and granted them freedom. Why he was here will be always a mystery. He may have been a fugitive from justice. He was a man of great scholarly attainments.

House Built By William Ewing, at Ewington, Ohio, 1812.

Enoch Ewing, 1799–1885.

XI

CAPTAIN JAMES EWING.

The Ewing family of Pocahontas County and vicinity was founded by James Ewing, born near Londonderry, Ireland, of Scotch parents, about 1720. He came to Virginia as a young man, and there married Margaret Sargent, of Irish birth, who bore him five children: Jennie, who married Clendennin, Susan who married Moses Moore, Elizabeth who married George Dougherty, John, and William. John was born in 1747. At the time of the Clendennin massacre in Greenbrier County, John, a mere lad, was taken prisoner by the Indians, and carried into the Ohio country. There he was adopted into an Indian tribe, baptized according to Indian custom, and given an Indian name. But John's Scotch-Irish blood was not easily converted to Indian, and when a returning party of warriors brought back as a curiosity an English Bible, he explained to them that it was the word of God. The Indians asked whether his God was an Indian or a white man, and when John answered that he was a white man, they would no longer listen to his reading the book.

John learned the Indian tongue, but he never loved the Indian. In his old age, at the mention of the word "Indian in his presence he would always say, "Curse and confound the Indian." He was released from captivity under a treaty with the Indians, probably in 1764, and delivered to the whites at Fort Pitt, from which point he made his way back to his old Virginia home. In 1774 he married Ann Smith, Irish. They had eleven children, namely: William, 1775–1858; Susannah Holcomb, 1766–; Hon. John Smith Ewing, 1778–1837; Janeat Howell, 1781–1855; Sarah Holcomb, 1782–1850; Ann Ewing, 1785–; Andrew, 1787–1868; Elizabeth; Nancy Mills, 1781–; Lydia Burris 1792–1872; Samuel, 1797–1855. The children of these gave John a list of grand children numbering sixty-five. In 1801, John emigrated from Pocahontas and located in Gallia County, Ohio, where he died in 1825. Of his family, his son William alone remained in Virginia, occupying lands on Stony Creek until the time of his death. John Smith Ewing represented his district in the Virginia Assembly in about 1812. Anselm T. Holcomb, son of Sarah, was a member of the Ohio Legislature. John Ewing, son of Andrew, and George Burris, son of Lydia, were members of the Missouri Legislature. Andrew, son of John S., was a member of the California Legislature.

John's living descendants are legion. They may be found in nearly every western state, and counted among the successful farmers, business men, and professional men of the country. Among them are John Ewing, lawyer, Grant City, Mo., Clay Ewing, York-

town, Kan., Jennie Sprouse, M. D. Greenview, Ill.,
M. Howell Finnegan- New London, Mo., P. H. Hol-
comb, lawyer, Butler, Mo., S. C. Holcomb, lawyer,
Yates Centre, Kan., A. T. Holcomb, Portsmouth, O.,
William Whitman, county clerk, Van West, O., S. G.
Burnside, merchant, Kansas City, Mo., Sumner Ew-
ing, teacher and author, Springfield, O., Mrs Homer
McCray, Kendallville, Ind., Laura Dunning, Ingomar
California.

The descendants of John Ewing reverently refer to
him as "Indian John."

William Ewing, brother of "Indian John," was
born in 1756. In 1774 he joined Arbuckle's company of militia, and pursued Chief Cornstalk and his
braves to the Ohio River, where he participated in the
famous battle of Point Pleasant. Here he was in the
thickest of the fight, but came out without a scratch,
narrowly escaping instant death. He had availed himself of the shelter of a sapling while firing at thr red-
skins, when an excited comrade rushed up to the place
pushing him from his shelter and occupying it himself.
William was scarcely out of the way before his comrade was struck in the head by an Indian bullet and
killed instantly. In after years he related that every
time he took deliberate aim at an Indian in that battle
his rifle flashed in the pan, and his Indian got away,
but when he fired at random his gun never missed fire.
If he killed an Indian he never knew it, but he tried
his level best to avenge the capture of his sister Mrs
Clendennin and his brother John.

In 1785 he married Mary McNeil, sister of Gabriel

McNeil, and daughter of Thomas McNeil. He settled on Swago Creek, near Buckeye, and was popularly known as "Swago Bill." It is said that he blazed a line of trees around the lands he selected, and afterwards had the tract patented. Once he was plowing when the alarm came that the Indians were preparing to attack the settlement. The shelter of the nearest fort was sought, but the Indians did not appear. After a few days of quiet, William ventured out to the farm, where he found everything about as he had left them, except that a brood of quails which had been hatched and mothered by a chicken had disappeared. On his return to the fort he shouldered his plow, thinking to hide it from the Indians in the woods. While proceeding through the woods he suddenly heard "thump, thump, thump," followed by "click, click, click," and turning to one side he saw three Indians behind a large log with their guns pointed at him. They had tried to shoot, but their powder was damp, and the guns had missed fire. William dropped his plow and started for the fort as fast as he could run, with the Indians after him. Going over a hill and into a gully, he suddenly changed his course, ran up the ravine a short distance and stopped, and shortly had the pleasure of seeing his pursuers trot by in the regular course. Ewing made his way to the fort in safety.

William and Mary Ewing were the parents of twelve children, all born on the Swago, near Buckeye, namely: Elizabeth Doddrill, 1787–1852; Thomas, 1788–1874; Jonathan, 1790–1850; William, 1792–; James, 1793–1824; John, 1795–; Sarah Wallace, 1797–1827;

Enoch, 1799–1885; Jacob, 1802–1878; Abram Mc-
Neel, 1804–1891; George, 1807–1883; Andrew, 1809–
1885. The children of these gave William and Mary
a list of grand children numbering eighty-one, twenty-
two of whom are still living. In 1810 William and
his family moved to Gallia County, Ohio, and the
town of Ewington was named in their honor. Thomas
served as Justice of the Peace for many years. Elizabeth, Thomas, William, James, John, Sarah, Abram,
George, and Andrew lived and died in or near
Gallia County. Jonathan and Jacob died in Hancock
County, Ill., Enoch died in Hillsdale County, Mich.,
and Andrew died in Iowa. Mary McNeal Ewing, the
mother, died in Mercer County, Mo., in 1858. Enoch
Ewing and his family went to Michigan in 1853, and
seven of his children are still living in that State, besides a host of grand children. William's descendants,
like John's, are counted among the successful men of
the country. Among them are Dr G. A. Ewing,
Jackson, O.; Dr G. K. Ewing, Ewington, O.; Dr U.
B. G. Ewing, Richmond, Ind.; Dr William Leonard,
Fostoria, O.; Rev Thomas E. Peden, President Theological Seminary, Ayden, N. C.; Rev M. L. Peden,
Temperance, Mich.; W. J. Aleshire, editor, Gibson-
burg, O.; E. E. Aleshire, lawyer, Stanberry, Mo.; Levi Howell, civil engineer, Luray, Mo.; Frank P. Mc-
Carley, civil engineer, Pittsburg, Pa.; Hon. W. S.
Matthews, President Insurance Company, Toledo, O.,
ex-member of the Ohio Legislature; E. B. Matthews,
manufacturer, Jackson, O.; G. W. Ewing, Plymouth,
Ill.; W. L. Ewing, Rutlege, Mo., J. K. Ewing, Port

Blakely, Wash.; John W., H. McK., James L., and Andrew A., of Camden, Mich.; E. C. White, White, Mich.: J. C. Jenkins, Cunningham, Kansas; Isaac Jenkins, White, Mich.; William H. Ewing, merchant, Camden, Mich.; I. E. Ewing, manufacturer, Reading, Mich.; W. J. Ewing, merchant, Kunkle, O.; Rev I. H. Ewing, Bristol, Ind.; J. C. Ewing, merchant, Pioneer. O.; L. P. Cravens, teacher, Lake City, Minn.; Ida M. Ewing, Pontoosuc, Ill.; A. L. Ewing, teacher, Wellston, O.; Smith H. Ewing, merchant, Frankfort, O.; John H. Ewing, county clerk, Gallipolis, O.; Rev Sadie P. Cooper, Detroit, Mich.; Prof. R. B. Ewing, Ewington, O.; Theresa Gilbert, Sioux Falls, South Dakotah.

The compiler is indebted to Hon. A. E. Ewing, of Grand Rapids, Mich., for most of the material contained in this sketch. He is a great-grandson of "Swago Bill," a grandson of Enoch, and a son of Henry McK. Ewing. His mother was a Miss Hank, of Monroe County. He is a lawyer, and a member of the House of Representatives of Michigan in 1893.

Captain James Ewing, the founder of these families, died probably about the year 1800. He was captain of a company of militia in Augusta County during the Revolutionary war, and tradition asserts that he received a large tract of land in consideration of his services. Tradition makes him the hero of more than one occasion. One of especial interest is told of how he captured an outlaw by the name of Shockley, who was a terror to the country, and who had stolen James' rifle from ever his cabin door.   His descendants have reached to the eighth generation, and numerically have reached into the thousands.   His Highland Scotch instinct made him to prefer the mountains to the plains, and it is probable that in his mountain home, surrounded by the perils of pioneer life, beset on the one hand by wild animals, and on the other by savage Indians, he found life quite to his liking.

His wife, it is said, lived to be one hundred years old.

XII.

CONCLUSION.

It may not be inappropriate at this time to embody in this book some facts concerning the development of the county in the last decade of the 19th century, which were momentous years for Pocahontas County.

In December, 1890, an epoch marking snow fell, making it the "winter of the deep snow." While it lay on the ground to the depth of three feet or more, Colonel John T. McGraw, of Grafton, made a visit to this county and purchased the farms known as Marlins Bottom for a town site. Five families lived on the land now occupied as the site of the town of Marlinton. The name of the postoffice had been changed a few years before from Marlin's Bottom to Marlinton. Mrs Janie B. Skyles, a Maryland lady, who was living here, being instrumental in effecting the change. It was bitterly opposed by some of the older citizens, who objected to the giving up of the descriptive and historic name of Marlin's Bottom.

The purchase of the town site by Colonel McGraw was the first intimation that county people had of proposed railway developments. The plan was that the

Camden System of railroads was to be extended up
Williams River, across the divide at the head of Stony
Creek, and to Marlinton. It was a part of the plan
that the C. & O. R. R. would build an extension from
the Hot Springs to Marlinton and connect with the
Camden Road at that place.

The town of Marlinton was laid off in town lots in
1891, and widely advertised as a place where a town
would be built. The building of the railroad was regarded as a certainty. The Pocahontas Development
Company was chartered and took a deed for 640 acres
on which the town was to be built. They put valuable
improvements on it. An offer of $5000 to be applied
on a new court house was made, if the people of the
county would change the county seat from Huntersville
to Marlinton. The election held in the fall of 1891
gave the county seat to Marlinton. At this time Marlinton had a population of about one hundred people.

The railroad was not built at that time because of
the money panic which came on the country at that
time. Colonel McGraw, who had invested largely in
lands elsewhere in the county, never ceased to try to
interest capitalists in this county and develop it with
a railroad. His attention being called to the natural
route for a railroad up Greenbrier River, he had a survey made from Marlinton to Ronceverte, at a cost of
$10,000, and it was on this location that the railroad
was afterwards built. The Greenbrier Railway was
commenced in 1899 and finished in 1901. The Coal
& Iron Railway is being built at the present time to
connect with it at Durbin. In two years Pocahontas

County changed from being one of the few counties in the State without a railroad, to the county having the greatest railwap mileage of any county of the State.

Marlinton began to improve at once. It was incorporated at the April Term of the Circuit Court, 1900, and held its first election of officers May 5th, 1900.

The first newspaper to be published in this county was the Pocahontas Times, founded in 1882 at Huntersville, and moved to Marlinton in 1892. The Pocahontas Herald was published in 1894 at Huntersville, and later at Marlinton, and ceased to be published in 1896. The Marlinton Messenger was first published in 1900.

The first telephone to be built in the county was the Marlinton and Beverly telephone line finished to Marlinton in August, 1899. That same year telephone lines were built along all the principal roads of the county.

The first bank to go into business in the county was the Bank of Marlinton in 1899, and later in the same year the Pocahontas Bank was opened. For more than a year these banks carried in large sums of money by special messengers from the nearest express stations from 45 to 57 miles distant, over lonely roads.

Writing at the time of the railroad development just beginning, the natural resources of the county have not been touched. No attention has been paid to the vast areas of iron ore land in the east of the county, which will some day make this county famous as an iron field.

In the nineties it was discovered that Pocahontas

County had a vast supply of marble which was equal in value to any marble ever found in the United States A company has been formed to develop this marble, and it will some day be ranked high among the marble deposits of the world.

The bulk of the timber is still standing, but an immense amount has been floated down the Greenbrier River, the St. Lawrence Boom & Manufacturing Company having removed in this manner a quarter of a billion feet of white pine. The walnut and cherry have been taken out in the last twenty-five years by rafting on the Greenbrier, which was once an important industry, rafting floods in the river being anxiously waited for. There were a number of skillful pilots who could thread their way with a raft of 50,000 feet of lumber between the rocks of this swift river.

We record these few facts in passing. It will require another book to do justice to the history of this county from the Civil War down, and there is much in that history that can better be reviewed by another generation.

The sketches which are embodied in this work have appeared in the Pocahontas Times, and have thus been scanned by the persons interested, and an opportunity afforded for correction that is invaluable, for history is nothing if not true. It has not been the work of a few months, but represents the work of ten years or more of preparation.

We wish to call attention to the fact that this book is a home product, written and printed in the county and published by reason of the hearty response of many Pocahontas people who desired to have the annals of the county in an enduring form. The paper on which this book is printed is from wood grown on Cheat Mountain, in this county, and very kindly furnished at a nominal price by the West Virginia Pulp & Paper Company.

In compiling this book the writer and publishers have endeavored to make it an honest history of Pocahontas County, and they have in no instance given undue prominence to any name in it for a consideration, though opportunities have presented themselves which were tempting to the publishers, who are at heavy expense in publishing so large a book.

In submitting this book to the public, we are aware that there are imperfections and omissions that will be apparent to many readers. To such we would say that no book or writer can cover so great a subject, but that you will find in this work so much pertaining to the history of this county that it can well lay claim to its title.

THE END.

- A -

----, Wallace 491
ADKINSON, Frances 371 Martha 307
ADKISON, 96
ADKISSON, Abel 201 Angelina 384 Barnett 201 Catherine 201 Daniel 202 385 Eleanor 201 202 Elizabeth 385 Frances 202 Henry 536 Isaac 202 James 201 Jane 384 John E 384 Lucinda 202 Maggie 536 Margaret 536 Martha 201 202 384 Martha Jane 202 Mary 202 Nancy 202 Oliver Blake 202 Susannah 201 202 William 201 536
AKERS, James H 582 Thomas 584
ALDERMAN, Andy C 582 John A 177 Martha 177
ALESHIRE, E E 615 W J 615
ALEXANDER, 8 498 John 588
ALKIRE, Ellen 436
ALLEN, Eliza 452 J J 590 Walton 452
ALTHAIR, Dr 200
American Indians, origin 3
AMISS, Adrew D 209 Effie May 381 Eveline 209
ANDERSON, _organ 117 Azelia 217 C M 157 217 Margaret 117 271 W S 157
ANGUS, Timolean 582
APPERSON, J R 295 296 Matilda 296
ARBAUGH, Eliza Jane 364 George Brown 364 Hannah 364 Jacob 364 365 369

ARBAUGH (continued)
James Marion 364 John Allen 364 Joseph Newton 364 Lauretta Frances 364 Nancy Caroline 364 Susannah Simms 364 William Hanson 364
ARBOGACT, Jacob H 125
ARBOGAST, 96 446 A M V 446 Abram 527 Ada 127 Adalaide Eleanor 148 Adam 122-128 131 133 446 449 487 Adam Jr 126 Alcinda 115 488 Alice 126 166 Allen 133 Allie 445 Amanda 125 Anna 132 429 444 Barbara 123 Benjamin 102 123-125 131-135 370 Benjamin Jr 124 134 Benjamin Sr 124 125 131 133 134 Brown 133 165 584 C C 126 Carlotta 131 Caroline 133 491 Catherine 123 Charles 133 Christopher 133 Clara 166 Clarissa 133 134 Daniel 582 David 123 Delilah 131 Dorinda 134 Earl 190 Eliza 126 134 Eliza A 447 Eliza Ann 446 Eliza Jane 125 Elizabeth 123 Elizabeth Wiison 125 Ella 126 Emma 134 George 123 132 133 488 584 Harriet Elizabeth 125 449 Henry 113 123 124 131 132 429 523 Hodie 127 Huldah 126 449 J C 429 585 Jacob 123 420 Jacob Hull 125 Jacob Lee 125 James 488 Jamieson 132 Jane 125 488 Joel 125 John 123-125 131 133 444 Lizzie 133 Margaret 123-125 132 133 444 446 488 523 Marshall 132 Mary 123 124 133 370 478 527

ARBOGAST (continued)
Michael 123 Minnie 190 Minta
132 Mrs Allen 133 Mrs
Benjamin 134 Mrs Brown 165
Nancy 133 Nancy Elizabeth
216 Nannie 488 Napoleon
Bonaparte 126 Newton 132
Otey 125 Paul McNeel 125
Peggy 123 Peter 123 Peter D
127 Polly 124 Rachel 126 132
133 Reed 134 Sallie 133 Sally
131 132 Sarah 126 132 Solo-
mon 124 131 133 Susan 123
Warwick 132 444 Washington
148 William 102 115 123 125
488 William Barton 125
ARBUCKLE, 613 Charles 516 J
W 591 Rebecca 516 Rosa 261
ARMENTROUT, John 152 Martha
152 Zechariah 152
ARMSTRONG, Jane 352 549
Lydia 169 Mr 377 481 549
Rachel 377 Thomas 352
ARTHUR, James 202 Martha
Jane 202
ASBURY, Bishop 521
ASHFORD, Anna 391 Craig 391
ATCHISON, 163
AULDRIDGE, 96 Allen 304 Caro-
line 454 Catherine 280 369
Charles 192 Eliza 282 369 536
Elizabeth 192 281 282 368-371
George 369 371 410 454
Hannah 371 Hanson 282 369
Henry 369 Huldah 369 410 Ida
369 James 186 368 369 371
James Edgar 370 John 303 304
368 370 Julia A 369 Kenney
192 Luther 192 Maggie 221
Malinda 369 Margaret 369
Martha 370 Mary 368 369 422
Mary Ann 186 281 369 370
Melinda 282 Miriam 185 186
369 370 Moffett 369 Mrs 305
Nancy 304 368 370 371 383
Olie 536 Rebecca 303 304 370
Richard 304 368 371 Samuel
185 186 192 368 370 Sarah 368
369 371 Susan 370 540 Susan
L 192 Thomas 221 280 368
369 461 Thomas Jr 369

AULDRIDGE (continued)
Thomas Sr 281 369 460 Tillot-
son 192 540 William 282 307
368-372 383 422 William Jr
370
AUSTIN, C L 488 Charles L 115
Mary 488 Mrs Charles L 115
AVERILL, Gen 314 599-606
William Woods 600
AVERILL'S Retreat, 599

- B -

BAILY, 580 Judge 591
BAKER, Elizabeth 300 Henry 463
464 558 James 108 109 121
231 383 463 John 115 Matilda
115
BALDWIN, Miss 182
BALLENGEE, Birdie 473 W H
473
BALLENGER, Mrs 503
BALTIMORE, Lord 301
BAMBRICK, George 191 Mantie
191 194
BARLOW, 96 470 A N 519
Alexander 184 185 Amos 185
186 229 396 404 464 505 510
519 588 Anderson 463 472
Andrew 185 Barbara 184 Davis
465 Effie 465 Elizabeth 185
421 Ellen 186 Francis 519
George 185 Henry 185 186 409
James 185 Jane 226 John 184-
188 226 276-278 480 Joseph
226 282 Josiah 185 Lula
Elizabeth 465 Martha 185 480
Mary 396 Mary Ann 186 369
464 Melinda 282 Miriam 185
370 Nancy Jane 409 Nathan
185 369 Wesley 584 William
185 186
BARNETT, Eleanor 364 Hannah
364 James 364 John Andrew
364 John Wesley 364 Josiah
364 Martha 364 Newton 364
Sabina Martha 176 Sarah Jane
364 Stephen 176 364 Thomas
364 Zechariah 364
BARRETT, Emanual 349 Rebecca 349

Battle, Point Pleasant 240
BAXTER, 96 470 Elizabeth 185
421 Geo A 256 George 103 285
310 396 410 420 421 469 Jane
280 419 John 50 100-103 268
280 355 369 373 393 419 420
469 590 591 Joseph 420
Margaret Jane 410 Martha 420
Mary 280 355 419 421 Miss
256 Mr 347 Mrs 420 Samuel
421 Sarah 420 Sarah Ann 396
William 185 280 419-421
BEALE, 96 Margaret 252 514
Margaret Elizabeth 262 514
Mary Vance 262 514 Mr 269
Nancy 280 Nancy Vance 496
Robert 262 495-497 Thomas
280
BEARD, 96 Abram 344 503 Arthur
447 Bertha 447 Bertie 447
Bessie 361 Blanche 447 Brown
447 C E 139 C Edgar 172
Charles W 436 514 Charles
Woods 262 Christopher 138
Clyde Yeager 447 Dr 138
Edgar 140 258 Edwin 262 548
Edwin S 584 Elizabeth 427 502
503 516 548 549 Emma Mil-
dred 447 Eveline Medora 447
Fannie 436 Harry 504 Henry
Moffett 262 Irbie 447 Irby 447
J Fred 504 J J 504 Jane 549
Janet 345 Jennie 118 Jesse
549 Joel 344 Joel Early 262
John 343 548 John G 503 584
John George 262 John J 584
591 John Jordan 504 Joseph
391 387 503 Josiah 101 183
261 343-347 440 502 514 516
542 549 591 Josiah O 447 Lee
140 Leslie 447 Luverta 448
Maggie 262 542 Margaret 138
548 Margaret Jane 504 Margie
447 Martha 503 504 Mary 140
262 Mary Agnes 183 Michael
O 447 Minerva 172 503 Miriam
138 Miriam Nancy 504 Miriam
Nannie 501 Miss 262 Moffett
584 Mollie 504 Monroe 447
Mrs Edgar 258 Mrs Thomas
545 Nellie Bly 447

BEARD (continued)
Rachel 514 549 Rachel
Cameron 261 345 Rosa 548
Ruby 447 Sabina 549 Samuel
440 502 549 Samuel J 262
Thomas 101 545 548 Thomas
III 549 Thomas Jr 548 W T
139 140 W W 584 Wallace
334 Wallace Warwick 118 262
William 138 549 William T
262
BEERY, Sallie Woods 300 Sally
W 266
BELL, David 235 F I 542 Frank
546 James 235 Mary 542
William 235 William A 235
BENNETT, Elizabeth 219 Marga-
ret 547 Mr 547 William 219
BENSON, Alexander 316 Eliza-
beth 207 Jane 316
BERRY, Rebecca 486 Widow 486
BEVERAGE, George 477 Hannah
281 Henry 166 Jacob 319 John
221 316 Levi 483 Margaret
Rebecca 166 Mary 221 316
Mary Ann 166 Mary Catherine
409 Nancy 477 Nancy Jane 483
Rachel 319 Thomas 409
BIAS, Caesereo 252 Catherine
252 James W 252 Kate 252
BIBLE, Jacob 324 360 445
Margaret 445 Rachel Bird 360
Susan 324
BIRD, Alcinda 317 Catherine
Hidy 431 Elizabeth 156 Elvira
Louisa 431 George 317 George
Newton 431 432 John 273 John
Henry 431 Mary 156 Ressie
474 Robert Craig 431 Susan
483 Uriah 107 483 W W 432
William 431 William Lee 432
BLACK, Margaret 545 546
BLACKBURN, Samuel C 591
BLAINE, Claiborne 117 John S
213 Lavinia 117 Margaret 213
BLAIR, Ann 503 Claiborne 503
Colbert 503 Doctor Franklin
503 Elizabeth 503 Frankie 437
503 Jane 503 John 503 Lavinia
503 Luther 532 Martha 184 503
Mary 514 532

BLAIR (continued)
Mary Elizabeth 532 Miriam
503 Morgan 503 Myra 532
Neva 532 William 102 437 503
BLAKE, Jennie 196 Mr 196
BLAND, Minerva 170
BLIZZARD, Jacob 356 Margaret
356
BOBLITT, Georgiana 193 194
Henry 193 194
BOGGS, Annie 406 Ezekiel 405
John 460 Martha 414 Sally 405
Susan 460
BOLAR, Esther 569
BOLES, Sally 413
BONAPARTE, Napoleon 587
BONNETT, Asbury 443 Caroline
443 Elizabeth 443 Jefferson
443 John 443 Sarah Ann 443
Serena Catherine 443
BOON, B B 582
BOONE, 353 Mary 374
BOSIER, 241
BOSWELL, Henrietta 342
BOSWORTH, Miss 257 Squier
257
BOULDIN, Mary 391 Randolph
Powhatan 391
BOWEN, Harriet 543 James 544
Margaret 544
BOWYERS, Catherine 194 Cicero
190 James Leonard 190 Jane
189 Leonard 194 Leonidas 189
BRADDOCK, 13 150 568 Gen 244
BRADFORD, T A 591
BRADLEY, James 582
BRADSHAW, 162 Elizabeth 506
508 Eveline 506 Franklin 506
Huldah Hickman 508 Isabella
506 James 506 Jane 487 506
509 Jane Elliot 507 John 100
103 198 268 323 397 505-510
528 586 607 Margaret 506 508
Martha 342 Martha Ann 508
Mary 473 Mary Ellen 508 Mary
Jane 508 Matilda Margaret 508
Nancy 198 506-508 Nancy
Makamie 508 R H 506 Rachel
Hannah 508 Rebecca Frances
508 Senilda 528 Senilda Eiler
508 Thomas 506 507

BRADSHAW (continued)
William 342 506 507 528
William James 508
BRADY, Margaret 193 Samuel
193
BRANNON, Mr 488 Nancy 488
BRATTON, W A 591
BRIDGER, 155 230 366 383 464
465 468 519 Elizabeth 458
James 129 178 179 558-560
John 558-560 Miss 138 Sallie
129 Sally 130
BRIGHT, Abram 544 David 435
542-545 David Jr 542 Eliza-
beth 437 543 Elizabeth Wiison
125 Francis 543 George 542-
544 Gordon 361 Harriet 543 J
K 502 James K 437 Jemima
437 Jesse 437 542 544 546
Jesse Jr 543 Jesse Sr 543 544
Julia 543 Lena 361 Maggie
542 Margaret 435 542-544
Martha 437 Mary 437 542 543
Michael 542 545 Mrs Abram
544 Mrs David 542 Mrs George
543 Rachel 542 Sally 545
Samuel 543 Sarah 543
BRINDLEY, James 285
BRINDLY, James 607
BRINKLEY, Andrew 542
BRITT, Mr 444 Virginia 444
BROCK, Daniel 231 Hannah 406
453 Isabella 337 John 337
Margaret 231 Mary 230 Mrs
Daniel 231 Rachel 363 Robert
231 Serena 152 Thomas 185
230 453 William 231 363 607
609
BROOKS, Mary Alice 320
BROWN, 96 Adalaide Eleanor
148 Ann 363 365 Anna 175
Cornelia 161 Eleanor 364
Elizabeth 363 Hannah 363 364
Jennie 176 364 365 480 John
364 367 398 400 Joseph 175
287 363-368 516 Josiah 103
176 179 242 336 341 364 366
367 461 480 Martha 341 365
Mary 336 366 Mary Hogsett
398 Miriam 366 Mr 552 Nancy
230 Polly 241 363 Rachel 363

626

BROWN (continued)
S L 591 Wesley 363 William
L 148
BROWNLEE, Mrs 254
BRUFFEY, Anna 146 Bradford
118 Caroline 490 591 Eliza
117 466 Elizabeth 117 165 532
Harriet 117 Ida 118 John 117
505 John Jr 118 Julia 117
Lavinia 117 503 Lizzie 118
Maggie 118 Margaret 117
Martha 117 Mary 118 162 Mrs
T A 120 Murray 118 Nancy 117
P 608 Patrick 146 162 165 237
238 491 T A 118 120
BUCHER, Amanda 125
BUCKHANNON, Mary Ann 155
BUCKLEY, 96 384 Elizabeth 195
Hannah 211 Hetty 211 293
John 211 230 385 Joseph 195
212 Joshua 202 210-213 230
293 499 Lucinda 202 Mary 230
Mrs John 385 Polly 230
BUMGARDNER, Adam 228
BURGESS, 155 Archibald 353
David 352 353 Eliza 536
Elizabeth 352 353 Hampton
352 Hannah 353 James 352
353 Jane 352 John 351-355
John Jr 352 354 Martha 352
353 Mary 352 353 Mrs Hamp-
ton 352 Mrs John 352 Nancy
352 Nathan 352 Paul 353
Susan 353
BURGOYNE, Gen 354
BURK, Jennie 221
BURKE, Virginia 392
BURNER, 96 Abram 426-428
Adam 426 Allen 427 Andrew
427 Caroline 391 427 Charles
427 Daniel 426 Elizabeth 191
392 426 427 515 Emma 427
Enoch 427 487 George 100 193
426 427 429 515 Harry 392
Henry 426 Hodie 127 Isabella
148 427 Jacob 426 Jennie 426
John 423 Joshua 426 Keziah
426 Lafayette 391 427 Lee 391
427 Lula 427 Margaret 426 428
Mary 193 426 Mary Jane 165
Miss 493 Nancy 427

BURNER (continued)
Nannie 427 Rachel Ann 427
487 Rebecca 391 423 427 Sally
427 429 Virginia 427
BURNSIDE, James 584 O S G 613
Asbury 540 Elizabeth 153 219
224 James 153 John 220
Margaret 219 438 Martha 501
Mary 220 William 438
BURR, 96 Aaron 119 Catherine
282 Elizabeth Jane 166 Fred-
erick 166 582 587 George 582
John 282 Mary 473 Sallie 119
Susan 183 William 183 582
BURRIS, George 612 Lydia 612
BUSSARD, 96 Adolphus 540
Alcinda 539 Armenius 290 538
Armnius 218 Arthelia 540
Asbury 540 Benjamin 538 Cora
539 Cornelius 131 540 Cronin
540 Eleanor 540 Eli 290 538
539 Ellis 216 539 Fannie 538
Frances 538 George 540 Henry
538-540 Hester 538 Jackson
356 Jerusha 540 Jesse Allen
539 John 593 Laura 539
Margaret 290 538 Martha 191
538 539 Mary 539 Mary Ann
540 Mildred 540 Minnie Ursula
216 Miss 334 Morgan 539
Moses 540 Mrs Eli 539 Mrs
Henry 540 Mrs Reuben 538
Mrs Wesley 539 Nancy 289
539 Perry 539 Perry Lee 539
Peter 289 539 Phoebe 539
Rachel 539 540 Reuben 538-
541 Reuben Jr 538 540 Reuben
Sr 191 Rhoda 539 Sally 540
Sampson 538 540 Samuel 540
Sarah 356 539 Sherman 539
Solomon 334 538-540 Susan
291 334 538-540 Virginia 539
Wesley 539
BUTCHER, Bayliss 138 F 138
Martha 138
BUZZARD, Armenius 584 Elean-
or 339 Eli 133 Henry 227
Hester 189 J H 356 Jane 373
John 373 Mary 227 Mary Ann
342 Perry 584 Rachel 189
Reuben 189 342 Sampson 339

BUZZARD (continued)
Solomon 189
BYRD, 236 Eveline 506 Rebecca
155
BYRNSIDES, Mary 334

-- C --

CACKLEY, 96 A M 198 Alice 129
197 Ann 199 Anne 118 197 198
Benjamin 197 199 Caroline
162 199 325 Claiborne 199
Davis 199 Frye 129 199
Hannah 199 Jacob 198 200 491
James 499 Jennie 129 198
John 199 Joseph 197 199 Leah
199 509 Lee 119 Levi 197 198
303 508 Levi Jr 334 Mary 197-
199 491 Nancy 198 303 508
Polly 129 Rebecca 119 197
198 Robert 199 Sarah Jane 199
Valentine 197-200 499 Valen-
tine Jr 199 Valentine Sr 118
197 199 William 73 102 119
129 197-199 334 407 William
H 199 William J 162
CADY, Hannah 355
CALAHAN, Miss 113
CALL, Susan 328 Thomas 328
CALLAHAN, Margaret 290
CALLISON, 596 Abbie 130 Abi-
gail 435 437 438 Abram 437
Anthony 435 437 438 502
Anthony Jr 437 Elisha 435 438
Elizabeth 434 435 437 438 502
Ellen 436 Fannie 436 Frankie
437 George 168 435 436 504
Hannah 435 Huldah 437 Ima
532 Isaac 172 435-437 503
Israel 437 542 James 102 434-
439 502 532 584 James B 503
Jane 436 Jemima 437 Jesse
435 Joseph 437 542 Josiah 436
437 Julia 130 265 438 515
Laura Frances 532 Mandie 436
Margaret 435 438 542 Martha
437 Mary 435 437 502 542
Minta 436 Miriam 503 Miss
190 Mrs George 504 Nancy 121
172 435 436 438 441 503 505
Quincy 532 Rebecca 435 436

CALLISON (continued)
Richard 347 423 424 436 Ruth
435 Samuel 435 Susan 435
Thomas 532 Thomas F 436
William 435 436 William H
532
CAMBRIAN, Era 30
CAMERON, Andrew W 251
Charles 249 251 269 John 251
John H 252 Miss 252 Mrs Dr
W T 253 Rachel 251 W T 253
CAMPBELL, Alcinda 182 Almira
162 Amos 509 Anna Laurie
161 Austin 551 Benjamin B
145 Brown 145 E 593 Effie 218
Hetty 294 Isabella 116 J E 218
James B 182 Judge 590 Levi
H 125 Lillie 551 Luther 145
Margaret 125 145 Martha Jane
509 Mattie 145 Mr 592 Mrs
Austin 551 Mrs Thomas 145
Mrs Wiliam Price 160 Sterling
294 Stuart 145 Thomas 116
145 372 373 509 Virginia 551
Walter P 551 William 162
William G 496 William P 546
William Price 160 161
CANAAN, Lewis 565 566
CANTER, J W 509 Martha Jane
509
CANTERBURY, Mary 341
CARAWAY, Mrs William 422
William 422
Carboniferout Era, 32
CARLYLE, 574
CARPENTER, Charles 192
Fletcher 192 Hanson 192 Hugh
192 I C 593 John 316 Margaret
192 316 Mary 316 Nancy 316
Peter 316 Rachel 192 Sydney
321 William 316 William H
582
CARROLL, Laura 444 Mr 444
CARSON, J C 378 Maggie 378
CARTER, Lee 369 472 Mary 369
Page 114
CARTMILL, Thomas 245
CASEBOLT, 96 Anna 176 Barbara
Ann 177 178 Hannah 177
Harvey 405 Henry 176 185
Jane 405 Jefferson 177

COCHRAN (continued)
Biddie 424 Bruffey 424 425
Catherine 425 Catherine Jane
282 Clark 424 425 584 Col 603
David 350 423 424 454 461
David J 426 David James 422
424 Deemie 423 Elisha 424
Eliza 423 Elizabeth 308 384
422-425 Eveline 424 Fannie
423 Franklin 423 George 348
349 351 424 George B 584
George Brown 424 Gordon 423
Hannah 424 454 Harriet 423
Isaac 384 423 Jackson 424
James 219 423 424 Jane 155
424 425 Jennie 349 423 424
Jesse 349 423 424 John 102
155 302 349-351 422-425 559
Joseph 424 Lewis Presley 424
Lincoln 349 Margaret 423 424
Mary 368 422-424 Melinda 282
425 Miss 422 Mrs David
James 422 423 Mrs John 424
Mrs Thomas 422 423 Nancy
219 422 424 425 Nellie 348-
350 423 424 Peggy 423 Phoebe
425 Porter William 424
Rachel 424 Rebecca 423 424
Richard 423 Robert 423 Sabrie
423 Sallie 155 Sally 336 423-
425 Samuel 423 424 Sarah 424
Solomon 384 423 424 Solomon
Salisbury 424 Susan 424
Thomas 336 337 348-350 422-
426 Thomas Jr 423 Washing-
ton 425 William 74 282 302
308 394 423-425 William Jr
425
COCKE, Margerie 161 Rev 161
COCRHAN, Fannie 302
COFFEE, Henry 285 Lizzie 285
COHN, M 554
COLAW, Elizabeth 210 J M 210
COLE, Rebecca 114 William 582
COLLINS, Adam 415 Alice 414
Amanda 415 Amanda Cather-
ine 414 Andrew 414 Andrew
Morgan 414 Barbara 412 415
Benjamin 411 413 414 Birdie
414 Caroline 415 Celia 415
Charles 412-415

COLLINS (continued)
Charley 109 241 Effie Alice
415 Elizabeth 412 413 Emma
414 Hannah 211 Henrietta 413
James 412 413 James Solo-
mon 414 Joanna Susan 415
John 289 412-415 John Riley
414 John William 415 Lewis
412 413 415 Luella May 414
Margaret 413-415 Martha 289
413 414 Mary 412-414 Mary
Elizabeth 414 Miss 402 Nancy
409 413 414 Nancy Jane 411
414 Peter 414 Sallie 414 Sally
413 Sally Joice 415 Samuel
414 415 Susan 414 Susannah
412 413 Vernie 414 W H 415
William 109 413 415 William
H 412 415 William Hunter 414
William Hutcheson 414
Composite Character, 96
CONAWAY, John 413 Martha 413
Conclusion, 618
CONRAD, Alice 398 Charles 398
David 398 400 Eliza 398
Elizabeth 398 Emory 398
Harmon 398 Huldah 398 John
398 John H 397-400 Margaret
398 528 Marietta 398 Mary 398
Mary Ann 398 399 Mary
Hogsett 398 Mrs Solomon 399
Nancy 398 400 Sally 398 400
Solomon 398-400 528
COOK, Elizabeth 372
COOL, Elizabeth 222 John 222
COOMBS, Mrs A 129
COOPER, 96 392 Agnes 478 Anna
392 Arthur 477 Charles 478
Charles Calvin 478 Elizabeth
477 Flora 477 George 478
George C 478 George Clark
478 Harriet 124 478 J W 478
James 101 476-479 James
Amos 478 James Harvey 478
Jane 477 John 478 John T 477
John William 478 Joseph W
478 Julia Ann 478 Lucinda 477
Margaret 477 Mary 133 478
Melinda 477 Nancy 477 Nancy
Agnes 476 Rachel 478 Rachel
Tallman 478 Rebecca 478

COOPER (continued)
Robert 478 Sadie P 616
Snowden 478 Thomas 477
Vivian 478 Walter 478 William 124 133
CORBETT, Mustoe H 582
CORBY, Miss 422
Corn, first ripe 69
County Records, 607
COURTNEY, Andrew 265 Andrew
Jackson 365 Ann 365 George
W 365 George Washington 365
Hannah 365 Hanson 365 James
365 Jane 365 Joe 375 Julia
365 Thomas 365
COX, Mary B 546
COYNER, Annette 261 Louisa
261
Crabbotom, battle of 575
CRAIG, 587 Caroline 259 Elizabeth 429 George E 259 John 12
23 343 Lizzie 118 Margaret
Ann 80 Nancy 431
CRAVENS, L P 616
CRAWFORD, A 593 Anna 175
Margaret Henderson 379 Nancy
486
CRIST, Susannah 284
CROCKETT, Mrs 253
CROOKMAN, Sarah Ann 443
Wasley 443
CROUCH, Andrew 564-567
Andrew Sr 565 Dolly 256
Elizabeth 209 Jacob 140 209
John 245 Joseph 564 Rachel
140
CROW, Miss 208
CROWLEY, Esta 399 J C 399
CROZET, 74
CRUIKSHANKS, Harriet 117
Rebecca 120 121 Wesley 117
CRUMMETT, William 312
CUMPSTON, Rebecca 190
CUNNINGHAM, 8 Eula Joe 448 J
M 448
CURLE, Clayton 552 Nellie 552
CURRY, 96 167 Abigail 492
Adam 311-315 Anna 492
Bessie 370 Caroline 217
Charles 493 Charlotte 493
Cyrus 102 Eliza Ann 456

CURRY (continued)
Elizabeth 492 493 Ellis 369
Emma 370 Enos 456 493 G H
396 Harvey 271 376 Isaiah
492-495 J H 316 J Harvey 218
369 James 405 492 493 John
492 493 584 Julia 407 Lucy
120 Margaret 270 405 492-494
Mary 164 370 Miss 133 Mrs
Charles 493 Mrs Ellis 369 Mrs
Enos 493 Mrs G H 396 Mrs
Harvey 376 Nancy 492 493
Robert 492 493 Sally 410 492
493 Sarah 369 Venie 493
Virginia 493 William 120 311
314 370 492 509 510 591
CURTIS, John 456 Mary Elizabeth 456
CUTLIP, Abram 348 David 348
Elizabeth 348 George 348 John
348 Martha 152 348 Sally 348
William 584

- D -

DAINGERFIELD, Foxhall A 585
Miss 554
DAMERON, Andrew 591
DAUGHERTY, 358 Andy 314
Elizabeth 401 Isabella 400
John 401 Margaret 400-402
Martha 400 Michael 400-403
Mrs William 402 Samuel 401
402 William 401 402
DAVIDSON, Henrietta 413 Judge
413
DAVIES, Margaret 514
DAVIS, Anne 477 Martha 137 142
Raymer 477
DAWSON, Major 265
DAY, Martha 150 Miss 460
DEAVER, James 482 Margaret
482 Mr 409 Sally 482
DELANEY, 464
DENNIS, R F 591 T H 591
DEPUTY, Lena 320
DEVER, 96 Alcinda Susan 381
Alice 324 Dennis 112 Dennis
W 324 Frances 395 Francis
112 114 115 181 Hugh 181 381
John 115 Margaret Jane 115

DEVER (continued)
Matilda 395
Devonian Era, 10 Rocks 32
DICKINSON, 8 Capt 575 576 Miss
258 Mrs 235
DIDDLE, Mrs 350
DILLE, 301
DILLEY, A L 527 Amanda 523
Amelia 433 523 Amos 524
Amos J 524 Andrew 113 419
521 522 524 525 Ann 300 524
Araminta 524 Birdie 221
Caroline 524 Clark 131 523
584 Clayton 523 527 Daniel
300 Davis 523 Elizabeth 300
445 523 524 Elizabeth Martha
524 Ellen 178 300 Ernest 524
Everett Amos 524 F M 360
527 Fletcher 221 523 Frances
300 Frank 520 George 433 523
525 Georgia 523 Hannah 112
290 522 Hannah Jane 523
Hanson 524 Henry 214 298-302
523 Howard Dennis 524 Ibbie
523 Iizzie 360 Isabel 523
Jeremiah 407 523 John 178
300 419 523 525 Joseph 176
299 Kenney 523 Margaret 132
214 299 407 523 Martha 113
290 518 521 524 Martin 102
112 290 298 300 419 522-526
Martin Clark 132 Mary 178 300
519 520 523 524 527 Mary Ann
176 299 Mary Jane 291 299
Missouri Francis 524 Mrs
Daniel 300 Nancy 221 523
Naomi 383 523 Noah Patterson
524 Peachy 299 Peter 523
Rachel 519 524 Ralph 291 299
416 524 Rebecca 523 Register
523 Summers 523 Thomas 299
Uriah Hevener 524 Virgie May
524 William 178 300 593
William Andrew 524 Wilson
523
DINWIDDIE, Sallie 146
DODDRILL, Elizabeth 614
DODS, Christina 114 Christine
472
DOLAN, Capt 328 Mrs Capt 328

DONAHUE, Barbara Ann 177 178
John 178
DONALDSON, Eliza Jane 386
DONIPHAN, Col 356
DORMAN, Frances 253 Mrs
General 253
DORR, C P 261 Mrs C P 261
DOTSON, Miss 177
DOUGHERTY, Elizabeth 611
George 611
DOYLE, 96 588 James H 597
DRENANN, 108 DRENNAN 96
108 121 420 Elizabeth 303
Jacob 303 Larry 560 Sally 296
560
DREPPARD, Clay 192 Ida
Missouri 192
DREPPERD, Ann 300
DRINNAN, Franklin 190 Law-
rence 231 Rebecca 190 Sally
231 Thomas 190
DRINNON, Bettie 460 Charles
459 460 462 463 Elizabeth 460
462 Jacob 462 James 460 462
John 460 461 Lawrence 459-
464 558 Mrs Lawrence 460
Mrs Thomas 462 Rebecca 460
Sally 460 Susan 460 Thomas
459-462 466 521 Walter 459-
464 William 462
DUFFIELD, 96 470 Abram 113
393 451-455 Andrew 230 452
453 464 Andrew Jr 452 Caroline 454 Catherine 452 Eliza
452 Emory 453 Hamilton 453
Hannah 113 424 452-454 Jane
230 464 John 453 454 John R
230 475 Margaret 231 Martha
453 Mary 454 473 McKendree
453 Nancy Ellen 453 Newton
231 452 453 Rebecca 230 453
454 Rebecca Jane 452 Robert
M 452 Sarah Jane 453 Wesley
453 William 231 452-454 584
DUNCAN, 96 470 Henry 282 294
420 J H 584 Julia A 369
Martha 420 Mary 294 Rachel
282 Sarah 420 William 420
584 William A 295
DUNKUM, 115 390

633

GALFORD (continued)
William Wellington 271
GALLAHER, Harriet 148 Patrick
148
GAMBLE, Eliza 257 Mary 257
Robert 257
GAMMON, C S 583 Cyrus 509
Elizabeth 148 509 Franklin
509 Jane 509 John 509 Martha
509 Martha Jane 509 Thomas
509 W T 590 William 509 583
William T 148 William
Tallman 509
GARDNER, Cornelia 285 286
William 285
GARVEY, John 315
GATEWOOD, 96 A C L 253 259
584 A L 582 Andrew 259 260
Catherine 252 Charles 261
Eliza 252 Eugenia 252
Frances 252 253 Hannah 261
Hannah Moffett 259 Jane 252
253 260 Margaret 252 Mary
259 Mary Jane 252 253 Mary
Pleasants 253 Miss 253 Nancy
260 261 514 Sally 261 Samuel
Vance 252 Susan 253 Thomas
260 Warwick 252 William 252
260 William Bias 253
GAWTHROP, Ida 166 John 166
GAY, 96 208 420 A P 281 Abbie
130 Abigail 438 Agnes 129 384
Alfred D 584 Alice 129 197
198 Andrew 129 384 Ann 503
Ann Maria 512 Bettie 464
Edward 511 Effie 281 Elizabeth 520 Flora 465 George 129
130 183 503 Hamilton B 334
Hannah 128 129 284 511 Harriet 511 520 James 129 130 429
438 511 Jennie 129 198 John
129 130 183 327 384 511-513
Joseph C 129 520 Levi 120
121 128 196 231 332 511 543
Margaret 429 Margaret B 130
511 Martha 453 Mary Catherine 464 Melinda 120 Miss 334
Mrs 513 Mrs Levi 543 Nancy
196 Polly 129 196 Rachel 334
Robert 100-103 128-131 178
198 284 334 464 511 591 608

GAY (continued)
Ruth 465 Sallie 129 Sallie
Hamilton 512 Sam 334 Samuel
129 Samuel M 196 198 342 511
Sarah Ann 129 342 Susan 130
183 310 511 William 129 453
William Sr 461
GEIGER, Adam 365 Annie 409
Godfrey 365 Hannah 365 Jane
365
Geographical, 51
GIBBONS, Miss 134 S B 134
GIBBS, James E A 54
GIBSON, 96 218 284 404 Caroline
329 Catherine 210 Clara 210
David 195-197 496 520 521
Elizabeth 195 196 209 210 Eva
Rebecca 209 George 182 198
225 Henry 394 Jacob 196
James 177 196 224 225 James
Sr 375 Jennie 196 John 195
196 281 Joseph 209 Kemper
209 Lizzie 521 Martha Susan
225 Mary 195 196 226 330 520
Mary Alice 216 Mary Ella
Frances 226 Mary Jane 177
Miss 219 Mrs George 182 Mrs
Jacob 196 Nancy 196 Polly
129 196 Rachel Ann 225
Robert 226 520 Sally 195 324
Samuel 128 226 Squire 351
Susan 281 William 19 56 65
73 196 209 330 350 519 593
William D 209 William Sr 329
GILBERT, Theresa 616
GILLESOIE, Joseph 124 Naomi
124
GILLESPIE, Amos 411 477 Jacob
426 486 Jennie 426 John 483
John Alexander 477 Lucinda
477 Margaret 426 477 Margaret
Virginia 483 Martha 477 Mary
477 Miss 133 377 508 Nancy
477 Rachel 477 486 Rachel
Ann 411 Rebecca 486 Taylor
477 Wise 477
GILLILAN, Agnes 129 Alexander
129 Catherine 464 Electa 118
Elizabeth 208 George 118
Jennie 118 John 118 208 436
480 Lydia 118 Margaret 118

RT Gay p 464
m. Bettie

GILLILAN (continued)
Martha 118 Mary 118 480
Mattie 118 Nancy 118 Rebecca
436 Richard 118 Samuel 118
Sarah 118 Shadrach Chaney
118 Talitha 118
GILLILAND, Catherine 469
Elizabeth 169 170 George 1699
James 168-170 James Sr 170
Jane 169 John 469 Lydia 168
169 Mary 168 169 Mrs James
168 Nancy 169 Nathan 169
Polly 168 169 Robert 169
Samuel 169 Sarah 169 William
169
GILLISPIE, 96 Jemima 488
GILMORE, 266 Alexander 145
Jemima 501 Sallie 145 Samuel
501
GINGER, G W 593 George W 489
Martha 489 Miss 489 Mr 489
GIRTY, Simon 227
GIVENS, Elizabeth 508 Mr 508
Rachel 145
GOELET, 356
GOFF, Margaret 488 Mr 488
GOODE, Mary Pleasants 253
Samuel 253
GOODMAN, 115
GOODRICH, John 309
GOULET, Reddy 395
GRAGG, Caroline 415 David 164
Luella May 414 Margaret 387
Mr 387 Mrs Zebulon 387 Sally
Ann 387 Zebulon 387 415
GRAHAM, 189 574
GRANDFIELD, John 583
GRANT, Major 244 Miss 542
Grasses, their value 79
GREAVER, Emma K 324
GREGG, Rachel 126 Zebulon 126
GREGORY, Clarissa 320 Isaac
275 Knapp 52 53 Samuel 273
GRIFFEY, Nancy 384
GRIFFIN, Abraham 332 336
Benoni 332 Jonathan 332 490
M P 583 Maggie 490 Margaret
385 Miss 332 336 Nancy 336
Rachel 332
GRIMES, Abraham 191 193
Addison 193 Allen 193

GRIMES (continued)
Amanda 190 216 Angeline 190
191 Arthur 189 190 194 195
317 332 Arthur Jr 190 Brumby
193 Bryson 194 Catherine 188
194 Charles 189 191-193 281
538 Clark 584 Cora 191 Crai-
gan 192 Craigin B 193 David
189 194 David G 190 Davis
189 Eleanor 194 Elizabeth 191
193 194 426 441 Elizabeth
Catherine 192 Elmer E 192
Esta 194 Ezra 193 Fannie 193
Felix 103 188-195 Fletcher
191 Francis 193 Frank 584
Franklin 189 George 194 426
George C 194 Georgiana 193
Granville 194 Hanson 190
Henry 189 191 193 287 538
Hester 189 538 Hugh 189 Ida
Missouri 192 J Barnett 194
James 189 190 193 194 Jane
189 191 John 189-191 426 441
John Wesley 191 Lavinia 190
Leah 190 226 Loretta 290
Loretta Jane 193 Lucy 194
Mantie 191 Margaret 189 190
192 193 196 Margaret Jane 317
Martha 191 538 Martha S 193
Mary 189 190 193 194 332 426
Mary Cullum 192 Minnie 190
Miss 113 Morgan 189 191 194
316 317 538 Mrs Abraham 191
Mrs Morgan 316 Nancy 176
189 191 194 Newton 190 Onie
Jane 191 Peter 189 583 Peter
H 193 584 Rachel 189 192 281
539 Rachel A 193 Rebecca 190
460 Rebecca Jane 190 Rettie
194 Sally 189 317 332 Sarah
132 Scott 194 Seba 193 Susan
370 Susan L 192 Thelia 193 W
C 191 Wesley 190 William
194 William Davis 192 Zane
189 Zane B 584 Ziona 194
GROGG, John 387
GROSE, William 592
GROVES, Ann Eliza 120 Mansfield 120 Martha 120 Oscar
120
GUM, Aaron 161 Agnes 391

636

GUM (continued)
Alice 398 Anna 392 395
Blanche 392 Brown 391 493
Caroline 391 427 Caroline
Amanda 388 Charles 392 482
Charlotte 493 Dolly Bell 482
Eliza 391 Elizabeth 325 387
392 Ella 391 Fannie 489
Filmore 391 Francis McBryde
387 Franklin 391 Gatewood
392 George 391 Harriet 392
482 Henry 395 396 Isaac 161
Jacob 386 390-393 Jacob Jr
392 James Floyd 387 James
Henry 387 Jane 392 Jennie 270
John 392 395 489 John E 392
482 Joseph 392 Lee 391
Lucretia 395 Margaret 391 482
Margaret Elsie 387 Margaret
Jane 395 Marietta 391 Martha
390 489 Martha Jane 391 Mary
161 391 Mary Etta 432
McBride Jackson 391 McBryde
388 389 Milton 391 398 Nancy
391 Nebraska 399 482 Nellie
391 Otho 270 Rebecca 391 427
Robert N 392 476 Sallie 391
Sally 396 488 Sally Ann 387
Samuel 391 Sarah 324 Tilda
387 Virginia 392 Virginia
Elizabeth 387 Warwick 482
William 391 392 427 482 488
William A 386-390 William
Alleghany 390 William M 391
Woods 391 Zachariah 396
GUMM, 96
GWIN, B Austin 508 David 508
Eliza 508 Elizabeth 508
Hester 295 James Sr 295 Jane
508 John 508 575 John Jr 508
Margaret 508 Mrs John Jr 508
Nancy 508
GWINN, John Sr 323 Nancy 323

- H -

HACKETT, Peter 244
HADDEN, Mary 405 Stephen 287
Susannah Crist 287
HAINES, J B 583 John 592 593

HALL, Abigail 492 Alexander 236
Elizabeth 401 John 225 Marga-
ret Elizabeth 225 Martha 515
HALTERMAN, 96
HAMBRICK, Amanda Pleasant
225 William Lee 225
HAMILTON, 96 A G 583 A H 263
Alice M 550 Bryson 520
Charles Atlee 550 Davis 593
Ellen Frances 550 Emma 395
Eugenia Gatewood 550 Gawyne
124 George 395 Georgia 523 J
M 592 John 236 457 John
William 550 Madora 124 554
Mary 520 Mary Sophia 550
Mary Winters 263 Medora
Sabina Beard 550 Mrs 236
Paul Price 550 Rose L 550
Sally 318 Sue Margaretta 550
Virginia Agnes 550 William
74 550 551
HAMPTENSTALL, Margaret 542
HANDLEY, Mary 118
HANK, Jehu 547 John 547 Miss
616 Rebecca 547
HANNA, Elizabeth 138 Julia 152
M A 208 Mark 169 Mary 515
Miss 424 S B 165 William 138
HANNAH, 96 196 Albert 225
Amanda 221 281 Amanda
Pleasant 225 Andrew 225
Andrew Warwick 225 Ann 219
Bessie 225 Birdie 221 Bryson
182 225 464 Burleigh 222
Carrie 225 Catherine 221 Clark
225 David 215 218-224 226
330 366 464 496 530 David Sr
219 Davis 225 Dora 225 Dr 219
Edgar Russell 221 Effie 225
Eliza Jane 215 Elizabeth 219
220 222 224 226 464 473
Emma Bell 225 Eugenius 221
Feltner 225 Forrest 225 Fred-
erick 225 George 226 George
Luther 225 George Preston 190
Georgiana 225 Henry 225 226
Hester 226 Hugh 225 Isabella
220 329 Ivie Viola 221 J B 584
J E 226 James 221 232 Jane
225 226 Jennie 219 221 530

HEROLD (continued)
B F 583 Benjamin 373 374 C
B 583 Catherine 373 Charles
373 374 Christopher 328 329
372-376 Christopher Jr 374
Daniel 374 Eliza 407 Eliza-
beth 208 372 373 Elizabeth
Ann 373 Eugenia 374 Henry
102 208 373 Horace F 374 Ida
Rebecca 374 Isaac Newton 374
Jane 373 John L 374 Joseph
374 Josiah 373 374 380 Kate
161 Katie 329 Lanty W 374
Lucy 374 Maria 209 373 374
Mary 374 Mary Ann 374 380
Millard F 374 Mrs L W 208
Myrta 374 Peter 329 373-375
Pruyn Patterson 374 Rachel
Ann 395 Sally Ann 374 Sarah
Ann 395 Susan 328 373
Washington 209 373 395
William 373 395 Wise 161
373
HERRING, Anna 161 Bethuel 161
HERRON, Elizabeth 528 Leonard
217 Mary Ann 217
HEVENER, 96 George 394 Harvey
410 John 146 Martha 254 410
Mrs Harvey 410 Nancy 493
Samuel 493 U S A 193 Uriah
254 256 376 388 527 Virgie
193
HEVNER, Anise 281 D 281
HICKLIN, 574
HICKMAN, Elizabeth 210 Huldah
437 Jane Elliot 507 Lanty 210
Martha 210 Mary 507 Roger
210 William 507
HICKS, Lizzie 474
HIDY, Sarah 443
HIGGINS, Comfort Slaven 388
Elizabeth 387 Henry 320
James 398 Nancy 320 William
273 274
HILL, 96 Aaron 119 406 501
Abraham 117 119 Abram 117
370 Alice 152 Allen 120 Ann
120 Ann Eliza 120 Anna 532
Anne 118 198 Archibald 120
Caroline 120 Chalmers 121
Claiborne 120 Cora 152

HILL (continued)
Davis 119 Doctor 119 Elizabeth 117 119 120 516 517
Elizabeth Araminta 406 Enoch
477 Ernest 532 Eveline 118
Franklin 120 George 117-120
370 440 502 532 Harriet 477
Henrietta 121 Isaac 117 119
120 151 153 440 Jennie 119
440 Joel 117 119-121 183 314
315 John 102 115 117 119-121
436 517 590 Joseph 120 Lavinia 119 Lena 532 Lucy 120
Maggie 118 Margaret 117-120
477 Margaret Jane 532 Martha
117 118 120 370 437 440 Mary
118 119 172 532 Mary Frances
120 183 Melinda 120 Minnie
121 Miriam 501 503 Miss 370
Nancy 117-120 138 436 501
Nannie 477 Peter 119 532 R W
314 Rebecca 119 120 121
Richard 116-122 138 154 228
463 466 517 558 Richard
Washington 120 Robert 119
Sallie 119 Sarah Ann 151
Sherman 532 Simon 532 Sterling 121 Thomas 117-119 152
172 198 Wallace 121 William
117 119 120 503 William P
516 Wilson 532
HILLERY, Frederika 270
HINER, Jane 319 John 319
HOGGSETT, J T 148 Martha 148
HOGSETT, 96 221 Eliza 509
Elizabeth 508 509 Elizabeth
Ann 373 Ina Josephine 456
John 199 509 Josiah T 490
Josiah Thomas 509 Kenney
151 Leah 199 509 Margaret
490 509 Mary 317 509 Nancy
509 Samuel 101 508 509
Samuel Jr 373 Samuel Renick
456 William Perry 509 Wil-
liam R 583
HOGSHEAD, Miss 155
HOLCOMB, A T 613 Anselm T
612 P H 613 S C 613 Sarah 612
Susan 316 Susannah 612
HOLDEN, Elizabeth 328 331
James 592

HOLDEN (continued)
John 328 329 592 593
HOLLOWELL, Israel 309
HOLMES, Mary 202
HOLSTOIN, Elizabeth 547 Mr 547
HOLT, E I 256 Judge 590 Mrs E I
256 Mrs Samuel 256 Samuel
256
HONEYMAN, Nancy 404
HOOKER, Levi 117 Nancy 117
HOOVER, Abel 387 Amanda
Catherine 414 Birdie 414
Nannie 477 Tilda 387 Vernie
414 Washington 477 William
414
HOUCHIN, Caroline Amanda 388
Comfort Slaven 388 Ellis 388
Martha 390
House raising, 61
HOWELL, Janeat 612 Levi 615
HUDSON, Bird 482 Clara Margie
484 Dallas 482 483 David
Warden 483 Davis 482 483
Edward Arbuckle 483 484
Elijah 482–485 Eliza 483
Elizabeth 481 Ethel Grace 484
Frank 483 Harriet 392 482
Hattie Jane 484 Henry Harper
483 Jackson 482 Jesse Arden
483 John L 477 481 John
Letcher 482 483 Keziah 481
Laura 482 Laura Mattie 484
Lucy Elizabeth 484 Luther
Gilbert 484 Madison 482
Maggie 483 Margaret 477 482
Margaret Virginia 483 Marion
Conner 483 Mary 483 Mary
Roxanna 483 Matilda 481
Minnie Ruth 484 Mrs Elijah
485 Nancy 482 483 Nancy Jane
482 483 Naomi 481 Paul
McNeel 482 483 Polly 481
Rachel 481 Rachel Cornelia
Margaret 483 Richard 481–485
Sally 481 Sarah 482 Susan 482
483 Thomas 482 Virginia 484
Warwick 482 Warwick B 481
Warwick Bird 483 William
482 483 William Frank 483
William McNeel 484
HUGES, Milburn 102

HUGHES, Andy 377 Eliza 165
Ellis 108 Frances 202 James
165 Milburn 151 Moses 151
Susanna 151 William 101
HULDER, John 245
HULL, 96 Adam 123 486 Alcinda
380 Andrew 379 434 Anise 443
Charlotte 380 Elizabeth 254
379 430 Esther 431 Eveline
380 Felix 254 Grace 445 Irene
Esther 434 Jesse 379 John 379
431 434 Margaret 123 379 431
434 Mary 426 Mary Ann 380
Nancy Jane 434 Nora 434
Peggy 123 Peter 443 487
Rachel 487 Robert 434 Tokey
381 William 434 William C
380 William Crawford 379
HUMPHREYS, Margaret 16
HUMPHRIES, J C 593 Laura 482
Madison 482 Matilda 481
Thomas 481
HUNTER, Gen 388
Huntersville, Notes 586
Husking Bees, 61
HUTTON, Dolly 257 John 257

– I –

IMBODEN, 602 Gen 387
INDIAN, Cornstalk 7 9 10 15 157
247 249 250 613 Crane 7
Killbuck 7 123 Logan 15
Pontiac 7–9 13 15
INGRAM, Ann 429 Peter 273 274
IRESON, Mary 381
IRVINE, 96 348 Amaziah 230
Cornelia 285 Ellen 230 Hannah
Jane 523 Herron 286 J Wesley
230 John 397 John Wesley 333
Kate 286 Leonard 285 Levi
285 Lizzie 285 Nancy 230
Rebecca 285 287 Robert 397
Susannah 286 Wesley 523
William 230 Wilton 286

– J –

JACKSON, 96 602 605 Amanda
Catherine 414 Anna 433
Louisa 407 Lytle Green 414

KELLISON (continued)
Luther 294 Margaret 294
Marietta Constance 217 Marietta Emmeretta Virginia 217
Mary 536 Nancy 370 Rachel
152 Susan 232 Thomas Bonar
217 Thomas R 217
KELLY, John 584 Magdalen 139
KENNEDY, Mary Jane 253
KENNISON, 96 Catherine 155
Davis 585 Jacob 155 Jane 383
John L 585
KENT, Mrs 253
KERCHEVAL, Col 248
KERR, 96 Adolphus 378 Andrew
377 477 Anne 477 Betsy 376
Caroline 477 D W 590 Daniel
376-378 David 376 David W
378 590 Eliza 378 Elizabeth
165 Fannie Elizabeth 447
George 377 Huldah 398 Jacob
377 398 James 376-378 James
D 447 Jane 477 John 376 377
477 Laura 399 Loring 399
Maggie 378 Mary 165 376-378
Mary Ann 377 Mrs Daniel 376
Mrs Thomas 377 Mrs William
377 Nancy 376 Nannie 477
Phoebe 377 Rachel 377 Rev
496 Robert 165 376 377 Robert
D 377 Thomas 376 377 William 376 377 477
KESSLER, Ella 411 Henry 411
KINCAID, 96 David 339 539 572
James 548 Mary 539 Miss 339
Mrs David 572 573 Nancy Jane
434 Peter H 434 Rosa 548
KINNISON, 137 460 Alice 152
Allen 151 154 Amos 151-153
Caroline 152 Catherine 151
Charles 136 149-154 352 Cora
152 David 151 152 348 David
Dyerly 151 Davis 153 334
Deida 153 Deida Gillespie 152
Doctor Morgan 152 Edward 136
Elizabeth 151 153 348 Elizabeth Ann 151 Esther 151
George Allen 152 Hannah 151
Hezekiah Bland 151 J B 154
Jacob 149-154 James 151
James Claiborne 152 Jane 151

KINNISON (continued)
John 153 John B 152 153 315
John Barlow 152 John Bland
151 John Wesley 152 Kenny
222 Lawrence 151 Margaret
222 Mark 151 Martha 150 152
352 Mrs Davis 334 Nancy 151-153 Nathaniel 151-153 441 442
Rachel 152 Rebecca 151 Sarah
153 Sarah Ann 151 Serena 152
Susanna 151 Thomas Franklin
152 William 151 153
KIRICOFE, Alexander 217 Alice
217
KIRKPATRICK, Miss 376
KNAPP, 247 A J 339 Ann 338
Caleb 338 540 Eleanor 339 540
Elizabeth 338 339 Margaret
339 Nancy 338 R W 339
KNIGHT, Alexander 532 Emma
532 Minnie 532 Susan Virginia
532 Thomas 532
KYLE, David 209 Eva Rebecca
209

- L -

LACEY, William L 399
LACKEY, 577 James 567
LACKEY'S Song, 577
LACKY, Thomas 245
LAFAYETTE, Marquis 384
LAMB, Hannah 337 Jennie 261
Miss 138 William 138
LANCASTER, Sarah 529
LANDES, Gabrielle 433 John 433
LANE, Edward 182 Sally Mildred
182
LARGE, 96
LARUE, James A 543 Lillian 543
Leasons from Stones, 81
LEDBETTER, Emma Mildred
447 Veva 447 W P 447
LEE, 605 Richard 9
LEIGH, Judge 252 Mrs Judge 252
LEONARD, Mary 413 William
615
LEPS, J C 448
LEVISAY, Addie 543 Allan S 543
Carnelis 543 Elizabeth 542
Emma 543 G W 542

LEVISAY (continued)
James W 543 Jennie 544
Jesse 543 Jesse A 542 John
543 544 John Brown 543 John
Granville 543 Joseph 542
Josephine 183 542 Julia 543
Letitia 542 Lillian 543 Louella 542 Louisa 543 Maggie 262
Margaret 543 544 Mary 542
544 Mary Margaret 543 Minnie
543 Miss 543 Mr 544 Rebecca
120 Sabina 543 Samuel Brown
542 Virginia 543 Washington
545
LEWIS, 8 237 Andrew 105 247
Ann 334 Capt 575 576 Charles
7 23 562 Col 106 James 334
339 Miss 339 Nellie 535
Rachel 424 Rebecca 334 Virgil
581
LIGHTNER, 96 247 Adam 145
325 Alcinda 130 181 182 Alice
182 Anthony 394 424 C A 391
Eliza 181 Elizabeth 182 217
324 325 393 Ellzabeth 114
Henry 195 Isabella 325 Jacob
114 181 182 432 Jacob Brown
432 James Cameron 432
Jennie 114 John 114 John
Adam 432 John M 181 182 324
Malcena Catherine 432 Mary
182 Mary Etta 432 Nancy Jane
432 Nellie 145 424 Peter 103
130 180-184 380 397 Peter H
432 Phebe Ann 184 Phoebe
Ann 380 Polly 183 Robert 432
Sally Mildred 182 Samuel M
182 Susan 130 183 Virginia
Rachel 432 William C 432
William Sr 393
LIGON, 96 Annette 261 Eva 261
Georgia 261 John 261 362
Louisa 261 Mabel 261 Rosa
261 Sally 261 Yancey 261
Limestone formed, 32
LINCOLN, Gen 556
LINDSAY, John 539 Sarah 539
LINGER, Matilda Margaret 508
Nicholas 508
LITTLEPAGE, Mr 547 Sally 547
LIVERMORE, Susan 466

LIVINGSTONE, Eliza 483
Location of first Court House,
103
LOCKE, John 297
LOCKHART, Miss 497
LOCKRIDGE, 96 574 Andrew 208
360 482 Augustus 208 Caroline
28 Caroline Elizabeth 381 Dr
260 Eleanor 147 285 Elizabeth
207 208 373 Elizabeth Youel
360 Florence 208 Harriet 208
209 Horace M 208 J B 54 208
James T 208 590 Lancelot 207
Lanty 207-210 381 Lanty Sr
147 Lee 208 Lillie 208 Martha
208 210 Matthias 208 Mrs Dr
260 Mrs Matthias 208 Mrs
Stephen 165 Nancy 482 Nellie
209 Nelly 208 Rebecca 208
209 Stephen 165
LOGAN, 15 Eliza Ann 456 Eliza-
beth 387 519 Ina Josephine
456 James A 387 John 455 493
John Commodore 387 Margaret
387 Mary Elizabeth 456 Miss
493 Nancy Jane 456 Preston
456 Rachel 455 Rebecca 456
Thomas 519 William 456
LONG, Margaret 257 Washington
257
LOOMIS, Aretas 240 Mr 242
LORING, Gen 492
LOURY, 96 J C 588 Joseph 129
Joseph C 334
LOVE, John 308
LOVELY, William Lewis 275
LUDINGTON, Francis 543 James
543
LUZADDER, Anna 444 John 444
LYONS, Enos 582
LYTTON, Nancy 492

- M -

M'AFFERTY, Hannah 363
MACE, Charles 391 Margaret 391
Phoebe 425
Machine, first threshing 65
MacKEMIE, Miss 422
MAD ANN, 579-581
MADISON, James 287 Jim 203

MADISON (continued)
President 252
MAGRUDER, T P W 594
MAHER, Patrick 582
MAKAMIE, 508 509
MALCOMB, James 396 John 339
Margaret 339 444 McCoy 338
339 Miss 339 Mr 444 Sally 396
Thomas 339
MALLETT, Prof 54
MANN, 363 Newton 544
Marble, 71
MARLIN, 52 Jacob 105-108
MARONY, 230 384
MARSHALL, 250 Cecil 256 F P
256 Georgiana 255 J W 360
392 Jacob W 255 585 L J 256
Miss 256
MARTIN, 428 Althea 519 Charles
398 Margaret 342 Mary 398
Samuel 342
MASSENGER, Mary 530
MASSIE, Ellen 259 Eugenia 252
253
MASTERS, Nancy 422
MASTIN, Agnes 547 548 William
A 547 548
MATHENY, Caroline 433 Daniel
432 Esther Ann 432 Mary
Amaret 433 Melissa 432 Miss
166 539 Morgan 433 Robert
432 Sarah Elizabeth 432
MATHEWS, Andrew G 102 115
254 257 Andrew Gatewood 253
Ann 498 Archie 498 Capt 247
Charles 254 482 Edward 255
Eliza 254 Elizabeth 253-255
Elizabeth Wood 265 Ellen 254
Gen 418 George 255 Hunter
255 J W 482 582 Jacob
Warwick 253 Jane 253 255
Joel 265 Lockhart 255 M G
481 Martha 254 Mary 253-255
257 498 Mary W 254 Mary
Warwick 253 254 Miss 254
Mrs 498 499 Mrs Jacob
Warwick 253 Mrs Sampson
497 Nancy 254 Naomi 481
Rachel 254 Sampson 103 199
253 310 497 Sampson Jr 498
Sampson L 101 254 450

MATHEWS (continued)
Sampson Lockhart 253 497-
500 Samuel 481 Withrow 255
MATTHEWS, 96 E B 615 Samp-
son Sr 175 W S 615
MAUPIN, 96 David 488 Harvey
488 Margaret 488 Thomas 488
MAXWELL, Hu 3 36
MAY, Calvin 356 Elijah 356 John
356 Lillie 356 Lizzie 356
Matilda 356
MAYS, Jennie 520
MAYSE, Ada 272 George 207 562
591 Joseph 107 248 249 561-
563 Jubal 272 Mrs 107 563
Mrs Richard 340 Nancy 352
Richard 340 William 352
McALLISTER, J T 591 William
591 William A 327
McALPIN, Margaret 399 Samuel
399
McATEE, Mr 509 Nancy 509
McCANDLISH, Maud Leps 448 R
C 448
McCARLEY, Frank P 615
McCARTY, 96 Albert Granville
406 Amanda 405 Amos Hed-
rick 406 Andrew 407 Annie 406
Calvin 405 Carrie Virginia 406
Catherine 407 Daniel 290 404
407 408 523 Della 396 407 Eli
286 404 405 Eliza 407 Eliza-
beth 290 405-407 Elizabeth
Araminta 406 Ella 407 Ellis
396 407 Fanny 406 Franklin
406 George 286 405-407
George W 584 Hannah 406
Jacob 404 406 James 404 405
James H 406 408 James
William 406 Jane 404 405 407
John 585 John D 396 John
David 407 Julia 406 407 Justin
404 Kate 286 Lanty 407
Leanna Frances 406 Lillie 407
Louisa 407 Mahala 406 Marga-
ret 286 405 407 523 Martha
404 407 Mary 286 405 413
Mary Price 406 Melissa 405
406 Milton 405 Nancy 404 405
Paul 286 Peter 54 290 405 406
584 Phoebe 290 405

McCARTY (continued)
Preston 404 Reuben 404 405
Robert 405 Sally 404 Samuel
290 404-406 Samuel Waugh
405 Sherman 407 Susan 407
Susie 406 Thomas 404 406
Timothy 103 286 404-408
Warwick 405 William 405
McCHESNEY, A G 584 Alexander
263 514 515 Dr 263 Mary
Winters 263 Rachel 263 515
Robert 515 Sally 514 515 Sally
Gatewood 263
McCLAIN, James 245 John 245
McCLARY, Nancy 405 Robert 405
McCLELLAND, Dr 591
McCLENACHAN, 8 Mr 107
McCLINTIC, 108 357 Alexander
579 Archibald 546 Dr 261
Emma 370 F T 575 Jacob 259
John 373 L M 591 Margaret
400 Maria 373 Mary 255 498
Mrs Archibald 546 Mrs Dr 261
Mrs Jacob 259 William 575
William H 255 William T 370
Withrow 382
McCLINTOCK, Robert 101
McCLUNE, Elvira Louisa 431
William 431
McCLUNG, Abigail 437 Charles
460 Cyrus 118 Elizabeth 373
Joseph 140 254 Mary 254
Mattie 118 Miriam 140 Miss
114 181 231 254 491 Mr 373
McCLURE, Arthur 221 225
Bessie 371 Caroline 264
Elizabeth 196 Emma Bell 225
Frances 371 Ida 369 James
196 371 374 Julia 117 Marga-
ret 221 226 Margaret Jane 221
Mary 371 Mrs James 371
Rachel 371 Sarah 371 William
117 371
McCOLLAM, 96 420 Absalom
232 Anna 214 230 Anna Jane
231 Daniel 214 229-234
Fletcher 231 George W 231
Isaac 231 499 Jacob 229
James 229 231 441 459 499
504 Jane 176 230 John 231 232
Lawrence 231 232

McCOLLAM (continued)
Margaret 231 Mary 229 230
Mary Anna 231 Matilda 231
232 Miss 114 Mrs 499 Nancy
230-232 Polly 230 Rachel 230
Rebecca 229-232 464 Ruth 231
232 295 296 499 Sally 231 296
460 463 560 Sarah 229-232 333
Susan 231 232 William 229
231 232 296 460 William
Morrison 232
McCOMB, Alice 282 Andrew
Beckley 282 Charles 282 Eliza
282 George 282 Henry 282
Miss 371 Nancy 282 Price 282
397 Wyllis 282
McCOY, 96 Anna Jane 231 Eliza-
beth 191 441 George 440
Margaret 440 William 191 440
McCRAY, Homer 613 Mrs Homer
613
McCUE, David 139 John 253 254
Martha 139
McCUTCHAN, Aunt Betsy 361
Christina Jane 361 Elizabeth
319 Elizabeth Eleanor 361
Elizabeth Y 361 Elizabeth
Youel 360 Iizzie 360 John
Blain 360 Luther 360 361
Margaret 360 Mary Martha 361
Nancy Caroline 361 Rachel
Bird 360 Robert 360 Robert D
359-362 Robert Dunlap 359
Samuel Hodge 360 William
Andrew Gatewood 360
McCUTCHEN, 239
McCUTCHEON, 96
McCDANIEL, Margaret 445 Sarah
126
McDANNALD, Martha 515
McDERMOTT, Margaret 379 380
Mr 379 380
McDOWELL, 353
McELHENNEY, Dr 156 309 496
John 156
McELHENNY, John 498
McELWEE, 96 B D 585 Bernard
433 527 Burton 527 D B 585
Divers 527 Eliza 126 Frank
126 John 134 527 Mahala 527
Mary Catherine 433

McFARLAND, Nancy 414
McGLAUGHLIN, H P 582
McGRAW, Col 275 J T 125 John
T 618 619
McGUIRE, Ann 338 343 Elizabeth
363 Mr 363 Rebecca 336
McKAMIE, Miss 376 Nancy 506
McKEEVER, Alcinda 295 George
295 Rachel 139
McKINLEY, William 431
McLAUGHLIN, 96 Abigail 281
316 317 Ada 318 Alcinda 317
Alice 324 Amanda 523 Andrew
M 264 325 Anna Margaret 264
Annie 320 Bertha 320 Brown
Letcher 320 Cameron 320
Caroline 199 325 Catherine
320 Charles 320 Christopher
320 Clarence 325 Clarissa 320
Daniel 191 281 316 317 520
David 110 316 456 Edgar 264
Edith 325 Edward 325 Eliza-
beth 234 242 320 324 520
Elmer 320 Emma K 324 Etta
325 445 Ewing 318 Fannie 325
Fred 325 G H 325 George 364
George H 324 George Henry
324 Grace 264 H P 317 321
582 H W 264 Hanson 335
Harper 199 325 445 Hugh 317
319-321 323-327 332 409 508
520 Huldah 510 Huldah
Hickman 508 Isabella 325 J A
317 J H 582 Jacob 321 Jacob
Andrew 324 Jacob C 321 323
Jacob Renick Cassell 320
James 317 318 320 321 James
Hickman 317 332 Jane 191 316
319 456 Jennie 270 319 320
John 315-323 325 520 John A
508 John C 325 John Calvin
324 John Jr 316 318 John M
317 Joseph 317 320 Lawrence
320 Lee 264 Lena 320 Letcher
318 Lola 320 Lovie 320 Lula
264 Lydia 320 Margaret 316
324 Margaret Jane 317 Mary
316 317 325 Mary Alice 320
Mary Elizabeth 317 Mary Jane
317 520 Mary Margaret 264
Mary Martha 520 Melissa 320

McLAUGHLIN (continued)
Minnie Belle 320 Minta 320
Mitchel D 324 Mrs Hanson 335
Mrs Samuel 317 Nancy 316
319 320 323 409 508 Nancy
Jane 324 Nannie 321 Nebraska
320 Rachel 319 Robert 318-
320 Ruhannah 325 Russell 320
Sally 317 318 324 332 Samuel
317 Sarah 324 Sarah Jane 364
Susan 316 324 Sydney 321
William 319 325 William
Andrew Gatewood 320 William
J 510 William Jacob 324
McMILLION, Nancy 119 Sallie
219 Sally 532 William 119
McNAIR, Daniel 353 David 353
Hannah 353 Martha 383
McNEAL, Mary 615
McNEEL, 96 156 A G 585 Abram
101 102 138 139 Andrew 474
Andrew G 584 Andrew Gate-
wood 258 Ann 140 Capt 263
Catherine 140 491 Eliza 258
Elizabeth 138 140 209 519
Esther 151 Eva 261 Eveline
209 George 258 262 Hannah
139 Harriet 209 Harvey Win-
ters 504 Henry 504 Henry
Washington 139 Isaac 101
138-140 195 200 209 464 501
504 507 559 Jacob 139 140 142
501 John 103 117 135-144 150
154 209 211 459 500 John A
141 John Adam 258 John
Henry 501 John Sr 141 143
John W 286 Joseph 504
Joseph B 286 Lanty 504
Louella 156 Lydia 170 M J
128 136 139 140 142 Magdalen
139 140 Maggie 504 Mandie
436 Margaret 138 Margaret
Jane 504 Martha 137-139 142
Mary 139 140 262 501 504
Mary Gold 504 Mathew 209
Mathew John 559 Miriam 138
140 500 Miriam Nancy 504
Miriam Nannie 501 Miss 258
491 Mrs Abram 138 Mrs
George 262 Nancy 117 138-140
Paul 135 139-143 172 257 258

McNEEL (continued)
Paul (continued) 327 450 590
Pauline 504 Peter 491 Phoebe
560 Rachel 139 140 142 209
Rachel Cameron 257 258
Richard 139 140 170 262
Samuel 501 Samuel Ellis 140
Thomas Summers 504 W L
491 Washington 138 William
101 151 William L 415 504
585 William Lamb 139
McNEIL, Absolem 382 Agnes 384
Angelina 384 Anna 383 Asa
385 Charles 383 Charlotte 385
Claiborne 154 336 384 385 499
Clark 383 Comfort 382 D T
385 Daniel 385 Doc 385
Douglas 385 Eliza Jane 386
Elizabeth 371 384 385 499
Enoch 382 385 Fannie 385
Gabriel 382 613 614 Jacob 371
James 384 385 Jane 151 382–
384 499 John 151 350 383 523
John Jr 383 Jonathan 382-384
499 Jonathan Sr 382 Joseph B
383 Joshua B 385 Little John
350 385 Margaret 385 Martha
383 Mary 381 382 613 Miss
385 Moore 371 383 384 386
Mrs Claiborne 336 N C 385
591 Nancy 371 383 384 Nancy
Jane 384 Naomi 382 383 523
Phoebe 382 383 Phoebe Ann
384 Preston 383 Rebecca 382
383 Sarah 385 Thomas 381-
386 614 Ulysses 385 Washington 383 William 353 381 384-
386 499
McNEILL, Anne 280 Daniel 294
James M 303 John 102 280
307 Jonathan 113 Little John
102 Milly 295 Mrs James M
303 Nancy 294 Phebe 113
Thomas 103 William 307
McNULTY, John 308 309 Joseph
309
McWHORTER, Florence Rebecca
166 Judge 590
MEEKS, Mary 332
MESSINBIRD, Henry 610

MILLER, 353 Bowyer 568 Eliza-
beth 255 551 Mr 255 Prof 594
MILLIGAN, Florence 208
MILLS, Nancy 612
Mills, the first 67
MINTER, Jane 401 Mary 401
MITCHE, Sylvester 582
MOFFETT, 8 353 G B 514 G H
585 George B 262 592 George
H 115 263 515 H M 591 Henry
487 Henry M 262 357 509 514
James 262 514 Margaret 514
Margaret Elizabeth 262 Martha
515 Mary Evelina 263 515
Mary Vance 514 Miss 603 Mrs
George H 115 Rachel 263 515
Robert 514 Sally 261 514 Sally
Gatewood 263
MOLLOHAN, John 219 Mary 219
MONROE, Jim 203
MONTGOMERY, 497 Henry 189
Margaret 189 Mary 189 Nancy
189 Samuel C 189 William
189
MOOMAN, Boone 488 Dr 487 E S
488 Flora 488 Frederick 488 J
P 488 James 488 L H 488
Lillian 488 Lucy 488 Mary 488
Nannie 488
MOORE, 96 185 366 558 A J 281
A Jackson 193 317 A Wash-
ington 396 Aaron 103 114 278-
284 288 475 Abigail 281 317
356 Adam C 290 Addison 226
300 453 472 473 Agnes 473
Alcinda 115 488 Alexander 454
472 473 508 Alfred 291 Allen
Taylor 464 Alwilda Nebraska
465 Amanda 221 281 Andrew
282 286 339 464 465 468
Andrew Jackson 280 281
Andrew Washington 112 115
Anise 280 281 Ann 370 465
519 Ann Maria 512 Anna 115
383 396 Anne 280 Annie 474
Aunt Teenie 475 Birdie 473
Brown 299 Bryson 473 C F 504
591 C Forrest 115 C L 507 520
Caroline Frances 290 Catherine 114 279 280 282 369 464

MOORE (continued)

Catherine (continued) 469
Charles King 290 Charles L
114 281 Chesley 115 Chesley
K 397 Chesley K K 456 Chesly
K 119 Christina 114 Christine
472 Clark 117 Col 603 604
Daniel 356 David 112 113 289
291 584 Davis 117 473 E O
387 Effie 281 465 Eliza 117
181 280 282 456 466 Elizabeth
114 226 280-282 290 369 370
387 396 407 464 473 520
Elizabeth Luena 395 Ella 220
330 396 473 Elliot 473 Ellis
281 Elmer 281 Enoch H 473
Ephraim 465 Ernest 115 260
281 Etta 281 Eveline 464 519
Fannie Amoret 290 Flora 465
Florence 473 Forest 281
Frances 280 Frank 474
Frankie 473 Franklin 466
Franklin D 466 George 280 284
287 466 George C 282 303
George Claiborne 280 George
Ellsworth 290 George P 114
117 396 466 Georgia Miami
465 Hannah 108 112 113 128
281 284 290 355 356 452 511
522 Harriet 520 Harry 115
Hattie 290 Henry 280 281 356
370 Henry Harrison 356 Hessie
528 Hester 290 I B 115 I
Brown 116 Ida Rebecca 374 Ira
H 290 Isaac 102 115 221 230
327 417 464 467-472 488 Isaac
Brown 112 Isaac Jr 115 Isaac
Sr 455 Isabella 116 J A 396
Jacob 281 512 520 Jacob S 114
520 James 108 215 280 291
353 464 523 527 James C 113
290 528 James E 114 176 242
395 473 474 James Elliot 472
James R 465 James W 291
Jane 230 280 382 419 420 452
464 465 472 Jefferson 113 291
Jennie 114 280 289 472 520
John 103 108 112-115 181 193
215 280 286 289-292 355 405
407 414 416 420 522 John Jr
291 John Kenney 465

MOORE (continued)

John Register 280 John S 491
John Sutton 473 Joseph 113
215 281 290 291 355-359 419
453 584 Julia 464 519 Kenney
280 Lee 473 474 Levi 103 194
195 284-289 302 582 Levi Jr
285 286 288 332 Levi Sr 128
Lillie 356 Lizzie 356 466 474
Lloyd 473 Loretta 290 Loretta
Jane 193 Lucas 280 Luemma
473 Lula Elizabeth 465 Malinda 115 395 Margaret 108 112-
115 119 280 286 289-291 355
356 405 472 473 527 538
Margaret Ann 490 Margaret
Jane 115 Martha 225 280 286
289 339 356 414 473 Mary 199
280 281 283 286 291 330 355
396 419 421 454 473 523 527
Mary Ann 281 370 464 Mary
Catherine 464 Mary Ellen 465
Mary Jane 285 287 291 299
317 508 520 Mary Martha 520
Mary Winters 473 Matilda 115
287 291 356 Matthias 281 520
Mattie Elizabeth 290 Melinda
280 282 425 Michael 582 Miss
115 290 300 Moffett 473
Mollie 504 Moses 103 108-116
181 278 289 382 452 464-466
472 507 611 Moses C 466
Moses Jr 108 114 Mrs Chesley
115 Mrs Ernest 260 Mrs Isaac
Sr 455 Mrs James C 113 Mrs
Jefferson 113 Mrs John 113
114 181 Mrs John S 491 Mrs
Moses 108 507 Mrs Robert 114
Mrs William 113 475 476
Myrtle Florence 290 Nancy
215 280 281 285 289 332 520
539 Naomi 280 Nelson 280
Newton 396 Pennsylvania John
289 522 Phebe 108 113 Phoebe
290 382 405 Polly 355 Porterfield 465 Preston 115 Price
396 Rachel 280-282 286 296
473 Rachel A 193 Rachel
Christine 176 Rebecca 114 215
221 230 281 285-287 290 339
464 520 Register 356

MOORE (continued)
Ressie 474 Rice 115 Robert
102 103 108 114 117 179 464–
467 469 Robert Jr 230 466
Robert Sr 230 452 Ruth 465
466 S B 464 519 Sallie 466
Sally 285 302 396 Samuel 280
281 Samuel B 114 Samuel
Bryson 465 Sarah 356 Sarah
Jane 453 Sheldon 290 407 507
Susan 281 291 466 611 Susan-
nah 284 Susannah Crist 287
Susie 473 Theodore 280
Thomas 280 281 Uncle Billy
474 Uncle Bobby 467 Virginia
281 W D 317 Wallace 473
Washington 112 115 280 330
396 William 108 113 114 280
290 291 299 355 370 416 417
464 465 472–476 527 William
Allen 473 William D 281 520
William Daniel 280 William
Jeff 290 William Jefferson
193 290 William Rives 465
William Thomas 280 Zane
396
MORGAN, William 102
MORIARTY, Pat 582
MORRISON, Deida Gillespie 152
Elizabeth 368 Hannah 151
James 368 Mr 191 Nancy 191
Sally 536 William 151
MOSER, Lillie 208
Mosses, 83
Mountains, 75
MOYERS, Philip 373 Susan 373
MULLINS, 228
MYLES, Jane 436 Minta 436

– N –

NAPOLEON, 74
Natural Curiosities, 58
Natural Scenery, 55
NEGRO, Aaron 346 610 Ben 608
Bill 610 Charlotte 610 Daffie
609 Daphne 391 Delph 391 609
Dick 228 Eveline 610 Green-
brier Ben 238 246 268 Joseph
212 Lewis 610 Nancy 610
Nathan 464 558 559 Peter 610

NEGRO (continued)
Rachel 610 Sam 246 Thyatira
212
NELSON, John 245 Mr 497 Mrs
497
NESBITT, Margaret 215
NEWCOMER, Nancy 304
NICHOLAS, Isabella 400 Miriam
366 Mrs Thomas 363 Nancy
Ann 456 P 456 Thomas 363
366 400 William 400
NICKEL, Miss 544
NORDAU, Max 418
NOTINGHAM, Emmett 194 Lucy
194
NOTTINGHAM, Adam 527 529
Addison 398 399 528 Amos
399 414 Caroline 528 Charles
269 Elizabeth 527 528 George
412 527 Harvey 190 527 528
Henrietta 529 Henry 456
Hessie 528 Hester 290 Jacob
527 James 527 Jennie 527
Mahala 527 Margaret 291 398
399 527 528 Martha 456 Mary
190 527 528 Mary Elizabeth
414 Miss 113 Mrs Harvey 190
Nancy 133 Rachel 132 Samp-
son 427 Senilda 528 Senilda
Eiler 508 Susannah 412
Washington 508 527 528
William 526–529 William Jr
527–529

– O –

O'FRIEL, Anna 175 Daniel 175
180 James 175 Jeremiah 175
William 175
O'NIEL, 97
OCHELTREE, Mother 228 Sally
195 Sampson 195
OLDHAM, Ann 219 Joseph 219
Lucinda 219 Nancy 153 Sarah
153 William 153 219
OLINGER, Bently 192 Josie
Loretta 192
OLIVER, 316
ORNDORF, Cassie 399 Cora Ella
166 Esta 399 Jesse 166 Laura
399 Lela 399 Mamie 399

ORNDORF (continued)
Margaret 399 Mary Ann 399
Mollie 399 Nebraska 399 482
Oscar 399 482 Oscar Conrad
399 Oscar L 398 William 399
OSBORNE, C 591 Elizabeth 146
OVERHOLT, 96 A J 119 Clara
218 Clarissa 491 George 371
Henry 218 Lee 270 Lydia 270
Mary 194 371 Mary Anna 231
232 Nancy Jane 384 Peter 491
Phoebe Ann 384 Rebecca 119
Reuben E 384 W H 384 Wil-
lard 194
OVERLY, Melissa 405

- P -

PALMER, Dr 594 Maggie 483
Margaret 215
PALSER, Mary J 296
PARKS, Catherine 348
PARSONS, Col 115
PATTERSON, Dr 317 593 F 269
Frank 320 H M 592 J H 149
591 Margaret Eveline 149 Mrs
S P 145 S P 592
PATTON, Frances 253 Lizzie
491 Miss 253
PAUGH, Margaret 192
PAYNE, 352 Dr 591 592 John 155
PECK, Caroline 120 D A 120 511
Daniel 442 Elizabeth 387
Susan 511 512
PEDEN, M L 615 Thomas E 615
PENCE, J W 582
PENICK, Daniel A 258 Eliza 258
PENN, William 301 555
PENNELL, Charlotte 385 Joseph
381 385
PERKINS, Fannie 385 Joseph 349
Mary 198 Miss 540 Rebecca
151 Travis W 103 Willette
198
PERRY, Lula 222
PETER, Simon 495
PEYTON, Howe 207 J Howe 498
591 J T 498
PHARES, Catherine 296 William
296

PHILIPS, Charles 165 Henrietta
529 John 539 Margaret Jane
165 Virginia 539
PHILLIPS, Mr 377 Phoebe 377
PILES, John 582 William L 582
PINNELL, Margaret 543
Pioneer characteristics, 12
POAGE, 96 397 596 Allen 287
Amanda 396 Ann 515 Anna 458
Catherine 519 Cyrus 515
Davies 442 Davis 515 Eliza-
beth 119 396 514-517 519 548
549 Elizabeth Wood 265
Frances 300 Franklin 515 G W
458 George 101 183 288 516
517 George W 353 428 487 516
549 George Washington 514
515 George Washington Jr 516
Henry 295 396 Henry M 300
Henry Moffett 266 Hester 295
J R 396 519 James 180 430
James R 396 515 John 513 514
548 John B 516 John R 130
368 John Robert 266 515 Julia
130 265 438 515 Lizzie 466
Margaret 827 430 514 Margaret
Davies 263 515 550 Martha
515 Mary 196 396 487 514 515
Mary Vance 262 496 514
Moses 515 517 Moses Hoge
514 515 Mrs 262 Mrs George
Washington 515 Mrs Patterson
380 Nancy 261 514 515 Nancy
Warwick 263 496 Nancy
Warwick-Gatewood 260 Pat-
terson 380 Quincy 130 Quincy
W 515 519 Quincy Woods 266
Rachel 514 549 Rachel
Cameron 261 345 Rankin 196
515 Rebecca 516 Robert 513
Sallie Woods 300 Sally Mil-
dred 182 Sally W 266 Samuel
Davies 441 514 516 Sarah Ann
396 William 69 100 103 261
295 345 396 496 513-518
William Anthony 266 William
Jr 101 514 William Sr 516 517
William Woods 265 515
Woods 438
POCAHONTAS, 100

Pocahontas, Streams 52 Mineral
Springs 54
POLLOCK, Mary 543
PORTER, Stephen 235
POST, Eber 443 Serena Catherine
443
POTTS, Carlotta 131 Jonathan
131
PRAY, Anthea 433 Ella 432
Margaret Ann 432 Nelson 272
432 Rebecca 444 Regina 432
PRESTON, 8 Elizabeth 514 J A
591 William C 260
PRICE, 96 Abraham 546 Addison
H 546 Agnes 547 Andrew 265
591 Andrew G 585 Andrew
Gatewood 263 264 Anna
Louise 265 Anna Virginia 265
Calvin W 265 Caroline 264
Elizabeth 427 543 547 Florida
256 Gen 553 George 546 Grace
Clark 549 Grandmother 554
Isaac Austin 546 J A 264 J
Calvin 256 J M 546 J W 519
547 J Woods 594 Jacob 545–
547 Jacob Jr 546 Jame Atlee
548 James 545 546 James A
263 427 515 550 James Atlee
548 James Henry 263 James
Ward 265 John 546 John
Calvin 263 John William 548
Josiah Woods 263 Lura 519
Margaret 545–549 Margaret
Colvert 546 Margaret Davies
263 515 550 Mary 325 546 547
Mary B 546 Mary D 264 Mary
Margaret 264 Medora 548
Medora Sabina Beard 550 Miss
545 546 Mrs Thomas 551
Nancy 140 Norman R 265
Rebecca 547 Sally 545 547
Samuel 545–557 591 Samuel
Davies 264 Samuel III 545
Samuel Jr 545 Sarah 546
Sophia 547 Sterling 552 Susie
A 265 Thomas 545 547–549
551 556 Thomas Jr 548 549
Thompson 548 549 Virginia
548 Virginia Agnes 551 W T
596 Washington 545 546
William 545 546

PRICE (continued)
William C 140 William T 264
265 Winneford 546
PRITCHARD, 96 Alcena 445
Charles 445 Col 250
PUGH, Delilah 132 Frederick 131
132 Marietta 398 Wilson 398
PULASKI, 254
PULLIN, 574
PYLES, J B 540 Jacob 371 Mary
334 Miss 371 Rachel 371 Sally
540 William 334

– Q –

QUEEN, Amanda 415 Elizabeth
412 Rev 415 William 412

– R –

RADER, Nannie 166
RALSTON, Dolly Bell 482 James
245 Robert 482
RANDOLPH, Anna Louise 265
Gov 101 Thomas Mann 100
RANKIN, 422 Abe 183 James 139
Miss 515 Nancy 139 Phebe
182 183
RAPP, Bayliss G 155
RATCLIFFE, Elizabeth 320
Harvey 320
RATLIFF, Bettie 460 Marcellus
453 Nancy 320 Nancy Ellen
453
RATLIFFE, Elizabeth 336 John
336
RAY, Ann 120 Hannah 435 Marion
165
REAGER, 442
RECTOR, George 553 George L
553 Jesse Nathaniel 553 John
Carlisle 553 Lenora 553 Lilli-
an Augusta 553 Nellie 553
William Henry 553 Willie 553
REDDEN, Elizabeth 481
REED, Alice 414 Andrew 248
John 414
REGER, Lorenza 437 Mary 437
Regiment, 127th 102
REID, Charles William 555
George 555 Lillian 555

REID (continued)
Miss 555
RENICK, 96 530 F A 130 183
James 254 Lydia 502 Mrs
James 254 Mrs William 170
Widow 502 William 170 502
REYNOLDS, Johnson 101 John-
ston 102 591
RHEA, James 102 365 Julia 365
Louella 554
RHINEHART, Caroline 443
Catherine 221
RICHARDS, Archie 584 Maria 553
RIDER, Alexander 214 Clark 224
Elizabeth 210 Isabella 214
Stuart 210 Wilson 404
RIDGEWAY, Florence 361
RIFFLE, Frank 567
RIGGLEMAN, Mattie 401
RIGSBY, Elizabeth 193 Thomas
193
RILEY, Amy 165 Anna 392 Ella
432 Joe 165 John 432 Joseph
429 Mary 148 Otey 125
RIMEL, America 395 R D 395
RITCHIE, Thomas 513
Roads, 73
ROBERTS, Gen 601 602
ROBEY, Walter H 582
ROBINSON, Emma 543
ROCK, Miss 369
RODGERS, A W 536 Alvin W 536
Chesley 536 Davis 536 Drury
535 Eliza 536 Elizabeth 535
Frances 202 G W 536 Hannah
536 James 535-538 James L
Jr 536 John 536 543 John H
536 Joseph 202 424 535 Jus-
tice N C 536 Laura 536 Lewis
536 Maggie 536 Margaret 536
Mary 535 536 Mary V 270 Mrs
James Sr 535 Mrs John 536
Mrs Robert 535 Nellie 535
Polly 536 Rebecca 536 Robert
305 535 Sabina 543 Sally 305
536 Sarah 535 Susan 424
Tabitha 535 William 536
ROGERS, Margaret 307 Sarah 307
RORKE, 96 John D 151 Nancy
151
ROSE, John 226 Melinda 226

ROUSS, Miss 479
ROWAN, Elizabeth 324 George
324
RUCKER, Dr 591 H S 591 593
RUCKMAN, 96 Almira 162 Anna
161 Anna Laurie 161 Ardelly
401 Asa 161 Caroline 133 162
490 491 Catherine 491 Charles
162 163 332 490 Clarissa 491
Cornelia 161 D L 198 David
159 160 162 David Glendye
161 David Jr 491 David Little
160 489-492 David Newton 162
David V 489 David Vanmeter
161 Elizabeth 160 161 401
Fannie 489 Hannah 160 Isabella 401 James 133 159-161 489
James Atlee 162 James Watts
490 491 Jane 401 Jesse 401
John 160 489 John H 159-164
John Hartman 159-164 John W
114 472 John Wade 490 Julia
Ann 490 Kate 161 Leonidas
490 Lizzie 162 491 Lucy 161
Lula 401 Maggie 490 Margaret
114 146 161 400 401 472 490
Margaret Ann 490 Margerie
161 Mary 160-163 401 491
Mary Ann 401 489 Mary
Frances 366 491 Mathews 198
422 489 490 Mattie 401
Michael Daugherty 401 Miss
160 491 Mrs Charles 332 Mrs
Otho Wade 491 Nancy 161 400
401 Nancy Priscilla 491
Nannie P 149 Otho 491 Otho
W 366 Otho Wade 491 Polly
Ann 162 Priscilla 490 Renick
491 Samuel 146 159 161 162
401 489 490 Sarah 161 Sidney
163 Sophia 160 Susannah 160
Sydney 162 Thomas 159 401
Wellington G 402 William 163
401 William Patrick 162
William Wallace 491
RUSH, Margaret 523
RUSKIN, 56
RUSMISELL, Lydia 320 Minta
320
RUST, Col 450
RYDER, Aaron 214 Nancy 334

RYDER (continued)
Robert 334 Rosa 214 Stewart
214 William J 214

- S -

SALISBURY, 425 Biddie 424
Jennie 423 John 348 Martha
348 Mary 348 423 Rebecca 423
Sarah 424 William 348 423
William Jr 350
SAPP, Elizabeth Ann 373 Mr 373
SARGENT, Margaret 611
SARVER, Ida 118
SAUNDERS, 247 Anna 201 207
Cyrus 201 Diana 201-207
Eleanor 201 Granny 202-205
Isaac 201 207
SCALES, 96 Caroline 133 Mi-
chael 133 422
SCHEMERHORN, John 220
SCHISLER, James 532 Rachel
Ann 532
Scotch-Irish, 97 Character 15
SCOTT, Alice 328 Anne W 546
Archie 592 Hiram 328 Howard
592 Mary 547 Miss 328 S B
448 Sallie Glenn 448 William
314 547
SEE, Adam 255 256 Charles 135
Charles Cameron 255 256
Chas S M 256 Christina 255
257 Dolly 255-257 Eliza 255
257 Florida 256 George 241
255 256 Georgiana 255 Hannah
255 257 Jacob 255 268 Jacob
Warwick 256 Lawyer 147
Margaret 255 257 Margaret
Warwick 255 257 Mary 255
257 Mary W 254 Mrs Charles
Cameron 256 Peter 257 Rachel
255 Rachel Cameron 257
Warwick 255
SEEBERT, Lanty S 583
SEIG, Judge 591
SEWALL, 52 Stephen 105-108
SEXTON, Dr 591
SEYBERT, Ann 140 Capt 123
Catherine 156 Eli 433 Eliza-
beth 209 Jacob 140 209 John
482 Joseph 209 374 Lanty 209

SEYBERT (continued)
Louisa Susan 433 Maria 209
374 Mary 209 Mary Amaret
433 Nancy 482 Rebecca 209
SHAFER, Mrs Robert 370 Robert
370
SHANNON, James 583 Michael
583
SHARATT, Adam 397 401 Elizabeth 401
SHARP, 96 284 366 Aaron Abraham 217 Aaron Uriah Bradford
216 Abraham 182 584 Abram
214 216 217 285 Albert 218
Alexander 333 519 524 Alice
217 Althea 519 Amanda 190
216 Anderson Butler 217
Andrew 215 334 Ann 334 465
480 519 524 Anna 214 230 333
520 Ashby 217 Austin John
216 Azelia 217 Barbara 176
Bernard 519 524 Bertha 218
Bessie 216 Bettie 217 C O W
216 584 Caroline 217 Carrie
216 Catherine 177 425 519
Catherine Jane 282 Charles
Hanson 216 Charles Letcher
216 Charles O W 190 Charles
Osborne Wade 216 Clara 218
Clifton Chalmers 216 Cora 191
Cuba Truxillo 217 Daisy 449
Daniel 177 215 David 520
David Franklin 216 Docia 218
Effie 218 Eliza Jane 215
Elizabeth 140 182 196 214 217
234 333 456 480 518-520
Elizabeth Rachel 217 Eliza-
beth Slaven 215 216 Ella 524
Ellen 216 230 333 520 Ellen
Susan 339 Ernest Gilmer 216
Esta Medora 216 Eveline 464
519 Ewing 520 Francis 519
Frank 190 George 519 George
Mervin 216 George Winters
216 Georgia Miami 465 Gilbert
218 Giles 242 282 519 Gilmer
133 216 Hannah 519 524
Hannibal Hamlin 216 Hanson
190 519 Harmon 519 524
Henderson Wickline 216 Henry
182 209 217 373 519 520 524

SHARP (continued)
Hugh 519 520 524 Ida Amanda
216 Isaac 465 519 Isabella 214
J B F 216 Jacob 140 266 333
Jacob Jr 519 Jacob W 519
Jacob Warwick 519 James 177
215 286 332-335 457 480 501
510 519 520 Jane 215 520
Jasper 217 Jasper N 191
Jeremiah 177 584 John 103
176 177 179 213-218 230 242
285 290 299 333 520 John
Benjamin Franklin 216 John Sr
453 456 John Washington 217
Joseph 182 215 217 225
Joseph Averill 217 Josiah 177
Julia 464 519 Julia Quebee
217 Lincoln 217 Lindsay 176
215 Lindsey 524 Lizzie 133
218 Lucinda 334 501 Lucy 218
Lura 519 Luther 519 524
Luther David 226 Malinda
Catherine 221 Margaret 213-
215 299 332 334 Margaret Ann
216 Marietta Emmeretta
Virginia 216 217 Martha 333
334 518 520 521 524 Martha
Ellen 216 Martin 317 Mary 176
189 196 225 230 332-334 519
520 524 Mary Alice 216 Mary
Ann 217 Mary Ella 519 Mary
Ella Frances 226 Mary Hannah
Susan 217 Mary Jane 317 Mary
Paulina 215 Matilda Ursula
216 Melinda Catherine 226
Milton 584 Minnie Ursula 216
Miss 266 335 Morris 177 Mrs
Andrew 334 Mrs John 218 Mrs
Josiah 177 Nancy 215 230 285
332-334 410 520 521 Nancy
Elizabeth 216 Nancy Elizabeth
Daisy 216 Oscar 217 339 Paul
333 464 519 Pearl 218 Peter
182 217 Phebe 182 Phoebe 395
Polly 182 214 Rachel 183 286
332 334 519 524 Rebecca 215
230 281 290 333 334 453 520
Robert 215 332 Rosa 214 Ruth
216 Sally 520 Samuel 217
Sarah 216 226 230 333 519
Silas 226 519 524

SHARP (continued)
Stewart Holmes 217 Summers
Hedrick 216 Susan 183 520 539
Trudie Montgomery 216 Upton
Porter 216 W B 449 William
102 114 179 189 196 215 217
234 242 285 331-335 367 410
462 464 467 480 518-522 524
539 William Alexander Gilmer
216 William Bradford 216
William Jr 333 524 William
Sr 518 524
Shawnees, 7 9
SHEARER, 275
SHEARS, David 134 Dorinda 134
SHEETS, 96 Asbury 377 George
477 Henry 377 477 Mary 477
Mary Ann 377 Rachel 477
SHELBY, Capt 248
SHINNEBERRY, Abram 540
Alcinda 539 Cora 539 Embry
539 Emma 414 Isaac 540
Jacob 413 Jerusha 540 John
414 Margaret 414 Mildred 540
Sarah 410 William 539
SHOWALTER, Ann 330
SHRADER, 96 B F 583 B Frank-
lin 339 Charles 339 Elizabeth
339 Ellen Susan 339 Enoch
339 Henry 338 Jacob 339 John
338 339 Julia Quebee 217
Luther 339 Margaret Ann 339
Mary 339 Mrs Jacob 339 Mrs
John 339 Mrs R C 334 339
Nancy 338 Peter 339 R C 334
339 Robert 342 William 217
339
SHUE, Jacob 423 Margaret 423
Peggy 423
SHUEY, Adam 125 Eliza Jane
125
SHULTZ, Mr 397
SICAFOOSE, Hester 226 Miss
538
Silurian Era, 31
SILVA, Elizabeth Ann 151 Fannie
193 Virginia 281 Frances 202
James W 202
SIMMONS, C A 583 John 285 286
405 Jonas 520 Margaret 286
408 Mary 270 Mary Ann 217

SIMMONS (continued)
Mrs John 285 Nancy 520
Nicholas 270
SIMMS, Dr 444 Josephine 444
Rhoda 539
SIMPSON, Ann 524 George 524
Sarah 524 William 524
SIMS, D K 584 John 539 Margaret
190 W H 190 584
SIPLE, 96 Anna 433 Capt 433 487
Clara Belle 433 G W 430
George 432 Hannah Rebecca
432 Joseph 433 Mary Cather-
ine 433 Nancy Jane 432 Wil-
liam 433
SIRON, Christine 444 Joel 444
Jonathan 444 Margaret 444
Milton 444
SITLINGTON, Andrew 235 245
Miss 235 Robert 235
SIVEY, Cain H 583
SKEEN, William 591
SKEENE, Gen 100 Miss 423
William 474
SKYLES, Janie B 618
SLANKER, Clinton 220 330
Margaret 220 330
SLATON, John 584
SLATOR, Patrico 463
SLAVEN, 96 429 Adalaide Elean-
or 148 Alice 149 Anna 146
Caroline 146 147 Charles 146
148 Daniel 144 Eleanor 147
149 285 Elizabeth 145 146 148
509 Ellen 176 Emmet 149
Frank 147 George 176 Gratz
148 Harriet 148 Henry 144 146
Isabella 148 427 Isaiah 144
Jacob 102 148 209 285 Jacob
Gillespie 147 James Cooper
146 Jesse 145 Jesse B 148
John 103 144-149 John Ran-
dolph 148 Lanty 147 427 Lanty
Lockridge 148 Lucy 147
Margaret 145 146 149 161
Margaret Eveline 149 Margaret
P 148 Martha 144 147 148
Mary 146 148 Mary P 148
Matilda 145 Mildred 149 Mrs
John 144 145 149 Mrs M P 146
Mrs Stuart 144 Nancy 146

SLAVEN (continued)
Nancy Priscilla 491 Nannie P
149 Naomi 270 271 Nathan 146
Nellie 145 209 Newlen 270
Perry 147 Peter H 149 Priscilla 146 Rachel 145 Rebecca
487 Reuben 144 145 487
Roland 147 Sallie 145 146
Sarah 146 149 Stuart 144 145
W W 583 Warwick 148 Wil-
liam 101 144-147 William
Patrick 146 Winfield 491
Winfield T 149
SLEATHE, Mary 530
SLOAN, 273 Mr 235 Mrs 561 563
SMITH, 470 Andrew 303 Ann 303
310 612 Ballard 154 159 Capt
491 Comfort 382 Elizabeth 303
462 Fannie 302 423 Hannah
304 371 Jane 168 169 John 174
285 302-306 370 371 423 462
535 John Jr 302 Joseph 196
Leah 366 Louis 583 Martha
305 Miss 352 535 Mr 580 Mrs
579-581 Nancy 303 Naomi 382
Pleasant 366 Rebecca 303 370
Sally 285 302 305 424 William
579
SNEDEGAR, Della 192 William
192
SNODGRASS, Catherine 553 Dr
554 Kate 554 Louella 554
Newton 554 William Edward
554 William N 553
SNYDER, Alice 126 Catherine
373 Early 126 Ellen 254 F J
183 591 Hamilton 220 330
Jennie 220 330 Susan 220
Virginia Susan 330 William
220 330
Soldiers, Union & Confederate
582-585
SPROUSE, Jennie 613
STALMAKER, Elizabeth 196
Hamilton 124 Mary 124 Minta
132 Polly 124 Warwick 196
STALNAKER, Alexander 520
Anna 520 Bud 132 Caroline
524 ELlen 520 Lizzie 521
Mary 520 Warwick 520
STARR, Jane 508 Mr 508

STEARNS, Nancy 425
STEENBERGER, Miss 543
STEPHENSON, Adam 568 Alcinda 380 Charlotte 568 David 569 Eliza 259 J W 259 591 L H 591 Mr 380 Mrs Washington 569 Rebecca 382 Susan 568 Washington 568 569
STEVENS, Isabella 506 Nancy 506 Robert 506
STEVENSON, Eliza 508 Rebecca 294
STEWART, Alice 220 330 Capt 248 E W 556 John 220 330 Kate Knox 556
STOCKLEY, 616
STOFER, D A 474 582 591
STRATHER, Dr 477
STUART, John 244 Martha 144 Miss 144 Sarah 118
STULTING, 220 Miss 339 Nicholas 339
STUMP, Keziah 426
SUMMER, the longest 32
SUTTON, 96 Anna 391 Caroline 477 Clara 410 Clarissa 133 Eldridge 391 Eliza 134 Gatewood 477 George 317 391 Henrietta 272 Huldah 398 India 409 James 134 John Jr 485 486 John Sr 485-486 Magnolia 391 Margaret 429 473 523 Martha Ellen 409 Mary 391 Mary Elizabeth 317 Nancy 391 Rachel 133 486 Rachel Tallman 478 Robert 391 409 Samuel 133 166 376 410 429 523 Sherman 391 Virgie 166 William 391
SWADELY, Jane 215 Nicholas 215
SWADLY, James 582
SWECKER, Lula 401
SWINK, Caroline 528 Elizabeth 493 Margaret Ann 410 Rachel 410 Zechariah 410 492
SWISHER, Miss 544
SYBERT, Abram 551 Kate 554 555 W C 554
SYDENSTRICKER, 96 D S 543 Mary Margaret 543

- T -

TACEY, 96
TALIAFERRO, Susan 253 William 253
TALLMAN, Benjamin 100 102 431 433 434 487 590 Boone 102 487 Caroline 430 Cyrus 410 434 487 Elizabeth 431 433 487 Enos 391 George 430 487 James 100 101 434 486-489 509 590 591 Jane 125 487 488 409 Jemima 488 Jennie 527 John 434 487 Margaret 488 Marietta 391 Mary 487 Mary Ann 410 Nancy 434 486-488 Rachel 487 Rachel Ann 427 487 Rebecca 487 Robert 434 487 Sallie 391 Sally 488 Samuel 488 William 434 487 509 527
TAYLOR, Andrew 473 Benjamin 202 Elizabeth 547 Elizabeth Jane 166 Judge 590 Martha 473 Nancy 202 William 166 529
TERREL, Rachel 236
TERRELL, W H 591
THARP, Jennie 178 Martha 348
THOMAS, Eliza 391 John 231 Margaret 231
THOMPSON, John 480 Mary Evelina 263 515 Maurice 54 Miriam 480 Mrs William P 603 William P 263 515 603
THRASHER, J 504 Mrs J 504
TIDD, Jack 593
TILLERY, Winneford 546
TOMLINSON, Eliza Valentine 410 Frances Elzedie 165 Henry 407 Jacob 165 Jane 407 Mary Ann 156
TOWNSEND, Elizabeth 320 Hannah 364 James 320 Margaret 196 William 364
TRACE, Emma 134 J 134
TRACY, George 165 Mary Ann 164 165
TRAINER, Brown 391 Ella 391
TRIMBLE, Bonaparte 167
TROTTER, Ann 579-581

WANLESS (continued)
Nancy 455 Nancy Ann 455 456
Nelson 455 584 Rachel 455
Ralph 131 155 156 394 455 458
515 Ralph Jr 458 Sally 131
Samuel 192 458 Stephen 215
455–457 Virgie 193 Virginia
493 William 317 455–459
WARD, Adam 257 Christina 257
Jacob 257 Margaret Eveline
381 Renick 257 381 Washing-
ton 257
WARE, Benjamin 583 Eugene
583 George 583 William T 583
WARREN, Docia 218
WARWICK, 96 Amelia 433 523
Amos 430 Andrew 145 237 258
259 427 428–431 429 431
Andrew Jackson 430 Ann 429
Anna 132 429 Anthea 433
Caroline 259 430 433 Cather-
ine Hidy 431 Cecil 433
Charles 433 Charles Cameron
258 259 Daniel 236 Elbert 433
Eliza 252 259 Elizabeth 145
234 260 429–431 433 387 Ellen
259 Emma 260 Esther 431
Forrest 433 Gabrielle 433
George 260 George Craig 433
Hannah 259 261 Hannah
Rebecca 432 Jacob 10 103 129
175 178 194 195 234–269 273
274 345 428 430 486 498 514
521 550 608 James 564–567
James W 234 252 James W Jr
585 James Woods 258 259
Jane 252 260 429 Jennie 433
Jesse 433 John 103 234 243
259 260 268 428–431 John
Andrew 259 585 John Jr 430
John R 428 John Robert 433
John W 261 Judge 249 Lieut
234 235 Lillie 259 Louisa
Susan 433 Louise Catherine
433 Margaret 255 429–431 434
Margaret Ann 432 Mary 234
240 253 259 262 429 433 498
Mary V 268 Mary Vance 266
486 Mathew Patton 430 Miss
259 260 Mrs 235–237 239 241
242 428 Mrs Andrew 258 431

WARWICK (continued)
Mrs Jacob 235 521 Nancy 260
429 431 433 514 Nancy Jane
432 Nelson 433 Otis 433 Paul
433 Peter 433 Peter H 428 431
Peter Hull 433 Pray 433
Rachel 250 430 Robert 102 433
Robert Craig 431 Sally 261 427
429 433 Sarah Elizabeth 432
William 145 429 431–434
William Craig 430 William
Fechtig 433
WASHINGTON, 23 130 206 516
Col 246
WATSON, Mary Ellen 508
WATTS, Margaret 120 Mary 118
WAUGH, 96 Alexander 341 Allen
337 Almira 365 Amanda 396
Ann 286 338 343 Annie 341
Arthur 341 Beverly 286 340
342 508 582 584 Brown 366
Clarissa Jane 337 Davis 365
Elizabeth 336 338 Enoch 366
Enos 365 Eveline 286 Hannah
337 Henrietta 342 Homer 366
Isabella 337 Jacob 129 336
342 366 452 James 103 336
423 James 3rd 336 James Jr
336–338 James Sr 338 Jane
404 Jane Miriam 365 John 286
310 339 340 John E 342 John
William 366 Leah 366 Levi
286 340 396 491 583 Lorenza
267 337 338 Marcus 337
Margaret 342 Martha 286 339
341 342 365 Martha Ann 508
Mary 336 338 341 366 Mary
Ann 342 365 540 Miriam 286
Miss 340 342 Morgan 337 Mr
608 Mrs Levi 491 Nancy 336
Ozias 365 Rachel 336 Rebecca
286 336 339 Robert 341 365 S
D 129 342 Sally 336 423
Samuel 103 286 310 338–343
365 404 540 Samuel Jr 340
Sarah Ann 129 342 Susan 337
William 341 365 William
Clark 365 Zane 365
WEAVER, C W 583 R L 583
WEBB, John 416–419
WEIFORD, Catherine 201

WEIFORD (continued)
Eleanor 194 Francis 193
Gratton S 523 Jacob 201
James 194 Rebecca 523
WEIMER, Celia 415
WEIR, Ann 338 Richard B 338
WETZEL, Christina Jane 361
David 361 Florence 361 Lena
361 Lizzie 361 Sallie 361
William 361
Wheat, Growing 64 Threshing 65
WHEELER, Agnes 473 Rufus 473
Whence rain and snow, 48
WHITE, 275 D 252 Dora 225 E C
616 Ella 473 Henry 225 373
John 564 565 Lake 361 Lizzie
361 Marion 473 Mrs D 252 Mrs
Thomas 252 Sarah 225
Thomas 252 William 564 565
WHITING, Bessie 532 Earle 532
Ebenezer 219 436 530 532 533
535 Elizabeth 532 Fannie 436
Floy 532 George W 530
George William 532 Grace 532
Harry 532 Jennie 219 530 John
Sherman 532 Laura Frances
532 Mabel 532 Margaret Jane
532 Mary 530 Mary Elizabeth
532 Mercy 530 Milton 532 Mrs
Ebenezer 533 534 Rachel Ann
532 Robert 530 Sallie 219
Sally 532 Samuel 219 529-535
Samuel Jr 530 Sarah 529 Sarah
Caroline 532 Susan Virginia
532 Thomas 532
WHITMAN, Eliza 378 Julia Ann
478 William 378 613
WHITMER, Jesse 65
WICKLINE, Joseph S 532 Sarah
Caroline 532
WILEY, Ruhannah 325
WILFONG, Ervine 520 Jacob 411
James 520 Jane 411 Margaret
Jane 411 Martha 520 Nancy
520 Serena 444 William 444
WILLIAMS, A D 519 Erasmus
190 J 593 Magdalen 140
Margaret 190 Nancy 507
Robert 140
WILLIHAN, Michael 583 Pat 583

WILLIS, Catherine 444 Josephine
444 Laura 444 Robert 444
Virginia 444
WILSON, Barbara 569 571 573
Bishop 135 Charlotte 568 Col
9 John 568-570 572 573
Margaret 115 Mary 163 220
330 Mrs 569 571 573 Nancy
455 Norval 135 Robert 220 330
Susan 568 569 571 572
Thomas 568-574 William 518
568 569
WISE, Michael 571
WITT, Dr 596 S B 595 S B JR
596
WODDELL, Delilah 124
WOLFENBARGER, Nancy 515
WOLFENBERGER, Joseph 102
Mary 378 Warwick 378
WOODDELL, 96 239 Aaron 125
Alice 410 Bessie 370 Caroline
444 Christine 444 Clark 124
Delilah 131 Eliza 398 Harriet
423 J K B 370 J S 146 James
429 Jane 429 John 146 147 410
Joseph 124 131 146 Margaret
146 Margaret P 148 Martha
Jane 391 Mary 146 163 377 Mr
238 377 Nancy 427 Nancy
Agnes 476 Nancy Jane 432 433
Nannie 427 Pierce 433 Preston
124 Priscilla 146 T C 423 W J
146 391 Warwick 125 William
427 444 William J 444
WOODS, Elizabeth 260 477
Elizabeth Warwick 260 George
255 Jane 255 Margaret 440
Miss 258 Mr 477 Phoebe 269
William 260
WOODSON, J C 591
Wool and Flax, 63
WRIGHT, Miss 317
WYLIE, Nancy 319

- Y -

YEAGER, 96 Alcena 445 Alice
445 Allie 445 Andrew 445
Anna 443 444 B M 125 Brown
McLauren 446

659

YEAGER (continued)
Brown McLaurin 449 Brownie
449 Bruce 449 Caroline 443
444 Catherine 443 444 Charles
445 Charles Andrew 445 Christine 443 444 Clinton 444 449
Daisy 449 Eliza A 447 Eliza
Ann 446 Elizabeth 443 445 523
Ella 445 524 Emma Mildred
446 447 Etta 325 445 Eula Joe
448 Eveline Medora 446 447
Fannie Elizabeth 446 447
Frederick 449 Gertrude 445
Goldie 449 Grace 445 H A 443
449 Harriet Elizabeth 125 449
Henry A 448 Henry Arbogast
446 Huldah 449 J Walker 449
Jacob 443 Jacob Brook 443
445 Jacob Reese 446 447 Jane
443 Jewell 449 Joel 443 444
John 124 127 443 446 450 451
John III 445 449 John Jr 443
446–451 John M 449 John Sr
442–446 Jonathan 214 Leah
Alice 446 447 Lewis A 449
Lucy 449 Luther 444 Luverta
448 Mabel 448 Mamie 449
Margaret 124 133 443–446

YEAGER (continued)
Martin 445 524 Maud Leps 448
Newton 444 Paris Dameron 448
Paul McGraw 449 Paul McNeel
123 126 446 449 Pearl 449
Peter 426 445 523 Peter D 443
445 Rachel 214 Rebecca 444
Sallie Glenn 448 Sarah 443
Sarah Jane 446 Serena 443 444
Sterling 449 Texie 449 Walter
H 448 William Asbury 446 448
William Edgar 448 William
Jacob 445
YOUNG, Adam 120 303 310 311
511 Alwilda Nebraska 465
Amy 306 Andrew 307 Ann 303
310 Charles 306 Elizabeth 307
308 352 384 425 George 425
585 James 307 352 Jane 307
425 John 302 303 306 307 311
465 511 Margaret 307 Martha
202 305 307 356 384 Mary 352
Miss 303 Mrs Adam 120 Sallie
466 Samuel 102 303 305–307
311 Sarah 307 385 Sarah Ann
307 Susan 310 511 Washington
425 William 102 303 306–311
352 356 369 425